THE NEW INTELLECTUALS

Advisory Editor: Alfred Harbage

The New Intellectuals

A Survey and Bibliography of Recent Studies in English
Renaissance Drama

Edited by

Terence P. Logan and Denzell S. Smith

UNIVERSITY OF NEBRASKA PRESS
LINCOLN AND LONDON

Library of Congress Cataloging in Publication Data

Logan, Terence P
  The new intellectuals.

  (Their A survey and bibliography of recent
studies in English Renaissance drama)
  Includes index.
  1. English drama—17th century—History and
criticism—Bibliography. 2. English drama—
Early modern and Elizabethan, 1500-1600—History
and criticism—Bibliography. I. Smith, Denzell S.,
joint author. II. Title. III. Series.
  Z2014.D7L817 [PR671]   106.822'3   75-38051
  ISBN 0-8032-0859-6

REF.

52,683

MANUFACTURED IN THE UNITED STATES OF AMERICA

CONTENTS

PREFACE

The New Intellectuals is the third volume of Recent Studies in English Renaissance Drama; when completed, the series will give a comprehensive account of recent scholarship on English plays and playwrights, exclusive of Shakespeare, from 1580 to 1642. The first volume, *The Predecessors of Shakespeare* (1973), deals with anonymous plays first performed between 1580 and 1593 and playwrights who wrote most of their plays in those years; *The Popular School* (1975) and the present volume jointly cover the period from 1593 to 1616. *The Popular School* includes dramatists primarily associated with the public open-air theaters, and anonymous plays first performed in them; *The New Intellectuals* treats dramatists who either wrote principally for the private theaters or were significantly influenced by them, and the anonymous plays first performed in them. The fourth and last volume, *The Later Jacobean and Caroline Drama,* will include plays and playwrights of both popular and private theaters for the period from 1616 to 1642. The division by type of theater and date of first performances was made principally by reference to Alfred Harbage, *Annals of English Drama,* revised by Samuel Schoenbaum (1964), to the *Supplements to the Revised Edition,* by Schoenbaum (1966, 1970), and by consultation with Professor Harbage.

The publication dates of E. K. Chambers's *The Elizabethan Stage,* 4 vols. (1923), and of the initial volumes of G. E. Bentley's *The Jacobean and Caroline Stage,* 7 vols. (1941–68), provided the anterior limits for the survey of scholarship and criticism in the series. Contributors to *The New Intellectuals* used annual bibliographies published from 1923 through 1974 and were encouraged to include especially important material published both before and after those limits. There are two exceptions to this policy. In the discussions of anonymous plays, only a few items published after 1967 have been included. The Jonson essay, because of the quantity and nature of the scholarship, uses an anterior limit of 1945 for the See Also section only; more important items dating from 1923, and earlier, are discussed in the other sections. The chief sources for the items included in this volume were the author and title

vii

entries in twelve bibliographies and lists: *Essay and General Literature Index, International Index* (since 1965, *Social Sciences and Humanities Index*), *MLA International Bibliography, Modern Humanities Research Association Annual Bibliography of English Language and Literature, Readers' Guide to Periodical Literature, Research Opportunities in Renaissance Drama, Shakespeare Quarterly, Shakespeare Survey, Studies in Bibliography, Studies in Philology, Yearbook of Comparative and General Literature,* and *The Year's Work in English Studies.* Those entries were supplemented by selected general studies of Elizabethan drama surveyed for discussions of individual playwrights, and by the additional research of individual contributors. Entries were restricted to published material except in the treatment of anonymous plays, where edition theses were included.

Each essay begins with a general section, including, when available, biographical material, general studies of the plays, and studies of the works at large. (It is assumed that later sections, particularly those dealing with individual plays, will be used in conjunction with this general section.) The next section discusses criticism of individual plays arranged in the order of their approximate critical importance, and concludes with a brief summary of the current state of criticism. The third section treats canon (including apocrypha), dates, and the state of the standard and other editions of the plays and nondramatic works. The arrangement of this section is chronological, following the preferred performance dates given in the *Annals of English Drama* and its *Supplements*; the play titles are cited as they appear in the *Annals* Index. At the contributor's discretion, items are either discussed in the commentary or listed in the See Also section. Contributors were free to modify these general guidelines to better accommodate the specific published material on a given author. Essays on the anonymous plays are organized independently according to the nature of the published studies; anonymous plays are discussed in the order of their performance date in the *Annals*. The section on minor named dramatists uses an annotated bibliography format arranged according to the date of publication of the criticism. Series titles are included only when they indicate the nature of the work or are useful as finding tools.

The choice of the year 1616 as the posterior limit for inclusion in this volume and in *The Popular School* was determined by the date of Shakespeare's death. While Ben Jonson rightly dominates the material in this volume, Shakespeare is never far from the foreground. The use of his career as an organizational guide for the series reflects both obvious facts of literary history and the hope that the series will contribute to an increased understanding of Shakespeare; the Shakespeare apocrypha, his associations, and his sources and influence are part of the series's subject matter.

The series owes a special debt to the librarians of more than a dozen colleges and universities and to the staffs of the Folger Shakespeare Library, Widener Library of Harvard University, and the Library of Congress, who located especially rare items. Professors Alfred Harbage and Samuel Schoenbaum gave permission to use information from the revised *Annals of English Drama* and the *Supplements to the Revised Edition* and to follow those works as principles of organization. Permission to use the Master List and Table of Abbreviations of the *MLA International Bibliography* was granted by the Bibliographer of the Association, Harrison T. Meserole. Our list of journal and series abbreviations conforms to the MLA list except that we include several older titles not in the current MLA tables.

Professor Alfred Harbage died on May 2, 1976, as editorial work on this volume was being completed. He gave to the series from its earliest stages. His books, especially the *Annals*, served as guidelines and scholarly benchmarks; he was the final arbiter on matters of policy and format; many of the contributors are his former students. There can be no capsule acknowledgment. He generously shared his learning and his humanity. Our final impression is of great joy in scholarship, passion for seeing it done *right*, and concern that human values be preserved in the process.

Terence P. Logan
Denzell S. Smith

LIST OF ABBREVIATIONS

AION-SG	*Annali Istituto Universitario Orientale, Napoli, Sezione Germanica*
AN&Q	*American Notes and Queries*
Archiv	*Archiv für das Studium der Neueren Sprachen und Literaturen*
ASNSP	*Annali della Scuola Normale Superiore de Pisa*
AUMLA	*Journal of the Australasian Universities Language and Literature Association*
AUR	*Aberdeen University Review*
BBr	*Books at Brown*
BFLS	*Bulletin de la Faculté des Lettres de Strasbourg*
BHR	*Bibliothéque d'Humanisme et Renaissance*
BJRL	*Bulletin of the John Rylands Library*
BLM	*Bonniers Litterära Magasin*
BNYPL	*Bulletin of the New York Public Library*
Boek	*Het Boek*
BRMMLA	*Bulletin of the Rocky Mountain Modern Language Association*
BUSE	*Boston University Studies in English*
CE	*College English*
CJ	*Classical Journal*
CL	*Comparative Literature*
CLAJ	*College Language Association Journal*
ClareQ	*Claremont Quarterly*
ColQ	*Colorado Quarterly*
CompD	*Comparative Drama*
CritQ	*Critical Quarterly*
CS	*Cahiers du Sud*
DA	*Dissertation Abstracts*
Drama	*Drama: The Quarterly Theatre Review*
DramS	*Drama Survey*
DUJ	*Durham University Journal*
EA	*Etudes Anglaises*
EDH	Essays by Divers Hands
EJ	*English Journal*

ELH	Journal of English Literary History
ELN	English Language Notes
EM	English Miscellany
E&S	Essays and Studies by Members of the English Association
ES	English Studies
ESA	English Studies in Africa
ESQ	Emerson Society Quarterly
ESRS	Emporia State Research Studies
ETJ	Educational Theatre Journal
Expl	Explicator
FK	Filológiai Közlöny
FurmS	Furman Studies
HAB	Humanities Association Bulletin
Hispano	Hispanófila
HLQ	Huntington Library Quarterly
HTR	Harvard Theological Review
IER	Irish Ecclesiastical Record
JEGP	Journal of English and Germanic Philology
JHI	Journal of the History of Ideas
JQ	Journalism Quarterly
JWCI	Journal of the Warburg and Courtauld Institute
KR	Kenyon Review
L&P	Literature and Psychology
LCrit	Literary Criterion
LHR	Lock Haven Review
Library	The Library
McNR	McNeese Review
MLN	Modern Language Notes
MLQ	Modern Language Quarterly
MLR	Modern Language Review
Month	The Month
MP	Modern Philology
MSpr	Moderna Språk
MuK	Maske und Kothurn
N&Q	Notes and Queries
Neophil	Neophilologus
NM	Neuphilologische Mitteilungen
NS	Die Neueren Sprachen
NSE	Norwegian Studies in English
NTg	De Nieuwe Taalgids

ShS	*Shakespeare Survey*
SJ	*Shakespeare-Jahrbuch*
SJH	*Shakespeare-Jahrbuch* (Heidelberg)
SJW	*Shakespeare-Jahrbuch* (Weimar)
SOF	*Sudöst-Forschungen*
SP	*Studies in Philology*
SQ	*Shakespeare Quarterly*
SR	*Sewanee Review*
SRen	*Studies in the Renaissance*
SSF	*Studies in Short Fiction*
SuAS	Stratford-upon-Avon Studies, ed. John Russell Brown and Bernard Harris
SzEP	Studien zur Englischen Philologie
TDR	*Tulane Drama Review* (since 1968, *The Drama Review*)
TEAS	Twayne's English Author Series
TFSB	*Tennessee Folklore Society Bulletin*
TLS	[London] *Times Literary Supplement*
TSE	*Tulane Studies in English*
TSL	*Tennessee Studies in Literature*
TSLL	*Texas Studies in Literature and Language*
UDR	*University of Dayton Review*
UFMH	University of Florida Monographs, Humanities Series
UMSE	*University of Mississippi Studies in English*
UTQ	*University of Toronto Quarterly*
VUSH	Vanderbilt University Studies in the Humanities
WF	*Western Folklore*
WSt	*Word Study*
WTW	Writers and Their Work
YWES	*Year's Work in English Studies*
ZAA	*Zeitschrift für Anglistik und Amerikanistik*

THE NEW INTELLECTUALS

BEN JONSON

William L. Godshalk

The standard edition is the Oxford *Ben Jonson*, ed. Charles H. Herford and Percy and Evelyn Simpson, 11 vols, (1925-52), hereafter cited as Herford and Simpson. Although faulty, Charles Crawford's unpublished "Concordance to the 1616 Folio of Jonson's *Works*" is useful and is available at the University of Michigan, the University of Virginia, and the Folger Shakespeare Library.

I. GENERAL

A. BIOGRAPHICAL

Drummond of Hawthornden is Jonson's first biographer (see Herford and Simpson, 1: 128-78). Charles Lewis Stainer, *Jonson and Drummond: Their Conversations: A Few Remarks on an 18th Century Forgery* (1925), questioned the authenticity of the *Conversations* and suggested that Sir Robert Sibbald, in whose transcription the *Conversations* are preserved, was a forger. Percy Simpson, "The Genuineness of the Drummond *Conversations*," *RES* 2 (1926): 42-50, defended the authenticity of the manuscript, discussing its character and history. J. R. Barker, "A Pendant to Drummond of Hawthornden's *Conversations*," *RES* 16 (1965): 284-88, reported that Drummond's copy of Jonson's 1616 Folio in the University Library, Dundee, contains Drummond's manuscript notes; his purpose in printing a number of these "jottings in Drummond's hand which also repeat information in the *Conversations*" is to help establish the authenticity of the Sibbald manuscript.

Herford and Simpson, vols. 1 and 2, examine the man and his works. Many older studies are still useful: M. Castelain, *Ben Jonson: l'homme et l'oeuvre* (1907), G. Gregory Smith, *Ben Jonson* (1919), and John

Palmer, *Ben Jonson* (1934). Marchette Chute, *Ben Jonson of West-minster* (1953), gives a full account of Jonson's life, though her study is often undocumented and her Selected Bibliography is dated. There is a convenient sketch in G. E. Bentley, *The Jacobean and Caroline Stage: Plays and Playwrights* (1956), vol. 4 (hereafter cited as *Jacobean Stage*). J. B. Bamborough, "The Early Life of Ben Jonson," *TLS*, 8 April 1960, p. 225, cites Fuller and Aubrey on Jonson's youth, and offers evidence to suggest that one "Roberte Brette" was Jonson's stepfather; Brette lived in Hartshorn Lane and was a bricklayer, as was Jonson's stepfather.

Discussing Jonson's conversion to Catholicism, Theodore A. Stroud, "Ben Jonson and Father Thomas Wright," *ELH* 14 (1947): 274–82, suggests that "the priest played a crucial role in Jonson's decision," and that probably Wright was that priest. Jonson knew Wright well, for he wrote a sonnet prefaced to Wright's *The Passions of the Minde in Generall* (1604). Wright completed this treatise immediately before the conversion, which, Stroud suggests, took place in Bridewell where both men were confined. Ian Donaldson, "Jonson's Italy: *Volpone* and Fr. Thomas Wright," *N&Q* 19 (1972): 450–52, suggests that Jonson read Wright's treatise on the passions in 1604 and that the book influenced *Volpone*. Jonson's Catholicism is also discussed by Barbara De Luna, *Jonson's Romish Plot* (see II,A, under *Catiline*), and by Heinrich Mutschmann and Karl Wentersdorf, *Shakespeare und der Katholizis-mus* (trans. 1952; German ed., 1950).

Although a recusant, Jonson possibly occupied a professorial chair for a time. C. J. Sisson, "Ben Jonson of Gresham College," *TLS*, 21 Sept. 1951, p. 604, announced that possibility: on 20 October 1623, Jonson gave evidence in the Court of Chancery for Lady Elizabeth Raleigh. The deposition gives his age as "50 yeares & upwards," fixing his date of birth between October 1572, and May 1573; in it Jonson describes himself as "Beniamin Johnson of Gresham Colledge in London gent." If Jonson was professor of rhetoric at the college—probably the deputy of Henry Croke—then his *Discoveries* and *English Grammar* may be lecture notes. George Burke Johnston, "Ben Jonson of Gresham College," *TLS*, 28 Dec. 1951, p. 837, adds support to Sisson by examining "An Execration upon Vulcan" in the light of a possible professorship. Jonson laments the loss of many pieces, includ-ing his translation of Horace's *Art of Poetry*, his *English Grammar*, and his notes (i.e., *Discoveries*). Why did these pieces get "rewritten" and not his translation of Barclay's *Argenis*? Johnston suggests that he needed them for his rhetoric course.

Jonson's connections with various publications have been described. J. M. Nosworthy, "Marlowe's *Ovid* and Davies's *Epigrams*—A Postscript," *RES* 15 (1964): 397-98, believes that Jonson was responsible for rehandling Marlowe's original translation in the Middelburg octavos. Jonson fought in the Low Countries (for which see Abraham Feldman, "Playwrights and Pike-Trailers in the Low Countries," *N&Q* 198 [1953]: 184-87); A. G. H. Bachrach, in "Sir Constantyn Huygens and Ben Jonson," *Neophil* 35 (1951): 120-29, argues that Jonson influenced Huygens, who occupied "a central place in the Anglo-Dutch cultural relations of the seventeenth century." Arthur Secord, "I.M. of the First Folio Shakespeare and Other Mabbe Problems," *JEGP* 47 (1948): 374-81, notes that Jonson was connected with Shakespeare's 1623 Folio and that he contributed verses for James Mabbe's *Rogue*. In an elaborate reconstruction, Thomas M. Parrott, "*Pericles*: The Play and the Novel," *SAB* 23 (1948): 105-13, suggests that Jonson may be blamed for the exclusion of *Pericles* from the First Folio. Mogens Muellertz, "De fire Shakespeare folioer," *Bogvennen,* 1949, pp. 1-59, believes that the fatal "merry meeting" of Jonson, Shakespeare, and Drayton at Stratford was to celebrate the publication of Jonson's 1616 Folio; Shakespeare supposedly died from a fever contracted during this drinking bout. (Other items of possible biographical importance are discussed under a section of Jonson-Shakespeare studies in I,B.)

Jonson's "taverns" and "clubs" have been discussed. Thomas Kirby, "*The Triple Tun,*" *MLN* 62 (1947): 191-92, begins with Herrick's poem and comments on the actual structure of the tavern. Later in *MLN* 63 (1948): 56-57, Kirby, with the help of Giles Dawson, makes certain adjustments to his earlier remarks. George Mackaness, "Literary Clubs," *American Book Collector* 14, no. 2 (1963): 23-26, lists Jonson's Apollo Club and the Mermaid. I. A. Shapiro, "The 'Mermaid Club,'" *MLR* 45 (1950): 6-17, reviews the case for Jonson's membership and looks at Beaumont's verse-letter describing some sort of meeting; Shapiro is skeptical about the existence of a literary club. Percy Simpson, "'The Mermaid Club': An Answer and a Rejoinder," *MLR* 46 (1951): 58-63, feels that Shapiro is wrong; he contends that there was a "tavern-tradition" among the poets and playwrights. Shapiro replies that he wishes to examine contemporary documents about the "Mermaid Club" and to clear away the nineteenth century mythology about these "meetings." Later, Simpson, "Francis Beaumont's Verse-Letter to Ben Jonson: 'The Sun, which doth the greatest comfort bring . . . ,'" *MLR* 46 (1951): 435-36, recounts the history of Beaumont's poem in print and manuscript, and suggests that it gives a vivid picture of the Mermaid Club. M. R. Woodhead, "Ben Jonson's Cup-Bearer," *N&Q* 20 (1973): 262, points out that a reference to Jonson in Hugh Crompton's poem "The Soliloquy" suggests that Crompton was a sometime cupbearer for the tribe of Ben.

Several items deal with Jonson's relationship to the Renaissance system of literary patronage. In three articles, Dick Taylor, Jr., discusses Jonson's relationship to the third Earl of Pembroke: "Clarendon and Ben Jonson as Witnesses for the Earl of Pembroke's Character," in *Studies in the English Renaissance Drama*, ed. Josephine W. Bennett et al. (1959), pp. 322-44; "The Masque and the Lance: The Earl of Pembroke in Jacobean Court Entertainments," *TSE* 8 (1958): 21-53; and "The Third Earl of Pembroke as a Patron of Poetry," *TSE* 5 (1955): 41-67. John F. Danby, "The Poets on Fortune's Hill: Literature and Society, 1580-1610," *Cambridge Journal* 2 (1949): 195-211 (rpt. in his *Poets on Fortune's Hill* [1952]), and Patricia Thomson, "The Literature of Patronage, 1580-1630," *Essays in Criticism* 2 (1952): 267-84, touch on Jonson. G. P. V. Akrigg, *Jacobean Pageant* (1962), notes Jonson's place in the court of James.

Marjorie L. Reyburn, "New Facts and Theories about the Parnassus Plays," *PMLA* 74 (1959): 325-35, believes that the Parnassus-poet is an anti-Jonsonian; the character "Furor Poeticus" is mainly a parody of Jonson. Edmund Blunden, "Shakespeare Oddities," *N&Q* 7 (1960): 334-35, observes that in the footnotes to an early nineteenth-century songbook is the comment "Chr. Marlow was killed by Ben Jonson." Equally odd is Edmund Wilson's contention, "Morose Ben Jonson," in *The Triple Thinkers* (1938; rev. ed. 1948; rpt. in *Ben Jonson: A Collection of Critical Essays*, ed. Jonas A. Barish [1963], pp. 60-74), that Jonson was an anal erotic and that most of his work can be explained by reference to that fact. Percy Simpson, "A Westminster Schoolboy and Ben Jonson," *TLS*, 27 Nov. 1953, p. 761, announces a hitherto unknown elegy on Jonson. Herbert Howarth, "Falkland and Duppa's *Jonsonus Virbius*," *Expl* 17 (1958): item 11, explains the ambiguity of the title: it is partly comic in that Jonson was quite unlike Hippolytus (the Greek name for Virbius) who so attracted Phaedra; partly a tribute to the chastity of Jonson's muse (Hippolytus died because he would not give his love to Phaedra); and partly a half-pun indicating that Jonson was both mentally and physically "vir bis," two men.

B. GENERAL STUDIES OF THE PLAYS

Although signs of the directions which twentieth-century criticism would take were evident as early as Charles R. Baskervill's *English Elements in Jonson's Early Comedy* (1911), T. S. Eliot's "Ben Jonson" (1919; frequent rpts.) has been seen as the seminal work for modern Jonson criticism. Jonson is the "legitimate heir of Marlowe"; he has "immense dramatic constructive skill" and creates "a *unique* world."

In *Apologie for Bartholmew Fayre: The Art of Jonson's Comedies* (1947), Freda Townsend argues against the idea that Jonson is a thoroughgoing classicist, and emphasizes the element of Renaissance variety and the interweaving of various plots into a unity: she uses the eighteenth-century revisions of Jonson's plays to reveal his break with the classical tradition. Examining the development of Jonson's constructive skill from his early plays, she sees *Bartholomew Fair* as the climax of his comic career. "The metaphor of the weaver seems almost inevitable when Jonson's drama is admired for what it truly is. The web in drama finds it[s] culmination in *Bartholmew Fayre*. In this play, the line has completely disappeared; no central interest can be found—except the Fair itself, which breaks down into a multiplicity of interest. Manifold, multiplex, multiform—these are the characteristics of Jonson's art." Townsend's "Ben Jonson's 'Censure' of Rutter's *Shepheards Holy-Day*," *MP* 44 (1947): 238-47, arrives at the same general conclusions from a different direction (see I,C). Marvin T. Herrick, *JEGP* 47 (1948): 305-6, feels that she overstates her case and misrepresents classical comedy; Jonson's constructive skills are "in large part a successful extension and elaboration of methods employed by the classical comic poets." See Herrick's *Comic Theory in the Sixteenth Century* (1950), *Tragicomedy: Its Origin and Development in Italy, France, and England* (1955), and *Italian Comedy in the Renaissance* (1960).

Helena Baum, *The Satiric and the Didactic in Ben Jonson's Comedy* (1947), examines Jonson's practice in relation to Renaissance theories of the function of poetry. "The course of the development of the didactic theory itself may be traced along an almost unbroken path from Horace to Jonson"; both poets say that poetry must both please and teach. Baum insists that Jonson's "didactic theory is more philosophical than moral, more literary than monitory," and that "the material of his plays is derived from the matter which interests him rather than from abstract heights of theology." The cardinal sins in his plays are ignorance and stupidity. While emphasizing the importance of esthetics to Jonson, she suggests that in the late 1590s "his aesthetic theories were not well established. . . . His problem in 1599 was to combine philosophical material, satire, and high comedy in dramatic form." After reviewing the objects of Jonsonian satire, she traces his development from *The Case Is Altered* (which she dates 1597) to the completion of *Volpone* (1605). *The Poetaster* is given special attention as "an attempt to combine undramatic, philosophical material on good poets and true poetry with satire on bad poets." In *Volpone*, Jonson strikes the balance between comedy and satire, a balance which leads to *The Alchemist* and *Bartholomew Fair*.

Alexander Sackton, *Rhetoric as a Dramatic Language in Ben Jonson* (1948), begins with a brief review of Renaissance rhetorical tradition. He emphasizes that Jonson is satirically akin to Aristophanes, Lucian, and Erasmus, and that Jonson divides his characters into three main classes, the buffoon, the ironist, and the impostor. By concentrating on Jonson's ironic use of jargon and hyperbole, Sackton reveals the growth and decline of Jonson's dramatic art; he feels that the last plays lack Jonson's former clarity, unity, and dramatic irony.

Bertil Johansson, *Religion and Superstition in the Plays of Ben Jonson and Thomas Middleton* (1950), tries to "show how the problems of religion and of its caricature, superstition, are reflected in the plays of Jonson and Middleton," and concludes that the two dramatists give a good idea of the religious interests of their age. Esko V. Pennanen, *Chapters on the Language in Ben Jonson's Dramatic Works*, Annales Universitatis Turkuensis, Series B, no. 39 (1951), deals with Jonson's vocabulary and tries to link his choice of words with his dramatic creativity. Pennanen notes that Jonson uses most classical loan words in the plays of his central period, and least in the final plays. He defends Jonson against the charge of using a too Latinate diction. The appendices collect Jonson's use of loan words, compounds, archaisms, and so on.

Two books by A. C. Partridge, *The Accidence of Ben Jonson's Plays, Masques, and Entertainments* (1953), and *Studies in the Syntax of Ben Jonson's Plays* (1953), constitute a complete examination of Jonson's linguistic usage. *The Accidence* is a historical account of the morphology of the plays with various parts of speech discussed in detail. One appendix treats dialectal forms in Jonson; the other compares the accidence of Jonson with that of Shakespeare. Jonson proves richer in colloquial, dialectal, and contracted forms. *Studies* is an examination of certain aspects of Jonson's syntax, e.g., his use of the periphrastic auxiliary verb "do."

John J. Enck, *Jonson and the Comic Truth* (1957), is perceptive and at times puzzling. He sees in Jonson's emblem of the broken compass an allusion to Perdix, whose "implements are not the wax and feathers of Daedalus but the saw and compass." "A willed acceptance of what he could reach permitted Jonson his expanding control over the comic truth, which eschews the Faustian ambitions of peering into hidden destinies. Rather, it revels in the knowable and disdains immoderate desire. . . . All else must ultimately be vanity." Enck surveys Jonson's development from *The Case Is Altered* to *The Sad Shepherd*. As Enck indicates, perhaps the best parts of his study are the individual analyses.

Edward Partridge, *The Broken Compass: A Study of the Major Comedies of Ben Jonson* (1958), treats *Volpone, The Alchemist, Epicoene, The Staple of News, The New Inn,* and *The Magnetic Lady*. This study of Jonson's imagery reveals "how his imagination works in his major comedies. The first three chapters define the nature and the functions of metaphorical language and show Jonson's awareness of decorum in the use of metaphor." Partridge also examines the concept of the "transchanged world" in the plays, that discrepancy between man's profession and his deeds, between his occasional verbalizations of piety and morality, and his regular practice of selfishness and folly. "In Jonson's plays, imagery is one means by which this inversion of the commonly accepted values of humanity is accomplished. . . . The use of terms taken from religion or love or classical mythology as either the tenor or the vehicle of images is an imaginative and economical way of showing how vicious or foolish or comic certain actions are." This sense of inversion is most evident in *Volpone* and *The Alchemist*. Part of Partridge's chapter on the last plays was published as "The Symbolism of Clothes in Jonson's Last Plays," *JEGP* 56 (1957): 396–409. He believes that an "analysis of the imagery of these plays may reveal to what extent" the traditional charges of lack of unity, inflexibility of dramatic pattern and design, and repetitious weakness are true. The final chapters "attempt to draw the conclusions concerning Jonson's language and the effect of his comedies which . . . most sensibly follow from the previous analyses."

After surveying prose usage before Jonson, Jonas Barish, *Ben Jonson and the Language of Prose Comedy* (1960), discusses Jonson's use of the "loose style," his idiosyncratic traits, and the relationship between his style and his structure. He traces Jonson's use of prose from *The Case Is Altered* to *Bartholomew Fair*. Jonson identifies language with character: words are the man. This concept "leads to an especially acute concern for decorum, the law which demands that a character speak like himself at all times. Mimicry, however, introduces a complication: a violation of decorum . . . on the part of the character." Barish sees Jonson's preoccupation with the viciousness of language beginning "within the old-fashioned 'romantic' plot" of *The Case is Altered*. Barish's last chapter is reserved for final considerations and the influence of Jonsonian prose comedy, especially on Restoration dramatists. His *Ben Jonson: A Collection of Critical Essays* (1963) contains an introduction to Jonson criticism by Barish himself and a selection of essays by various critics, including T. S. Eliot, L. C. Knights, Harry Levin, Edmund Wilson, Arthur Sale, Paul Goodman, Edward Partridge, Ray Heffner, Joseph A. Bryant, Jr., and Dolora Cunningham. It was designed "to represent the state of Jonson criticism over the past forty years, both in its excellences and in its defects."

Calvin G. Thayer, *Ben Jonson: Studies in the Plays* (1963), gives a thorough introduction to the plays, summarizing current critical thought. He identifies certain characters as multidimensional symbols and details their symbolic functions. "In some of the earlier plays it has been possible to discern two groups of characters—those whose realistic presentation carries a symbolic value, and those whom we might describe as more or less purely realistic. Thus Volpone and Mosca as opposed to Voltore, Corvino, and Corbaccio. . . . That is to say, there has been one group of characters that we might describe as poet-figures, set up in opposition to another group of characters whose quintessence they expose. . . . I wish to insist that the poet-figures are also realistic figures and that their symbolic identity does not 'make' any particular play but enriches the satirical comedy in which they appear."

Robert E. Knoll, *Ben Jonson's Plays: An Introduction* (1964), attempts "to define Jonson's dramatic ideas by close examination of the plays and to deal with some of the principal scholarly controversies touching them." He believes that the plays are "elaborations of the Tudor morality drama," that Jonson "enriches the simplicity of his drama by setting his contemporaneous world within a mythic one," and that "Jonson is a . . . Christian humanist." Knoll begins his analyses with *Tale of a Tub* (which he considers an early play) and ends with a brief look at *The Sad Shepherd*. His book is a complete introduction to the plays.

Challenging Dryden's pronouncement that Jonson's "last plays were but dotages," Larry S. Champion, *Ben Jonson's "Dotages": A Reconsideration of the Late Plays* (1967), contends "that Jonson's comic intent, his theory of art, and his manipulation of material for both instruction and entertainment, is precisely that of his acknowledged masterpieces and that the plays can hardly be branded 'dotages' of a 'washed-out brain.'" Excluding *Tale of a Tub*, he suggests that the late comedies should be seen as "attempts to revivify satiric comedy and to broaden its appeal through adaptation of aspects of the native dramatic tradition."

In *Vision and Judgment in Ben Jonson's Drama* (1968), Gabriele Jackson suggests that Jonson's plays "might justly be called drama of revelation." The difference "between, and union of, real and ideal which occupies Jonson's drama occupies his thought about poetic composition as well. As theorist and as creator he sees double. The components of this doubleness I have called 'vision' and 'judgment'. . . . Jonson's perfect poet is simultaneously visionary and judge—superhuman seer and public man of action. . . . The conclusion of this study attempts very briefly to sum up the significance, both as strength and as weakness, of Jonson's simultaneous devotion to vision and judgment."

Pointing out that the brilliance and wealth of meaning in Machiavelli's political and historical writings have diverted attention from his comedies and esthetic thought, Daniel C. Boughner, *The Devil's Disciple: Ben Jonson's Debt to Machiavelli* (1968), argues that Jonson is indebted to Machiavelli's dramatic theory and practice for the structure of his comedies. He analyzes *Volpone, Sejanus, Every Man in His Humour, Epicoene, The Alchemist, Bartholomew Fair*, and *The Devil Is an Ass* to support his contention. He concludes that "*The Devil Is an Ass* stands as an impressive final tribute to Machiavelli."

Coburn Gum, *The Aristophanic Comedies of Ben Jonson* (1969), sees Aristophanes as the major inspiration for Jonson's comedy and compares the two dramatists, indicating their similarity in plot structure, in the comic function of low-class characters, in the distortion of accepted reality, in their vocabulary, and in their serious intention disguised by the comic mode. Jonson himself liked to be appreciated as a follower of Aristophanes, and Gum attempts to present the plays in that light.

In *Jonson's Moral Comedy* (1971), Alan C. Dessen sees Jonson's comedy in the light of the morality tradition. Beginning with a survey of "the dramatic legacy of one sizeable group of Elizabethan moralities, a group which in purpose and technique might have appealed to a dramatist of Jonson's inclinations," Dessen touches briefly on Jonson's early plays and gives his major attention to *Volpone, The Alchemist,* and *Bartholomew Fair*; "Jonson's three great comedies represent the culmination of the English morality tradition." He sees *The Devil Is an Ass* and *The Staple of News* as a falling away from this achievement.

Judd Arnold, *A Grace Peculiar: Ben Jonson's Cavalier Heroes* (1972), feels that a major structure in Jonsonian comedy is the opposition of three major groups of characters: the fools and knaves; the railing critics; and, between these two, the cavalier gallants. He traces this pattern from the early plays through *Bartholomew Fair*. The final plays are touched on briefly. Arnold emphasizes the role of the gallants in the action of the comedies.

During recent years an important concern of Jonson criticism has been the tone of his comedies—the attitude of the playwright toward his characters and the world he has created for them, and the relationship of both of these to the world outside that Jonson criticized so thoroughly. *The Compassionate Satirist: Ben Jonson and His Imperfect World* (1972), by Joseph A. Bryant, Jr., is a product of that concern. Bryant traces a change in Jonson's attitude toward satire from *Every Man in His Humour* and the "comical satires" to the mature comedies, which receive greatest attention. "What he did maintain throughout his career was a hardheaded, orthodox belief in the fundamental goodness of creation . . . and the belief usually manifested itself in one way or another in all but his most somber work. *A Tale of a Tub* presen.₅ it without embarrassment." The other late comedies are dismissed as dotages, Champion notwithstanding.

Franz Fricker, *Ben Jonson's Plays in Performance and the Jacobean Theatre* (1972), examines "the theatrical physiognomy of Ben Jonson's 'mature' comedies, courtly masques, and later plays," and concludes that "the dramatist suited his plays to the Jacobean theatres, their methods of production and audiences. . . . The conditions of the public and private theatres are integrated in the plays, whereas those of the stage at Whitehall . . . are less deeply embodied in the speeches of the masques."

Mary C. Williams, *Unity in Ben Jonson's Early Comedies*, Salzburg Studies in English Literature: Jacobean Drama Studies, no. 22 (1972), deals with "Jonson's methods of unifying his early comedies and the relationship of these methods to his critical statements about unity." After analyzing Jonson's various unifying methods in *A Tale of a Tub, The Case Is Altered, Every Man In* and *Every Man Out, Cynthia's Revels*, and *Poetaster*, Williams concludes: "The early plays reveal Jonson learning methods of unity to the point where he did not find 'comick law' a constricting and out-of-date tyranny but simply a means of artistic control. At this point he was ready to write both the play *Volpone* and the critical statements appended to it." Annette Drew-Bear, *Rhetoric in Ben Jonson's Middle Plays: A Study of Ethos, Character Portrayal, and Persuasion*, Salzburg Studies in English Literature: Jacobean Drama Studies, no. 24 (1973), argues that "an examination of Ben Jonson's use of rhetoric in four of his middle plays—*Sejanus, Volpone, The Alchemist,* and *Bartholomew Fair*—helps to illuminate the persuasive arts of Jonson's orators and his portrayal of their characters." William D. Wolf, *The Reform of the Fallen World: The "Virtuous Prince" in Jonsonian Tragedy and Comedy*, Salzburg Studies in English Literature: Jacobean Drama Studies, no. 27 (1973), analyzes *Catiline* and *Sejanus* to "provide a useful perspective" on *Volpone, The Alchemist,* and *Bartholomew Fair.* "Only *Catiline* of the five plays ends 'happily,' and it alone contains a sufficient prince. . . . Each of the other plays contains at least one potential 'virtuous prince,' but for various reasons these figures fall short. . . . Jonson uses these figures to explore the prince's opportunities and his shortcomings."

James E. Savage, *Ben Jonson's Basic Comic Characters and Other Essays* (1973), makes a case against the tendency to consider Jonson as a writer tied to the theory of humours. Instead he divides Jonson's basic comic characters into three groups: the choric, the broker, and the humourous. There are also chapters on the personal elements in the plays and on Jonson's relationship to Shakespeare.

Mary Olive Thomas, "Editor's Comment," in *Ben Jonson: Quadricentennial Essays*, a special issue of *Studies in the Literary Imagination* 6 (1973): x–xi, groups the essays in this volume by genre: "The first six treat the major plays, the next one traces Jonson's career as a writer of court masques, and the final four consider representative poems." The critics are Alvin B. Kernan, George A. E. Parfitt, Marvin L. Vawter, L. A. Beaurline, David McPherson, Richard Levin, M. C. Bradbrook, Ian Donaldson, Edward Partridge, William Kerrigan, and Richard S. Peterson. *A Celebration of Ben Jonson*, ed. William Blissett et al. (1973), contains critical essays by Clifford Leech, Jonas Barish, George

Hibbard, D. F. McKenzie, Hugh Maclean, and L. C. Knights, on Jonson's plays and poetry.

Aliki Lafkidou Dick, *Paedeia Through Laughter: Jonson's Aristophanic Appeal to Human Intelligence* (1974), emphasizes "the importance both dramatists placed upon the fact that human intelligence is to be used rightly if man wants to have a happy life on earth." He compares the two "in terms of common ideas, thoughts, intentions, tone, methods, and techniques," and concludes that "Jonson's attempt to educate through laughter is shaped and influenced by Aristophanes' art and spirit."

Douglas Duncan, "Ben Jonson's Lucianic Irony," *Ariel* 1, no. 2 (1970): 42-53, contends "that the satiric standpoint of Lucian and his humanist imitators decisively influenced, or at least authoritatively supported, Jonson's approach to dramatic art, especially following his withdrawal from the Poetomachia in 1601-2." He feels that "the Lucianic tradition offers the best parallel for the particular kinds of irony" Jonson practiced, and that the "channelling of the didactic urge into irony was vital to the success of his greatest work." H. R. Hays, "Satire and Identification: An Introduction to Ben Jonson," *KR* 19 (1957): 267-83, suggests that the twentieth century wants to identify with the major character in a work of art; Jonsonian comedy prohibits this kind of identification by presenting characters with whom we do not wish to identify. Although Jonson's characters may be contemporary caricatures, they are also psychologically true and universal; by laughing at their faults, we purge ourselves of the same faults. To illustrate this point, Hays analyzes *Bartholomew Fair*.

Alvin Kernan, *The Cankered Muse: Satire of the English Renaissance* (1959), feels that "what Jonson did in *Every Man Out* was to develop in dramatic terms the relationship between author and satirist which is axiomatic in both Elizabethan formal verse satire and critical discussions of the genre," but that "the satiric plays of Ben Jonson written after 1604, and after a number of unsuccessful efforts on Jonson's part to include the figure of the satirist in his drama, constitutes a movement away from the use of the satirist." Although his characters are all "satiric portraits of Renaissance aspiration," Jonson keeps them all tied to a "dense substratum of primal matter." His characters satirize themselves, and it is their "willingness . . . to accept the apparent for the real that makes them immediately ridiculous." Kernan's "Alchemy and Acting: The Major Plays of Ben Jonson," in *Ben Jonson: Quadricentennial Essays* (above), pp. 1-22, points out that the "surface of Jonson's plays is bright, bubbling, lively. The characters are great optimists. . . . But latent in this same world is the Jonsonian nightmare of disorder and death, a 'zany' version of meaningful life, into which the characters tumble by their very efforts at transcendence." Jonson's answer to this vision of horror "is the provisional one of accepting your own limitations and realizing that no warrant confers very much authority."

Two studies discuss Jonson's satire in relation to other authors. D. J. Enright, "Poetic Satire and Satire in Verse: A Consideration of Jonson and Massinger," *Scrutiny* 18 (1951-52): 211-23, included with minor changes in his *The Apothecary's Shop* (1957), compares *Volpone* with *A New Way to Pay Old Debts*. Enright concludes that "Jonson wrote poetic satire, Massinger wrote satire in verse." Edwin Honig, "Notes on Satire in Swift and Jonson," *New Mexico Quarterly* 18 (1948): 155-63, suggests that Jonson and Swift gave "satire that personal emphasis which existed neither before their times nor ever again after their deaths." Honig compares their satire in terms of "repudiation of zeal, pride, religious enthusiasm, clothes-fetishism, and poetasting; a stoical defense of reasonableness; and the use of allegory, hyperbole, invective," and concludes with generalizations about Swiftian and Jonsonian satire.

Brian Gibbons, *Jacobean City Comedy: A Study of Satiric Plays by Jonson, Marston and Middleton* (1968), sees Jonson's satire as "City Comedy"—"a distinct dramatic genre with a recognisable form and conventions of theme, setting and characterization," which developed between 1597 and 1624. Gibbon traces the interaction between the three playwrights studied, and since city comedy satirizes the age, he examines the socioeconomic background. He suggests that Jonson's comic world is Machiavellian and Hobbesian, and not at all like the ideal world of Tudor myth.

Wallace A. Bacon, "The Magnetic Field: The Structure of Jonson's Comedies," *HLQ* 19 (1956): 121-53, surveys the plays from *Every Man In* to *The Magnetic Lady*. "For Jonson, structure *is* something like a 'Center attractive' . . . drawing unto it a diversity of characters and humours. The magnetic center determines the pattern—the structure—of elements. . . . This center may be a person, as in *Volpone*; or a profession, as in *The Alchemist*; or a unified body of activities, as in *Bartholomew Fair*. . . . we have demonstrated that in the major successes of Jonson, this kind of structure has been attained." Ray L. Heffner, Jr., "Unifying Symbols in the Comedy of Ben Jonson," *English Stage Comedy*, ed. W. K. Wimsatt, Jr., *English Institute Essays*

1954 (1955), pp. 74–97 (rpt. in Barish, *Ben Jonson: A Collection of Critical Essays,* pp. 133–46, above), feels that the "essential unity of Jonson's comedy is thematic," and that Jonson, given to the interplay of fantasy and realism, united each play around a comic conceit, extravagant in nature, which he turns into a unifying symbol. Lawrence L. Levin, "Replication as Dramatic Strategy in the Comedies of Ben Jonson," *RenD* 5 (1972): 37–74, proposes that Jonson utilizes "a central analogue, occurring primarily in Act IV, but sometimes in Act III or V, which reflected upon the play's catastrophe. . . . Jonson fashioned one or two significant pieces of analogous action as a key structural block with a dual purpose: to help unify the play by bringing into focus theme, incident, and character, and to anticipate . . . elements of the denouement and conclusion." To illustrate this proposition, Levin examines Jonson's method of construction from the earliest plays to *The Staple of News.*

L. A. Beaurline, "Ben Jonson and the Illusion of Completeness," *PMLA* 84 (1969): 51–59, suggests that in all Jonson's work there is an impulse toward a kind of controlled completeness. Along with the more advanced writers of his age, he chose to be less cosmic than his predecessors and less quantitative, more selective and exhaustive. His comic plots are like the working out of a series of permutations with a fixed number of constants and one variable. By this method, Jonson was able to replace copiousness by a more selective variety and contrast, and by gradations within strict limits. See also Ejner J. Jensen and L. A. Beaurline, "L. A. Beaurline and the Illusion of Completeness," *PMLA* 86 (1971): 121–27, a reply and an exchange. Thomas M. Greene, "Ben Jonson and the Centered Self," *SEL* 10 (1970): 325–48, believes that the dual image of circle and center is an important organizing principle in Jonson's work. The circle, symbolic of perfection, harmony, cosmic balance, society, the household, soul, is doubled by the center, symbolic of the governor, the king, the inner self. In the masks, the images represent achieved ideals. In most of Jonson's other work, the circle is broken, and the center is isolated in solitary and upright independence.

In "Feasting and Judging in Jonsonian Comedy," *RenD* 5 (1972): 3–35, Jonas A. Barish points out that each of Jonson's plays grapples anew with the question of justice and "propounds its own experimental answers. Glancing over Jonson's output as a whole, we can perceive a gradual abandonment of the attempt to embody justice in figures of authority or public institutions, and an increasing reliance on the happy conjunctions of wit and chance. We discover also a rough inverse correlation between severity of judgment and feasting. Where judicial stringency prevails, the festive element tends to remain tentative and muted. Where the festive note is strongly struck, judgment tends toward leniency." John Thatcher French, "Ben Jonson: His Aesthetic of Relief," *TSLL* 10 (1968): 161-75, discusses Jonson's "appropriation of the ancient Greek concept of physical purgation as a form of relief (literal and figurative) for the passions." Surveying the plays from *Every Man In* to *The Staple of News*, French concludes: "If this view of purgation as an aesthetic formula which satisfies physical and epistemological demands be accepted, we may conclude that Jonson did have something like a philosophical development which he refused to push beyond the humanistic formula of his concept of art. Had he done this he would have been writing comedies of the absurd to the tune of Ionesco or Pirandello."

Leona Dale, "Jonson's Sick Society," *BRMMLA* 24 (1970): 66-74, contends that, "through a complex method of equating social and cultural diseases with physiological ills, Jonson created a medical imagery which is inextricably a part of the development of character, the working of plot, and the maintenance of an underlying theme which is basically the theme of all his comedies—the deviation of man from the accepted norm." Dale uses *Every Man In*, *Every Man Out*, and *Volpone* to illustrate her point. Kirsty Northcote-Bade, "The Play of Illusion in Ben Jonson's Comedies," *Words: Wai-Te-Ata Studies in Literature*, no. 2 (1966), pp. 82-91, believes that "illusion itself is the basic theme of his major comedies *Volpone, The Alchemist,* and *Bartholomew Fair*," and tries to explain the "bewilderment" of the latter by explaining its use of "a new handling of illusion in the structure of the play." Gail Kern Paster, "Ben Jonson's Comedy of Limitation," *SP* 72 (1975): 51-71, argues that "what Jonson called the law of place is in his plays a useful dramatic technique and the basis for comic statements about the nature of actuality." Using *Volpone, Epicoene, Bartholomew Fair*, and *The Alchemist*, she shows that there is a contrast between the megalomania of the characters and the very limited space they are made to occupy.

George A. E. Parfitt, "Virtue and Pessimism in Three Plays by Ben Jonson," in *Ben Jonson: Quadricentennial Essays* (above), pp. 23-40, examines "virtue" in *Volpone, Bartholomew Fair,* and *Sejanus*. He believes that "behind adverse criticism of Jonson's virtuous characters there lies a Christian assumption that 'virtue' is a meaningful and convincing concept in relation to human experience," and suggests that the

weakness of Jonson's virtuous characters reveals his "inherent pessimism." In an eighteen-page essay bound with Sanford Sternlicht's *John
Webster's Imagery and the Webster Canon*, Derek de Silva, "Jonson:
Wit and the Moral Sense in *Volpone* and the Major Comedies," *Salzburg
Studies in English Literature: Jacobean Drama Studies*, no. 1 (1972),
argues that, in *Volpone, The Alchemist,* and *Bartholomew Fair,* Jonson
"tends to exhibit an indulgence to crook and sybarite which is
grounded in his admiration for the refinement of intelligence and taste
their professions require." Jonson's admiration and moral sense are in
greatest tension in *Volpone* where de Silva finds a striking pattern of
"inflation and deflation" in the protagonist's career. At the end of the
play, "Volpone pops back irrepressibly alive to make the Epilogue.
. . . He reminds us . . . what Jonson held instinctively—that in a work of
art aesthetic pleasure need not be identified with moral wholesome-
ness."

Constantine J. Gianakaris, "The Humanism of Ben Jonson," *CLAJ*
14 (1970): 115-26, emphasizes Jonson's broadly humanistic background which allowed him to unite classical with contemporary
standards in order to create enlightening comic plays. W. David Kay,
"The Shaping of Ben Jonson's Career: A Reexamination of Facts and
Problems," *MP* 67 (1970): 224-37, investigates the success of Jonson's
early drama, especially the *Every Man* plays, in terms of his contemporary audience. Percy Simpson's "The Art of Ben Jonson," *E&S* 30
(1944): 35-49 (rpt. in his *Studies in Elizabethan Drama* [1955]), is of
interest as a summary statement by one of the editors of the Oxford
Ben Jonson. Other introductory essays are: J. B. Bamborough, *Ben
Jonson,* WTW, no. 112 (1959), and his *Ben Jonson* (1970); Una Ellis-
Fermor, "Ben Jonson," in her *The Jacobean Drama: An Interpretation*
(4th ed., 1958); and Louis Kronenberger, *The Thread of Laughter:
Chapters on English Stage Comedy from Jonson to Maugham* (1952).

Joseph A. Bryant, Jr., "The Significance of Ben Jonson's First
Requirement for Tragedy: 'Truth of Argument,'" *SP* 49 (1952): 195-
213, glances at Jonson's critical thought generally before turning to a
specific discussion of his criteria for tragedy, especially "Truth of
Argument." This criterion "meant to him just what it had always
meant in Renaissance criticism," but Jonson goes a step further: "the
argument of a tragedy must not only be drawn from history; it must
also be historically verifiable." Bryant accounts for this emphasis by
citing Jonson's high regard for history *per se* and the Puritan attacks on
fictional drama. Robert Ornstein's essay on Jonson in *The Moral*

Vision of Jacobean Tragedy (1960) is reprinted in *Elizabethan Drama: Modern Essays in Criticism,* ed. R. J. Kaufmann (1961), pp. 187-207. Ornstein sees Jonson's tragedy as closest to Chapman's, and suggests that Jonson's were unsuccessful because he could not come to terms with his own view of politics. He feels that Jonson "did not see his tragic theme steadily," and concludes that Jonson lacks "moral vision" in the tragedies. Geoffrey Hill, "The World's Proportion: Jonson's Dramatic Poetry in *Sejanus* and *Catiline,*" in *Jacobean Theatre,* SuAS, vol. 1 (1960), pp. 112-31, stresses the closeness of Jonsonian tragedy to the Jacobean political situation and the resulting ambiguity of presentation.

Ralph Nash, "Ben Jonson's Tragic Poems," *SP* 55 (1958): 164-86, suggests that *Catiline* and *Sejanus* are "experiments, . . . being exemplars of a variety of tragic poem that never flourished well and consequently has not been widely noticed." He goes on to discuss Jonson's use of historically verifiable material and denies the relevance of Aristotelian pity to Jonson's tragedy. A conservative in politics, Jonson did not believe in the overthrow of authority, and this belief influences his art in both plays. Nash especially notes the parallels between Cicero and Catiline. In using political material, Jonson has a rough and ready grasp of political realities, a fact which Nash illustrates by quoting Machiavelli (see Boughner, above). For Nash, Jonson's plays raise two important questions: how far may tragedy deal with the political nature of man? how shall we classify Jonson's plays? Nash feels that the plays are "Renaissance tragedies" in the widest sense of the phrase and suggests that we simply call them "Renaissance tragic poems." Other treatments of the tragedies are: Jacob I. DeVilliers, "Ben Jonson's Tragedies," *ES* 45 (1964): 433-42; Irving Ribner, *The English History Play in the Age of Shakespeare* (1957; rev. ed. 1965); and Anselm Schlösser, "Ben Jonson's Roman Plays," *Kwartalnik neofilologiczny* 8 (1961): 123-59. Louis C. Stagg, *Index to the Figurative Language of Ben Jonson's Tragedies* (1967), includes such topics as "animals," "arts," "body," "learning," and "nature."

Various critics have linked the concept of humours to Jonsonian comedy, and Baum, *The Satiric and the Didactic in Ben Jonson's Comedy* (above), gives a partial bibliography of the subject. Henry L. Snuggs, "The Comic Humours: A New Interpretation," *PMLA* 62 (1947): 114-22 (abridged in *Shakespeare's Contemporaries,* ed. Max Bluestone and Norman Rabkin [1961], pp. 172-77), suggests that Jonson used the word "humours" in two different ways: (1) "a genuinely ingrained temperament in accord with humoral psychology," and (2) "the prevalent extension and misconception of the term, an assumed or temporary characteristic, the assumption of which was itself absurd and demanded satirical treatment." In his plays, Jonson generally uses "humours" in the second sense in order to "show the age its vices and vanities." In "The Source of Jonson's Definition of Comedy," *MLN* 65 (1950): 543-44, Snuggs suggests Minturno's *De Poeta,* Book IV, as the source for Cordatus's Ciceronian definition of comedy in *Every Man Out.*

James D. Redwine, Jr., "Beyond Psychology: The Moral Basis for Jonson's Theory of Humour Characterization," *ELH* 28 (1961): 316-34, believes that Jonson saw his "humours" as moral in basis, and to support this contention he examines Jonson's early statements about humours. He sees Jonson's interest in humour characterization lasting throughout his career and suggests that decorum in Renaissance thought "is based in good part upon moral philosophy." James H. Clancy, "Ben Jonson and the 'Humours,'" *Theatre Annual* 11 (1953): 15-23, maintains that Jonson uses his humours in a theatrical way, comparing O'Neill's use of Freudianism. Hiram Haydn, *The Counter-Renaissance* (1950), supposes that Jonson "drew his new satiric version of this famous concept from current individualistic philosophies." Charles O. McDonald, "Restoration Comedy as Drama of Satire: An Investigation into Seventeenth Century Aesthetics," *SP* 61 (1964): 522-44, examines "Ben Jonson and the humours tradition," E. E. Stokes, Jr., "Jonson's 'Humour' Plays and Some Later Plays of Bernard Shaw," *Shavian* 2, no. 10 (1964): 13-18, believes that Shaw's later plays reveal a change in the direction of Jonson, in that the characters become "representatives of types or classes of men or of abstract 'qualities,' theories, or attitudes." Although Joseph A. Bryant's article, "Jonson's Satirist out of His Humor," *Ball State Teacher's College Forum* 3, no. 1 (1962): 31-36 (incorporated in Bryant's *The Compassionate Satirist,* above), is only tenuously linked to a discussion of humours; it deals with the early humours comedies. He suggests that *Every Man Out, Cynthia's Revels,* and *The Poetaster* are illustrative fables showing that the satirist is a healthy member of society only when supported by an enlightened, moral ruler.

De Witt T. Starnes and Ernest W. Talbert, *Classical Myth and Legend in Renaissance Dictionaries: A Study of Renaissance Dictionaries in Their Relation to the Classical Learning of Contemporary English Writers* (1955), consider Jonson's use of Renaissance compendia of classical learning, and point out that "examples might be multiplied of instances in the plays and poems wherein the dictionary entries could have supplied Jonson with particular details of phraseology and association or could have directed him to classical passages that seem to be reflected in his lines." James A. Riddell, "Seventeenth-Century Identifications of Jonson's Sources in the Classics," *Renaissance Quarterly* 28 (1975): 204–18, reveals that, in "a copy of the 1616 folio of Jonson's *Works*," a seventeenth-century hand has identified 250 passages in which Jonson has borrowed from the classics. Ellen M. T. Duffy, "Ben Jonson's Debt to Renaissance Scholarship in *Sejanus* and *Catiline*," *MLR* 42 (1947): 24–30, feels "the fact that Jonson used contemporary aids to the study of the classics does not detract from his scholarship. . . . Jonson . . . was making use of the most authoritative material at his disposal and at the same time linking himself with European scholarship." Harold A. Mason, *Humanism and Poetry in the Early Tudor Period* (1959), treats Jonson's humanistic scholarship in his translation of Vives and in "To Penshurst"; "Jonson's Humanism . . . not only shows us what was potentially there in the writings of More and Wyatt, it is also the finest possible test for assessing the Humanism of Milton." Sir Roland Syme, "Roman Historians and Renaissance Politics," in *Society and History in the Renaissance: A Report of a Conference Held at the Folger Library on April 23 and 24, 1960* (1960), pp. 3–12, notes the influence of the Roman historians on Jonson. Esther C. Dunn, *Ben Jonson's Art* (1925), comments on Jonson's antiquarianism.

Evaluating Jonson's knowledge of the criminal underworld, Normand Berlin, *The Base String: The Underworld in Elizabethan Drama* (1968), writes: "Jonson so effectively manipulates his underworld that the audience leaves the play thinking that the victims are inferior to the cheaters. . . . He calculatingly, even arrogantly, justles his audience's moral standards. In doing so his comedy provides a valid satiric commentary on man's folly. . . . The dramatist who sees humanity divided between rogues and fools seems content to let his rogues play their parts and go their way."

Jonson's knowledge of Italian is investigated by Simonini and Praz. Rinaldo C. Simonini, Jr., *Italian Scholarship in Renaissance England* (1952), believes that "Ben Jonson's remarkable and much celebrated breadth of learning encompassed some knowledge of Italian scholarship." Pointing out the personal connections between Jonson and John Florio, Simonini presents evidence to suggest that Jonson knew Florio's "scholarly work." Jonson may have known Bruno's *Candelaio,* a possible source for *The Alchemist,* through Florio, as well as Tomaso Garzoni's *Piazza universale* (1587), a possible source for the background of *Volpone.* Simonini's "Ben Jonson and John Florio," *N&Q* 195 (1950): 512-13, supports the view that Jonson was the chief author of *Eastward Ho!,* Act V. In *The Flaming Heart* (1958), Mario Praz suggests that the Italian names of the early plays are a simple veneer, but that "a great change came about with *Volpone* (1606). Here the Venetian local colour is rendered with such accuracy as to leave behind any other contemporary dramatist fond of picturesque allusion." Praz feels that Jonson's knowledge of Italian literature is not wide, and he believes Florio to be the source of that knowledge.

Jonson's use of poetry in the drama has received some attention. After discussing the wide use of rhymed couplets in Elizabethan dramatic verse, Alexander H. Sackton, "The Rhymed Couplet in Ben Jonson's Plays," *Studies in English* (Univ. of Texas) 30 (1951): 86-106, observes that for Jonson "the couplet was a familiar and sympathetic form," especially in *Poetaster* (420 lines of rhyme), *Sejanus* (303) and *The Sad Shepherd* (299). Sackton feels that a chronological review of the plays will tell us something about Jonson's use of the couplet. A more general survey of Jonson's dramatic poetry is Rufus Putney's "Jonson's Poetic Comedy," *PQ* 41 (1962): 188-204. Putney feels that Jonson's fusion of dramatic and lyric poetry reaches its high point in *Volpone,* III.vii.

Several items concern Jonson's prose and his use of language. In a seminal article, Jonas Barish, "Baroque Prose in the Theatre: Ben Jonson," *PMLA* 73 (1958): 184-95, points out the music of "brusque dissonances and irregular rhythms" in Jonson's prose. Robert Beum, "The Scientific Affinities of English Baroque Prose," *EM* 13 (1962): 59-80, identifies three types of baroque prose: loose, ornate, and terse or stringy; Jonson uses the terse style. Marco Mincoff, "Baroque Literature in England," *Annuaire de l'Université de Sofia,* Faculté Historico-Philologique, 43 (1946-47), also treats this aspect. Dave Rankin, "Ben Jonson: Semanticist," *Ect* 19 (1962): 289-97, argues that Jonson understood the general principles of semantics. Tore Jungnell's "Notes on the Language of Ben Jonson," *Studier i Modern Språkvetenskap* 1 (1960): 86-110, is a collection of grammatical-syntactical phenomena from Jonson's First Folio. Wesley Trimpi's "Jonson and the Neo-Latin Authorities for the Plain Style," *PMLA* 77 (1962): 21-26, is incorporated in his *Ben Jonson's Poems* (I, C).

Henry W. Wells, "Ben Jonson, Patriarch of Speech Study," *SAB* 13 (1938): 54–62, is still valuable.

In "Ben Jonson and Jacobean Stagecraft," in *Jacobean Theatre*, SuAS, vol. 1 (1960), pp. 42–61, William A. Armstrong sets out to "survey Jonson's criticisms of the stagecraft of contemporary plays and masques and then to discuss the main characteristics of the stage-craft of his comedies and tragedies." Jonson's personal stagecraft is "distinguished by its clarity, economy, and discrimination, and many of his finest effects are obtained by the simplest of means." "At his best, Jonson integrates stage business, properties, and dialogue with remarkable finesse and subtlety." Matthew W. Black, "Enter Citizens," in *Studies in the English Renaissance Drama*, ed. Josephine W. Bennett et al. (1959); pp. 16–27, makes some interesting comments on Jonson's use of humour names which in his drama tend to replace the numbered groups used by earlier playwrights. A. V. Cookman, "Shakespeare's Contemporaries on the Modern English Stage," *SJ* 94 (1958): 29–41, discusses Jonson and others on the modern stage.

"The War of the Theaters" is at best a nebulous event. Nevertheless, Jonson's place in it has been examined. Josiah H. Penniman, *The War of the Theatres* (1897), and Roscoe A. Small, *The Stage-Quarrel between Ben Jonson and the So-Called Poetasters* (1899), are seminal studies, though Baum (see above) feels they have "been too lavish in their identifications." Robert Boies Sharpe, *The Real War of the Theaters* (1935), takes a more balanced approach. John J. Enck, "The Peace of the Poetomachia," *PMLA* 77 (1962): 386–96, believes that about 1600 Shakespeare and Jonson became professionally aware of each other. "Because at this period Jonson experimented more boldly . . . than Shakespeare did, to list as objectively as possible what Jonson introduced and then to detect how Shakespeare adapted it may help isolate elements which will comprise a measure for *Troilus and Cressida.*" "The Poetomachia, as a struggle about correctness . . . explains more than any other conjecture why a school of talented professional writers should all, inside two years, experiment with a style which forcefully yokes lightness and intensity, and then aban-dons it." F. G. Fleay, *A Chronicle History of the Life and Work of William Shakespeare* (1886), suggested that Ajax in *Troilus* was a satire on Jonson. William Elton, "Shakespeare's Portrait of Ajax in *Troilus and Cressida*," *PMLA* 63 (1948): 744–48, comes to the same conclusion, using internal and external evidence. Other identifications are made in Fleay's *A Biographical Chronicle of the English Drama, 1559–1642*, 2 vols. (1891).

Basing his conclusions partly on Ralph W. Berringer's "Jonson's *Cynthia's Revels* and the War of the Theatres," *PQ* 22 (1943): 1-22, and Ernest Talbert's "The Purpose and Technique of Jonson's *Poetaster*," *SP* 42 (1945): 225-52, W. L. Halstead, "What 'War of the Theatres'?" *CE* 9 (1947-48): 424-26, feels that it was not a quarrel, but a friendly feud aimed at gaining an increased drawing power for the plays; in his opinion, it failed. Robert Withington, "What 'War of the Theatres'?" *CE* 10 (1948-49): 163-64, suggests that the event had more meaning than Halstead admits. One result "seems to have been that, perhaps unconsciously, Jonson shifted . . . from classical to realistic satire." In *Shakespeare and the "War of the Theatres"* (1957), Henryk Zbierski sees the war as a struggle between the private and public theaters. He is determined to prove Jonson the prime enemy of the popular theater, and he searches Shakespeare for allusions to Jonson and the war. For a different point of view, see Alfred Harbage, *Shakespeare and the Rival Traditions* (1952). (See II,A, under *Poetaster.*)

Jonson and Shakespeare are often linked, and much scholarship has been devoted to examining and clarifying that relationship. G. E. Bentley, *Shakespeare and Jonson: Their Reputations in the Seventeenth Century Compared,* 2 vols. (1945), concludes that "Jonson's general popularity was greater than Shakespeare's from the beginning of the century to 1690." Bentley's list of allusions may be supplemented by William R. Keast, "Some Seventeenth-Century Allusions to Shakespeare and Jonson," *N&Q* 194 (1949): 468-69. Ernest Sirluck, "Shakespeare and Jonson among the Pamphleteers of the First Civil War: Some Unreported Seventeenth-Century Allusions," *MP* 53 (1955-56): 88-99, points out that Bentley did not examine the pamphlets of the Civil War and that they contain Jonson-Shakespeare allusions. Sir Politic Would-Be is the most popular of Jonson's characters in the century and first alluded to in a Puritan pamphlet of 1642. Documenting the change of taste in the early eighteenth century which preferred Addison to Swift, "and, most important, Shakespeare to Jonson," Stuart M. Tave, "Corbyn Morris: Falstaff, Humor, and Comic Theory in the Eighteenth Century," *MP* 50 (1952): 102-15, believes that Corbyn Morris's *An Essay towards Fixing the True Standards of Wit, Humour, Raillery, Satire, and Ridicule* (1744), is important in that change. If Dryden begins the process away from Jonson, Morris completes it.

In the view of Bentley and the scholars who follow him, Jonson reigned supreme in the earlier seventeenth century, but was replaced by Shakespeare in the eighteenth. However, David L. Frost, "Shakespeare in the Seventeenth Century," *SQ* 16 (1965): 81-89, and *The School of Shakespeare: The Influence of Shakespeare on English Drama 1600-42* (1968), challenges Bentley's use of rigid principles in selecting allusions. Frost concludes that "Shakespeare was widely appreciated in his own day and appealed to the public of the seventeenth century more than did Jonson." E. Honigmann, "Who Did Like Shakespeare," *New Saltire,* no. 11, April 1964, pp. 47-50, also feels that Bentley has exaggerated his case. John Freehafer, "Leonard Digges, Ben Jonson, and the Beginning of Shakespeare Idolatry," *SQ* 21 (1970): 63-75, traces the beginnings of bardolatry to Digges's poetic defense of Shakespeare against the opposing dramatic principles of Jonson. Although these studies do not completely destroy Bentley's thesis, a complete review of the facts is needed.

Sydney Musgrove's *Shakespeare and Jonson* (1957), considers several areas of contact and concludes that it is best to think of the two dramatists as closely allied in aims and methods, rather than in any way opposed. G. E. Bentley's *The Swan of Avon and the Bricklayer of Westminster,* Inaugural Lecture at Princeton University, 15 March 1946 (1947), and Robert Ornstein's "Shakespearian and Jonsonian Comedy," *ShS* 22 (1969): 43-46, are succinct comparisons. Although primarily a study of Shakespeare, Milton Crane's "*Twelfth Night* and Shakespearian Comedy," *SQ* 6 (1955): 1-8, suggests that Nevill Coghill may be wrong in distinguishing between Shakespearean and Jonsonian comedy. Peter G. Phialas, "Comic Truth in Shakespeare and Jonson," *SAQ* 62 (1963): 78-91, believes there is a distinct difference between the two types of comedy. Rejecting romance, Jonson invents plot to exhibit human imperfections; on the other hand, Shakespeare is unafraid of romantic themes and emphasizes man's reaching toward perfection. David Bevington, "Shakespeare vs Jonson on Satire," in *Shakespeare 1971: Proceedings of the World Shakespeare Congress,* ed. Clifford Leech and J. M. R. Margeson (1971), pp. 107-22, concludes that Jonson satirized all popular forms while limiting himself to a neoclassical drama. Shakespeare experimented with Jonsonian satire, but retained a more flexible attitude. Northrop Frye, "Comic Myth in Shakespeare," *PTRSC,* ser. 3, 46, no. 2 (1952): 47-58, believes that "Jonson established, by conscious effort and will, the tradition of modern comedy; Shakespeare achieved a far deeper affinity with dramatic tradition in the manner recommended by some Chinese philosophers, by not doing anything about it." Mary Lascelles, "Shakespeare's Comic Insight," *PBA* 48 (1962): 171–86, contrasts Shakespeare's "inclusiveness" with the "exclusiveness" of Jonson.

Harry Levin, "Two Magian Comedies: *The Tempest* and *The Alchemist,*" *ShS* 22 (1969): 47–58, believes that the "conjunction of Jonson and Shakespeare was never closer or more productive than in the successive seasons of 1610 and 1611, when His Majesty's Servants introduced *The Alchemist* and *The Tempest*. . . .That *The Tempest* came after *The Alchemist* means, of course, that Shakespeare had the opportunity to reflect and reply. . . . He responded to Jonson's brilliant example not through imitation or refutation but, we might opine, through sublimation—remembering that this notion was held by the alchemists long before it was adopted by the psychoanalysts." Daniel C. Boughner, "Jonsonian Structure in *The Tempest,*" *SQ* 21 (1970): 3–10, suggests that Shakespeare uses the neoclassical four-part structure introduced by Jonson to the English stage. John Hollander, "*Twelfth Night* and the Morality of Indulgence," *SR* 67 (1959): 220–38, deals with the relationship of Shakespeare's play to Jonson's comic theory. Madeleine Doran's *Endeavors of Art: A Study of Form in Elizabethan Drama* (1954) contains a section on "Jonsonian and Shakespearean Comedy." J. Dover Wilson, "Ben Jonson and *Julius Caesar,*" *ShS* 2 (1949): 36–43, feels that Jonson's line, "Reason long since is fled to animals, you know," in *Every Man Out* (III.iv), is a fling at *Julius Caesar* (cf. Antony's "O judgment! thou art fled to brutish beasts"), as also is Carlo Buffone's "Et tu Brute!" (V.vi). Antony's eulogy of Brutus may have influenced the description of Crites in *Cynthia's Revels,* and Jonson in turn may have influenced certain changes in *Julius Caesar.* James E. Savage, "Ben Jonson and Shakespeare: 1623–1626," *UMSE* 10 (1969): 25–48 (incorporated in his *Ben Jonson's Basic Comic Characters,* above), sees the influence of Shakespeare's *Timon of Athens, Julius Caesar,* and *Troilus and Cressida* on Jonson's *Staple of News.*

Jonson's influence on later authors has been traced. T. McAlindon, "Yeats and the English Renaissance," *PMLA* 82 (1967): 157–69, investigates Yeats's comment that he was "deep in Ben Jonson" in 1906. Jonson's influence on Joyce is noted by J. B. Bamborough, "Joyce and Jonson," *REL* 2, no. 4 (1961): 45–50, and Herbert Howarth, "The Joycean Comedy: Wilde, Jonson, and Others," in

A James Joyce Miscellany: Second Series, ed. Marvin Magalaner (1959), pp. 179-94. In the nineteenth century, Jonson influenced Scott (George Burke Johnston, "Scott and Jonson," *N&Q* 195 [1950]: 521-22), and in the eighteenth century, Pope (Stanley S. Wronker, "Pope and Ben Jonson," *N&Q* 196 [1951]: 495-96). William Peery, *"Eastward Ho!* and *A Woman Is a Weathercock,"* *MLN* 62 (1947): 131-32, and "The Influence of Ben Jonson on Nathan Field," *SP* 43 (1946): 482-97, points out Jonson's influence on Field. Ralph J. Kaufmann, *Richard Brome, Caroline Playwright* (1961), deals with Jonson's value system and his struggle against the cash nexus; "It is likely that Jonson's verve and spirited attack are the very things that most powerfully influenced Brome." Rufus A. Blanshard, "Carew and Jonson," *SP* 52 (1955): 195-211, feels that Carew follows Jonson in the genres used and in the lucidity of style and thought; at times, one may point to direct influence. F. S. Boas, "Edward Howard's Lyrics and Essays," *Contemporary Review* 174 (1948): 107-11, touches on Howard's tributes to Jonson and Shakespeare. Thomas B. Stroup, "George Daniel: Cavalier Poet," *RenP,* 1958, pp. 39-51, and his edition of Daniel's poems (1959), points out Daniel's references to Jonson. Douglas Bush, "Jonson, Donne, and Their Successors," in his *English Literature in the Earlier Seventeenth Century, 1600-1660* (1945; 2nd ed. 1962), gives a broad view, as do Joe Lee Davis, *The Sons of Ben: Jonsonian Comedy in Caroline England* (1967), and Joseph Summers, *The Heirs of Donne and Jonson* (1970). Ronald Pearsall, "The Case for Shadwell," *Month* 216 (1963): 364-67, believes Shadwell's comedies are comparable to Jonson's, and Egon Tiedje, *Die Tradition Ben Jonsons in der Restaurationskomödie* (1963), closely examines the relation between Jonsonian comedy and the comedy of the Restoration.

Jonson's influence on Milton is the subject of several items. Robert C. Fox, "A Source for Milton's *Comus,"* *N&Q* 9 (1962), 52-53, suggests *Poetaster* (III.iv. 114-16). M. F. Moloney, "The Prosody of Milton's *Epitaph, L'Allegro,* and *Il Penseroso,"* *MLN* 72 (1957): 174-78, touches on Jonson's "Epitaph on Elizabeth, L. H.," and "On My First Daughter," noting that "it is a commonplace that Ben Jonson is the great master in the 17th century of funerary verse"; from him the century learned "stateliness in the four-stress line." W. Lawrence Thompson, "The Source of the Flower Passage in *Lycidas,"* *N&Q* 197 (1952): 97-99, suggests *Pan's Anniversary.* Jonson's possible influence on Oldham and Massinger is touched on elsewhere (II, A, *Catiline* and *Sejanus).*

Herford and Simpson (vols. 1 and 11) attempt a reconstruction of Jonson's library, which is listed by Sears Jayne, *Library Catalogues of the English Renaissance* (1956). C. B. L. Barr, "More Books from Ben Jonson's Library," *Book Collector* 13 (1964): 346–48, deals with Jonson's copies of Lucan and his use of the *Pharsalia* (see William Blissett, II,A, *Catiline*). H. C. Fay, "Critical Marks in a Copy of Chapman's *Twelve Bookes of Homers Iliades*," *Library* 8 (1953): 117–21, describes the marginalia and suggests they are Jonson's. "If the copy was Jonson's, it takes its place in a very interesting series with his copies of *Seaven Bookes* and *Shield* of 1598 . . . and his copy of the *Whole Works* of 1616." F. C. Francis, "The Shakespeare Collection in the British Museum," *ShS* 3 (1950): 43–57, discusses some of Jonson's books. See also "John Aubrey's Books—I, II," *TLS,* 13, 20 Jan. 1950, pp. 32, 48; James M. Osborn, "Ben Jonson and the Eccentric Lord Stanhope," *TLS,* 4 Jan. 1957, p. 16; R. A. Sayce, *TLS,* 11 Oct. 1957, p. 609; G. P. V. Akrigg, "The Curious Marginalia of Charles, Second Lord Stanhope," in *Joseph Quincy Adams Memorial Studies,* ed. James McManaway et al. (1948), pp. 785–801; and W. Todd Furniss, *RES* 5 (1954), discussed below.

Jonson's career as a writer of masks is marked and perhaps marred by his association with Inigo Jones. In the introduction to *The Symbolic Persons in the Masques of Ben Jonson* (1948), Allan Gilbert suggests that the quarrel emanated from Jones's wish to simplify the symbolism of Jonson's masks and from Jonson's contrary wish to load every aspect with meaning both moral and intellectual. Jonson was following the allegorizing tendency of his age. The main portion of Gilbert's book is an alphabetically arranged, annotated catalogue of symbolic characters: classical gods, personified abstractions, mythological and legendary characters, historical and semihistorical figures. There is a bibliography, with a list of books which Jonson may have used to create his symbolic characters. This may be supplemented with Starnes and Talbert, *Classical Myth,* mentioned above, and the earlier study by Charles F. Wheeler, *Classical Mythology in the Plays, Masques, and Poems of Ben Jonson* (1938). Along with Ernest Talbert, "The Interpretation of Jonson's Courtly Spectacles," *PMLA* 61 (1946): 454–73, and D. J. Gordon, "The Imagery of Ben Jonson's *The Masque of Blacknesse* and *The Masque of Beautie*," *JWCI* 6 (1943): 122–41, and "Poet and Architect: The Intellectual Setting of the Quarrel between Ben Jonson and Inigo Jones," *JWCI* 12 (1949): 152–78, Gilbert is one of the seminal figures in recent studies of the Jonsonian masque.

W. Todd Furniss, "Ben Jonson's Masques," in *Three Studies in the Renaissance: Sidney, Jonson, Milton,* by Richard Young, W. Todd Furniss, and William Madsen (1958), pp. 89-179, is a full examination of Jonson's masks. Jonson concentrates on monarchy in his masks, and we should see this concentration as an emphasis on a hypothetically ideal kingship. Spectacle is used especially to express the excellence of the two principal figures: "the person in whose honor the Triumph is held and the god to whom the hero offers his thanks. And in every case . . . the full effect demands the presence of the king. At the center of each of these performances is not the spectacle itself but the idea that the king is a hero or god in whose person are to be seen reflected the virtues which have their seat in heaven." Furniss combines with his analysis "a study of those elements which deserve attention in every masque—verse, music, scenery, dancing, Jonson's use of the king as the central symbol. Although these are handled separately, they apply equally to all the masques."

Outlining the growth of the mask from the time of Richard II to the reign of Elizabeth I, Stephen Orgel, *The Jonsonian Masque* (1965), details Jonson's development as a mask-maker. He sees the central problem of the Jonsonian mask as one of unity—on many levels—and his study traces Jonson's progress in unifying his material. He underlines the functions of the antimask and the royal presence. In conclusion, Orgel suggests that "the masques are a link between the playwright of *Volpone* and that of *The New Inne.* The idea of theater that Jonson conceived, he could perfect only in the masque."

Method and Meaning in Jonson's Masques (1966), by John C. Meagher, is "an attempt at placing the Jonsonian masques in their rather complicated context in order to elucidate their meaning and explicate their design." Meagher links Jonson to the continental, European tradition. Practically Jonson may have been beaten by Inigo Jones and his insistence on spectacle, but in the long run, Jonson's masks survive as a species of poetry. "It is as a humanistic poet that we must finally view Jonson the Mask-writer." Although the study has no formal bibliography, there is a succinct review of recent scholarship in the footnotes.

Stephen Orgel's *The Illusion of Power: Political Theater in the English Renaissance* (1975), is "an essay about theater at court" in which Jonson plays a major part. M. C. Bradbrook, "Social Change and the Evolution of Ben Jonson's Court Masques," in *Ben Jonson: Quadricentennial Essays* (above), pp. 101–38, offers a survey of the Jonsonian mask and its background. Dolora Cunningham, "The Jonsonian

Masque as a Literary Form," *ELH* 22 (1955): 108-24, begins with a complete definition of the form, which is analyzed under the three chief principles of the Jonsonian mask: decorum, hierarchical unity, and instruction joined with pleasure. She concludes that the final effect of the mask, admiration or wonder, is analogous to fear and pity in tragedy. Her essay is reprinted in *Ben Jonson: A Collection of Critical Essays,* ed. Barish, pp. 160-74 (above). Irene Janicka, "The Popular Background of Ben Jonson's Masques," *SJW* 105 (1969): 183-208, examines the background and the dual function of Jonson's mask: the mask extols the magnificence of the royal person while the antimask amuses and satirizes. "The parallels . . . show that Jonson's grotesque antimasque vision owes a great deal to the popular tradition. The elfin spirit, the fairy-tale imagery, the witches and their charms, the acting of Robin Goodfellow . . . ; the vice symbolism; the antithetical style and other devices used in folk-plays, mysteries and moralities—all these contributed." Catherine M. Shaw, "The Masques of Ben Jonson: Editions and Editorial Criticism," *Genre* 3 (1970): 272-88, considers the growth of a fair evaluation of Jonson's masks through the 1616 and 1640 Folios, P. J. Walley's *Works* (1756), Gifford's edition (1816), Cunningham's revision (1875), Herford and Simpson's edition (1925-52), and Stephen Orgel's *The Complete Masques* (1969). David Bergeron, *English Civic Pageantry, 1558-1642* (1971), deals with Jonson's creation of civic pageants.

MacDonald Emslie, "Three Early Settings of Jonson," *N&Q* 198 (1953): 466-68, adds songs to the list of musical settings of the mask in Herford and Simpson. John P. Cutts, "Robert Johnson and the Court Masque," *Music and Letters* 41 (1960): 111-26, discusses the composer of music for some of Jonson's masks. (See Emslie, II,A, *Mask of Augurs,* for Nicholas Lanier.) Liselotte Dieckmann, "Renaissance Hieroglyphics," *CL* 9 (1957): 308-21, notes that "Jonson himself once called the masque a court-hieroglyphic," and briefly discusses his use of the hieroglyphic, as does D. C. Allen, "Ben Jonson and the Hieroglyphics," *PQ* 18 (1939): 290-300. Jack E. Reese, "Unity in Chapman's *Masque of the Middle Temple and Lincoln's Inn,"* *SEL* 4 (1964): 291-305, suggests that Jonson's praise of Chapman's masks stems from his admiration of their unity. Albert Wertheim, "James Shirley and the Caroline Masques of Ben Jonson," *Theatre Notebook* 27 (1973): 157-61, finds a reference to the Jonsonian mask in Shirley's *Love's Cruelty,* II.ii. "The picture of the Jonsonian masque in *Love's Cruelty* provides a sense of what Ben Jonson and Inigo Jones' masques must in general have been like."

C. THE WORKS AT LARGE

George Burke Johnston's *Ben Jonson: Poet* (1945), is a brief study. Wesley Trimpi's *Ben Jonson's Poems: A Study of the Plain Style* (1962), is a detailed and complex study of Jonson's poetry and its backgrounds in the "plain" style. He begins by discussing the history and precepts of the plain style as it originated in the classical writers and was perpetuated in the Renaissance. Since Jonson applied a passage on letter writing in John Hoskyns to style in general and since "he regarded the epistolary treatise as a general rhetorical statement, he found ample contemporary justification for using the plain style to treat any subject, either human or divine." The last two chapters contain analyses of Jonson's poems, by genre, with emphasis on the plain style. (Cf. Barish, *Ben Jonson and the Language of Prose Comedy*, I,B.) J. G. Nichols's *The Poetry of Ben Jonson* (1969), contains four chapters in which Nichols attacks "unprofitable ways of approaching Jonson's poetry," indicates "Jonson's salient attitudes and those features of his style which seem . . . to be conditioned partly by those attitudes," and discusses Jonson's occasional and his lyric poetry. Judith Kegan Gardiner, *Craftsmanship in Context: The Development of Ben Jonson's Poetry* (1975), gives a complete study of the nondramatic poetry, placing it "first in the context of [Jonson's] three published collections of poetry, then in comparison with his plays and masques."

Arthur F. Marotti, "All About Jonson's Poetry," *ELH* 39 (1972): 208-37, believes that Jonson wrote two kinds of poetry: "the first a poetry of explosive imagery and perverse imagining, the second a poetry of more visible control, imagistically spare, prosodically tight, and intellectually lucid." William V. Spanos, "The Real Toad in the Jonsonian Garden: Resonance in the Nondramatic Poetry," *JEGP* 68 (1969): 1-23, feels that Jonson's poetry has received little attention because of a Romantic bias in New Criticism which has found Jonson's classical style lacking in cogent spontaneity. The verbal equivalent of a formal sixteenth-century garden, a Jonson poem is a highly-wrought artifact, the linguistic structure of which is activated by what superficially seems to be an imperfection of one kind or another in it. George A. E. Parfitt, "The Poetry of Ben Jonson," *Essays in Criticism* 18 (1968): 18-31, believes that Jonson's attachment to classicism has misled critics to think that he was alienated from the English tradition of thought and language and that he lacked inspiration. An examination of his poetry shows that his integrity to the experience he is trying to communicate and his sense of linguistic appropriateness make him an important poet. In "Ethical Thought and Ben Jonson's Poetry,"

SEL 9 (1969): 123-34, Parfitt argues that "To Penshurst" indicates the extent to which Jonson's poetry is based on ethical discriminations and anchored to a contemporary environment, while a general survey shows that most of the ethical views in the poetry are familiar Elizabethan attitudes and that what Jonson thought does not make him a classical writer, even where his poetry owes a verbal debt to classical literature. In "Compromise Classicism: Language and Rhythm in Ben Jonson's Poetry," *SEL* 11 (1971): 109-23, Parfitt distinguishes between the plain style and the genuinely classical in Jonson's poems. In "The Nature of Translation in Ben Jonson's Poetry," *SEL* 13 (1973): 344-59, Parfitt discusses the ways Jonson incorporated material borrowed from classical sources into his poetry. As a creative borrower, Jonson had a strong tendency to borrow ethical concepts rather than images and allusions.

Hugh Maclean, "Ben Jonson's Poems: Notes on the Ordered Society," in *Essays in English Literature from the Renaissance to the Victorian Age, Presented to A. S. P. Woodhouse, 1964*, ed. Millar MacLure and F. W. Watt (1964), pp. 43-68, suggests that "while the plays deal principally in the satiric recognition and description of the factors that contribute to social disorder, we find in the poems (with the *Discoveries* behind, as theory to practice), not an explicit and detailed outline of the social order Jonson admired, but rather 'notes' on particular elements that ought to mark a society properly ordered, as well as suggestions for conduct in the midst of a disordered one." Jonson stresses three things in the poems: friendship, monarchy, and the ruling class. Anthony Mortimer, "The Feigned Commonwealth in the Poetry of Ben Jonson," *SEL* 13 (1973): 69-79, points out that, in *Timber*, Jonson describes the function of the poet as a creator of a commonwealth in which the conflict between virtue and vice is delineated. In his commendatory poems, the vicious are not named because vice destroys the personality; the virtuous are named for recognition and imitation. These verses "express Jonson's aristocratic social ethic." Robin Skelton, "The Masterpoet and the Multiple Tradition: The Poetry of Ben Jonson," *Style* 1 (1967): 225-46, believes that "in his lyric and satiric verse . . . Jonson attempted to present an example of the ideal poet." Geoffrey Walton, "The Tone of Ben Jonson's Poetry," in his *Metaphysical to Augustan: Studies in Tone and Sensibility in the Seventeenth Century* (1955), pp. 23-44 (rpt. in *Seventeenth-Century English Poetry*, ed. William R. Keast [1962], pp. 193-214), feels that "a social spirit of a clear and peculiarly noble kind was present in poetry from the start [of the seventeenth century] and that this spirit is exemplified particularly in Ben Jonson."

Lester A. Beaurline, "The Selective Principle in Jonson's Shorter Poems," *Criticism* 8 (1966): 64-74, points out that for Jonson the ideal in poetry is "fitness or propriety." "The principles of selection, rejection, subduing and heightening, in order to affect meaning, to project thoughts and feelings—these seem to bring us closer to the ineffable grace of Jonson's best verse." Edwin Honig, "Examples of Poetic Diction in Ben Jonson," *Costerus* 3 (1972): 121-62, takes "poetic diction to be the whole structural design of poetic achievement," and studies Jonson's meter and verse form, rhetoric and syntax, imagery and poetic functions. Morag Hollway, "Jonson's 'Proper Straine,'" *Critical Review* 13 (1970): 51-67, believes that "Jonson's poetry reveals his deep connection with the general life most clearly whenever his own self is most quickened and distinct. Indeed, although he was not the first English poet to grow aware of his self and his world as distinct entities, it seems to me he was the first to make the relationship between them central to his poetry." Bruce Babington, "Ben Jonson's Poetry of the Surface," *Words: Wai-Te-Ata Studies in Literature*, no. 2 (1966), pp. 66-81, sees the Jonsonian poem as "an image of the clarity of ordered life." F. W. Bradbrook, "Ben Jonson's Poetry," in *From Donne to Marvell* (1956; vol. 3 of the Pelican *Guide to English Literature*, ed. Boris Ford), pp. 131-41, is a brief survey.

More specifically, Paul M. Cubeta, "Ben Jonson's Religious Lyrics," *JEGP* 62 (1963): 96-110, traces the influence of medieval and Renaissance meditative exercises on Jonson's moderately pitched and quietly confident devotional lyrics. He concludes with a comparison of Jonson and Herbert. Anne Ferry, *All in War with Time* (1975), discusses Jonson's love poetry. Paul Cubeta, "'A Celebration of Charis': An Evaluation of Jonsonian Poetic Strategy," *ELH* 25 (1958): 163-80, contends that a history of English love poetry between Spenser and Pope must consider Jonson's series of ten poems. "Because of his remarkable feat in combining the mode of much Greek and Latin love poetry with the manner of Spenser, Donne, and Pope, this poem holds a pivotal position halfway between the traditions of the sixteenth and eighteenth centuries." G. J. Weinberger, "Jonson's Mock-Encomiastic 'Celebration of Charis,'" *Genre* 4 (1971): 305-28, points out the ways in which the poem is a paradoxical encomium. Charis is not praised at all. Trimpi's discussion (*Ben Jonson's Poems*, above) places it solidly in the neo-Platonic tradition, relating it to the literary convention of the "*discorso* or *questione d'amore*," and comparing it "in subject and structure to the general discussions of love as exemplified in *The Courtier*." Richard Peterson, "Virtue Reconciled to Pleasure: Jonson's 'A Celebration of Charis,'" in *Ben Jonson: Quadricentennial Essays* (above), pp. 219-68, discusses Jonson's use of mythological emblems and concludes that "these lyrics to Charis remind us of the moral concern typical of all his best work."

"To Penshurst" is Jonson's most popular poem. Mason, *Humanism and Poetry* (I,B), discusses the poem's classical background, and Paul Cubeta, "A Jonsonian Ideal: 'To Penshurst,'" *PQ* 42 (1963): 14-24, offers an analysis in terms of a social ideal. Jonson "more than any other poet of his age must be understood as a moral and social critic as well as a man of letters." His technique in poetry is to establish an ideal which he contrasts with empirical reality. "In 'To Penshurst' and its companion piece 'To Sir Robert Wroth' . . . Jonson defines an area of experience where ideal human activity can still thrive even though urban society has become morally corrupt." Gayle E. Wilson, "Jonson's Use of the Bible and the Great Chain of Being in 'To Penshurst,'" *SEL* 8 (1968): 77-89, sees the poem as a "'fable' in which Jonson, a poet-priest, demonstrates that man can perpetuate his society if he uses and governs nature in accordance with the metaphysical 'truth' contained in the Bible and inherent in the Great Chain of Being." Commenting on Jonson's use of the epigram and emphasizing his concern for words, Harris Friedberg, "Ben Jonson's Poetry: Pastoral, Georgic, Epigram," *English Literary Renaissance* 4 (1974): 111-36, discusses "To Penshurst," underlining the poet's "search for a language of praise that will discriminate the invisible values present at Penshurst and yet tie those values to a world of fact." Judith K. Gardiner, "Line Counts, Word Counts, and Two Jonson Epistles," *Style* 7 (1973): 30-38, points out that line-count and word-count analyses of "To Penshurst" and "To Sir Robert Wroth" corroborate the impression that in the former details of structure and of verbal texture reflect the ideal of the ordered life that the poem praises. By examining the correspondence of Sir Robert Sidney, J. C. A. Rathmell, "Jonson, Lord Lisle, and Penshurst," *English Literary Renaissance* 1 (1971): 250-60, proves that Jonson had an intimate knowledge of Penshurst and suggests that the poem is a subtle reminder to Sir Robert concerning the true nature of his family fortune. Charles Molesworth, "'To Penshurst' and Jonson's Historical Imagination," *Clio* 1, no. 2 (1972): 5-13, suggests that Jonson uses metonymy to embody his own image of history.

Basically a study of "To Penshurst," Jeffrey Hart's "Ben Jonson's Good Society," *Modern Age* 7 (1962-63): 61-68, begins with a discussion of the poetry of place, and more specifically of those poems written "under the aspect of a potentially tragic danger, in which the very existence of the things celebrated is seen to be threatened." G. R. Hibbard, "The Country House Poem of the Seventeenth Century," *JWCI* 19 (1956): 159-74, examines "To Penshurst" as both ode and "country-house poem." Charles Molesworth, "Property and Virtue: The Genre of the Country-House Poem in the Seventeenth Century," *Genre* 1 (1968): 141-57, contrasts Jonson and Marvell. "Jonson's technique is more emblematic, whereas Marvell's . . . is allegorical." Elizabeth McCutcheon, "Jonson's 'To Penshurst,' 36," *Expl* 25 (1967): item 52, explains that "*Officiously*" is a pun on "fish."

In "Ben Jonson's 'Chast Booke': The *Epigrammes*," *RMS* 13 (1969): 76-87, David Wykes suggests that Jonson altered the traditionally accepted moral stance of the epigrammatist by making him a praiser as well as a censurer. Rufus Putney, "'This so Subtile Sport': Some Aspects of Jonson's Epigrams," *University of Colorado Studies*, Series in Language and Literature, 10 (1966): 37-56, is a discursive essay on the epigrams. Martial's influence is explored by Thomas King Whipple, "Martial and the English Epigram from Sir Thomas Wyatt to Ben Jonson," *University of California Publications in Modern Philology* 10 (1925): 279-414, and Kathryn A. McEuen, *Classical Influence upon the Tribe of Ben* (1939). Karen Holum, "The Epigram: Semantic Basis for the Pointed Ending," *Linguistics* 94 (1972): 21-36, finds Jonson's plays important in understanding the satirical point of his epigrams. The epigrams have two structures: a single meaning and a second meaning in context. The epigram to Sir Henry Saville is studied by Paul J. McGinnis, "Ben Jonson on Savile's Tacitus," *CJ* 55 (1959): 120-21; Jonson "turned to ancient history, rhetoric and literary correspondence in order to find a philosophy of history which accorded with his own, and a statement of the qualities which the ideal historian should cultivate." Ronald E. McFarland, "Jonson's *Epigrams*, XI ('On Something, That Walkes Some-where')," *Expl* 31 (1972): item 26, comments on Jonson's creation of the courtier's image as lifeless or life-in-death, using allusions and poetic caesuras. Laurence Perrine, "Jonson's *Epigrams*, XI ('On Some-thing, That Walkes Some-where')," *Expl* 32 (1973): item 30, suggests an emendation to McFarland's comment. According to him, the last five words of the poem are addressed by the poet to the courtier, not as direct speech, but as apostrophe. Two epigrams were addressed by Jonson to Lady Mary Wroth; Peter Fellowes, "Jonson's *Epigrams*, CIII ('To Mary Lady Wroth')," *Expl* 31 (1973): item 36, suggests that the first of these epigrams (CV) is full of floridity while the second (CIII) is a model of tact and wit. The success of the poem is a result of Jonson's choice of an appropriate emblem for his subject.

Robert B. White, Jr., "A Reading of Jonson's 'Epitaph on Elizabeth, L.H.,'" *Notre Dame English Journal* 9, no. 1 (1973): 9–14, finds "in the 'Epitaph' a continuous conceptual development throughout, particularly across the crucial terminal pointing at the end of line six, thus giving the poem a unity which has not otherwise been attributed to it"; the poem "is typically Jonsonian in its control, its precision, and its realistic recognition of Elizabeth's humanity." Howard S. Babb, "The 'Epitaph on Elizabeth, L.H.' and Ben Jonson's Style," *JEGP* 62 (1963): 738–44, observes that most of the discussion of the epitaph has centered about the naming of the lady; Fleay and Newdigate have suggested Elizabeth, Lady Hatton. Babb emphasizes the compression of meaning in the poem, "for compression, the quality that he really claims for the poem in the opening couplet, is one hallmark of Jonson's style." Objecting to the identification of "L.H." as Lady Hatton, James McKenzie, "Jonson's 'Elizabeth, L.H.'," *N&Q* 9 (1962): 210, suggests Elizabeth, Lady Hunsdon, who married Sir George Carey, the lord chamberlain. She was known as a patroness of poets. (But, as Herford and Simpson note, no identification can be absolutely certain.)

Jonson's "To Celia" ("Drink to me only") has evoked a plethora of notes and articles. Marshall Van Deusen, "Criticism and Ben Jonson's 'To Celia,'" *Essays in Criticism* 7 (1957): 95–103, examines interpretations of "But might I of *Iove's Nectar* sup/ I would not change for thine." Basically, it is either a complimentary hyperbole to the lady, or a realistic admission that he would not exchange Jove's nectar (if obtainable) for the lady's. Gerald Bullett, *TLS*, 1 June 1956, p. 329, suggests an emendation of "for" to "fro" (meaning "from"): "I would not change from thine." E. A. Horsman, *TLS*, 8 June 1956, p. 345, notes that "change" means "exchange." See also the letter by Daniel George, *TLS*, 8 June 1956, p. 345, and the exchange between Frank Allen, "'Drink to Me only . . . ,'" *N&Q* 197 (1952): 161, and J. Burke Severs, *N&Q* 197 (1952): 262. More substantial is A. D. Fitton Brown, "'Drink to Me, Celia,'" *MLR* 54 (1959): 554–57, who discusses the source, Philostratus's *Epistles* and its Latin translation by Bonfini

(1606). Brown believes "that it was in the revision of the first and third quatrains that literalism got the better of " Jonson.

Osborne B. Hardison, *The Enduring Monument: A Study of the Idea of Praise in Renaissance Literary Theory and Practice* (1962), discusses a number of Jonson's poems as part of a tradition in both literary criticism and practice. Barbara Hutchison, "Ben Jonson's 'Let Me Be What I Am': An Apology in Disguise," *ELN* 2 (1965): 185–90, argues that the poem is "a step-by-step argument furnished with satiric *exempla*, by means of which Jonson has sought to justify himself on moral as well as artistic grounds, and to establish the respectability of legitimate poetry of compliment."

Frederick M. Combellack, "Jonson's 'To John Donne,'" *Expl* 17 (1958): item 6, feels that the poem is dependent on the word "wit" in line 3 and offers a prose paraphrase. Stanley M. Wiersma, *Expl* 25 (1966): item 4, thinks that Combellack's interpretation is essentially correct, but that he misses much of the ironic ambiguity. According to Walter R. Davis, in "Jonson's 'An Ode' (*Under-wood* 28)," *Expl* 31 (1973): item 70, "the poem is a tactful piece of advice on marriage and presents friendship as a fitting prelude to marriage." George Hemphill, in "Jonson's 'Fit of Rime against Rime,'" *Expl* 12 (1954): item 50, says that many problems are solved by redefining "rime" as "all the conventions of verse, particularly the modern ones"; Roger L. Clubb, in "The Paradox of Ben Jonson's 'A Fit of Rime against Rime,'" *CLAJ* 5 (1961): 145–47, feels that the poem contains a genuine paradox, attacking rhyme when Jonson himself often used it.

Judith Gardiner, "'To Heaven,'" *Concerning Poetry* 6, no. 2 (1973): 26–36, sees that poem as "a prayer for the cessation of doubt and a partial demonstration of its cure through faith. At the same time, and persistently, 'To Heaven' is an expression and portrait of religious melancholy." In "The Christian Wisdom of Ben Jonson's 'On My First Sonne,'" *SEL* 11 (1971): 125–36, W. David Kay points out that, though the poem is basically Christian, Jonson fully recognizes the dilemma of the human situation in which spiritual consolation is in tension with physical loss. Francis Fike, "Ben Jonson's 'On My First Sonne,'" *Gordon Review* 11 (1969): 205–20, believes that Jonson "implies the continuity of human experience. . . . By confessing his sin of idolatry, Jonson places his poem in a theological context which the reader must not ignore." Jonson's "Epitaph on Solomon Pavy" is discussed by Louis F. May, *Expl* 20 (1961): item 16, as a use of the topos *puer senex*; in this traditional pattern of exaggeration, the accomplishments of an old man are paradoxically attributed to a young boy. Suggesting another aspect of Jonson's poetry, Phyllis Rackin, "Poetry without Paradox: Jonson's 'Hymne' to Cynthia," *Criticism* 4 (1962): 186-96, emphasizes "decorum" rather than polarity.

Peter Steese, "Jonson's 'A Song,'" *Expl* 21 (1963): item 31, deals with the classical influence on "Oh do not wanton with those eyes." The primary reason for the poem's lack of warm vitality is the negative approach to love necessitated by its Aristotelean form. Jack Shadoian, "'Inviting a Friend to Supper': Aspects of Jonson's Craft and Personality," *Concerning Poetry* 3, no. 2 (1970): 29-35, closely analyzes the poetic strategy of the poem and its moralist persona. Lisle Cecil John, "Ben Jonson's 'To Sir William Sidney, on His Birthday,'" *MLR* 52 (1957): 168-76, sketches in the background of Sir William's upbringing in order to indicate the reason for Jonson's words of warning. Discussing "To the Immortall Memorie, and Friendship of That Noble Paire, Sir Lucius Cary, and Sir H. Morison," George Held, "Jonson's Pindaric on Friendship," *Concerning Poetry* 3, no. 1 (1970): 29-41, suggests that the friendship between Cary and Morison serves as an example of the ethical values Jonson cherished most: bravery, integrity, disinterested affection, and virtue of conduct.

George Burke Johnston, "'An Epistle Mendicant' by Ben Jonson," *N&Q* 1 (1954): 471, notes that Jonson uses the image of his "wants" in a punning sense as "moles or underminers" in his verse petition to Lord Weston, Lord High Treasurer in 1631, and in the dream-fable sent to the Earl of Newcastle on December 20, 1631. In "An Apocryphal Jonsonian Epigram," *N&Q* 5 (1958): 543-44, Johnston discusses a four-line satire written upon the ill-fated performance of *Catiline* and ascribed to Jonson; although it cannot be placed in the canon, the poem has a certain Jonsonian spirit. Mary Morrison, "A Possible Source for Ben Jonson's 'Execration Upon Vulcan,'" *RLC* 29 (1955): 349-50, suggests a source in Nicolas Bourbon, and Charlotte Winzeler, "Curse upon a God: Classical and Elizabethan Thought Blended," *Brigham Young University Studies* 5 (1964): 87-94, also discusses the genesis of the poem. (See Johnston, I,A.) Daniel O'Connor, "Jonson's 'A Hymne to God the Father,'" *N&Q* 12 (1965): 379-80, observes that Herford and Simpson trace the poem back to 1635 in manuscript, and suggests that John Cosin's *A Collection of Private Devotions*, written before 1 March 1627, may contain a reminiscence of the 'Hymne,' lines 17-20, 29, 32. George Burke Johnston, "Jonson's 'Perseus upon Pegasus,'"

RES 6 (1955): 65–67, points out that Jonson's poem to the Earl of Newcastle (*Underwood* 53) places Perseus on the back of Pegasus; Perseus replaced Bellerophon on Pegasus even in classical times and the confusion lasted into the Renaissance. "Presumably the scholar Jonson knew better; if so, he felt free to follow the art and letters of his own day when such a practice suited his poetic needs." See John D. Reeves, "Perseus and the Flying Horse in Peele and Heywood," *RES* 6 (1955): 397–99, and John M. Steadman, "'Perseus upon Pegasus' and *Ovid Moralized*," *RES* 9 (1958): 407–10, which also deal with Perseus's steed.

Charles G. Osgood, "Epithalamion and Prothalamion: 'and theyr eccho ring,'" *MLN* 76 (1961): 205–8, discusses Spenser's influence on Jonson and other seventeenth-century epithalamists. Jackson I. Cope, "Jonson's Reading of Spenser: The Genesis of a Poem," *EM* 10 (1959): 61–66, believes that Jonson's *Epistle to Elizabeth, Countess of Rutland* has its chief source in *The Ruines of Time* and is influenced by *Mother Hubberd's Tale* and *The Visions of Bellay*. Steven Zwicker, "Dryden's Borrowing from Ben Jonson's 'Panegyre,'" *N&Q* 15 (1968): 105–6, points out that Dryden's borrowing from Jonson in "A Song to St. Cecilia's Day" and "To His Sacred Majesty, A Panegyrick on His Coronation" have been noted. But Dryden also used line 162 from Jonson's "Panegyre on the Happy Entrance of James" for the last line of his "Prologue to John Banks' *The Unhappy Favorite*." Edward Doughtie, "Ferrabosco and Jonson's 'The Houre-glasse,'" *Renaissance Quarterly* 22 (1969): 148–50, notes that Alfonso Ferrabosco's collaboration with Jonson was of long duration, and suggests that one of Ferrabosco's musical settings was for "The Houre-glasse."

John W. H. Atkins, *English Literary Criticism: The Renascence* (1947; 2nd ed. 1951), provides a detailed discussion and a general summary of Jonson's critical position. "Apart from earlier theorists, he is in fact the first to give criticism an important place in his creative work, and to expound, as a conscious artist, his main ideas and principles." As a literary critic, Jonson is only superficially in the classical tradition, though in his work as poet he seems to have inborn classical tendencies. His posthumous *Discoveries* (1641) are the most classical of his criticisms. Atkins also discusses Jonson's casual remarks on poetic theory preserved in the *Conversations with Drummond*, noting Jonson's emphasis on subject matter. On the epigram, Jonson's insights are most helpful and constructive. Jonson's memorial verses are seen as critical pieces, and, in summary comment, Atkins states that Jonson's incisive critical comments are indicative of a general development of the English critical faculty. He was the "first great English critic" and his position may be described as "liberal classicism." David Klein's *The Elizabethan Dramatists as Critics* (1963) may be used to supplement Atkins; Klein allows Jonson to speak for himself with only brief intercommentary by the author. See also William K. Wimsatt, Jr., and Cleanth Brooks, *Literary Criticism: A Short History* (1957), who devote a chapter to Jonson and Dryden.

In an attempt to reconstruct Jonson's critical principles, Freda L. Townsend, "Ben Jonson's 'Censure' of Rutter's *Shepheards Holy-Day*," *MP* 44 (1947): 238-47 (see Townsend, I,B), begins with Jonson's poem of praise prefixed to Rutter's play. "Examination of the structure of *The shepheards holy-day* . . . should yield a twofold reward: (1) it should broaden our knowledge of the form that the pastoral play took in England; and (2) it should throw light on the kind of plot that was likely to earn Jonson's critical commendation." Since the plot is "multiplex" and seems to disregard classical principles of regularity, "Jonson's dramatic laws were most probably original in their formulation and had little to do with ancient prescriptions." (Cf. Herrick's remarks on Townsend's *Apologie*, I,B.) Eleanor Withington, "Nicholas Briot and Jonson's Commendation of Joseph Rutter," *N&Q* 198 (1953): 152-53, examines the numismatic imagery of Jonson's poem, referring it to Briot's new method of coinage. Jonson seems to be warning Rutter to make distinctions in language according to the decorum of character, and Rutter seems to misinterpret his meaning.

It is traditional to see Jonson as the father of English classicism. This view is set forth by Felix Schelling, "Ben Jonson and the Classical School," *PMLA* 13 (1898), 221-49 (rpt. in *Essential Articles for the Study of English Augustan Backgrounds*, ed. Bernard N. Schilling [1961], pp. 173-97). Louis Bredvold believes that Schelling's essay is indispensable for a study of Jonson's classicism, and in his own article, "The Rise of English Classicism: Study in Methodology," *CL* 2 (1950): 253-68, emphasizes Jonson's place in the growth of English neoclassicism: "the reputation and influence of Jonson as the master literary craftsman, the English Virgil in the sense that he was the pattern of 'elaborate' or laborious writing, is of primary importance to the student of English literature of the seventeenth century." Bredvold's point is that English classicism is not largely French in origin; the actual source is Jonson.

The major text of Jonson's criticism is the *Discoveries* or *Timber*. Frank B. Fieler, "The Impact of Bacon and the New Science upon Jonson's Critical Thought in *Timber*," *RenP*, 1961, pp. 84–92, contrasts Jonson's independence of judgment with Sidney's reliance on classical authority and feels that this independence is a product of the new science and especially Bacon's writings. Ted-Larry Pebworth, "Jonson's *Timber* and the Essay Tradition," in *Essays in Honor of Esmond Linworth Marilla*, ed. Thomas A. Kirby and William J. Olive (1970), pp. 115–26, believes that the essays in *Timber* "point the direction that the genre was to take"; in contrast, Bacon's essays stand outside the mainstream. Atkins (above) contends that Jonson's concept of "imitation" is essentially "non-Aristotelian." Daniel G. Calder, "The Meaning of 'Imitation' in Jonson's *Discoveries*," *NM* 70 (1969): 435–40, argues that Jonson's theoretical statements in *Discoveries* prove that this contention is misleading; Jonson defines a poetic that contains the very elements that Atkins finds lacking. Ralph S. Walker, "Ben Jonson's *Discoveries*: A New Analysis," *E&S* 5 (1952): 32–51, suggests that the materials in *Discoveries* were confused in the printing and gives a tentative rearrangement. In his introduction to the rearranged edition, *Ben Jonson's "Timber" or "Discoveries"* (1953), Walker somewhat modifies his original classifications. As appendices, he reprints his "Ben Jonson's Lyric Poetry," *Criterion* 13 (1933–34): 430–48, and "Literary Criticism in Jonson's Conversations with Drummond," *English* 8 (1951): 222–27.

The sources of Jonson's *Discoveries* have been of interest since Castelain's edition (1906). Herford and Simpson trace many of them. Paul J. McGinnis, "Ben Jonson's *Discoveries*," *N&Q* 4 (1957): 162–63, finds a source in Vives's *Libri de Disciplinis*. W. A. Murray, "Ben Jonson and Dr. Mayerne," *TLS*, 2 Sept. 1960, p. 561, traces a Jonsonian quotation to the Preface of Turquet de Mayerne's *Famosa Responsio*; a defender of "chemical" medicine, Mayerne came to England in 1609. Joseph K. Houck, "An Unidentified Borrowing in Jonson's *Discoveries*," *N&Q* 15 (1968): 367–68, points to a source in Quintillian and comments on Jonson's arrangement of translated quotations. Teikan Yamoto, "Ben Jonson and His *Discoveries*," *Bunka* (Tohoku University, Sendai) 20, no. 3 (1956), points out the personal elements in the *Discoveries* and relates them to Jonson's life and work. Frank Caldiero, "Ben Jonson's Course in Freshman English," *CE* 19 (1957): 7–11, deals very lightly with *Discoveries*. Paul R. Sellin,

Daniel Heinsius and Stuart England (1968), believes that "nearly half of Ben Jonson's critical remarks on poetry" in *Discoveries* are translations or paraphrases of Heinsius. He concludes that Jonson does "not present a system of ideas on poetry" and is "not a Heinsian critic."

Ben Jonson (A Concise Bibliography) by Samuel A. Tannenbaum was published in 1938, followed by a supplement, compiled with Dorothy R. Tannenbaum, in 1947; both are reprinted in *Elizabethan Bibliographies,* vol. 4 (1967). In 1966, Robert C. Steensma published "Ben Jonson: A Checklist of Editions, Biography, and Criticism, 1947-1964," *RORD* 9 (1966): 29-46, followed by Anthony Nania's "Addenda: Ben Jonson: A Checklist of Editions, Biography, and Criticism, 1947-1964," *RORD* 10 (1967): 32. George Guffey, *Robert Herrick, Ben Jonson, Thomas Randolph,* Elizabethan Bibliographies Supplements, vol. 3 (1968), updates Tannenbaum. D. Heyward Brock and James Welsh, *Ben Jonson: A Quadricentennial Bibliography, 1947-1972* (1974), give a comprehensive listing of criticism and editions along with some annotation. Irving Ribner's *Tudor and Stuart Drama,* Goldentree Bibliographies (1966), provides a selected list. For accounts of the history of Jonson criticism, see Robert Gale Noyes, *Ben Jonson and the English Stage, 1660-1776* (1935); Stuart M. Tave, "Corbyn Morris: Falstaff, Humor, and Comic Theory in the Eighteenth Century," *MP* 50 (1952): 102-15, discussed above; Jonas A. Barish, ed., "Introduction," in *Ben Jonson: A Collection of Critical Essays* (1963), pp. 1-13, discussed above; Freda L. Townsend, *Apologie for Bartholmew Fayre* (above); Dolores Sarafinski, "Book-Length Studies of Ben Jonson Since 1919: A Review," *RORD* 17 (1974): 67-83; Paul L. Gaston, "Commendation and Approbation: Recent Ben Jonson Scholarship," *Papers on Language and Literature* 9 (1973): 432-49.

II. CRITICISM OF INDIVIDUAL PLAYS AND STATE OF SCHOLARSHIP

A. INDIVIDUAL PLAYS

Volpone

A good introduction is Alvin Kernan's chapter in *The Plot of Satire* (1965), which serves in an expanded version as the introduction to the Yale Ben Jonson edition (1962). Kernan sees Jonson as a traditionalist critic, who "attacked the new [Renaissance] dream of man that he was free to make himself and his world over in the image of his desires, rather than working slowly and patiently with a stubborn Nature." Volpone is an apostle of the "dumb god," wealth, and both he and Mosca make gold their deity, the center of their world. Materialists, they are also consummate actors, who enjoy their improvising. At the end of the play, those who would aspire beyond just limits are taught to know what they truly are. Alexander Leggatt, "The Suicide of Volpone," *UTQ* 39 (1969): 19-32, also deals with Volpone as an actor and points out the problems he encounters after his role has been exhausted. Volpone's suicide, his self-revelation, is due to an impulse deeply rooted in his nature, and the implications of the suicide reflect not merely on the final scene, but on the play in general and its judgment of human nature.

Ralph Nash, "The Comic Intent of *Volpone*," *SP* 44 (1947): 26-40, defends the play against adverse judgments of its comedy. He concludes that the "amount of subordinate comedy . . . coupled with the comic treatment of the gulls, suggests that the effect of the play, at least up to the second trial scene, should be far from that of tragic foreboding." Essentially the play is comic, and the final catastrophe occurs because the audience expected wrongdoers to be punished. In the same vein, William Empson, "*Volpone*," *Hudson Review* 21 (1968): 651-66, feels that Jonson intended *Volpone* to be an exhilarating comedy, not a painful tragedy. Volpone could not have been detained by English law, except possibly for impersonating a policeman; Jonson indicts the laws of Venice which "inherently produce" characters like Volpone. "No English audience would want to cripple Volpone, as the Venetian bench did, for making Venice ridiculous." Ian Donaldson, "*Volpone*: Quick and Dead," *Essays in Criticism* 21 (1971): 121-34, also argues against a too moral interpretation, pointing out that Celia and Bonario are not powerful forces in the play. The amoral energies of Volpone and Mosca are placed against a background of sickness and death; this juxtaposition yields the particular tone of the play. See George Parfitt's reply, "*Volpone*," *Essays in Criticism* 21 (1971): 411-12, and Donaldson's rejoinder, 22 (1972): 216-18. John Creaser, "*Volpone*: The Mortifying of the Fox," *Essays in Criticism* 25 (1975): 329-56, comments on Volpone's epilogue: "Volpone—speaking for the author as well as the Fox—makes his judicial sentence subsidiary in importance to the theatrical pleasure he has given, and he ends in full command." Also defending the play as comic, Robert Ornstein,

"Volpone and Renaissance Psychology," *N&Q* 3 (1956): 471–72, suggests that the play belongs to an earlier tradition. "The psychological portrait of the rich man given by F. N. Coeffeteau, in his *Table of Humane Passions,* is strikingly similar" to Volpone.

S. L. Goldberg, "Folly into Crime: The Catastrophe of *Volpone," MLQ* 20 (1959): 233–42, feels that the punishment of Volpone and Mosca is emotionally ambiguous, an ambiguity necessary in Jonson's satire. The play contains multiple levels of "folly," from the "simple folly of Sir Politic Would-be with his absurd pretensions" to the folly of Celia and Bonario, "perhaps a distant reminiscence of the 'folly' of Lear's Fool, which is the unworldly wisdom of the simple and innocent." Folly is also the object of the play's satire. Jonson's dramatic problem is "how to enforce a proper judgment on the most fundamental moral perversions while still retaining the effects of comedy." At the catastrophe, "our judgment may assent, but our feelings are still lagging." That folly is the major theme is also the contention of John Weld, "Christian Comedy: *Volpone," SP* 51 (1954): 172–93. The plot is basically that of "the deceiver deceived; the wisdom of the world is made foolish." For the worldly fool, the pleasures of the earth do not last or satisfy; folly leads into irrational action, and the love of the world is motivated by self-love. These ideas are the basis of "Christian comedy," as in Erasmus's *Praise of Folly; Volpone* "can be seen to illustrate this theme with almost fable-like clarity." Harriett Hawkins, "Folly, Incurable Disease, and *Volpone," SEL* 8 (1968): 335–48, stresses the relationship between folly and incurable disease which Jonson establishes. "From the 'praise of folly' sung by Volpone's permanently impaired retainers in the first scene, to the consignment of Volpone's wealth to the Hospital of Incurables at the end, Jonson's insistence on the connection between folly and disease gives thematic unity to the action."

By comparing *Volpone* and *The Alchemist,* Tinsley Helton, "Theme as a Shaping Factor in *Volpone* and *The Alchemist," English Record* 13, no. 4 (1963): 38–46, suggests that Jonson forms each play around a major theme, greed in *Volpone,* fraud in *The Alchemist.* The contrasting themes indicate the reasons for the contrasting denouements. Greed is a personal sin; through *Volpone,* Jonson dramatizes its debasement of human relations and thus the punishment of greed is appropriately and justifiably severe. C. J. Gianakaris, "Identifying Ethical Values in *Volpone," HLQ* 32 (1968): 45–57, notes that in this play "no trustworthy character steps forth to comment on misdeeds, and formal

representatives of legal standards . . . are for the first time unreliable."
Analyzing the way Jonson indicates ethical values, he concludes that
"sound, reasonable conduct turns out to be the sum of values within
Volpone. . . .When good reason is violated by one of his characters,
Jonson is prompt in bringing to bear his instrument of ridicule, the
comic manager within a play." Discussing Jonson's "rhetorical
method," Douglas Duncan, "Audience-Manipulation in *Volpone*,"
Wascana Review 5, no. 2 (1970): 23-37, argues that the ideal audience
must have a dual reaction to the play: "Wryly [Jonson] forces the
spectators to acknowledge that their approval of his play . . . depends
on their refusing to recognise that it has been directed against them."

Jonas A. Barish, "The Double Plot in *Volpone*," *MP* 51 (1953):
83-92, believes that the Would-bes are justifiable on the thematic level
and that their antics are related to the play's major motifs. First, they
are part of the beast fable in the play, Sir Pol being a parrot; he is also
a comically inverted picture of Volpone. His first scene with Peregrine
develops three major themes: monstrosity, folly, and mimicry. Seriously used in the main plot, these themes are parodied in the subplot.
Elaborating on Barish, Judd Arnold, "The Double Plot in *Volpone*:
A Note on Jonsonian Dramatic Structure," *Seventeenth-Century
News* 23 (1965): 47-52, concludes: "The action of *Volpone* is determined by its theme, but the full statement of that theme is realized
only by the mutually dependent progressions of multiple actions."
Lloyd L. Mills, "Barish's 'The Double Plot' Supplemented: The Tortoise Symbolism," *Serif* 4, no. 3 (1967): 25-28, points out that the
tortoise is a symbol of silence. "While the tortoise may stand for
polity . . . it seems that Jonson's more immediate aim was to effect a
dramatic economy by having Sir Pol climb into a device which, because
it is so crude, illustrates the shallowness of his intellect, even while it
represents symbolically the silence to which he has been reduced."
John Canuteson, "Sir Politic Would-Be's *Testudo*," *AN&Q* 11 (1973):
117-18, notes that a "testudo" is both a tortoise and a Roman engine
of war. The double meaning deflates Sir Pol from his would-be heights
of statesmanship to the level of a common soldier. Suggesting that
"self-deception is actually the key to the play," Dorothy Litt, "Unity
of Theme in *Volpone*," *BNYPL* 73 (1969): 218-26, argues that
"through this theme the subplot may be seen to mirror the main plot;
the would-be sophisticate operates in a world of folly, while the would-
be heirs operate in a world of vice."

The animal fable is examined fully in several items. D. A. Scheve,
"Jonson's *Volpone* and Traditional Fox Lore,"*RES* 1 (1950): 242-44,

notes that there was a "very specific tradition about the fox" and his ability to catch birds of prey by feigning death. Jonson uses the feigning fox as an emblem for the deceiving of the legacy hunters, drawing parallels between the action and the fable; he may have read the story in Conrad Gesner's *Historia Animalium* (1557), which was in his library. Malcolm H. South, "Animal Imagery in *Volpone*," *TSL* 10 (1965): 141–50, attempts "to give a more thorough analysis of the structural and thematic function of the animal imagery . . . and to show how this particular fox story . . . shaped Jonson's composition of the play." Jonson builds most of his animal imagery around the fable of the deceptive fox, and "the entire play turns on deceptions. . . .Volpone's world is one of deceit and inhumanity, a world where animal values have replaced human ones and each creature is the prey of another." That Volpone is finally "outwitted through his own cleverness is in keeping with the literary and oral traditions concerning the fox." Robert Knoll, *Ben Jonson's Plays* (I,B), believes that the play is a morality disguised as beast fable. The fly (Mosca) was associated with devils in folklore; ironically the crow (Corvino) was an emblem of Christian constancy; the raven (Corbaccio) forsook its children who were cared for by Divine Providence; and the tortoise (into whose shell Sir Pol crawls) was a symbol of polity. The animal imagery suggests that the play is about Nature and unnatural perversions. See Ian Donaldson, "Jonson's Tortoise," *RES* 19 (1968): 162–66, for the emblematic significances available to Jonson, and Kenneth Varty, *Reynard the Fox: A Study of the Fox in Medieval English Art* (1967), for the background of the fox fable.

Rainer Pineas, "The Morality Vice in *Volpone*," *Discourse* 5 (1962): 451–59, believes that most scholars have seen classical models behind Volpone and Mosca, and proposes "to trace the influence of a native tradition on these two arch-villains, namely, that of the morality Vice." That Mosca, the prime Vice of the play, "derives many traits from the morality Vice can be seen by examining some of their respective characteristics"; even the fact that Mosca and Volpone turn upon and delude each other is a feature of the morality play. Alan C. Dessen, "*Volpone* and the Late Morality Tradition," *MLQ* 25 (1964): 383–99, incorporated in *Jonson's Moral Comedy* (I,B), demonstrates "how the theme, structure, and techniques of a group of late moralities provide a valuable key to the distinctive Jonsonian 'comedy' found in *Volpone*." To answer the question of the power of gold in society—a typical morality concern—Jonson uses a dramatic structure similar to that of the late morality play. There are three sets of characters which resemble those in the moralities: Corvino, Corbaccio, and Voltore function as "estates," Celia and Bonario are the "Faithful Few," and Volpone and Mosca are the "Vices." *Volpone* is not simply a morality play, but the late moralities are "closer in form and intent to *Volpone* than are most 'comedies.' " Gerrard H. Cox, III, "Celia, Bonario, and Jonson's Indebtedness to the Medieval Cycles," *EA* 25 (1972): 506–11, argues that Jonson's treatment of Celia and Bonario is remarkably similar to that of the sacred figures in the Corpus Christi plays. These consciously stylized characters are the standards of virtue in a corrupt world. Charles Hallett, "Jonson's Celia: A Reinterpretation of *Volpone,*" *SP* 68 (1971): 50–69, emphasizes Celia's major role as Heavenly Justice in Volpone's fall, and in "The Satanic Nature of Volpone," *PQ* 49 (1970): 41–55, he associates the character of Volpone with that of the devil who acts as a tempter, tormentor, and high priest of a diabolical religious cult centered around the worship of gold.

Peter H. Davison, "*Volpone* and the Old Comedy," *MLQ* 24 (1963): 151–57, proposes that the play is "a special kind of comedy, the ultimate source of which is to be found in the Old Comedy of Greece." Jonson's critical comment, "The parts of a Comedie are the same with a *Tragedie,* and the end is partly the same. For, they both delight, and teach," points to the fact that for him "the *hybris* of tragedy is equated with the *alazōneia* of Aristophanic comedy, giving in *Volpone* the appearance of the hubristic hero wreaking his own downfall." In Sir Pol and Peregrine, one can identify the Impostor and the Ironical Buffon of Old Comedy, and these characters are comparable to Mosca and Volpone in the main plot. (See Coburn Gum, I,B.) In contrast, W. Speed Hill, "Biography, Autobiography, and *Volpone,*" *SEL* 12 (1972): 309–28, emphasizes Jonson's own humor and personality as a key to the ethical intention of this morally ambiguous play. Since the good are helpless, society's only hope is that evil will destroy itself. Basing his argument on De Luna (see below, under *Catiline*), James Tulip, "Comedy as Equivocation: An Approach to the Reference of *Volpone,*" *Southern Review: An Australian Journal of Literary Studies* 5 (1972): 91–101, feels that the play "reaches into the political life of the time"; *Volpone* "was written at the very crisis of the Gunpowder Plot," and Sir Pol is actually a parody of Cecil.

In "Lewkenor and *Volpone,*" *N&Q* 9 (1962): 124–30, Daniel Boughner proposes that a primary source for Jonson's details of Venetian life and customs is Lewis Lewkenor's *The Commonwealth and*

Gouernment of Venice (1599), a translation of Contareno's *Della Repvblica et Magistrati di Venetia* (1564). Shakespeare also uses Lewkenor, and Boughner theorizes: "The presence in Jonson's play of some details from *The Commonwealth,* but also of others from sources unmentioned by the translator and outside Contareno, shows how the emulative research stimulated by Shakespeare's Venice plays and charted by Lewkenor enriched his Venetian masterpiece with marvellous local colour." In *The Devil's Disciple* (I,B), Boughner discusses Machiavellian irony in the play. Ian Donaldson, "Jonson's Italy: *Volpone* and Fr. Thomas Wright" (I,A), points out Wright's influence.

Sources have been sought for set pieces within the play. F. W. Bradbrook, "John Donne and Ben Jonson," *N&Q* 4 (1957): 146–47, hears an echo of Donne's "The Sunne Rising" in the opening lines, and compares *Volpone,* V.i, with Donne's Satire III. Examining I.i.30–40, R. P. Draper, "The Golden Age and Volpone's Address to His Gold," *N&Q* 3 (1956): 191–92, notes that the source of the lines is Ovid's description of the Golden Age (*Metamorphoses,* 1. 89–112). Edward Partridge, *The Broken Compass* (I,B), points out the discrepancy between the language of Christian worship and the actual adoration of gold. A general study of the language, L. A. Beaurline's "Volpone and the Power of Gorgeous Speech," in *Ben Jonson: Quadricentennial Essays* (I,B), pp. 61–75, emphasizes "Mosca and Volpone's exuberant style." "The rogue and the comic artist make a seemingly self-contained and self-generating world of tempting fantasy that we must participate in, although we may finally acknowledge its essential ugliness."

Arguing against the source suggested by Herford and Simpson, John P. Cutts, "Volpone's Song: A Note on the Source and Jonson's Translation," *N&Q* 5 (1958): 217–19, contends that the source for both Volpone's main song and the four-line catch that follows is Catullus's fifth poem. William Sylvester, "Jonson's 'Come, My Celia' and Catullus' 'Carmen V,' " *Expl* 22 (1964): item 35, points out that "a significant dimension is added to . . . 'Come, My Celia,' if it is set against the background of the darker poem, Catullus' fifth ode, which it emulates."

Frederick W. Sternfeld, "Song in Jonson's Comedy: A Gloss on *Volpone,*" in *Studies in the English Renaissance Drama in Memory of Karl Julius Holzknecht,* ed. Josephine W. Bennett et al. (1959), pp. 310–21, indicates that Jonson had determined ideas about music. He uses song in many ways, and "certainly the music with which Mosca arranges to entertain Volpone or with which Volpone endeavors to seduce Celia is tawdry and debasing and not the manifestation of a divine skill." Nevertheless, Volpone's song displays three prominent characteristics of Jonson's poetry: rationalism, classicism, and sensitivity to native English idiom. Sternfeld's "Lasso's Music for Shakespeare's 'Samingo,'" *SQ* 9 (1958): 105-16, touches on Jonson's use of the song "Monsieur Mingo."

Pierre Han, "'Tabarine' in Ben Jonson's *Volpone*," *Seventeenth-Century News* 28 (1970): 4-5, suggests that Jonson is not alluding merely to Tabarin the Italian zany who visited France in 1572, but to "a whole tradition of improvised buffoonery that characterized the Italian *commedia dell'arte* whose influences were . . . felt in France." Frank N. Clary, Jr., "The Vol and the Pone: A Reconsideration of Jonson's *Volpone*," *ELN* 10 (1972): 102-7, argues that the name is a "compounded Figure." "Vol" may be defined as a lure, while "pone" is "a writ requiring the sheriff to secure the appearance of the defendant by attaching his goods or by causing him to find sureties for his appearance." "The specialized definitions of the terms vol and pone provide the keys to Jonson's wit at the end of *Volpone*."

Charles Hallett, "*Volpone* as the Source of the Sickroom Scheme in Middleton's *Mad World*," *N&Q* 18 (1971): 24-25, believes that *Volpone* is not only the source of the feigned death of Quomodo at the end of *Michaelmas Term*, but also the source of Act III of *A Mad World, My Masters*. Cecil Seronsy, "Sir Politic Would-Be in Laputa," *ELN* 1 (1963): 17-24, thinks that Sir Pol's penchant for fantastic projects and supposed conspiracies may be a direct source for parts of *Gulliver's Travels*, Book III. Jay H. Hartman, "*Volpone* as a Possible Source for Melville's *The Confidence Man*," *Susquehanna University Studies* 7 (1965): 247-60, argues that Melville's character "could very easily be the Venetian confidence man transplanted to an American setting, so similar is his manner of swindling those about him. . . . Melville could have drawn on Ben Jonson's *Volpone* for ideas as he wrote *The Confidence Man*." Jackson I. Cope, "*Volpone* and the Authorship of *Eastward Hoe*," *MLN* 72 (1957): 253-56, uses *Volpone* to suggest Jonson's authorship of *Eastward Hoe*, II.ii.92-124. David McPherson, "Rough Beast into Tame Fox: The Adaptations of *Volpone*," in *Ben Jonson: Quadricentennial Essays* (I,B), pp. 77-84, finds it "one of the ironies of dramatic history that Jonson, the only Elizabethan playwright who meticulously edited many of his own works to insure preservation of an accurate text, has been known since 1771 to many audiences of his most famous play through the interesting but inevitably distorting versions of his many adapters." Annabella

Cloudsley, *"Volpone* in Germany," *Twentieth Century* 168 (1960): 66-69, deals with the premiere of Francis Burt's operatic adaptation; *Volpone* on stage is discussed by Priscilla Sellman, "The Old Globe's Sixth Season in San Diego," *SQ* 7 (1956): 419-22. C. J. Gianakaris, "Jonson's Use of 'Avocatori' in *Volpone,"* *ELN* 12 (1974): 8-14, feels Jonson's use of "Avocatori" indicates his possession of a sophisticated grasp of "Venetian justice as it existed during the republican period of that city." T. W. Craik, "Volpone's 'Young Antinous,'" *N&Q* 17 (1970): 213-14, suggests that III.vii.157-64 is an allusion to the unwelcomed suitor of the *Odyssey* rather than Emperor Hadrian's favorite. Arthur Freeman, "The Earliest Allusion to *Volpone,"* *N&Q* 14 (1967): 207-8, believes *The Mous-Trap* (1606) to be the earliest datable reference to the play.

Jonas A. Barish, *Ben Jonson and the Language of Prose Comedy*, John Enck, *Jonson and the Comic Truth*, J. A. Bryant, Jr., *The Compassionate Satirist*, Helena Baum, *The Satiric and the Didactic in Ben Jonson's Comedy*, and D. J. Enright, *The Apothecary's Shop* (all in I,B), also treat the play. Jonas A. Barish, ed., *Jonson: "Volpone": A Casebook* (1972), offers a selection of critical essays previously printed and reviews of productions from 1930 to 1972. See also Lawrence Levin (below, under *Sejanus*).

The Alchemist

Paul Goodman, *The Structure of Literature* (1954), analyzes the play into the component parts of comedy, using a structural approach. Calvin G. Thayer, "Theme and Structure in *The Alchemist,"* *ELH* 26 (1959): 23-35, incorporated in *Ben Jonson: Studies in the Plays* (I,B), feels that much of the play is symbolic. With his suggestive name and ever-shifting identity, Face becomes the embodiment of the "comic spirit," while Subtle, as the alchemist, is the "comic artist." In Subtle's speech (II.iii.133-98), alchemy is identified as "a metaphor for art" in general and comic art in particular. The plague indicates a sick society, and the unity of place in Jonson's classical structure is calculated. Lovewit's house is close to Blackfriars, and thus close to the audience. As alchemy is used to influence the gulls, so the play should influence the audience.

Judd Arnold, "Lovewit's Triumph and Jonsonian Morality: A Reading of *The Alchemist,"* *Criticism* 11 (1969): 151-66, believes the play is not so much about alchemy as it is about people who will transmute themselves and others into that which they are not. These creatures cannot or will not accept the world as it is, or their place in it. Lovewit triumphs over the world of gulls, and his triumph is consistent with Jonson's tolerant but satirically unsentimental portrayal of the world. Vincent F. Petronella, "Teaching Ben Jonson's *The Alchemist:* Alchemy and Analysis," *HAB* 21, no. 2 (1970): 19-23, and Edgar Hill Duncan, "Jonson's *Alchemist* and the Literature of Alchemy," *PMLA* 61 (1946): 699-710, introduce fundamental concepts of alchemy to facilitate a reading of the play. David Woodman, *White Magic and English Renaissance Drama* (1973), places it in the context of Shakespeare's *Tempest* and the Jacobean court mask. "More extensively than any other playwright of the English Renaissance, [Jonson] explored the tenets of white magic and the magicians who held them." James V. Holleran, "Character Transmutation in *The Alchemist,*" *CLAJ* 11 (1968): 221-27, deals "with the play in terms of the relationship between the theme of alchemy and the methods of characterization." "The scientific inadequacy of alchemy is paralleled thematically by the psychological inadequacy of the characters." Holleran points out the problems in Lovewit's success; it is not unqualified. "Lovewit's apparent success may be interpreted as the final attempt at transmutation in the play. The circumstances of his life have changed, and now he must endure them." "In a sense, every character in Jonson's play is an alchemist; but no one, including Lovewit, actually succeeds in transmuting himself."

Barry Targan, "The Dramatic Structure of *The Alchemist,*" *Discourse* 6 (1963): 315-24, sees Face, Subtle, and the gulls corresponding to the modern "roper," "inside man," and "the mark." "Now as then, the bait is the promise of something for nothing." Jonson is not interested in moral judgments, but in moral truths, and the theme of the play may be called "ingenuity." "Each man in the play with the exception of Love-wit wins or loses according to his intellectual merit." "Jonson emphasizes these various gradations of wit by setting up indicative relationships between representatives of the levels and Pliant, for she is the richest prize and in this play money is the measure." Targan concludes with a brief analysis of the relationship of the members of the triumvirate to each other.

Robert Knoll's "How to Read *The Alchemist,*" *CE* 21 (1960): 456-60, included in his *Ben Jonson's Plays* (I,B), is also concerned with structural aspects. Knoll points out that the first scene introduces two important facts: the gulling takes place in the house of Face's master who is away in the country; and the triumvirate's alliance is precarious. The play is a series of repeated comic events, and Jonson's technique is the one used in fairy tales and nursery rhymes—reduplication. The pattern consists of a primary introduction followed by a waiting period and a final gulling. The difference in the pattern is the degree of seriousness, and only Surly and Lovewit stand outside the web of reduplication; both the gullible and the confidence men who take them in are satirized. Moreover, the play is a retelling of the Parable of Talents; ironically, Face put his master's talents to work. And finally the play is a commentary on human aspirations and religious humility.

Alan Dessen, *"The Alchemist:* Jonson's 'Estates' Play," *RenD* 7 (1964): 35-54, incorporated in his *Jonson's Moral Comedy* (I,B), observes the play's affinities in dramatic structure to a group of late morality plays, such as *A Knack to Know a Knave*; although Jonson does not slavishly follow the tradition, these allegorical plays "are closer in form and intent to *The Alchemist* than are most 'comedies.'" William Blissett, "The Venter Tripartite in *The Alchemist," SEL* 8 (1968): 323-34, points out that the cheaters who make up the "Venter tripartite" are the old enemies of mankind—the World, the Flesh, and the Devil—put into a realistic London setting. "The conclusion of the play is as bland as that of *Volpone* is severe. The householder Lovewit gains riches and a young wife, and condones the actions of his unjust steward. The respectable worldling is the winner in this world."

Cyrus Hoy, "The Pretended Piety of Jonson's *Alchemist," RenP,* 1958, pp. 15-19, included in his *The Hyacinth Room* (1964), pp. 119-27, discusses the multiple ironies involved in the assertions of piety. The basic irony stems from the discrepancy between the ideal concepts which provide a background of significant truths and the grim realities of the actual situation. Jonson thus suggests the thorough corruption of the characters. Ian Donaldson, "Language, Noise, and Nonsense: *The Alchemist,"* in *Seventeenth-Century Imagery,* ed. Earl Miner (1971), pp. 69-82, sees the play as centrally concerned with the problems and questions of language. Jonson's use of Puritans in the play is investigated by Maurice Hussey, "Ananias the Deacon: A Study of Religion in Jonson's *The Alchemist," English* 9 (1953): 207-12. Hussey's main point is that Jonson was not simply attempting to satirize Puritans as fanatics and hypocrites; his satire is much more universal. Myrddin Jones, "Sir Epicure Mammon: A Study in 'Spiritual Fornication,'" *Renaissance Quarterly* 22 (1969): 233-42, proposes that by associating himself with Solomon in terms of wealth, wit, and sexual potency, Mammon fails to understand that the Hebrew king also epitomizes apostasy and idolatry.

M. A. Shaaber, "The 'Vncleane Birds' in *The Alchemist*," *MLN* 65 (1950): 106-9, reports that an anonymous tract on "diuerse vnknowne Foules" (1586) throws light on IV.vii.50 ff. Knoll, *Ben Jonson's Plays* (I,B), summarizes the history of opinion about these birds and concludes that they are "Ibises," which were supposed to give clysters to each other with their bills. Malcolm South, "The 'Vncleane Birds, in Seuenty-Seuen': *The Alchemist*," *SEL* 13 (1973): 331-43, argues that there is anti-Catholic feeling behind Ananias's comparison of the huge ruff worn by Surly to the "vncleane birds, in seuenty-seuen"; he traces the origin of the allusion to Catholic priests as birds and explains the topicality of Ananias's remark.

C. J. Sisson, "A Topical Reference in *The Alchemist*," in *Joseph Quincy Adams Memorial Studies,* (I,B), pp. 739-41, feels that the basis of Jonsonian comedy—to satirize the follies of the times—invited Jonson to draw upon contemporary events for his material. Since *The Alchemist* is a topical play, Sisson compares the character of Dapper with young Thomas Rogers who gave one Greene, a tool of the Asheleys, five or six pounds to meet the Queen of Fairies. Both Dapper and Rogers were gulled in 1610. Franklin Williams, Jr., "Thomas Rogers as Ben Jonson's Dapper," *Yearbook of English Studies* 2 (1972): 73-77, helps to confirm Sisson's identification. See Joseph McCullen, Jr., "Conference with the Queen of Fairies: A Study of Jonson's Workmanship in *The Alchemist*," *Studia Neophilologica* 23 (1951): 87-95.

Arthur Colby Sprague, "*The Alchemist* on the Stage," *Theatre Notebook* 17 (1962-63): 46-47, surveys the stage performances of the play from 1610 to 1962. For *The Alchemist* on the Restoration stage, see A. L. D. Kennedy-Skipton, "John Ward and Restoration Drama," *SQ* 11 (1960): 493-94, and his note, *SQ* 12 (1961): 353. "The Alchemist," in *Manchester Guardian Weekly*, 23 Jan. 1947, p. 9, merely recounts a performance of the play. First published in *PQ* 24 (1945): 85-89, Johnstone Parr's "Non-Alchemical Pseudo-Sciences in *The Alchemist*," is reprinted in his *Tamburlaine's Malady, and Other Essays on Astrology in Elizabethan Drama* (1953). Enck, *Jonson and the Comic Truth* (I,B), and Bryant, *The Compassionate Satirist* (I,B), deal extensively with the play. Partridge, *The Broken Compass* (I,B), discusses the play's functional imagery and its relation to alchemy. Richard Levin, "'No Laughing Matter': Some New Readings of *The Alchemist*," in *Ben Jonson: Quadricentennial Essays* (I,B), pp. 85-99, discusses recent criticism of the play and decries the trend toward "instant seriousness" which it represents. "If it continues we will be asked to surrender the joyous pleasures that the immediate, felt experience of comedy can give us, in all its rich and complex particularity, for a mess of platitudinous pieties."

Bartholomew Fair

Freda Townsend's seminal study, *Apologie for Batholmew Fayre* (I,B), sees the play as the culmination of Jonsonian comedy. Richard Levin, "The Structure of *Bartholomew Fair*," *PMLA* 80 (1965): 172-79, incorporated in *The Multiple Plot in English Renaissance Drama* (1971), believes that one should be able to see the construction of the play on the level of plot, "the organizing principle that accounts for and connects the separate parts of the play." "The major division of the characters will be between the people who make up the fair and, consequently, the special dramatic world in which the action takes place, and the outsiders whose visit to this world constitutes the action itself, the plot, of the play." In broad outline, the play is built thus: each group begins in solidarity and then gradually disintegrates. "Each member is joined to his counterpart in the other party, and then is brought to the puppet-show that assembles all the visitors, in their new relationships, for the resolution."

Jacqueline E. M. Latham, "Form in *Bartholomew Fair*," *English* 21 (1972): 8-11, points to "the four planes of reality presented in sequence from the Induction to the puppet play-within-a-play in Act V." "Not only has Jonson given his play the form of a Chinese box in which one plane of reality is enclosed within another, but he has made one character symbolic of each." Thus, Adam Overdo symbolizes "the respectable world of spiritual and intellectual shortcomings"; Ursula represents the fair, and Bartholomew Cokes, the world of the puppets. (Apparently she neglects the world of the Induction.) Barry Targan, "The Moral Structure of *Bartholomew Fair*," *Discourse* 8 (1965): 276-84, claims that "in *Bartholomew Fair* the mimetic structure—the 'imitation of an action'—is carried not only to the limit of Jonson's concern but perhaps to the very limit of the concept of mimesis." The play does not have the same kind of moral or dramatic center found in the early plays, but deals broadly with pervasive human frailty. Its structure "is comparable, metaphorically, to that of a dance." "Each movement begins as an attempt on the part of various parties to accomplish some personal thing, and through a mounting confusion that results when the aims collide, the movement ends in symbolic chaos." The play resolves nothing, underscoring Jonson's point, "the futility of attempting change." Guy Hamel, "Order and Judgement in *Bartholomew Fair*," *UTQ* 43 (1973-74): 48-67, observes that the "construction of *Bartholomew Fair* achieves a fine balance of delicately opposed obligations. In its multiplicity the play reflects the disorder that is its matter. In bringing shape to its sprawling action it illustrates its informing concerns: the scope and limits of order in human affairs, the role of right judgement in establishing such order, and the adjustments that the wise allow in recognition of the irrational and chancy."

James E. Robinson, *"Bartholomew Fair:* Comedy of Vapors," *SEL* 1, no. 2 (1961): 65-80, suggests that "the center of the structure and meaning" of the play "lies in the symbolism of vapors that pervades the play's imagery, characterization, and action." All the intrigues grow and converge into one whole; the world of the fair joins with the world outside and forms a universal, a symbol of Vanity Fair. It is in this merging of "imagery, character, scene, and action to produce a universal comic truth that the structure and unity of the play lies." Starting with a comparison of Jonson and Dekker, Joel Kaplan, "Dramatic and Moral Energy in Ben Jonson's *Bartholomew Fair*," *RenD* 3 (1970): 137-56, feels that "the same skepticism towards extravagant energy and mimesis that appears in both *Volpone* and *The Alchemist* is brought to bear upon the roaring spirit of Smithfield, revealing a grotesque turbulence that coarsens as it liberates, creating tumult and heightening antagonisms while moving characters towards a reconciliation at the level of flesh and blood, where all are united by a common participation in human folly." He emphasizes the complexity of Jonson's vision of the fair.

Ray L. Heffner, Jr., "Unifying Symbols in the Comedy of Ben Jonson" (I,B, and see below, *Epicoene*), feels that *Bartholomew Fair* deals with the problem of warrant. The focus of the play is upon the concrete symbols of legal sanction, and the entire play may be seen under this aspect, the most important symbol of which "is the 'warrant' which the madman Troubleall demands of almost all the characters in the fourth act." Ian Donaldson, *The World Upside-Down* (1970), suggests that it is a festive comedy, and that the main theme is the recoil of justice on those who try to administer it. Calvin C. Smith, *"Bartholomew Fair:* Cold Decorum," in *Essays in the Renaissance in Honor of Allan H. Gilbert,* ed. Philip Traci and Marilyn Williamson, special issue of *SAQ* 71 (1972): 548-56, argues that Grace Wellborn is thematically and structurally the central character. The major movement is toward marriage, and Grace is the object of this movement. Vincent Petronella, "Jonson's *Bartholomew Fair:* A Study in Baroque Style," *Discourse* 13 (1970): 325-37, believes that Jonson's baroque technique is instrumental to the success of the play, while William McCollom, *The Divine Average: A View of Comedy* (1971), sees the play as Jonson's representation of a deranged world.

John M. Potter, "Old Comedy in *Bartholomew Fair,"* *Criticism* 10 (1968): 290-99, notes that Jonson's editors discuss a lost "apologie" that he wrote for *Bartholomew Fair* which they believe contained Jonson's explanation for his "glaring disregard of classical structure" in the play. On the contrary, Potter thinks the "apologie" probably explained the type of classical structure borrowed from Old Comedy which he used here. For further comment on the "apologie," see Mary C. Williams, "Ben Jonson's 'Apology' for *Bartholomew Fair,"* *ELN* 10 (1973): 180-85. Don Mager, "The Paradox of Tone in *Bartholmew Fayre,"* *Thoth* 9 (1968): 39-47, points out that Jonson's great comedies are not denials of his moralistic ideals for art; rather the moralistic function is so fused into the total structure of these plays that their brilliance is inseparable from their didacticism. He explores the ways in which this fusion works in *Bartholomew Fair.*

Jonas Barish, *"Bartholomew Fair* and Its Puppets," *MLQ* 20 (1959): 3-17, explains that the puppet show is an integral part of the play. "If the Fair is in this play a microcosm of the world, and the puppet show, in its turn, a microcosm of the Fair, then the squalid bickering of the puppets, their pettiness and emptiness, merely reproduce in concentrated form the same qualities distributed among the live inhabitants of Smithfield, and in the world at large. In addition . . . the puppet show serves as an instrument of correction." The play's corporeality and carnality, its procreative imagery, its use of vapors, all culminate in the puppet show. The puppets "reflect still another trait peculiar to the denizens of the world and the Fair: human littleness and childishness." Finally, the puppets are Jonson's defense of the theater against magistrates (Overdo) and Puritans (Busy); the theater must be "defended even in its vilest and rowdiest manifestations." James E. Savage, "Some Antecedents of the Puppet Play in *Bartholomew Fair,"* *UMSE* 7 (1966): 42-64, points to the influence of Nashe's *Lenten Stuffe,* and George Speaight, *The History of the English Puppet Theatre* (1955), believes that they must have been "glove puppets."

Eugene M. Waith, "The Staging of *Bartholomew Fair,*" *SEL* 2 (1962): 181-95, argues that the most notable element of Jonson's theater technique is the use of "the principles of simultaneous staging." Beginning with the facts that *Bartholomew Fair* was performed at the Hope Theatre on 31 October 1614 and at court the following night, and that it needed "Canvas for the Boothes," Waith offers a reconstruction of the staging as medieval and intimate. "In the last act the puppet booth becomes what the 'pig-box' earlier was—the chief locus of the action." The play is "one of the clearest examples of the survival in the Elizabethan public theater of the essentially medieval tradition of staging." See Waith's edition of the play in the Yale Ben Jonson (1963), Appendix II: "The Staging." R. B. Parker, "The Themes and Staging of *Bartholomew Fair,*" *UTQ* 39 (1970): 293-309, demonstrates that the stage techniques of the play add to the themes and the overall excellence.

W. J. Olive, "A Chaucer Allusion in Jonson's *Bartholomew Fair,*" *MLQ* 13 (1952): 21-22, suggests that Jonson emended Chaucer's line from "new to begynne" to "now . . . to begin." Calvin Thayer, "Ben Jonson, Markham, and Shakespeare," *N&Q* 1 (1954): 469-70, points out that Jonson was following Markham's *Cavelarice* in his description of Win Littlewit and that he was probably also thinking of Shakespeare's description of the horse in *Venus and Adonis,* ll. 295-300. Umphrey Lee, "Jonson's *Bartholomew Fair* and the Popular Dramatic Tradition," *Louisburg College Journal of Arts and Sciences* 1 (1967): 6-16, argues that parts of the play are "deliberate parodies" of Chettle and Day's *The Blind Beggar of Bednal Green.* He sees Jonson turning from classical to popular themes and thus beginning a new phase in his work. Eugene Waith, "A Misprint in *Bartholomew Fair,*" *N&Q* 10 (1963): 103-4, contends that V.v.50-51 should be spoken by Grace Wellborn, not by Quarlous as in *Works* (1640).

Other studies include Jackson I. Cope, "*Bartholomew Fair* as Blasphemy," *RenD* 8 (1965): 127-52, and chapters in Barish, *Ben Jonson and the Language of Prose Comedy,* Enck, *Jonson and the Comic Truth,* Knoll, *Ben Jonson's Plays,* Thayer, *Ben Jonson,* Bryant, *The Compassionate Satirist,* and Dessen, *Jonson's Moral Comedy* (all in I,B).

Epicoene, or The Silent Woman

Edward B. Partridge, "The Allusiveness of *Epicoene,*" *ELH* 22 (1955): 93-107, incorporated in his *The Broken Compass* (I,B), begins with a discussion of the play's allusive language and then underlines the theme of hermaphroditism which runs through the play. For the seventeenth century, "epicoene" suggested "the abnormal no man's land . . . between the normal male and the normal female. This meaning is . . . central to *The Silent Woman*," where nearly every character is epicoene in some way. The play is concerned with deviations from a norm and the comic effect of these deviations: it is about "nature, normality, and decorum." In "Ovid, Juvenal, and *The Silent Woman*," *PMLA* 71 (1956): 213–24, Jonas Barish maintains that the play is only a limited success and tries to explain why by examining Jonson's use of Ovid and Juvenal. Jonson was emotionally split in his use of these sources; though trying to be polished and Ovidian, his natural bent was toward the Juvenalian tone. John Ferns, "Ovid, Juvenal, and *The Silent Woman:* A Reconsideration," *MLR* 65 (1970): 248–53, feels that Barish misses the point: "Jonson the dramatist simply uses Ovid and Juvenal as salt for his comic broth and both True-wit and Morose strike this reader at least as independent comic creations who reveal no signs that surly authorial interference has maimed them." The play is unified by its plot, not by classical sources. Mark Anderson, "The Successful Unity of *Epicoene:* A Defense of Ben Jonson," *SEL* 10 (1970): 349–66, suggests that the two metamorphoses of Epicoene reveal the two stages of the play's unified plot. Dauphine incites the action of the play to discredit Morose's judgment and to reveal his folly; Truewit organizes the deceptions and exposures of the play's second part, acting successfully in a society where deception is the accepted norm.

L. G. Salingar, "Farce and Fashion in *The Silent Woman*," *E&S* 20 (1967): 29–46, believes that modern critics have underrated the originality of Jonson's farcical scheme. Though Jonson may have borrowed the main idea from Aretino (see Oscar J. Campbell, "The Relation of *Epicoene* to Aretino's *Il Marescalco*," *PMLA* 46 [1931]: 752–62), he was the first playwright in England to use a similar surprise in his plot. Having established that the mode of the play is farce, Salingar shows that its material is topical. Charles A. Carpenter, "*Epicoene* Minus Its Secret: Surprise as Expectation," *Xavier University Studies* 7, no. 3 (1968): 15–22, suggests that the effect of the play depends on the pleasure we derive as acquainted spectators, through expectation and anticipatory suspense.

Ian Donaldson, " 'A Martyrs Resolution': Jonson's *Epicoene*," *RES* 18 (1967): 1–15, incorporated in his *The World Upside-Down* (1970), interprets the play as a festive comedy. The theme of secrecy runs throughout, and the contrast between secret people and open people, between private action and public action, is central. At the play's center is the festive invasion of the private world by the public. These scenes should be seen "in relationship to certain festive and wedding customs common in Jonson's time." The discordant music of III.vii may symbolize the discordant marriage and world of Morose, but it is also reminiscent of the custom of charivari in which an "old dotard" is derided by "a foule noise made" for his marrying a "young wanton." The charivari scene seems to celebrate "the larger theme of sexual reversal in the play."

In "Unifying Symbols in the Comedy of Ben Jonson" (I,B), Ray Heffner concludes: "The essential movement of *The Silent Woman . . .* is the exploration of themes implicit in the central comic conceit of a noise-hating man married to a noisy woman. Noise and the hatred of noise take on the proportion of symbols as they are given ever-widening meanings." Bryant, *The Compassionate Satirist* (I,B), feels sympathy for Morose. The play "reminds us how close we are to our ancestral jungle." Michael Shapiro, "Audience vs. Dramatist in Jonson's *Epicoene* and Other Plays of the Children's Troupes," *English Literary Renaissance* 3 (1973): 400–417, posits that the audiences in the private playhouses were condescending in their attitude to the stage and liked to dramatize themselves with the play as background. Using Marston and Chapman as examples, Shapiro points out that Jonson gives his audience the most complex picture of its aristocratic self-dramatization in Truewit, Dauphine, and Clerimont. By using these characters, Jonson attempts to win the attention and sympathy of the audience. William Slights, "*Epicoene* and the Prose Paradox," *PQ* 49 (1970): 178–87, argues that the Renaissance genre of the prose paradox informs the language and action of the play. Used against folly, the prose paradox allows Jonson to question stereotyped judgments and to indicate the complexity of responsible moral action.

Enck, *Jonson and the Comic Truth* (I,B), feels that the play begins a "new rationale" for Jonson. Barish, *Ben Jonson and the Language of Prose Comedy* (I,B), believes that "the persistence with which living creatures are identified with blocks of stone and metallic artifacts corresponds to a certain frigidity at the heart of the play." Thayer, *Ben Jonson* (I,B), sees it as "another step forward in Jonson's development as a comic writer." Knoll, *Ben Jonson's Plays* (I,B), comments that it is "a farce by a thoughtful man reaffirming conventional values."

Sejanus His Fall

Sejanus has gained in popularity since the early 1950s. Joseph A. Bryant, Jr., "The Nature of the Conflict in Jonson's *Sejanus*," in *Vanderbilt Studies in the Humanities,* ed. Richmond Beatty et al. (1951), pp. 197-219, begins with "an assumption which takes into account all the elements" of the play: "that the basic conflict is between good and evil, rather than between two evils, and that the 'good' characters in the play have a valid function as protagonists." All the characters representing "good" are related in some way—blood or sympathy—to the murdered hero Germanicus, a symbol of good in the past. Set against this good remnant are the evil characters, who, in a series of intrigues which continue beyond the play proper, struggle against and overthrow each other. Classical peoples, just as Renaissance Christians, felt that a bad ruler was a punishment of God and that passive obedience was the best way to oppose such a ruler. "To summarize, Jonson's play shows us a trial of the small remnant of virtue in a Roman commonwealth that is degenerate and, in fact, all but doomed to destruction. The issue for that remnant, and for the commonwealth, is death or survival, and the only favorable solution is set forth in terms of the Stoic concept of virtue."

Barbara N. Lindsay, "The Structure of Tragedy in *Sejanus*," *ES* 50 (Anglo-American Supplement, 1969), xliv-1, defines three levels of tragedy in the play: the personal, the "parochial but historically instructive level," and "the universal or ontological level." An analysis of the levels reveals that Jonson's theme is "the reality of chaos." Precisely because this is his theme, he can present it "only by the exact ordering of his material. Otherwise he will be left with no theme at all: Chaos will inherit the stage itself." In "*Sejanus* and *Coriolanus*: A Study in Alienation," *MLQ* 12 (1951): 407-21, Edwin Honig suggests that Jonson views the problem of tragedy as social and moral, while Shakespeare views it as psychological. Neither play suggests that the willful assertion of power by a single ruler is evil, but both suggest that tyranny is inevitable when traditional authority is dislodged. Sejanus is alienated because he acts without the two traditional sanctions of political authority and accepted religion. Another aspect of *Sejanus*'s relationship to Shakespearean tragedy is explored by W. J. Olive, "*Sejanus and Hamlet*," in *A Tribute to George Coffin Taylor,* ed. Arnold Williams (1952), pp. 178-84. Eugene W. Waith, *The Herculean Hero* (1962), believes that Sejanus belongs with Shakespeare's Antony and Marlowe's Tamburlaine in a category where the hero-villain is "not only wicked but monumental."

K. M. Burton, "The Political Tragedies of Chapman and Ben Jonson," *Essays in Criticism* 2 (1952): 397-412, maintains that these tragedies "have often been misjudged because they have been measured by the wrong yardsticks," and analyzes Chapman's *Tragedy of Chabot* and Jonson's *Sejanus.* Both playwrights are "interested in the problem of social decadence and its political implications," and in these plays, their views on the propagation of evil within the political realm are presented most completely. This kind of tragedy is non-Aristotelean, and both dramatists find their tragic flaws not in individual men, but in the social order. Jonson sees corruption in general; Chapman sees corruption growing from the top of the order. Contrasting *Sejanus* with Chapman's *Caesar and Pompey,* J. W. Lever, *The Tragedy of State* (1971), sees Jonson's play as denying the moral preconceptions which underlie the medieval idea of tragedy. Evil continues unabated here, and this is a tragedy of "a whole society in the political inferno of its own creation." G. R. Hibbard, "Goodness and Greatness: An Essay on the Tragedies of Ben Jonson and George Chapman," *RMS* 11 (1967): 5-54, traces the development of the theory of tragedy in Renaissance England and shows how the concepts of goodness and greatness entered that theory. The tragedies of Jonson and Chapman are examined against this background.

Moody E. Prior, *The Language of Tragedy* (1947), prefaces his remarks with a brief consideration of Jonson's critical principles. In *Sejanus,* Jonson's imagistic language is mainly used by the opposing Romans, Arruntius, Lepidus, and their friends, and very rarely by Sejanus and Tiberius. This separation leads to a disjunction between the elevated speech of Sejanus (V.i.6-9) and the "scale on which the play is drawn." Enck, *Jonson and the Comic Truth* (I,B), analyzes the play's imagery at length, discussing images of size, rising and falling, light which resembles darkness, and animals. Christopher Ricks, "*Sejanus* and Dismemberment," *MLN* 76 (1961): 301-8, points out that "in its imagery—the imagery of the parts of the body—the play anticipates and works towards the final scene. For not only is Sejanus dismembered, but the play shows the tragic dislocation of Roman life, the dismemberment of the body politic." Jonson rarely uses this kind of recurrent imagery, but here it is used with skill and subtlety.

K. W. Evans, "*Sejanus* and the Ideal Prince Tradition," *SEL* 11 (1971): 249-64, believes that Jonson was unaware of radical social changes taking place in his day and that his play appeals to an outdated concept of political hierarchy which renders the dramatic tensions simplistic. Arthur Marotti, "The Self-Reflexive Art of Ben Jonson's

Sejanus," TSLL 12 (1970): 197–220, supposes that the self-conscious artificiality of *Sejanus* is both a major cause of its failure as a tragedy and a characteristic of Jonson's dramaturgy. Irving Ribner, *Jacobean Tragedy: The Quest for Moral Order* (1962), comments that the play is merely a scholarly attempt "to achieve a classical ideal in tragedy"; it is "moralistic rather than moral."

By studying Jonson's annotations, Ellen Duffy, "Ben Jonson's Debt to Renaissance Scholarship in *Sejanus* and *Catiline," MLR* 42 (1947): 24–30, proves that not all his debts are directly to Tacitus; many are to Lipsius. Daniel Boughner also discusses Jonson's use of Lipsius's edition in "Jonson's Use of Lipsius in *Sejanus," MLN* 73 (1958): 247–55. Percy Simpson assumed that the dramatist followed Tacitus, but Boughner contends that Tacitus was, for Jonson, essentially uncongenial; Jonson's Tiberius, for example, is not Tacitus's Tiberius. However, Boughner feels that the impression of servility to Lipsius is "momentary and superficial," for in the larger aspects Jonson differs widely from his source. In " 'Rhodig.' and *Sejanus," N&Q* 5 (1958): 287–89, Boughner points out that Jonson's note to IV.283–87 refers to Rhodiginus, and investigates the possibility of Jonson's debt to the *Antiqvarivm Lectionvm libri xvi* (Venice, 1516). Boughner's "Juvenal, Horace and *Sejanus," MLN* 75 (1960): 545–50, discusses Jonson's use of Juvenal, who is "throughout the play a pervasive influence, but decidedly not a predominant source. The emotion that inspired his poems . . . becomes in Jonson's drama a moral fervor deliberately limited to Arruntius and his like-minded companions, whose tongues it sharpens by its bitter raillery." See Boughner's *The Devil's Disciple* (I,B).

Jonson's Caesar is a thoroughly Machiavellian prince (cf. Ralph Nash, I,B). Boughner, "Sejanus and Machiavelli," *SEL* 1, no. 2 (1961): 81–100, feels that the passage expressing indignation over the spies at Tiberius's court has a source in Machiavelli. *Sejanus's* relationship to "the contemporary political situation" is pointed out in Geoffrey Hill's "The World's Proportion," in *Jacobean Theatre* (I,B), pp. 113–31. Gary Hamilton, "Irony and Fortune in *Sejanus," SEL* 11 (1971): 265–81, proposes that the concept of Fortune is used ironically; what the characters allude to as the acts of Fortune are really the machinations of Tiberius.

Allan H. Gilbert, "The Eavesdroppers in Jonson's *Sejanus," MLN* 69 (1954): 164–66, disagrees with the staging suggested by Herford and Simpson (vol. 9); a possible alternative is indicated by Tacitus. Knoll,

Ben Jonson's Plays (I,B), Appendix A, believes that the "seeling" in IV.95–97 should be interpreted "arras."

Lawrence L. Levin, "Justice and Society in *Sejanus* and *Volpone*," *Discourse* 13 (1970): 319–24, believes that *Sejanus* influenced Jonson's later creation of *Volpone* and that the two plays act as tragic and comic counterparts in their portrayal of ethical and judicial degeneracy. J. C. Maxwell, "The Relation of *Macbeth* to *Sophonisba*," *N&Q* 2 (1955): 373–74, notes parallels between *Sejanus* (III.257–58), Marston's *Sophonisba* (I.ii), and *Macbeth* (I.ii.50–51), and suggests that Marston borrowed from Jonson, and Shakespeare from Marston. After indicating Massinger's classical borrowings, C. A. Gibson, "Massinger's Use of His Sources for *The Roman Actor*," *AUMLA* 15 (1961): 60–72, notes sources in *Sejanus* and Webster's *Duchess of Malfi*. D. C. Gunby, "Webster: Another Borrowing from Jonson's *Sejanus*?" *N&Q* 17 (1970): 214, suggests that *The Duchess of Malfi* (I.i.124–26) was influenced by *Sejanus* (I.33–34), since Webster borrowed heavily from *Sejanus* for several of his works.

In "William Strachey," *N&Q* 195 (1950): 508–11, Geoffrey Ashe suggests that Strachey was Jonson's collaborator in *Sejanus*. The leading contenders for this disputed place have been Chapman and Shakespeare. See Herford and Simpson (vol. 9), who support Chapman's claim; George Taylor, in *Joseph Quincy Adams Memorial Studies* (I,B), pp. 22–23 (below, under *Every Man In*), who suggests Shakespeare; and Samuel Schoenbaum, *Internal Evidence and Elizabethan Dramatic Authorship* (1966). Discussion continued in *N&Q* 196 (1951): 19–20 (Muir and Eagle), 85–86 (Huxley).

Catiline His Conspiracy

In *Jonson's Romish Plot: A Study of "Catiline" and Its Historical Context* (1967), Barbara N. DeLuna supposes that, to be completely intelligible, the play must be seen as a commentary on the Gunpowder Plot of 1605. It is a "parallelograph." The character Quintus Curius is Jonson himself; Cicero is Sir Robert Cecil; Catiline, Robert Catesby; Cethegus, Thomas Percy; and so on. The winter imagery is a reference to "the Winter-faction in the Powder Plot." DeLuna is able to connect most of the play's details to her reconstruction of the Plot.

Joseph A. Bryant, Jr., "*Catiline* and the Nature of Jonson's Tragic Fable," *PMLA* 69 (1954): 265–77, holds that "the basic and distinctive fact about Jonson's tragic fable is that it depends upon a verifiable historical context," and Bryant investigates the play in light of its historical sources. The conspiracy is only nominally Catiline's; actually it is Caesar's. The play magnifies and distorts Caesar's true historical role to indicate what lies ahead. Catiline is a symptom, "Caesar the disease, Cicero the will of the state, Cato its all but submerged conscience." They all exist in a body politic which seems to be flourishing, but which is inwardly rotten and spiritually doomed. Jonson is writing the tragedy of an entire society. Michael J. C. Echeruo, "The Conscience of Politics and Jonson's *Catiline*," *SEL* 6 (1966): 341-56, repeats Gosson's claim for his own lost *Catiline* and shows that the Catilinarian conspiracy was part of popular history. It follows that Jonson was not vitally interested in ends and conclusions, but in the analysis of the processes of politics. The issues of the play are the "deeper, more permanent questions of the nature of political success and political morality." In the end, no character can be said to be the moral center of the play. Jonson was trying to show that history was as true as life, and "he looked with a sophisticated and critical eye at the concept of politics as a game of 'Policy.'" "We are allowed to watch both the noble and the criminal follow the rather attractive path of exigency and of policy." This is the paradox of politics. Michael J. Warren, "Ben Jonson's *Catiline:* The Problem of Cicero," *Yearbook of English Studies* 3 (1973): 55-73, emphasizes Cicero's complex character and his limited achievements. Cicero may be a "superior man," but "the menace of individual ambition which threatens Roman society has received only a temporary check. The pervasiveness of this vice which is almost a virtue makes the outlook bleak, despite the rejoicing." Angela G. Dorenkamp, "Jonson's *Catiline:* History as the Trying Faculty," *SP* 67 (1970): 210-20, believes that Jonson follows the Renaissance concept of history as a teacher of important political lessons.

Ellen Duffy, "Ben Jonson's Debt to Renaissance Scholarship in *Sejanus* and *Catiline*," *MLR* 42 (1947): 24-30, investigates Jonson's use of Durantinus's *Historia* and the commentaries of the Basel edition of Sallust (see I,B and *Sejanus,* above). William Blissett, "Lucan's Caesar and the Elizabethan Villain," *SP* 53 (1956): 553-75, and "Caesar and Satan," *JHI* 18 (1957): 221-32, points out that the monstrous figure of Caesar in Lucan's *Pharsalia* may have contributed to Jonson's picture of Catiline. (See Barr, I,B.) Michael Warren, "The Location of Jonson's *Catiline,* III.490-754," *PQ* 48 (1969): 561-65, suggests that this scene occurs at the house of Lecca rather than at Catiline's.

Weldon Williams, "The Genesis of John Oldham's *Satyrs upon the Jesuits,*" *PMLA* 58 (1943): 958-70, and "The Influence of Ben

Jonson's *Catiline* upon John Oldham's *Satyrs upon the Jesuits,*" *ELH* 11 (1944): 38-62, suggests Jonson's influence on Oldham. Although agreeing with Williams, Chester Cable, "Oldham's Borrowing from Buchanan," *MLN* 66 (1951): 523-27, believes that Oldham was also influenced by Buchanan's *Franciscanus.*

Geoffrey Hill, Ralph Nash, Enck, *Jonson and the Comic Truth,* and Thayer, *Ben Jonson* (all in I,B), also treat the play.

Every Man in His Humour

Although discussed in general works by Barish, Bryant, Dessen, Enck, Knoll, and Thayer (all in I,B), this play has elicited few individual studies. Boughner, *The Devil's Disciple* (I,B), feels that it is "a pioneering achievement in design. . . .In it Jonson introduced to the Elizabethan stage a play built on the four-part structure that cuts across the five-act division in an unimpeded dramatic movement. Moreover, he attempted in the Quarto or Italian version to write a comedy that is, like Machiavelli's, at once satiric and romantic." In "Jonson's Revision of *Every Man in His Humor,*" *SP* 59 (1962): 641-50, Joseph A. Bryant shows "what happened to the structure of *Every Man in* in [the] revision" of the Quarto for the 1616 Folio. Jonson "established for himself the possibility of using the intrigue of Roman comedy," the Terentian structural pattern, "in a new and significant way." In the first version, the structure of intrigue is little more than "a correctly constructed showcase designed to hold attention and exhibit the contents." In revision, Jonson makes two major structural changes: the deletion of Lorenzo's defense of poetry and the integration of the "humor business with the action and the structure of the play." The second change is of prime importance since it leads to two further changes: (1) to a change in Old Knowell's character-humour, and (2) to a new structural design. In revising, Jonson subordinates all to a single humour study and to a single intrigue-structure. Lawrence Levin, "Clement Justice in *Every Man in His Humor,*" *SEL* 12 (1972): 291-307, discusses Judge Clement who functions as priest, educator, reformer, and magistrate, and who looks forward to similar characters in Jonson's four succeeding plays. A departure from the conventional dull-witted justice of Elizabethan drama, Clement is a shrewd humanist who mirrors Jonson himself.

George C. Taylor, "Did Shakespeare, Actor, Improvise in *Every Man in His Humour?*" in *Joseph Quincy Adams Memorial Studies* (I,B), pp. 21-32, supposes that Shakespeare may be responsible for various passages in the play, which he improvised while acting in it. Taylor suggests that Shakespeare acted Kitely, improvising that role, for many of Kitely's expressions seem to be Shakespearean. He compares *Every Man In* with *The Merry Wives of Windsor,* and Kitely with Ford and Brooke. He believes that some of Kitely's speeches could not have come from Jonson's pen, and compares, as does Baskervill, *English Elements in Jonson's Early Comedy* (I,B), and Gifford before him, Kitely with Shakespeare's King John. Claire McGlinchee, "'Still Harping . . . ,'" *SQ* 6 (1955): 362-64, points out that Old Knowell's advice to his nephew Stephen (I.i) is comparable to Polonius's "precepts" to Laertes.

J. C. Maxwell, "Comic Mispunctuation in *Every Man in His Humour,*" *ES* 33 (1952): 218-19, suggests that Matheo's mispunctuation of quotations from *Hero and Leander* is comically intended by Jonson. J. D. Aylward, "The Inimitable Bobadill," *N&Q* 195 (1950): 2-4, 28-31, identifies Bobadill with Rocco Bonetti, the fashionable Italian master of the rapier in London, who is mentioned in George Silver's *Paradoxes of Defence* (1599). K. T. Butler, "Some Further Information about Rocco Bonetti," *N&Q* 195 (1950): 95-97, adds further details about his career from the state papers. Barbara DeLuna, *Jonson's Romish Plot* (above, under *Catiline*) suggests that "Jonson's absurd braggart," sometimes called "Captain Bob," is actually Robert, Earl of Essex. More pertinent is G. Geoffrey Langsam, *Martial Books and Tudor Verse* (1951), who considers Bobadill a *miles gloriosus.*

Alice Scoufos, "Nashe, Jonson, and the Oldcastle Problem," *MP* 65 (1968): 307-24, notes that editors and critics of Renaissance drama have been perplexed by Shakespeare's use of the fifteenth-century Lollard's name in a satiric mode. But Shakespeare was not alone in treating Oldcastle satirically; ramifications of the Oldcastle satire are found in Nashe's *Lenten Stuffe* and Jonson's *Every Man In.* James L. Jackson, "Sources of the Subplot of Marston's *The Dutch Courtezan,*" *PQ* 31 (1952): 223-24, believes that the episode about "the apprehension of Mulligrub in the lost cloak, is much like the incident in Jonson's *Every Man in His Humour* in which Stephan [sic] retrieves Downright's lost cloak and is then arrested in place of Downright." Roger Rollin, "Images of Libertinism in *Every Man in His Humor* and 'To His Coy Mistress,'" *Papers on Language and Literature* 6 (1970): 188-91, presents the possibility that Jonson's play figured in the creation of Marvell's seriocomic poem. Carl J. Stratman, "Scotland's First Dramatic Periodical: *The Edinburgh Theatrical Censor,*" *Theatre Notebook* 17 (1963): 83-86, notes that the anonymous editor discusses the play.

Poetaster, or The Arraignment

Both Charles Baskervill, *English Elements in Jonson's Early Comedy* (I,B), and Oscar J. Campbell, *Comicall Satyre and Shakespeare's "Troilus and Cressida"* (1938), have influential discussions of the play. Arthur King, *The Language of Satirized Characters in "Poëtaster": A Socio-Stylistic Analysis, 1597-1602* (1941), deals with the play's language. Ernest W. Talbert, "The Purpose and Technique of Jonson's *Poetaster*," *SP* 42 (1945): 225-52, suggests that the play is a dramatic *ars poetica.* Stressing the same point, Leonard B. Terr, "Ben Jonson's *Ars Poetica:* A Reinterpretation of *Poetaster*," *Thoth* 11, no. 2 (1971): 3-16, sees that the defense underlines the poet's moral duties in society. Norbert Platz, "Ben Jonson's *Ars Poetica:* An Interpretation of *Poetaster* in Its Historical Context," *Salzburg Studies in English Literature: Elizabethan Studies,* no. 12 (1973), pp. 1-42, suggests that the "meaning and purpose of the play are revealed in a new perspective if we focus on the complex relationships between society and literature or the state and literature as they are portrayed or alluded to in the play." From such an analysis, we better understand "Jonson's subtle attempt to justify satire as a necessary literary form from which both state and society might profit." Basically Jonson is a Christian humanist. Robert C. Jones, "The Satirist's Retirement in Jonson's 'Apologetical Dialogue,'" *ELH* 34 (1967): 447-67, feels that the "Apologetical Dialogue" appended to the *Poetaster* reveals Jonson's essentially ambivalent attitude: the poet is both splendidly isolated from the world and an active worker in the world. Jones traces this idea through the early plays and in Jonson's poetry. He feels that this ambivalence mars Jonson's total artistic achievement.

In "The Poet's Morals in Jonson's *Poetaster*," *MLQ* 12 (1951): 13-19, Eugene M. Waith investigates the "perplexing scene" in which Ovid parts with Julia. Waith concludes: "If the good poet must be a good man, it is understandable that a defense of poetry should present the case of the morally irresponsible poet, in order to show that he is not reckoned among the good." Starting as a defender of poetry, Ovid is later contrasted with Horace in III.v. The trial in which Ovid is found guilty is parallel with that in which Horace is judged innocent. The contrast between the poets is completed in Act IV, making clear Ovid's inadequacy. *The Poetaster* is a defense of poetry in which the poet's relations with society are emphasized. According to Waith, as the play progresses it becomes increasingly evident that Ovid's defense in Act I is deficient in the recognition of social responsibility.

An answer to Waith's analysis, Ralph Nash's "The Parting Scene in Jonson's *Poetaster* (IV,ix)," *PQ* 31 (1952): 54–62, also finds an understanding of the parting scene essential to an understanding of the play; Nash relates the sometimes unclear language of the scene to the imagery and ideas of the whole play. Since Jonson uses the legend of Ovid and Julia's mismatched love, the observer is led to question what his attitude to the lovers is. The major concern of the parting scene is the nature of "true virtue" and its "prerogative of place." Ovid and Julia echo the language of Caesar, but they do not agree with his evaluations. Although "Caesar is right," Jonson's view of Ovid is generally favorable; he stands midway between the poetasters, Crispinus and Demetrius, and the good poets, Virgil and Horace. "Jonson insinuates the feeling that mercy perhaps should be extended to those who are on the threshold of true virtue."

Part of the commentary on *Poetaster* has centered on its place in the "War of the Theatres" (see I,B). Believing that most critics agree that the Chamberlain's Men were being attacked in III.iv, Henry David Gray, "The Chamberlain's Men and the *Poetaster*," *MLR* 42 (1947): 173–79, seeks to identify the actors whom Jonson was satirizing. Gray identifies Aesop as Shakespeare, and concludes: "What the *Poetaster* tells us, I believe, is that Jonson's hopes for a Court performance of *Cynthia's Revels* were thwarted by the intervention of Shakespeare, and the play rejected on the ground that it was treasonable." Percy Simpson, "A Modern Fable of Aesop," *MLR* 43 (1948): 403–5, attacks Gray's conclusions, first noticing that his identifications are similar to those of T. W. Baldwin, *The Organization and Personnel of the Shakespearean Company* (1927). Simpson points out that Shakespeare and Jonson were friends, that *Cynthia's Revels* was probably performed at court by the Children of the Chapel on 6 January 1601, and that "politician" was slang for the actor who carries on transactions on behalf of his company with outside persons or authorities. The "politician" for the Chamberlain's Men was Heminges, not Shakespeare. In "Shakespeare or Heminge? A Rejoinder and a Surrejoinder," *MLR* 45 (1950): 148–52, Gray reiterates his case and questions certain points in Simpson's attack, while Simpson supports his original case and emphasizes the point that Gray's conclusions are founded on conjecture rather than fact.

A portion of K. Gustav Cross's argument, "The Authorship of *Lust's Dominion*," *SP* 55 (1958): 39–61, that Marston had a hand in *Lust's Dominion*, rests on the identification of Marston with Crispinus. Cross's attribution of partial authorship to Marston is supported by an analysis of Jonson's (supposed) linguistic satire of him in *Poetaster,* part of which satire can only refer to the language of *Lust's Dominion.* Donald H. Reiman, "Marston, Jonson, and the *Spanish Tragedy* Additions," *N&Q* 7 (1960): 336-37, believes that the existing additions to the *Spanish Tragedy* are "earlier than those additions for which Jonson was paid by Henslowe in 1601 and 1602." He argues that *Poetaster,* III.ii.230-35 (Quarto, 1602), is a parody of Marston's *Antonio's Revenge,* V.iii.1-4, and that the latter play obviously postdates *Antonio and Mellida,* which in turn parodies a scene from the additions to the *Spanish Tragedy.*

Frank Kermode, "The Banquet of Sense," *BJRL* 44 (1961): 68-99, and Donald K. Anderson, "The Banquet of Love in English Drama (1595-1642)," *JEGP* 63 (1964): 422-32, supply background for the banquet scene in Act IV. G. Blakemore Evans, "Dryden's *MacFlecknoe* and Dekker's *Satiromastix,*" *MLN* 76 (1961): 598-600, replaces Jonson's *Poetaster* with Dekker's *Satiromastix* as an influence on Dryden. Enck, *Jonson and the Comic Truth*, Barish, *Ben Jonson and the Language of Prose Comedy*, Knoll, *Ben Jonson's Plays*, Thayer, *Ben Jonson*, Dessen, *Jonson's Moral Comedy*, and Bryant, *The Compassionate Satirist* (all in I,B), discuss the play.

The Staple of News

Richard Levin, "*The Staple of News,* The Society of Jeerers, and Canters' College," *PQ* 44 (1965): 445-53, incorporated in *The Multiple Plot in English Renaissance Drama* (1971), argues that "the Staple of News," the "Society," and the "College" do not fit into the view of the play as a "monolithic study of money-worship." In the main action, there is an allegorical opposition between "prodigality" and "miserliness" symbolized in Pennyboy Junior and Pennyboy Senior; and all three institutions of the play are aligned with prodigality. "Pennyboy Junior's increasing involvement in them is the principal means of dramatizing his growing recklessness." Nevertheless, "the portrayal of the abuses of language that was found in them still stands in its own right, independent of, and parallel to, the portrayal of the abuses of wealth in the Pennyboy-Pecunia plot." Devra Kifer, "*The Staple of News:* Jonson's Festive Comedy," *SEL* 12 (1972): 329-44, argues that the play is best understood as a festive comedy with festivals as the main theme; at the play's conclusion, Jonson's ideal society is momentarily realized.

Although the play is linked with the morality tradition, the Prodigal Son motif, and the theme of covetousness, Irena Janicka, "Jonson's *Staple of News:* Sources and Traditional Devices," *Kwartalnik neofilologiczny* 15 (1968): 301-7, points out that there is an earlier play, *The Trial of Treasure* (1567), where the theme of adoring "treasure" is expressed allegorically on a sexual level as it is in Jonson's play. Moreover, the personification of riches, Treasure, in *Trial* is a woman whose lover is Lust, and thus she is a closer analogue to Jonson's Pecunia than the male Money in *The Contention between Liberality and Prodigality* (1601). Alan Dessen, "Jonson's 'Knaue of Clubs' and *The Play of the Cards,*" *MLR* 62 (1967): 584-85, notes that Jonson calls his audience's attention to the difference between "the old way" of the defunct morality tradition and his new method by which the Vices "are attired like men and women o' the time." In making his spokesman describe the traditional Vice as appearing in "a Iuglers ierkin, with false skirts, like the Knaue of Clubs," it appears certain that Jonson had in mind a specific play or type of play like *Terminus et Non Terminus* (1586) and the lost *Play of the Cards.* In *Jonson's Moral Comedy* (I,B), Dessen comments: "In spite of the various faults of *The Staple of News*, . . . the play can still provide revealing insights for the reader seeking better understanding of the major comedies. Ideas and techniques implicit in . . . earlier plays, such as the power of money or the modernization of the Vice, here become explicit, even blatant, thereby helping us understand what has gone before."

Bentley, *Jacobean Stage,* vol. 4, notes that the Office of the Staple is "a satire on the English newspapers or corantos" of the early 1620s and that the play in general outline and many details resembles *The London Prodigal.* Although DeWinter in his edition of *The Staple of News* (1905), suggested that Jonson had written *The London Prodigal,* Bentley feels that "the evidence does not seem . . . sufficient to settle reasonable doubts."

L. C. Knights, *Drama and Society in the Age of Jonson* (1937), studies Jonson's relationship to the growing emphasis on the cash nexus in capitalism. Robert Ashton, "Usury and High Finance in the Age of Shakespeare and Jonson," *RMS* 4 (1960): 14-43, notes that the dramatic statements on socioeconomic problems were usually conservative. Keith Salter, "Of the Right Use of Riches," *E&S* 16 (1963): 101-14, uses *The Staple,* III.ii, as an example of the older tradition in the use of riches. Lloyd Mills, "A Clarification of Broker's Use of 'A Perfect Sanguine' in *The Staple of News,*" *N&Q* 14 (1967): 208-9, explains the reference in II.ii by using the money imagery with which the play abounds. A parallel is cited by J. C. Maxwell, "Dryden's Paraphrase of Horace and *The Staple of News*," *N&Q* 197 (1952): 389.

Enck, *Jonson and the Comic Truth* (I,B), touches on the play. Knoll, *Ben Jonson's Plays* (I,B), feels that it is a summarizing document, a succinct statement of Jonson's ethics. Thayer, *Ben Jonson* (I,B), argues that the play is well-structured; Champion, *Ben Jonson's "Dotages"* (I,B), defends it as an allegory of the golden mean. Edward Partridge, "The Symbolism of Clothes in Jonson's Last Plays," *JEGP* 56 (1957): 396–409, and *The Broken Compass* (I,B), considers the clothes symbolic. Savage, *Ben Jonson's Basic Comic Characters* (I,B), examines Shakespeare's influence on the play. See Peter Ure (below, under *The Devil Is an Ass*).

The New Inn, or The Light Heart

Rayburn Moore, "Some Notes on the 'Courtly Love' System in Jonson's *The New Inn*," in *Essays in Honor of Walter Clyde Curry* (1954), pp. 133–42, believes that one of the most interesting aspects of the play is the dramatist's use of the "courtly love" convention. Moore traces this background in both its historical and contemporary aspects and suggests that Jonson's purpose is satiric. The satiric courtly love relationship between Lovel and Frances fits in with Jonson's other barbs thrown at contemporary manners in the play, and what we have is a satire on the manners of the time "in which the 'courtly love' tradition and the Platonic love doctrine play an important part." Larry S. Champion, "The Comic Intent of Jonson's *The New Inn*," *Western Humanities Review* 18 (1964): 66-74, and *Ben Jonson's "Dotages"* (I,B), reviews the adverse criticism of the play and underscores that the play's intent is basically parodic and satiric. "If the major theme of the drama is intended to set off comically the ridiculous pretensions of false concepts, what more logical framing device could be selected than one in which an equally ridiculous exaggeration and artificiality would be apparent?" The plot, however, is too complex for successful performance. In the same vein, Douglas Duncan, "A Guide to *The New Inn*," *Essays in Criticism* 20 (1970): 311-26, examines the design of the play in terms of Jonson's ironic intentions. Duncan interprets the play's conclusion as a deliberate spoofing of romantic comedy. He deplores a recent trend in criticism to rehabilitate plays by proving they are to be taken ironically.

Harriett Hawkins, "The Idea of a Theater in Jonson's *The New Inn*," *RenD* 9 (1966): 205-26, notes that "the world of the theater is based upon the acceptance of certain illusions, and in *The New Inn* Jonson uses theatrical terms and conventions to call our attention to this acceptance, to emphasize the illusory nature of the world of the theater." Though the "play may be said to err on the side of experiment," the "experiment is there for a specific and significant purpose, for the sake of Jonson's comic exploration of an idea of a theater which, through feigning and illusion, can inform men in the 'theater of the world' of their own nature." Calvin Thayer, *Ben Jonson* (I,B), suggests that the split level of the play is complexly symbolic. The upper level versus the lower level may indicate a tension between idealism and realism, or New Romantic Comedy and Old Satiric Comedy. Social distinctions are also hinted at: "The two comic worlds . . . represent two social worlds and two kinds of comedy, associated in the play through symbolic and thematic cross-references." A proper understanding of the significance of the two levels of the inn may lead to a better appreciation of the play's art.

Oliver Lodge, "A Ben Jonson Puzzle," *TLS*, 13 Sept. 1947, p. 465, suggests that Jonson changed the name of Lady Frampul's chambermaid from *Cis* to *Pru* because of the hissing sound in the former name. Edward Partridge, "A Crux in Jonson's *The New Inne*," *MLN* 71 (1956): 168-70, analyzes V.ii.13-23, finding several complexities of meaning and sexual puns. "The Lady's words betray her into suggesting not merely that the tainting of the clothes may call forth Lovel's chivalry and hence his love, but also that the grease on the gown, warmed by Pru's buttocks, may prove an aphrodisiac miraculous enough to arouse him to his old passion." A lyric from the play is examined by Barbara Everett, "Ben Jonson's 'A Vision of Beauty,' " *CritQ* 1 (1959): 238-44, who feels that the short poem satisfies us because of its mastery, discipline, and that "fine vitality found throughout Jonson's work." Bentley, *Jacobean Stage*, vol. 4, provides a brief commentary.

Every Man out of His Humour

Hallett Smith, *Elizabethan Poetry: A Study in Conventions, Meaning, and Expression* (1952), observes that the classic analysis of the play was made by Charles Baskervill, *English Elements in Jonson's Early Comedy* (I,B). Revealing the connection between Jonson's play and the nondramatic satiric poetry of the 1590s, Baskervill relates Jonson's characters "though undoubtedly finished from life" to character-types from earlier English literature. Oscar J. Campbell, *Comicall*

Satyre (above, under *Poetaster*), emphasizes critical theory. And see Alvin Kernan, *The Cankered Muse* (I,B). Hallett Smith approaches the play from the nondramatic satires and from the difficulty with point of view which satirists faced at the end of the sixteenth century. "Jonson analyzes the problem by presenting three different characters who fill the role of artist": Asper, Macilente, and Carlo Buffone. Macilente is an envious malcontent; Carlo, an irresponsible railer; and Asper, a more or less detached critic. None of these alone will do; so Jonson suggests a solution by purging Macilente, transforming him into "one with the impersonality of Asper." Whatever we may think of the play as comedy, the revised conclusion is a "major piece of criticism."

Thomas L. Watson, "The Detractor-Backbiter: Iago and the Tradition," *TSLL* 5 (1964): 546-54, believes there is a connection between *Every Man Out* and Shakespeare's *Othello*. Shakespeare undoubtedly knew Jonson's play, and Iago is perhaps the direct descendent of Carlo. Both characters are similar in function and conception, and stem from the same tradition. Allan H. Gilbert, "The Italian Names in *Every Man out of His Humour*," *SP* 44 (1947): 195-208, and Robert H. Selby, "The Italian Names in Ben Jonson's *Every Man out of His Humour*," in *Of Edsels and Marauders,* ed. Fred Tarpley and Ann Moseley (1971), pp. 97-106, note that the charactonyms are to be found in, and were probably taken from, John Florio's Italian-English dictionary, *A Worlde of Wordes* (1598). They examine the meaning of the names in the light of Florio.

Thomas H. McNeal, *"Every Man out of His Humour* and Shakespeare's *Sonnets," N&Q* 197 (1952): 376, finds echoes of the sonnets in Jonson's play, and William W. Main, " 'Insula Fortunata' in Jonson's *Every Man out of His Humour*," *N&Q* 1 (1954): 197-98, notes that Jonson is following a tradition in choosing the island; "Insula Fortunata" is the birthplace of Erasmus's Folly and thus in Jonson it signifies the land of fools. Richard Hosley, "The Discovery-Space in Shakespeare's Globe," *ShS* 12 (1959): 38-39, discusses Jonson's walk-on stage directions. Enck, *Jonson and the Comic Truth*, Knoll, *Ben Jonson's Plays,* Thayer, *Ben Jonson*, Dessen, *Jonson's Moral Comedy*, and Bryant, *The Compassionate Satirist* (all in I,B), discuss the play.

Cynthia's Revels, or The Fountain of Self-Love

Enck, *Jonson and the Comic Truth* (I,B), writes: "Despite this careful patching into patterns" which he describes, "Jonson does not bring off the whole. *Cynthia's Revels* remains paralyzed." The playwright's "dogged refusal to allow the empty heads an iota's wit beyond their powers betrays the work, Jonson's only one which can be so blamed, into what one critic has termed the imitative fallacy. Effete boredom . . . produces, in general, boredom." Barish, *Ben Jonson* (I,B), feels that the play fails as a dramatic whole. "The final act . . . is stupe- fyingly dull." Thayer, *Ben Jonson* (I,B), believes that Jonson is continu- ing and expanding in *Cynthia's Revels* the techniques he used in *Every Man Out*. The play is "experimental work" in which "comical satire is joined with allegory and the masque to do two separate but related things: to satirize courtly society and to show how the artist can effect changes in that society." Knoll, *Ben Jonson's Plays* (I,B), suggests that the play is "united thematically," and that the chief theme of the play is "presumption born of self-love." Modesty and humility governed by reason are the remedies indicated by Jonson. However, Knoll finds the play "repugnant," E. M. Thron, "Jonson's *Cynthia's Revels:* Multiplic- ity and Unity," *SEL* 11 (1971): 235-47, argues that Criticus and Cynthia are unifying characters and describes the basic concerns of the play as fame and self-love. Robert M. Wren, "Ben Jonson as Producer," *ETJ* 22 (1970): 284-90, discusses the care taken by Jonson in the pro- duction of his plays, especially *Cynthia's Revels*, noting how his stage- craft affected contemporaries and successors. Bryant, *The Compassion- ate Satirist* (I,B), finds the Narcissus episode "one of the really arresting things in this generally tiresome play." Dessen, *Jonson's Moral Comedy* (I,B), treats the play.

Abbie Findlay Potts, "*Cynthia's Revels, Poetaster,* and *Troilus and Cressida*," *SQ* 5 (1954): 297-302, suggests that the play is useful in interpreting some cruxes in Shakespeare's play. Andrew Sabol, "A Newly Discovered Contemporary Song Setting for Jonson's *Cynthia's Revels*," *N&Q* 5 (1958): 384-85, announces the discovery of a manu- script of the song "The Kisse" (IV.iii), through which Jonson satirizes artificial, modish wooing. In "Two Unpublished Stage Songs for the 'Aery of Children,'" *RN* 13 (1960): 222-32, Sabol reproduces manu- script settings for songs in *Cynthia's Revels* and *The Dutch Courtesan* and discusses the way in which song helps to establish atmosphere.

The Devil Is an Ass

Thayer, *Ben Jonson* (I,B), argues that the play exhibits Jonson's changed technique, "probably through the influence of his own career as a writer of masques and through the influence of his extensive read- ing in English drama, including the morality play." Knoll, *Ben Jonson's Plays* (I,B), also sees the morality influence and traces the dramatic background of the play in the theme "The Devil Abroad." Dessen, *Jonson's Moral Comedy* (I,B), deals with the tradition of dramatic diabolism. "Jonson's devil play . . . exhibits a proliferation of individuals and a weakening of satiric control reminiscent of his early plays. Still one cannot help admiring Jonson's ingenuity and skill in adapting the devil play of popular tradition to his own ends." Champion, *Ben Jonson's "Dotages"* (I,B), supposes that "an awareness of the structure of the play and the manipulations of morality elements to sharpen the satiric exposure of the earth's vices indicates that Jonson has neither allowed his comedy to deteriorate under a heavy didacticism, nor suffered any serious decline in inventiveness and ingenuity." Enck, *Jonson and the Comic Truth* (I,B), contends that the play "falters with doubts." Jonson "fails to define effectively the number of levels on which it operates and their relative values."

Edward Partridge, *The Broken Compass* (I,B), notes that the implication "of the whole play is that the human mind, so adept at concealment and hypocrisy, can outwit a devil who is committed wholly to vice." Savage, *Ben Jonson's Basic Comic Characters* (I,B), suggests that the "Ass," Fitz-dottrell, is the "Devil." Jonson "appears to be saying that folly itself . . . when accompanied by greed, is evil of a large order. In fact, when compared with the enormities of Fitz-dottrell, the professional efforts of Satan and Pug become almost innocuous. And this folly is manifested over and over in the play by the acceptance of the cloak for the man, of the dressing for the woman, of appearance for reality."

Robert R. Reed, "Ben Jonson's Pioneering in Sentimental Comedy," *N&Q* 195 (1950): 272-73, points out that the subplot foreshadows sentimental comedy. Richard Levin, "'The Ass in Compound': A Lost Pun in Middleton, Ford, and Jonson," *ELN* 4 (1966): 12-15, suggests that in II.i.30-31 there may be a pun on "alas" and "all ass." Cecil Seronsy, "A Skeltonic Passage in Ben Jonson," *N&Q* 198 (1953): 24, notes that V.vi.25 ff. is reminiscent of the description of Elynour Rummyng. Peter Ure, "A Simile in *Samson Agonistes*," *N&Q* 195 (1950): 298, notes a parallel between *Samson* and Jonson's *The Devil* and *The Staple of News*. Bentley, *Jacobean Stage*, vol. 4, discusses the play briefly.

The Magnetic Lady, or Humours Reconciled

Knoll, *Ben Jonson's Plays* (I,B), places *The Magnetic Lady* among the "dotages"; although the basic plan does not differ from that of the great plays, Jonson's "genius had burned out." Enck, *Jonson and the Comic Truth* (I,B), blames uncongenial subject matter for the play's failure: "comedy can do little with romantic love." Thayer, *Ben Jonson* (I,B), admires the play and feels that "in tone it is the most Chaucerian of all his plays." Larry S. Champion, "*The Magnetic Lady*: The Close of Ben Jonson's Circle," *Southern Humanities Review* 2 (1968): 104-21, incorporated in *Ben Jonson's "Dotages"* (I,B), defends it as a tour de force. "Nothing in it is more evident than the immutability of Jonson's artistic principles." Ronald E. McFarland, "Jonson's *Magnetic Lady* and the Reception of Gilbert's *De Magnete*," *SEL* 11 (1971): 283-93, demonstrates Jonson's command of the principles of magnetism and argues that a fundamental knowledge of these principles is necessary to understand the play fully. Jackson I. Cope, "Jonson on the Christ's College Dons," *MLN* 74 (1959): 101-2, notes that I.v.10-20 alludes to the three rival groups in a theological controversy at Christ's College, Cambridge. There are brief commentaries in Bentley, *Jacobean Stage*, vol. 4, and Partridge, *The Broken Compass* (I,B).

A Tale of a Tub

Joseph A. Bryant, Jr., "*A Tale of a Tub*: Jonson's Comedy of the Human Condition," *RenP*, 1964, pp. 95-105, feels that the play has a wide application and is not merely an "English modification of Roman comedy." The structure may resemble Roman comedy, but in contrast to classical practice, the marriages seem to have no discernible purpose or consequence in Jonson's play. The major difference between the play and Roman comedy is the underlying action which here is neither specifically pagan nor Christian, "but antecedent to civilization itself." Nature overcomes the social conventions, and the contrivances of man, "prematurely invoked and applied," serve only to underline their ineffectiveness. These views are modified and used as a conclusion to Bryant's *Compassionate Satirist* (I,B).

Mortimer His Fall

Rather surprisingly, Jonson's incomplete *Mortimer* was published in the 1640 Folio. Leo Kirschbaum, "Jonson, Seneca, and *Mortimer*," in *Studies in Honor of John Wilcox*, ed. Alva Dayle Wallace and Woodburn Ross (1958), pp. 9-22, believes that "what *is* very important" is seeing where it "fits into Jonson's slowly evolving theory and practice of tragedy." "*Mortimer His Fall* had it been completed would have been the most purely Senecan" of Jonson's tragedies. Kirschbaum notes a tendency "on Jonson's part, when what he had done was not appreciated, to exaggerate rather than to eliminate those very attributes which had bored or irritated his auditors"; after the failure of *Catiline*, Jonson becomes even more Senecan in *Mortimer*. As in the traditional Senecan play, there is a very small cast; little happens on stage; and undoubtedly all the unities were to be observed. It is Jonson's last and most Roman play.

The Case Is Altered

John J. Enck, "*The Case Is Altered*: Initial Comedy of Humours," *SP* 50 (1953): 195-214, and *Jonson and the Comic Truth* (I,B), argues that the play is a pilot study for the comedy of humours. Enck notes that Jonson took two entire plots from literary sources: Plautus's *Captivi* and *Aulularia*. A detailed analysis of the plot reveals the changes made from the sources and suggests that Jonson had already hit on the idea of humours comedy. The play is a "not untalented effort in a construction with a satiric bias." The basic themes are "identity" and "recognition of the truth about one's self and others." Robert Knoll, *Ben Jonson's Plays* (I,B), feels that it is a play of contrasts and comparison, and, like Enck, argues that it looks forward structurally and thematically to Jonson's later work. Tucker Brooke, in *A Literary History of England*, ed. Albert C. Baugh (1948; rev. ed. 1967), calls it "a comedy comparable with Chapman's *All Fools*, though more romantic in tone." Dessen, *Jonson's Moral Comedy* (I,B), believes that Jonson wanted to disown the play. It has not been widely appreciated.

The Mask of Blackness

Orgel, *The Jonsonian Masque* (I,B), and Meagher, *Method and Meaning in Jonson's Masques* (I,B), touch on this mask. In "The Falling 'Curtain' in Jonson's *Masque of Blacknesse*," *N&Q* 7 (1960): 174-75, and in "The 'Artificiall Sea' in Jonson's *Masque of Blacknesse*," *N&Q* 7 (1960): 419-21, D. D. McElroy discusses production techniques and devices. D. J. Gordon, "The Imagery of Ben Jonson's *The Masque of Blacknesse* and *The Masque of Beautie*," *JWCI* 6 (1943): 122-41, shows that "these Masques are images, whose significance is to be apprehended in the light of the doctrines of Beauty and Love held by the Platonists of the Renaissance." Marvin Rosenberg, "On the Dating of *Othello*," *ES* 39 (1958): 72-74, feels that the desire of Queen Anne for blackamoors on the stage accounts for both *The Mask of Blackness* and *Othello*.

Hymenaei

D. J. Gordon, "*Hymenaei*: Ben Jonson's Masque of Union," *JWCI* 8 (1945): 107-45, explains the implications of the mask. Written for the marriage of the young Earl of Essex to Frances Howard, it also celebrates the union of thistle and rose in James. "Jonson takes this marriage, which is the marriage of the kingdoms, as type and instance of universal union." In "A Note on Ben Jonson's *Hymenaei* (ll. 56-58 and 182-85)," *N&Q* 3 (1956): 510-11, Inga-Stina Ekeblad points out the unusual description of the bride's hair as "sprinckled with grey." The explanation seems to lie in Jonson's mistranslation of *senis crinibus* ("with six locks") as "locks of an old woman." Jackson I. Cope, "The Date of Middleton's *Women Beware Women*," *MLN* 76 (1961): 295-300, uses *Hymenaei* (1606) to help date Middleton's play in 1613-14. Meagher, *Method and Meaning in Jonson's Masques* (I,B), suggests that it may be "Jonson's most complex and difficult masque."

The Mask at Lord Haddington's Marriage or *The Hue and Cry after Cupid*

D. J. Gordon, "Ben Jonson's *Haddington Masque*: The Story and the Fable," *MLR* 42 (1947): 180-87, describes the mask and suggests that the antimask is a dramatization of Moschus's *Amor Fugitivus*. "Jonson has, as usual, based his representations of the classical deities on the accounts given in the hand-books of mythology." The mythological figures convey a general truth which makes the mask into more than an elegant marriage celebration; it becomes "a fable about marriage, or, specifically, about procreation which is the fulfillment of marriage." Perfection is emphasized in the song, the globe, and the signs of the zodiac. Meagher, *Method and Meaning in Jonson's Masques* (I,B), discusses the function of Cupid in the mask.

The Mask of Beauty

Thomas N. Ross, "Expenses for Ben Jonson's *The Masque of Beauty*," *BRMMLA* 23 (1969): 167-73, reproduces the "official record of accounts" for this mask; outrageously expensive, it cost £4000 or (its approximate modern equivalent) $400,000. "James's Court was less interested in the verse than in Inigo Jones's designs, in the dancing, and in the preposterous structures of jewels, silks, laces, gold, and silver that were the symbolic costumes."

The Mask of Queens

W. Todd Furniss, "The Annotation of Ben Jonson's *Masqve of Qveenes*," *RES* 5 (1954): 344-60, feels that "a study of the annotation not only widens our knowledge of Jonson's library and tells us something of how he used it, but suggests another dimension of the *Masque of Queenes* in which the central theme [i.e., "that knowledge is virtue and that ignorance is sin"] is further developed." Books on witchcraft such as James I's *Daemonologie* (1597) form the background for the antimask, while the main mask is particularly indebted to Charles Stephanus, *Dictionarium Historicum, Poeticum, & Geographicum* supplemented by Robert Stephanus, *Thesaurus Linguae Latinae.* Orgel, *The Jonsonian Masque* (I,B), feels that the mask "displays a new sort of coherence." Meagher, *Method and Meaning in Jonson's Masques* (I,B), also discusses it.

Oberon the Fairy Prince

The music is discussed by John P. Cutts in "Le Rôle de la musique dans les masques de Ben Jonson et notamment dans *Oberon* (1610-1611)," in *Les fêtes de le Renaissance,* ed. Jean Jacquot (1956), 1: 285-303, and in "Original Music to Browne's Inner Temple Masque, and Other Jacobean Masque Music," *N&Q* 1 (1954): 194-95. Robert Goldsmith, "The Wild Man on the English Stage," *MLR* 53 (1958): 481-91, sees *Oberon* at the end of a tradition; Jonson's wild men "are porters rather than actors in the masque." A more complete study is found in Orgel, *The Jonsonian Masque* (I,B).

The Vision of Delight

W. Todd Furniss, "Ben Jonson's Masques," in *Three Studies in the Renaissance* (I,B), thoroughly discusses this mask. Harriett Hawkins, "Jonson's Use of Traditional Dream Theory in *The Vision of Delight,*" *MP* 64 (1967): 285-92, emphasizes that Jonson treats the spectators as dreamers and exhibits the participants as dream figures; he explores traditional ideas concerning the nature of dreams in order to lend high symbolic importance to the invocation of the king at the end. Macrobius's classification of dreams in *In Somnium Scipionis* seems to be a probable source for the different kinds of dreams presented by Jonson. John P. Cutts, "Ben Jonson's Masque *The Vision of Delight,*" *N&Q* 3 (1956): 64-67, describes a contemporary musical setting for the epilogue.

The Gypsies Metamorphosed

Dale B. J. Randall, *Jonson's Gypsies Unmasked: Background and Theme of "The Gypsies Metamorphos'd"* (1975), believes it to be "Jonson's finest achievement as a writer of masques." He interprets it as an elaborate admonition; "in the process of praising the King [Jonson] has managed here both to amuse and give a public warning [against George Villiers], something like a jester who aims to make his master laugh while serving up a trencher of truth." The mask is also discussed fully by W. Todd Furniss, "Ben Jonson's Masques," in *Three Studies in the Renaissance* (I,B). Dick Taylor, Jr., "Clarendon and Ben Jonson as Witnesses for the Earl of Pembroke's Character," in *Studies in the English Drama* (I,A), pp. 322-44, mentions the mask's description of Pembroke. Allan Gilbert and C. F. Main discuss the relationship between the libelous poem *For the Kinge* and Jonson's litany on the king's senses (ll. 1327-85). Gilbert, "Jonson and Drummond or Gil on the King's Senses," *MLN* 62 (1947): 35-37, notes that the libel is sometimes attributed to Drummond and points out the parallels between the two pieces. Main, "Ben Jonson and an Unknown Poet on the King's Senses," *MLN* 74 (1959): 389-93, suggests that the libelous song, perhaps written by James Johnson, is a parody of Jonson's litany.

The Mask of Augurs

There is a brief description in Barish, *Ben Jonson and the Language of Prose Comedy* (I,B). Its "learning" is discussed by Ernest Talbert, "Current Scholarly Works and the 'Erudition' of Jonson's *Masque of Augurs* [corrected]," *SP* 44 (1947): 605-24, who proposes to "point out in some detail how the Stephanus dictionaries and kindred compilations [e.g., Comes, Rosinus, Peucer] throw light upon the learning and the composition of a particular masque." Jonson "first seems to have collected a body of notes with which to develop a central invention that would fit the great persons in the realm who would be participants and spectators. From such notes might arise other inventions 'to furnish the inward parts,' and from the notes his glosses might be made. Once sufficient material was gathered, he presumably" wrote everything in prose. "After turning the material into verse, he would presumably" revise. MacDonald Emslie, "Nicholas Lanier's Innovations in English Song," *Music & Letters* 41 (1960): 13-27, notes that one of the datable declamatory airs by Lanier is Apollo's song, "Do not expect," in *The Mask of Augurs*.

The Mask of Owls

John J. McAleer, "Captain Cox: Paragon of Black-Letter Antiquaries," *Drama Critique* 5 (1962): 34-38, notes that a character in this mask was a historical person.

Chloridia: Rites to Chloris and Her Nymphs

R. I. C. Graziani, "Ben Jonson's *Chloridia:* Fame and Her Attendants," *RES* 7 (1956): 56-58, suggests that Fame symbolizes the art of the mask, while Poesy and History represent Jonson's contributions, and Architecture and Sculpture the contributions of Inigo Jones.

Love's Welcome at Bolsover

John P. Cutts, "'When were the *Senses* in such order plac'd?'" *CompD* 4 (1970): 52-62, examines clues in the mask which provide a means of proving the influence of specific works of art upon the design of the dramatic performance.

Prince Henry's Barriers

W. Todd Furniss, "Jonson, Camden, and the Black Prince's Plumes," *MLN* 69 (1954): 487-88, finds a source for the Black Prince's feathers in William Camden's *Remaines* (1614) and feels that Camden probably located his source (the MS "Medica" by John of Arderne) between 1605 and 1614.

B. OVER-ALL STATE OF CRITICISM

With a solid edition of the complete works by Herford and Simpson and a full background of basic studies, Jonson criticism has flourished. Studies of his career, his attitudes, and his individual plays have been steadily forthcoming. Almost every aspect has been discussed, if only briefly, and with the appearance of well-annotated editions of his individual plays, the continued growth of Jonson criticism seems assured.

The central comedies and *Sejanus* have received a generous share of critical attention, but the early and the late comedies have been less fortunate. *Every Man In, Every Man Out,* and *Cynthia's Revels* are generally neglected. Although in 1963 Calvin Thayer called for a re-evaluation of the final plays, only Larry Champion, *Ben Jonson's "Dotages"* (I,B), has responded with a positive appreciation of the late comedies. More work needs to be done in these areas.

Textual studies of Jonson have not been far-reaching. DeVocht's work (III,D) has been questioned by Herford and Simpson, and by Enck. Johan Gerritsen, T. H. Howard-Hill, and J. A. Lavin are notable exceptions to the general neglect of textual problems. Along with more textual studies, a reliable one-volume edition of the complete works, with introductions and annotations, is needed.

Although Jonson has found a large scholarly audience in the past decades, one may still look for a more appreciative, tolerant response. Many of the best Jonson critics, including Barish, Enck, and Knoll, have been unable to give wholehearted praise to the majority of his plays.

III. CANON

A. PLAYS IN CHRONOLOGICAL ORDER

The source for the type of play, the acting date (in italics preceding semicolon), and the original date of publication is Alfred Harbage, *Annals of English Drama, 975-1700*, rev. S. Schoenbaum (1964), and the *Supplements* by Schoenbaum (1966, 1970). The form and spelling of first titles is that used in the *Annals* Index. Readers are also directed to Herford and Simpson, vols. 1, 2, 9, 10; W. W. Greg, *A Bibliography of the English Printed Drama to the Restoration*, 4 vols. (1939–59); G. E. Bentley, *The Jacobean and Caroline Stage* vol. 4 (1956); and E. K. Chambers, *The Elizabethan Stage*, 4 vols. (1923).

A Tale of a Tub, comedy (*1596-1633*; 1640)

Herford and Simpson, vols. 1 and 9, discuss the dating. Although first performed in 1633, it "is a composite play in which work of a much earlier date can be clearly traced": "the delineation of character" which we expect in the mature Jonson is "entirely lacking here"; the play has "two entirely different styles," two correspondingly different kinds of poetry, and it exhibits the "fitful intrusion of rhyme"; the archaisms of the play are "carried to a point where the allusions would hardly be intelligible in 1633." They conclude: "Each of these points is significant: collectively they constitute a powerful case." Chambers, *Elizabethan Stage*, vol. 3, arguing for a later date, suggests that the archaisms give the play a consciously historical setting and place it in the time of Queen Mary. Florence May Snell, ed., *A Tale of a Tub* (1915), and "The Date of Jonson's *Tale of a Tub*," *MLN* 30 (1915): 93-94, and W. W. Greg, "Some Notes on Ben Jonson's Works," *RES* 2 (1926):

133-36, hold for a late date. Esko V. Pennanen, "On the Date of Ben Jonson's *A Tale of a Tub*," *NM* 53 (1952): 224-40, concludes: "An early date of composition of *A Tale of a Tub* may be accepted as practically certain, for not only its motive, style, verse, and plot-structure, characters and chronological allusions but also its language and diction show decidedly early features." Bentley, *Jacobean Stage*, vol. 4, suggests a late dating by implication of the fee charged by Sir Henry Herbert for licensing it (the fee was the standard one for new plays) and the satire on Inigo Jones. Enck, *Jonson and the Comic Truth* (I,B), asks how the old manuscript of the play could have survived the fire of 1623 and points out that "the metaphoric language . . . matches the later works." Most scholars, e.g., Bryant, *The Compassionate Satirist* (I,B), favor a late date, though Knoll, *Ben Jonson's Plays* (I,B), discusses it as early.

The Case Is Altered, comedy (*1597-98*; 1609)

Nashe refers to the play in *Lenten Stuffe* (1599), but according to Herford and Simpson, "the play which has come to us shows clear signs of interpolation, which can only have been made for a revival." It is possible that II.vii.26-82, along with various touches here and there, is an interpolation. These additions "could not have been written before 1600" because of their relation to the "Humour Play." J. M. Nosworthy, "*The Case Is Altered*," *JEGP* 51 (1952): 61-70, and Frank L. Huntley, "Ben Jonson and Anthony Munday, or, *The Case Is Altered* Altered Again," *PQ* 41 (1962): 205-14, argue that Jonson did not write all of the play. Nosworthy sees Porter's hand in the Aurelia-Phoenixella scenes, and Huntley supposes that Munday wrote most of the play. Anyone who would take the play from the Jonson canon must explain the findings of Enck (II,A, under *The Case Is Altered*), who shows that it is an "initial comedy of humours."

Every Man in His Humour, comedy (*1598*; 1601)

Every Man out of His Humour, comedy (*1599*; 1600)

See W. W. Greg, "The First Edition of Ben Jonson's *Every Man out of His Humour*," *Library* 1 (1920): 153-60.

Cynthia's Revels, or The Fountain of Self-Love, comedy (*1600*; 1601)

Poetaster, or The Arraignment, comedy (*1601*; 1602)

The 1602 Quarto carries the subtitle "The Arraignment." Jonson changed it to "His" in the 1616 Folio.

A Particular Entertainment of the Queen and Prince Their Highness at Althorp (The Satyr), royal entertainment (*25 June 1603*; 1604)

Sejanus His Fall, tragedy (*1603*; 1605)

The Coronation Triumph, part by Jonson; coronation entertainment (*15 March 1604*; 1604)

This entertainment, done in collaboration with Dekker, confusingly goes by several names, e.g., *Part of the King's Entertainment in Passing to His Coronation* (Bentley, *Jacobean Stage*, vol. 4), and *The King's Entertainment* (Herford and Simpson, vol. 10). Dekker's share is called *The Magnificent Entertainment Given to King James*. For details, see Greg, *Bibliography*, vol. 1.

A Panegyre, royal entertainment (*19 March 1604*; 19 March 1604)

Omitted by Harbage and Schoenbaum, this piece was "composed for James when he opened Parliament" (Herford and Simpson, vol. 2). See Greg, *Bibliography*, vol. 1; Bentley, *Jacobean Stage*, vol. 4; and Herford and Simpson, vol. 10.

The Entertainment of the King and Queen at Highgate (The Penates), royal entertainment (*1 May 1604*; 1616).

The Mask of Blackness (The Twelfth Night's Revels), mask (*6 Jan. 1605*; ca. 1608 and MS)

Hymenaei, mask and barriers (*5 Jan. 1606*; 1606)

Volpone, or The Fox, comedy (*1605-6*; 1607)

The Entertainment of the Two Kings of Great Britain and Denmark (The Hours), royal entertainment (*24 July 1606*; 1616)

The Entertainment of the King and Queen at Theobalds (The Genius), royal entertainment (*22 May 1607*; 1616 and MS)

The Entertainment at Merchant Taylors, royal entertainment (*16 July 1607*; lost)

The Mask of Beauty, mask (*10 Jan. 1608*; ca. 1608)

The Mask at Lord Haddington's Marriage (The Hue and Cry after Cupid), wedding mask (*9 Feb. 1608*; ca. 1608)

This is sometimes called *Lord Haddington's Mask* (Bentley, *Jacobean Stage*, vol. 4).

The Entertainment at Salisbury House for James I, royal entertainment (*5-11 May 1608*; lost)

The Entertainment at Britain's Burse for James I, royal entertainment (*11 April 1609*; lost)

Epicoene, or The Silent Woman, comedy (*1609*; 1616 earliest extant)

Gifford was sure that he had seen a 1612 quarto, which, if he was correct, is lost. Thomas Kranídas, "Possible Revisions or Additions in Jonson's *Epicoene*," *Anglia* 83 (1965): 451-53, proposes that the play was reworked during or after 1613; until now, the text in the 1616 Folio was thought to date from about 1609. Kranídas points to two passages which are strongly reminiscent of the Essex divorce trial of 1613 (V.iii and iv), and concludes that it is highly probable "that Jonson added or revised these passages . . . in order to teach and delight his readers with hilarious parodies of the grim history of Frances Howard." W. W. Greg, "Was There a 1612 Quarto of *Epicene*?" *Library* 15 (1934): 306-15, discusses the possibility of a lost quarto, and Gerritsen (III,D) offers evidence that the play was not printed before 1616.

The Mask of Queens, mask (*2 Feb. 1609*; 1609 and MS)

The Alchemist, comedy (*1610*; 1612)

Prince Henry's Barriers (The Lady of the Lake), speeches at barriers (*6 Jan. 1610*; 1616)

This is also called *Speeches at Prince Henry's Barriers* (Bentley, *Jacobean Stage*, vol. 4).

Catiline His Conspiracy, tragedy (*1611*; 1611)

Oberon the Fairy Prince, mask (*1 Jan. 1611*; 1616)

Love Freed from Ignorance and Folly, mask (*3 Feb. 1611*; 1616)

Love Restored, mask (*6 Jan. 1612*; 1616)

A Challenge at Tilt, tilt (*27 Dec. 1613, 1 Jan. 1614*; 1616)

The Irish Mask, mask (*29 Dec. 1613*; 1616)

The May Lord, comic pastoral (*1613-19*; lost)

W. W. Greg, ed., *Ben Jonson's Sad Shepherd, with Waldron's Continuation* (1905), believes that *The May Lord* is nondramatic and refutes Fleay's contention, *Biographical Chronicle of the English Drama, 1559-1642* (1891), vol. 1, that it and *The Sad Shepherd* are the same play. Greg's points are summarized in his *Pastoral Poetry and Pastoral Drama* (1906). Bentley, *Jacobean Stage*, vol. 4, generally follows Greg. Herford and Simpson feel that *The May Lord* was a play, but follow Greg in asserting that it was not the extant *Sad Shepherd* (vol. 2). Our knowledge of the piece rests on Jonson's reference in his *Conversations with Drummond*.

Bartholomew Fair, comedy (*31 Oct. 1614*; 1631)

The Golden Age Restored, mask (*6 Jan. 1615*; 1616)

Mercury Vindicated from the Alchemists at Court, mask (*1 Jan. 1616*; 1616)

The Devil Is an Ass, comedy (*Oct.-Nov.?, 1616*; 1631)

Christmas His Mask (Christmas His Show), Christmas show (*Christmas 1616*; 1641 and MSS)

The Vision of Delight, mask (*6 Jan. 1617*; 1641)

The dating is based on a letter from John Chamberlain to Dudley Carleton, *Letters of John Chamberlain*, ed. Norman E. McClure (1939), vol. 2. Bentley, *Jacobean Stage*, vol. 4, adds the date "19 [?] January

1616/17" to the one above, but feels unsure: "Since Jonson does not give the precise date of performance and Chamberlain does not give the name of the masque nor the author, one could wish for other evidence that *The Vision of Delight* really was the piece performed on Twelfth Night, 1616/17."

Lovers Made Men (*The Mask at Lord Hay's*; called *The Mask of Lethe* by Gifford), mask (*22 Feb. 1617*; 1617)

Gifford was unacquainted with (or had forgotten) the title on the 1617 quarto (Herford and Simpson, vol. 9). Bentley calls it *Lord Hay's Masque* (*Jacobean Stage*, vol. 4).

Pleasure Reconciled to Virtue, mask (*6 Jan. 1618*; 1641 and MS)

See Bentley, *Jacobean Stage*, vol. 4. Unfavorably received, the mask was revised (see below, next item).

For the Honour of Wales, antimask (*17 Feb. 1618*; 1641)

This is a revision of *Pleasure Reconciled to Virtue* (above). Herford and Simpson, vols. 2, 10, comment: "The elaboration of the antimasque begins with this piece." The label "antimask" is misleading; this is still officially a mask, though it marks a turning point in Jonson's technique.

News from the New World Discovered in the Moon, mask (*7 Jan. 1620*; 1641)

Bentley, *Jacobean Stage*, vol. 4, comments: "There has been a deal of confusion about this masque because it has been dated 1620/1, and a number of references to the masque produced on 6 January and 11 February 1620/1 have been taken as applying to it." Herford and Simpson, vol. 10, note that "Jonson himself tells us that this was his first masque at Court after he walked back from Scotland." They believe that "the performance was on 17 January and 29 February." The references to a mask on 6 January and 11 February are not to *News from the New World*.

The Entertainment at Blackfriars (*The Newcastle Entertainment*), entertainment (*May?, 1620;* MS)

Pan's Anniversary, or The Shepherds' Holiday, mask (*19 June? 1620;* 1641)

See Bentley, *Jacobean Stage*, vol. 4, for a discussion of the date.

The Gypsies Metamorphosed (The Metamorphosed Gypsies), mask (*3, 5 Aug., Sept. 1621*; 1640 and MSS)

This is also called *The Gypsies' Metamorphosis* (Harbage and Schoenbaum) and the *Masque of Gypsies* (Bentley, *Jacobean Stage*, vol. 4).

The Mask of Augurs, mask (*6 Jan. 1622*; 1622)

Bentley, *Jacobean Stage*, vol. 4, notes that the "various records, strictly interpreted, give contradictory dates for both the original performance and the revival of this masque." He concludes that "the 6th is probably the correct date" for the first performance.

Time Vindicated to Himself and to His Honours, mask (*19 Jan. 1623*; 1623)

See Bentley, *Jacobean Stage*, vol. 4, for a discussion of the date.

Neptune's Triumph for the Return of Albion, mask (*6 Jan. 1624*; 1624)

This mask was not performed, even though both the quarto and the Folio say it was. See Herford and Simpson, vol. 10.

The Mask of Owls, entertainment (*19 Aug. 1624*; 1641)

The date given in the 1640 Folio is 1626. See Herford and Simpson, vol. 10, and Bentley, *Jacobean Stage*, vol. 4.

The Fortunate Isles and Their Union, mask (*9 Jan. 1625*; 1625)

A revision of *Neptune's Triumph* (above), this mask was called *Virtue and Beauty Reconciled* in Hazlitt's *Manual*. Bentley, *Jacobean Stage*, vol. 4, discusses this question and concludes that "*Virtue and Beauty Reconciled* is an odd and inaccurate reference to *The Fortunate Isles*."

The Staple of News, comedy (*Feb. 1626*; 1631)

The New Inn, or The Light Heart, comedy (licensed *19 Jan. 1629*; 1631)

Bentley, *Jacobean Stage*, vol. 4, comments: "Malone's extract from the manuscript of Sir Henry Herbert's office-book [from which we have the licensing date] is presumably as reliable as all his others, though the quotation is indirect in this instance. The date he gives is clearly the one Herbert attached to his license, a date which Malone several times in other instances assumed to be the date of first performance. In this assumption he must have been wrong, for companies would surely not have been so foolish as to do all their rehearsing and advertising before the Master of the Revels had allowed the play."

Love's Triumph through Callipolis, mask (*9 Jan. 1631*; 1630-31)

Chloridia: Rites to Chloris and Her Nymphs, mask (*22 Feb. 1631*; 1631)

The Magnetic Lady, or Humours Reconciled, comedy (licensed *12 Oct. 1632*; 1641)

See Bentley, *Jacobean Stage*, vol. 4, and compare his comment above, under *The New Inn*.

The King's Entertainment at Welbeck (Love's Welcome at Welbeck), royal entertainment (*21 May 1633*; 1641 and MS)

Love's Welcome at Bolsover, royal entertainment (*30 July 1634*; 1641 and MS)

Mortimer His Fall (incomplete), history (*1595-1637*; 1641)

See Herford and Simpson, vol. 2, and Bentley, *Jacobean Stage*, vol. 4. The fragment is too slight to justify any firm conclusions about the date, but see Leo Kirschbaum (II,A, under *Mortimer*) for a late dating.

The Sad Shepherd, or A Tale of Robin Hood (incomplete), comic pastoral (ca. *1612-37*; 1641)

The date is in dispute. Bentley, *Jacobean Stage*, vol. 4, believes that a late date is indicated by Lucius Cary's lines in *Jonsonus Virbius* (1638) and suggests a date between 1635 and 1638. Joan Rees, *Samuel Daniel* (1964), sees a possible reference to Daniel's *Hymens Triumph* in the play; if so, one terminal date is established: February 1614 when

Daniel's play was produced. See Herford and Simpson, vol. 2. No final conclusion can be reached; the stylistic argument is weak.

B. UNCERTAIN ASCRIPTIONS; APOCRYPHA

The Jonson Apocrypha has not been important to the criticism of his known plays. See Herford and Simpson, vol. 2, Index under "Lost Plays," and G. E. Bentley, *Jacobean Stage*, vol. 4.

The Spanish Tragedy (Hieronimo Is Mad Again), tragedy (*1582-92*; ca. 1592)

Jonson revised this play, perhaps in 1601-2. See Herford and Simpson, vol. 2. Donald Reiman, "Marston, Jonson, and the *Spanish Tragedy* Additions," *N&Q* 7 (1960): 336-37, supports the view that the extant additions are earlier than those for which Jonson was paid. Warren Stevenson, "Shakespeare's Hand in *The Spanish Tragedy* 1602," *SEL* 8 (1968): 307-21, argues that the extant revision is not by Jonson because of the incongruity of his style with that of the additions. Schoenbaum, in the second *Supplement*, indicates that the Jonson revisions posited in earlier editions of the *Annals* are not present in the extant text. (See II,A, under *Poetaster*.)

The Isle of Dogs, satirical comedy (*July 1597*; lost)

The play was possibly completed by Jonson. Chambers, *Elizabethan Stage*, vol. 3, comments: "It is hardly possible to doubt that Jonson was one of the actors who had a hand with Nashe . . . in that play."

Hot Anger Soon Cold, with Chettle and Porter, comedy (*18 Aug. 1598*; lost)

Nosworthy's suggestion (see above, III,A) that this play is an earlier version of *The Case Is Altered* has not been generally accepted.

Page of Plymouth, with Dekker, tragedy (*10 Aug.-2 Sept. 1599*; lost)

Robert II King of Scots (The Scot's Tragedy), with Chettle, Dekker (and Marston?), history (*3-27 Sept. 1599*; lost)

Richard Crookback, history (*22 June 1602*; lost)

This play may never have been completed.

The London Prodigal, comedy (*1603-5*; 1605)

This anonymous play has been claimed for Shakespeare, Dekker, Drayton, and Marston, as well as Jonson. De Winter, ed., *The Staple of News* (1905), details the numerous parallels between *Staple* and *London Prodigal*. Since Jonson did not usually borrow from contemporary sources, De Winter felt that the parallels indicated Jonson's hand in this play. The ascription has not received general acceptance. See Herford and Simpson, vol. 2, and Bentley (II,A, under *Staple of News*). The play is discussed in the Anonymous Plays section of *The Popular School* in this series.

Eastward Ho, with Chapman and Marston, comedy (*1605*; 1605)

Herford and Simpson, vol. 2, comment: "*Eastward Ho* has, in strictness, no title to be included, as a whole, in an edition of the works of Jonson. He certainly did not write it all. . . . But it is no less certain that he contributed something to it." See Percy Simpson, "The Problem of Authorship of *Eastward Ho*," *PMLA* 59 (1944): 713-25; Jackson I. Cope, "*Volpone* and the Authorship of *Eastward Hoe*," *MLN* 72 (1957): 253-56 (II,A, under *Volpone*); and Rinaldo Simonini, Jr., *N&Q* 195 (1950): 512-13 (I,B), who gives evidence to support Jonson's authorship of Act V.

The Widow, by Middleton (with Jonson and Fletcher?), comedy (ca. *1615-17*; 1652)

Bentley, *Jacobean Stage*, vol. 4, comments that "the evidence for Jonson's collaboration is negligible."

Love's Pilgrimage, by Fletcher (with Beaumont?), tragicomedy (*1616?* rev. *1635*; 1647)

Passages from Jonson's *New Inn* (1629) are incorporated in I.i. See Bentley, *Jacobean Stage*, vol. 4, and Baldwin Maxwell, "The Date of *Love's Pilgrimage* and Its Relation to *The New Inn*," *SP* 28 (1931): 702-9. There is a possibility of Jonson's collaboration.

A Mask Presented at Coleoverton, mask (*2 Feb. 1618?*; MS)

Rudolf Brotanek, *Die englischen Maskenspiele* (1902), argues for the above acting date through biographical analysis and ascribes the anonymous mask to Jonson. The ascription has not been generally accepted. See Bentley, *Jacobean Stage*, vol. 5.

The Bloody Brother (Rollo, Duke of Normandy), by Fletcher (with Massinger? Jonson? and another? rev. 1627-30 by Massinger?), tragedy (*1616-24*; 1639)

Cyrus Hoy, "The Shares of Fletcher and His Collaborators in the Beaumont and Fletcher Canon (VI)," *SB* 14 (1961): 45-67, suggests that Jonson's hand is "perhaps" in the play. See Richard Garnett, "Ben Jonson's Probable Authorship of Scene 2, Act IV, of Fletcher's *Bloody Brother*," *MP* 2 (1905): 489-95, and C. Crawford, "Ben Jonson and *The Bloody Brother*," *Jahrbuch der Deutschen Shakespeare-Gesellschaft* 41 (1905): 163-76. J. D. Jump, ed., *Rollo Duke of Normandy or The Bloody Brother* (1948), ascribes IV.i and ii to Jonson.

C. CRITIQUE OF THE STANDARD EDITION

The eleven-volume Oxford *Ben Jonson* (1925-52), edited by C. H. Herford and Percy and Evelyn Simpson, is the standard edition. The first two volumes discuss the man and his work in general; volumes three to seven are editions of the plays, masks, and entertainments, with textual variants at the bottom of each page; eight contains the poems and the prose; nine has a historical survey of the text, a stage history, and commentary on the plays; ten has commentary on the masks and entertainments. The final volume contains Jonson's Literary Record, supplementary notes, and an index. The textual work is definitive, while the commentary, notes, appendices, and scholarly materials are invaluable as repositories of information about Jonson. Unfortunately, the editors felt obligated to defend their conclusions against such scholars as Henry DeVocht, Henry David Gray, and I. A. Shapiro; these literary debates seem dated. Also there are minor errors throughout the annotations. An updated edition which takes into account recent scholarship and corrects these minor errors is needed. For further and more particular criticism, the reader is directed to the various reviews which have appeared over the years, e.g., W. W. Greg, *RES* 2 (1951): 275-80, who is very incisive, and Johan Gerritsen, *ES* 38 (1957): 120-26.

D. TEXTUAL STUDIES

Johan Gerritsen's "Stansby and Jonson Produce a Folio: A Preliminary Account," *ES* 40 (1959): 52-55, is a brief pilot study for an account of the printing of the 1616 Folio. "What is certainly known is that the volume contains work produced up to 1615 (or even 1616 if *Mercury Vindicated* is correctly dated to that year), that some other works from before 1616 are omitted (notably *Bartholomew Fayre*), and that Stansby registered copy for it on 20 January 1615 and produced the volume some time in 1616." Gerritsen disputes Herford and Simpson's contention that the Folio was begun in 1612-13. Though it is uncertain when the volume was planned, it was printed over 1615-16, and was halfway completed by the spring of 1616; probably work was started in late 1615, and the printing was completed near the beginning of the following summer. Josephine Waters Bennett, "Benson's Alleged Piracy of *Shake-speares Sonnets* and of Some of Jonson's Works," *SB* 21 (1968): 235-48, discusses Benson's publication of some of Jonson's work in 1640 and tries to vindicate his tarnished reputation as publisher. D. F. McKenzie, "The Printer of the Third Volume of Jonson's *Workes*," *SB* 25 (1972): 177-78, produces evidence that the printer was John Dawson Junior. The factotum used in the Jonson printing was also used in other well-known Dawson printings. J. A. Lavin, "Printers for Seven Jonson Quartos," *Library* 25 (1970): 331-38, argues that Adam Islip printed *Every Man Out* (1600), Simon Stafford printed *Every Man In* (1601), Richard Read printed *Cynthia's Revels* (1601), George Eld printed *Volpone* (1607), *The Masque of Blackness* (1608), and part of *The King's Entertainment* (1604). As Greg earlier suggested, Richard Braddock is the printer of *Poetaster* (1602).

Herford and Simpson, vol. 9, disagree with Henry DeVocht, who questions the authority of the 1616 Folio. DeVocht feels that, in certain cases, the quarto texts are superior. For Enck, "his tedious misreadings are effectually repudiated by the Jonson editors" (*Jonson and the Comic Truth*, I,B). DeVocht's studies have continued in *Comments on the Text of Ben Jonson's "Cynthias Revels"* (1950), and *Studies on the Texts of Ben Jonson's "Poetaster" and "Sejanus"* (1958). The older study by Bastiaan A. P. Van Dam and Cornelius Stoffel, "The Authority of the Ben Jonson Folio of 1616," *Anglia* 14 (1903): 377-92, anticipates DeVocht's arguments. See also W. W. Greg, "Jonson's Masques—Points of Editorial Principle and Practice," *RES* 18 (1942): 144-66, and Fredson Bowers, *On Editing Shakespeare* (1966).

E. SINGLE-WORK EDITIONS OF THE PLAYS

Volpone has been edited by Arthur Sale (1951), Louis Kronenberger (1952), and Jonas Barish (1958). The Yale Ben Jonson text (1962) is introduced and edited by Alvin Kernan (see II,A, under *Volpone*). David Cook edited the play for Methuen English Classics (1962), and J. B. Bamborough has an edition (1963) with an introduction and notes. Louis B. Wright and Virginia A. LaMar are the editors of the Folger Shakespeare Library edition (1970). Jay L. Halio's critical old-spelling edition (1968) has an introduction, textual apparatus, commentary, and selected bibliography. Scolar Press printed a facsimile of the 1607 quarto (1968), which also was edited by Henry DeVocht (1937). Vincent F. Hopper and Gerald B. Lakey's *Volpone* (1959), and the Chandler Editions text, introduced by Henry G. Lee (1961), are not well annotated.

The Alchemist has been edited by Douglas Brown (1966) with a complete critical apparatus; the text is that of the corrected First Folio. F. H. Mares' Revels edition (1967) contains a thorough introduction and notes. J. B. Steane's edition (1967) has a sound introduction and is fully annotated. S. Musgrove has edited a critical old-spelling text (1968). Alvin Kernan's edition for the Yale Ben Jonson (1974) has an appendix on Jonson's use of alchemy. G. E. Bentley's Crofts Classics edition (1947) has a brief introduction. Alfredo Obertello's Italian translation with introduction and notes appeared in 1948; Henry De Vocht's edition, based on the 1612 Quarto, in 1950; and Jiří Levý's Czech edition, with a preface contrasting the techniques of Jonson and Shakespeare, in 1956.

Bartholomew Fair is edited with a full introduction for the Revels series by E. A. Horsman (1960). Although there are a few errors, the text is completely annotated. The play is edited for the Regents series by Edward B. Partridge (1964); for the New Mermaids by Maurice Hussey (1964); and for Yale by Eugene M. Waith (1963). Waith's edition has two appendices, one on the text, the other on the staging.

Epicoene has been edited by L. A. Beaurline (1966) for the Regents series and by Edward Partridge (1971) for the Yale Ben Jonson. *Sejanus* is introduced and edited for the Yale Ben Jonson by Jonas A. Barish (1965) and for the New Mermaids series by W. F. Bolton (1966).

Catiline, edited by W. F. Bolton and Jane F. Gardner (1973) for the Regents series, contains a solid appendix on Jonson's classical sources. The New Mermaids edition of *Every Man in His Humour* (1966) is by Martin Seymour-Smith; the Yale Ben Jonson text with introduction, notes, and appendices is by Gabriele Bernhard Jackson (1969). J. W. Lever's *Every Man in His Humour: A Parallel-Text Edition of the 1601 Quarto and the 1616 Folio* (1971), in the Regents series, prints the two texts on facing pages. *The Divell is an Asse* edited by Maurice Hussey (1967) contains an old-spelling text with introduction and explanatory notes. *The Staple of News* is edited for the Regents series by Devra R. Kifer (1975).

In the Yale Ben Jonson, *The Complete Masques* (1969) and *Selected Masques* (1970) are edited by Stephen Orgel. *Jonson's "Masque of Gipsies" in the Burley, Belvoir, and Windsor Versions* (1952) is an "attempt at reconstruction" by W. W. Greg and contains a complete discussion of textual matters. Andrew J. Sabol transcribes and introduces *A Score for "Lovers Made Men": A Masque by Ben Jonson* (1963). *Oberon, the Fairy Prince* edited by Richard Hosley, *Love Freed from Ignorance and Folly* edited by Norman Sanders, *Lovers Made Men* edited by Stanley Wells, and *Pleasure Reconciled to Virtue* edited by R. A. Foakes are included in *A Book of Masques in Honour of Allardyce Nicoll* (1967).

The apocryphal *Rollo Duke of Normandy or The Bloody Brother* has been edited by J. D. Jump (1948).

The Brinsley Nicholson and C. H. Herford volumes are available in paperback. Volume 1 has an introduction by Herford, an editor's preface by Nicholson, and the plays *Volpone, Epicoene,* and *The Alchemist.* Volume 2 contains *Every Man In, Sejanus,* and *Bartholomew Fair.* Michael Jamieson's *Three Comedies: Ben Jonson* (1966) has a general introduction and prints *Volpone, The Alchemist,* and *Bartholomew Fair.* Felix Schelling's dated, two-volume edition is available in the Everyman Library.

F. EDITIONS OF NONDRAMATIC WORKS

The nondramatic works are included by Herford and Simpson in the Oxford *Ben Jonson.* The Oxford Standard Authors edition of the poetry is by Ian Donaldson (1975). William B. Hunter, Jr., ed., *The Complete Poetry of Ben Jonson* (1963), has a brief introduction, notes, glosses, some musical settings for the poems, and a selected bibliography. George Burke Johnston's edition, *The Poems of Ben Jonson*

(1954), appeared in the Muses' Library, and John Hollander's *Ben Jonson* (1961), in the Laurel Poetry Series. A generous selection of the poetry with a sound introduction is included in *Major Poets of the Earlier Seventeenth Century* (1973), edited by Barbara K. Lewalski and Andrew J. Sabol.

Ben Jonson's Literary Criticism in prose and poetry is selected and edited by James D. Redwine, Jr., for the Regents Critics Series (1970). *Timber or Discoveries* has been rearranged and edited by Ralph S. Walker (1953). Walker's rearrangement is discussed above (I,C).

IV. SEE ALSO

Because of the large amount of published scholarship on Jonson, this See Also section is comprehensive only for the years between 1945 and 1973. Selected studies published before and after those dates have been included.

A. GENERAL

Adams, Robert P. "Transformations in the Late Elizabethan Tragic Sense of Life: New Critical Approaches." *MLQ* 35 (1974): 352-63.

Allen, Don Cameron. *The Star-Crossed Renaissance: The Quarrel about Astrology and Its Influence in England.* 1941.

Anderson, Ruth L. "Kingship in Renaissance Drama." *SP* 41 (1944): 136-55.

Angell, C. F. "A Note on Jonson's Use of Sir Edward Dyer's 'My mynde to me a kyngdome is.'" *Papers on Language and Literature* 10 (1974): 417-21.

Arden, John. "An Embarrassment to the Tidy Mind." *Gambit* 6, no. 22 (1973): 30-46.

Asthana, R. K. "The Dynamics of Jonson's Comedies." *Criticism and Research* (Banaras Hindu Univ., 1964), pp. 46-55.

Aubrey, John. *Brief Lives*, ed. Oliver L. Dick. 1957.

Babb, Lawrence. *The Elizabethan Malady: A Study of Melancholia in English Literature from 1580 to 1642.* 1951.

Bamborough, J. B. "Jonson and Chapman." In *English Drama (excluding Shakespeare): Select Bibliographical Guides*, ed. Stanley Wells (1975), pp. 54-68.

Barber, C. L. *The Idea of Honour in the English Drama, 1591-1700.* 1957.

Barish, Jonas A. "Jonson's Dramatic Prose." In *Literary English Since Shakespeare*, ed. George Watson (1970), pp. 111-55.

———. "Jonson and the Loathèd Stage." In *A Celebration of Ben Jonson*, ed. William Blissett et al. (1973), pp. 27-53.

Barker, Richard H. *Thomas Middleton.* 1958.

Barnes, Peter, et al. "Ben Jonson and the Modern Stage." *Gambit* 6, no. 22 (1973): 5-30.

Barnes, T. R. *English Verse: Voice and Movement from Wyatt to Yeats.* 1967.

Baskervill, Charles R. *The Elizabethan Jig and Related Song Drama.* 1929.

Bastiaenen, Johannes Adam. *The Moral Tone of Jacobean and Caroline Drama.* 1930.

Bateson, Frederick W. *English Poetry and the English Language: An Experiment in Literary History*. 1934.

Benham, Allen R. "Horace and His *Ars Poetica* in English: A Bibliography." *Classical Weekly* 49 (1956): 1-5.

"Ben Jonson's Poems." *TLS*, 5 July 1947, p. 336. [Review article]

Bentley, G. E. "Seventeenth-Century Allusions to Ben Jonson." *HLQ* 5 (1941): 65-113.

————. *Shakespeare and His Theatre*. 1964.

Bergeron, David. "The Emblematic Nature of English Civic Pageantry." *RenD* 1 (1968): 167-98.

————. *Twentieth-Century Criticism of English Masques, Pageants, and Entertainments: 1558-1642*. 1972.

Bergman, Joseph A. "Shakespeare's 'Purge' of Jonson, Once Again." *ESRS* 15 (1966): 27-33.

Bevington, David M. *Tudor Drama and Politics: A Critical Approach to Topical Meaning*. 1968.

Bluestone, Max, and Norman Rabkin, eds. *Shakespeare's Contemporaries*. 1961; 2nd ed., 1970.

Blumenthal, Walter Hart. *Paging Mr. Shakespeare: A Critical Challenge*. 1961. [Questions authorship]

Boas, F. S. "The Soldier in Elizabethan Drama." *EDH* 19 (1942): 121-56.

————. "Charles Lamb and the Elizabethan Dramatists." *E&S* 29 (1943): 62-81.

————. *An Introduction to Stuart Drama*. 1946.

————. *Ovid and the Elizabethans*. 1947.

————. *Queen Elizabeth in Drama and Related Studies*. 1950.

Boas, Ralph P. "Ben Jonson's 'To Celia.'" *Expl* 1 (1942-1943): item 28.

Boughner, Daniel C. *The Braggart in Renaissance Comedy: A Study in Comparative Drama from Aristophanes to Shakespeare*. 1954.

Bowden, William R. *The English Dramatic Lyric, 1603-42: A Study in Stuart Dramatic Technique*. 1951.

Bowen, Elizabeth. *Collected Impressions*. 1950.

Bowers, Fredson Thayer. "Ben Jonson the Actor." *SP* 34 (1937): 392-406.

Boyd, John D. "T. S. Eliot as Critic and Rhetorician: The Essay on Jonson." *Criticism* 11 (1969): 167-82.

Bradbrook, Muriel C. *Themes and Conventions in Elizabethan Tragedy*. 1935.

————. *The Growth and Structure of Elizabethan Comedy*. 1956.

————. "The Nature of Theatrical Experience in Ben Jonson with Special Reference to the Masques." In *Expression, Communication and Experience in Literature and Language*, ed. Ronald G. Popperwell (1973), pp. 103-17.

Bridges-Adams, William. *The Irresistible Theatre: Growth of the English Stage*. 1957.

Briggs, Katharine M. *The Anatomy of Puck: An Examination of Fairy Beliefs among Shakespeare's Contemporaries and Successors*. 1959.

Broadbent, John B. *Poetic Love*. 1964.

Brooks, Harold F. "'A Satyricall Shrub.'" *TLS*, 11 Dec. 1969, p. 1426.

Brown, Arthur. "Citizen Comedy and Domestic Drama." In *Jacobean Theater*, SuAS, vol. 1 (1960), pp. 66-83.

Brown, Huntington. *Rabelais in English Literature*. 1933.

Brown, Ivor. *Shakespeare in His Time*. 1960.

———. "Not So Big Ben." *Drama* (Winter 1970), pp. 44–46.

Brown, John Mason. "Inigo Jones." *Theatre Arts Monthly* 12 (1928): 353–57.

Brunoski, Janet. *Ben Jonson: "Volpone," "The Alchemist."* 1970. [Study notes]

Bush, Douglas. *Mythology and the Renaissance Tradition in English Poetry*. 1932; rev. ed. 1963.

Buxton, John. *Elizabethan Taste*. 1963.

———. "The Poets' Hall Called Apollo." *MLR* 48 (1953): 52–54.

Camden, Carroll. "Spenser's 'Little Fish That Men Call Remora.'" *Rice Institute Pamphlet* 44 (1957): 1–12.

Cannon, Charles K. "The Relation of the Additions of *The Spanish Tragedy* to the Original Play." *SEL* 2 (1962): 229–39.

Capone, Giovanna. *Ben Jonson: L'Iconologia verbale come strategia di commedia*. 1969.

Caputi, Anthony. *John Marston, Satirist*. 1961.

Cazamian, Louis. *The Development of English Humor*. 1952.

Cejp, Ladislav. "Allegorical Terms in Jonson's Plays." *Sborník Vysoké školy pedagogické v Olomouci, Jazyk a literatura* 5 (1959): 123–29.

Chambers, E. K. *William Shakespeare*. 2 vols. 1930.

Chetwood, William Rufus. *Memoirs of the Life and Writings of Ben Jonson Esq.* 1756.

Chew, Samuel C. *The Virtues Reconciled: An Iconographic Study*. 1947.

Child, Harold. *Essays and Reflections*, ed. S. C. Roberts. 1948.

Churchill, Reginald Charles. *Shakespeare and His Betters*. 1958.

Chute, Marchette. *Shakespeare of London*. 1949.

———. "'If Ben Jonson Returned . . .'" *Library Journal* 78 (1953): 1595–96.

Clark, Donald. "Ancient Rhetoric and English Renaissance Literature." *SQ* 2 (1951): 195–204.

Clausen, Wendell. "The Beginnings of English Character-Writing in the Early Seventeenth Century." *PQ* 25 (1946): 32–45. [Emphasis on Jonson]

Coiseault-Cavalca, M. "Les Romantiques français et les Elisabethains." *Les Lettres Romanes* 20 (1966): 334–55.

Craig, Hardin. *The Literature of the English Renaissance. A History of English Literature*. Vol. 2. 1954.

Crane, Milton. *Shakespeare's Prose*. 1951.

Cruttwell, Patrick. *The Shakespearean Moment and Its Place in the Society of the 17th Century*. 1954.

Cunningham, J. *Elizabethan and Early Stuart Drama*. 1965.

Currey, R. N. "Jonson and *The Tempest*." *N&Q* 192 (1947): 468.

Curry, John V. *Deception in Elizabethan Comedy*. 1955.

Cutts, John P. "British Museum Add. MS. 31432 William Lawes' Writing for the Theatre and the Court." *Library* 7 (1952): 225–34.

———. "Jacobean Masque and Stage Music." *Music & Letters* 35 (1954): 185–200.

————. "Seventeenth-Century Illustrations of Three Masques by Jonson." *CompD* 6 (1972): 125–34.

Davenport, Arnold. "The Quarrel of the Satirists." *MLR* 37 (1942): 123–30.

————, ed. *The Poems of John Marston.* 1961.

Demaray, John G. *Milton and the Masque Tradition: The Early Poems, "Arcades," and "Comus."* 1968.

Donaldson, Ian. "Ben Jonson." In *English Drama to 1710,* ed. Christopher Ricks. *History of Literature in the English Language,* vol. 3 (1971).

————. "Jonson's Ode to Sir Lucius Cary and Sir H. Morison." In *Ben Jonson: Quadricentennial Essays,* ed. Mary Olive Thomas; special ed. of *Studies in the Literary Imagination* 6, no. 1 (1973): 139–52.

————. "Damned by Analogies: Or, How to Get Rid of Ben Jonson." *Gambit* 6, no. 22 (1973): 38–46.

Douglass, James W. "'To Penshurst.'" *Christian Scholar* 44 (1961): 133–38.

Duncan, Douglas. "Synge and Jonson (with a Parenthesis on Ronsard)." In *Sunshine and the Moon's Delight: A Centenary Tribute to John Millington Synge, 1871–1909,* ed. Suheil B. Bushrui (1972), pp. 205–18.

Dunfey, Francesca. "'Mighty Showes': Masque Elements in Jacobean and Caroline Drama." *Shakespeare Studies* (Univ. of Tokyo) 6 (1967–68): 122–46.

Dunlap, Rhodes. "The Allegorical Interpretation of Renaissance Literature." *PMLA* 82 (1967): 39–43.

Dutton, A. Richard. "*Volpone* and *The Alchemist*: A Comparison in Satiric Techniques." *RMS* 18 (1974): 36–62.

E., A. C. "Ben Jonson." *N&Q* 193 (1948): 323. [Biographical]

Earley, Robert, "Sir Luckless Woo-All's 'Wast Wife' and the *OED* (Jonson's Epigramme XLVI)." *ELN* 12 (1975): 265–68.

Eccles, Mark. "Jonson's Marriage." *RES* 12 (1936): 257–72.

————. "'Memorandums of the Immortal Ben.'" *MLN* 51 (1936): 520–23.

————. "Jonson and the Spies." *RES* 13 (1937): 385–97.

Eddy, William Alfred. "Dryden Quotes Ben Jonson." *MLN* 46 (1931): 40–41.

Edwards, A. S. G. "Libertine Literature." *TLS*, 18 Feb. 1972, p. 189.

Elliott, Robert. *The Power of Satire: Magic, Ritual, Art.* 1960.

Ellrodt, Robert. *L'inspiration personelle et l'esprit du temps.* 1960. Vol. 3.

Enck, John J. "A Chronicle of Small Latin." *SQ* 12 (1961): 342–45.

Enright, D. J. "Crime and Punishment in Ben Jonson." *Scrutiny* 9 (1940): 231–48.

Esdaile, Katharine A. "Ben Jonson and the Devil Tavern." *E&S* 29 (1943): 93–100.

Evans, A. J. *Shakespeare's Magic Circle.* 1956.

Evans, B. Ifor. *A Short History of English Drama.* 1948; rev. ed., 1965.

Evans, G. Blakemore, ed. *The Plays and Poems of William Cartwright.* 1951.

Evans, K. W. "The Political Philosophy of Ben Jonson's Masques." *Work in Progress* 1 (Zaria, Nigeria, Ahmadu Bellow University) (1972).

Evans, W. M. *Ben Jonson and Elizabethan Music.* 1929.

Ewbank, Inga-Stina. "'These Pretty Devices': A Study of Masques in Plays." In *A Book of Masques in Honour of Allardyce Nicoll* (1967), pp. 407–48.

————. "'The Eloquence of Masques': A Retrospective View of Masque Criticism." *RenD* 1 (1968): 307-27.

Farmer, Norman K., Jr. "A Theory of Genre for Seventeenth-Century Poetry." *Genre* 3 (1970): 293-317.

Farnham, Willard. "Medieval Comic Spirit in the English Renaissance." In *Joseph Quincy Adams Memorial Studies*, ed. J. G. McManaway et al. (1948), pp. 429-37.

Feldman, Sylvia D. *Morality-Patterned Comedy of the Renaissance.* 1970.

Findeisen, Helmut. "'Humour' und Satire bei Ben Jonson." *SJW* 109 (1973): 47-50.

Finney, Gretchen L. "Music: The Breath of Life." *Centennial Review of Arts & Science* 4 (1960): 179-205.

————. *Musical Backgrounds for English Literature, 1580-1650.* 1962.

Fisher, William. "*Occupatio* in Sixteenth- and Seventeenth-Century Verse." *TSLL* 19 (1972): 302-22.

Frajnd, Marta. "Teorijski stavovi Bena Dzonsona [Theoretical Viewpoints of Ben Jonson]." *Filoloski Pregled* (Belgrade), no. 1-2 (1964): 231-45.

Fraser, Russell. "Elizabethan Drama and the Art of Abstraction." *CompD* 2 (1968): 73-82.

Freeman, Arthur. "A Jonson Attribution." *N&Q* 8 (1961): 195.

Friedman, William F. and Elizebeth S. *The Shakespearean Ciphers Examined.* 1957.

Fuller, David. "The Jonsonian Masque and Its Music," *Music & Letters* 54 (1973): 440-52.

Funke, Otto. "Ben Jonsons *English Grammar.*" *Anglia* 52 (1940): 117-34.

Furniss, W. Todd. "Jonson's Antimasques." *RN* 7 (1954): 21-22.

Gamberini, Spartico. *Poeti metafisici e cavalieri in inghilterra.* 1959.

Gardiner, Judith K., and Susanna S. Epp. "Ben Jonson's Social Attitudes: A Statistical Analysis." *CompD* 9 (1975): 68-86.

————. "Jonson's Friend Colby." *N&Q* 22 (1975): 306-7.

Gardner, Thomas. "'A Parodie! A Parodie!': Conjectures on the Jonson-Daniel Feud." In *Lebende Antike: Symposion für Rudolf Sühnel*, ed. Horst Meller and Hans-Joachim Zimmermann (1967), pp. 197-206.

Gassner, John. *Masters of the Drama.* 1940; 3rd ed., rev., 1954.

Gibson, H. N. *The Shakespeare Claimants.* 1962.

Goldsmith, Robert H. "Did Shakespeare Use the Old Timon Comedy?" *SQ* 9 (1958): 31-38.

Gollancz, I. "Ben Jonson and Richard Greneway." *TLS*, 21 June 1928, p. 468.

Gossett, Suzanne. "Masque Influence on the Dramaturgy of Beaumont and Fletcher." *MP* 69 (1972): 199-208.

Gotch, John Alfred. *Inigo Jones.* 1928.

Gottwald, Maria. "Ben Jonson's Theory of Comedy." *Germanica Wratislaviensia* 10 (1966): 131-53.

————. "Koncepcja 'Humorów' u Beniamina Johnsona." *Germanica Wratislaviensia* 12 (1968): 3-14.

————. *Satirical Elements in Ben Jonson's Comedy.* 1969.

Graham, C. B. "An Echo of Jonson in Aphra Behn's *Sir Patient Fancy.*" *MLN* 53 (1938): 278-79.

————. "Jonson Allusions in Restoration Comedy." *RES* 15 (1939): 200–204.

————. "The Jonsonian Tradition in the Comedies of Thomas D'Urfey." *MLQ* 8 (1947): 47–52.

Gray, Arthur. *How Shakespeare "Purged" Jonson: A Problem Solved.* 1928. [Jaques was a satire on Jonson.]

Gray, Henry David. "The Date of *Hamlet.*" *JEGP* 31 (1932): 51–61.

Greene, Thomas M. "Ben Jonson e l'io accentrato." *Strumenti Critici* 3 (1969): 236–62.

Greg, W. W. "Some Notes on Ben Jonson's Works." *RES* 2 (1926): 129–45.

————. "Shakespeare and Jonson." *RES* 22 (1946): 58.

————. *The Collected Papers of Sir Walter W. Greg,* ed. J. C. Maxwell. 1966.

Hagstrum, Jean H. *The Sister Arts: The Tradition of Literary Pictorialism and English Poetry from Dryden to Gray.* 1958.

Halio, Jay L. "The Metaphor of Conception and Elizabethan Theories of the Imagination." *Neophil* 50 (1966): 454–61.

Hall, Vernon, Jr. *Renaissance Literary Criticism: A Study of Its Social Content.* 1945.

Halliday, Frank E. *Shakespeare in His Age.* 1956.

————. *The Cult of Shakespeare.* 1957.

Hankins, John E. "Jonson's 'Ode on Morison' and Seneca's *Epistulae Morales.*" *MLN* 51 (1936): 518–20.

Harbage, Alfred. *Sir William Davenant.* 1935.

————. *Cavalier Drama.* 1936.

Hartnoll, Phyllis. "Library Drama Comes to Life." *Theatre Arts* 43, no. 12 (1959): 79–81, 83.

Hayahi, Tetsumaro. "Ben Jonson and William Shakespeare: Their Relationship and Mutual Criticism." *East-West Review* 3 (1966–67): 23–47.

Heltzel, Virgil B. "The Dedication of Tudor and Stuart Plays." In *Studies in English Language and Literature Presented to Professor Karl Brunner on the Occasion of His Seventieth Birthday.* Special ed. of *Wiener Beiträge zur Englischen Philologie* 65 (1957): 74–86.

Hemphill, George, ed. *Discussions of Poetry: Rhythm and Sound.* 1961.

Heninger, S. K., Jr. *A Handbook of Renaissance Meteorology: With Particular Reference to Elizabethan and Jacobean Literature.* 1960.

Henry, Hélène. "Charles Dullin et le théâtre élisabéthain." *EA* 13 (1960): 197–204.

Herrick, Marvin T. *Poetics of Aristotle in England.* 1930.

————. *The Fusion of Horatian and Aristotelian Literary Criticism, 1531–55.* 1946.

Hett, Francis P., ed. *The Memoirs of Sir Robert Sibbald, 1641–1722: Edited, with an Introduction and a Refutation of the Charge against Sir Robert Sibbald of Forging Ben Jonson's "Conversations."* 1932.

Hibbard, G. R. "Ben Jonson and Human Nature." In *A Celebration of Ben Jonson,* ed. William Blissett et al. (1973), pp. 55–81.

Hilberry, Clarence B. *Ben Jonson's Ethics in Relation to Stoic and Humanistic Ethical Thought.* 1933.

Hobsbaum, Phillip. "Elizabethan Poetry." *Poetry Review* 56 (1965): 80–97.

Hogan, Jerome W. "Two Jonson Allusions." *N&Q* 22 (1975): 248.

Holden, William P. *Anti-Puritan Satire, 1572-1642.* 1954.

Holland, Norman N. *The First Modern Comedies: The Significance of Etherege, Wycherley, and Congreve.* 1959.

Hollander, John. *The Untuning of the Sky: Ideas of Music in English Poetry, 1500-1700.* 1961.

———. *Vision and Resonance: Two Senses of Poetic Form.* 1975.

Holzknecht, Karl J. *Outlines of Tudor and Stuart Plays.* 1947. [*Every Man, Sejanus, Volpone, Epicoene, Alchemist, Bartholomew Fair, Staple of News*]

Honda, Kensho. "Ben Jonson to Sheikusupia [i.e., and Shakespeare]." *Journal of English Literature* (Hosei Univ., Tokyo) 3 (1960): 1-2.

Horn, Robert D. "Shakespeare and Ben Jonson—Ashland, 1961." *SQ* 12 (1961): 415-18.

Howarth, Herbert. "Shakespeare's Gentleness." *ShS* 14 (1961): 90-97.

Howarth, R. G. *A Pot of Gillyflowers: Studies and Notes.* 1965.

Howell, A. C. "A Note on Ben Jonson's Literary Methods." *SP* 28 (1931): 710-19.

Hoy, Cyrus. "The Shares of Fletcher and His Collaborators in the Beaumont and Fletcher Canon (VII)." *SB* 15 (1962): 71-90.

Hunt, Clay. "The Elizabethan Background of Neo-Classic Polite Verse." *ELH* 8 (1941): 273-304.

Hunter, G. K. "English Folly and Italian Vice: The Moral Landscape of John Marston," In *Jacobean Theatre,* SuAS, vol. 1 (1960), pp. 85-111.

Hussey, Maurice. *The World of Shakespeare and His Contemporaries: A Visual Approach.* 1972.

Hyde, Mary Crapo. *Playwriting for Elizabethans, 1600-1605.* 1949.

Ing, Catherine. *Elizabethan Lyrics: A Study in the Development of English Metres and Their Relation to Poetic Effect.* 1951.

Inglis, Fred. "Classicism and Poetic Drama." *Essays in Criticism* 16 (1966): 154-69.

———. *The Elizabethan Poets: The Making of English Poetry from Wyatt to Ben Jonson.* 1969.

Ingram, R. W. "Editions of English Drama in Progress and Planned: A Rough Checklist." *RenD* 7 (1964): 13-49.

———. "Editions of English Renaissance Drama in Progress." *RenD* (Supplement) 7 (1964): 15-28.

Irmscher, Johannes. "Die klassische Bildung zur Zeit Ben Jonsons." *SJW* 109 (1973): 51-55.

Ishibashi, Kotaro. "Ben Jonson's English Grammar." *Urn* (Japan) 1 (1949): N.P.

Jacquot, Jean, et al. *La lieu théâtral à la renaissance.* 1964.

———. *Dramaturgie et societé: Rapports entre l'oeuvre théâtrale, son interprétation et son public aux xvie siècles.* 2 vols. 1968.

Johansson, Bertil. *Law and Lawyers in Elizabethan England as Evidenced in the Plays of Ben Jonson and Thomas Middleton.* 1967.

John, Lisle Cecil. "Ben Jonson's Epigram CXIV to Mistress Philip Sidney." *JEGP* 45 (1946): 214-17.

Johnson, Carol Holmes. *Reason's Double Agents.* 1966.

Johnson, Stanley. "Donne's 'Autumnall Elegy,'" *TLS,* 30 April 1931, p. 347.

Johnston, George B. "Notes on Jonson's *Execration upon Vulcan.*" *MLN* 46 (1931): 150-53.

———. "An Apocryphal Jonsonian Epigram." *N&Q* 5 (1958): 543-44.

Joly, A. *William Drummond de Hawthornden, 1585-1649.* 1934.

Jones, Thora Burnley, and Bernard de Bear Nicol. *Neo-Classical Dramatic Criticism, 1560-1770.* 1976.

Jones-Davies, M. Thomas. *Inigo Jones, Ben Jonson, et le Masque.* 1967.

Jost, François. "Ludwig Tieck: English and French Sources of His *William Lovell* (1795-96). In *Studies in Eighteenth-Century Culture,* ed. Harold E. Pagliaro. *Proceedings of the American Society for Eighteenth-Century Studies* 2 (1972): 181-93.

Kallich, Martin. "Unity of Time in *Every Man in His Humour* and *Cynthia's Revels.*" *MLN* 57 (1942): 445-49.

Keller, Wolfgang. "Ben Jonson und Shakespeare." *SJ* 73 (1937): 31-52.

Kelliher, W. Hilton. "Anecdotes of Jonson and Cleveland."*N&Q* 19 (1972): 172-73.

Kelty, Jean McClure. "The Frontispiece of Ben Jonson's 1616 Folio: A Critical Commentary on the Elizabethan Stage." *Theater Annual* 17 (1960): 22-35.

Kenner, Hugh. *The Poetry of Ezra Pound.* 1951.

Kerr, Mina. *Influence of Ben Jonson on English Comedy: 1598-1642.* 1912.

Kerrigan, William. "Ben Jonson Full of Shame and Scorn." In *Ben Jonson: Quadricentennial Essays,* ed. Mary Olive Thomas. Special ed. of *Studies in the Literary Imagination* 6, no. 1 (1973): 199-217.

Kim, Seyong. "Ben Jonson the Playwright." *English Literature and Language* (Tokyo) 5 (1958): 28-50.

Kirsch, Arthur C. "A Caroline Commentary on the Drama." *MP* 66 (1969): 256-61. [*Staple of News, Bartholomew Fair.*]

———. *Jacobean Dramatic Perspectives.* 1972.

Kliegman, Benjamin. "A 'Jonson-Shakespeare' Portrait." *ShN* 2 (1952): 35.

Knight, G. Wilson. *The Golden Labyrinth: A Study of British Drama.* 1962.

Knights, L. C. "Tradition and Ben Jonson." *Scrutiny* 4 (1935): 140-57. Rpt. in his *Drama and Society in the Age of Jonson* (1937), pp. 179-99.

———. "Ben Jonson, Dramatist." In *The Age of Shakespeare,* ed. Boris Ford (1956), pp. 302-11.

———. "Ben Jonson: Public Attitudes and Social Poetry." In *A Celebration of Ben Jonson,* ed. William Blissett et al. (1973), pp. 167-87.

Knowlton, Edgar C. "The Plots of Ben Jonson." *MLN* 44 (1929): 77-86.

Kreider, Paul V. *Elizabethan Comic Character Conventions as Revealed in the Comedies of George Chapman.* 1935.

Krishnamurthi, M. G. "The Ethical Basis of Ben Jonson's Plays." *Journal of the Maharaja Sayajirao University of Baroda* 11, no. 1 (1962): 139-57.

Kroejer, Maxim. "Ben Jonson en Zijn Tijd." *Autotoerist* 16 (1963): 909-11.

LaFrance, Marston. "Fielding's Use of the 'Humor' Tradition." *Bucknell Review* 17, no. 3 (1969): 53-63.

La Regina, Gabriella. "Ben Jonson e la sua fortuna nel seicento." *EM* 16 (1965): 37-86.

Lascelles, Mary. "Shakespeare's Comic Insight." *PBA* 48 (1962): 171-86.

Latham, Agnes. "Ben Jonson." In *Critics Who Have Influenced Taste (From "The Times"),* ed. A. P. Ryan (1965), pp. 3-5.

Leavis, F. R. "English Poetry of the 17th Century." *Scrutiny* 4 (1935): 236-56.

———. *Revaluation: Tradition and Development in English Poetry.* 1936.

LeComte, Edward. *The Notorious Lady Essex.* 1969.

Leech, Clifford. *Shakespeare's Tragedies and Other Studies in Seventeenth-Century Drama.* 1950.

―――. "The Incredibility of Jonsonian Comedy." In *A Celebration of Ben Jonson,* ed. William Blissett et al. (1973), pp. 3–25.

Lees-Milne, James. *The Age of Inigo Jones.* 1953.

Leggatt, Alexander. *Citizen Comedy in the Age of Shakespeare.* 1973.

Leishman, James B., ed. *The Three Parnassus Plays (1598–1601).* 1949.

―――. *The Monarch of Wit: An Analytical and Comparative Study of the Poetry of John Donne.* 1951.

Lemay, J. A. Leo. "Jonson and Milton: Two Influences in Oakes's *Elegie.*" *New England Quarterly* 38 (1965): 90–92.

Levin, Harry. "Jonson, Stow and Drummond." *MLN* 53 (1938): 167–69.

―――. "Jonson's Metempsychosis," *PQ* 22 (1943): 231–39.

―――. *The Myth of the Golden Age in the Renaissance.* 1970.

Levin, Richard. "Thematic Unity and the Homogenization of Character." *MLQ* 33 (1972): 23–29.

Levý, Jiří. "Divadelní prostor a čăs v dramatech Williama Shakespeara a Bena Jonsona [Dramatic space and time in the plays of Shakespeare and Ben Jonson]." In *F. Wollmanovi k sedmdesátínam* (1958), 648–56.

Lindsey, E. S. "The Music in Ben Jonson's Plays." *MLN* 44 (1929): 86–92.

Linklater, Eric. *Ben Jonson and King James: Biography and Portrait.* 1931.

Linthicum, M. Channing. *Costume in the Drama of Shakespeare and His Contemporaries.* 1936.

MacCarthy, Desmond. *Humanities.* 1953.

McCarthy, Mary Therese. *Sights and Spectacles, 1937–1956.* 1956.

McClennen, Joshua. *On the Meaning and Function of Allegory in the English Renaissance.* 1947.

McDiarmid, Matthew P. "The Stage Quarrel in *Wily Beguiled.*" *N&Q* 3 (1956): 380–83.

McEuen, Kathryn A. "Jonson and Juvenal." *RES* 21 (1945): 92–104.

McGalliard, John C. "Chaucerian Poetry: The *Merchant's Tale,* Jonson, and Moliere." *PQ* 25 (1946): 343–70.

McGuire, Philip C. "Private Prayer and English Poetry in the Early Seventeenth Century." *SEL* 14 (1974): 63–77.

Maclean, Hugh. "'A More Secret Cause': The Wit of Jonson's Poetry." In *A Celebration of Ben Jonson,* ed. William Blissett et al. (1973), pp. 129–66.

―――. "Ben Jonson's *Timber,* 1046–1115, and Falstaff," *Papers on Language and Literature* 10 (1974): 202–6.

McMillan, Scott. "Jonson's Early Entertainments: New Information from Hatfield House." *RenD* 1 (1968): 153–66.

McPeek, James A. S. *The Black Book of Knaves and Unthrifts in Shakespeare and Other Renaissance Authors.* 1969.

McPharlin, P. "Ben Jonson and Inigo Jones, Inventors." *Mask* 12 (1927): 10–14.

McPherson, David. "Some Renaissance Sources for Jonson's Early Comic Theory." *ELN* 8 (1971): 180–82.

―――. *Ben Jonson's Library and Marginalia: An Annotated Catalogue. SP* 71, no. 5 (1974): 1–106.

Maddison, Carol. *Apollo and the Nine: A History of the Ode.* 1960.

Main, C. F. "Two Items in the Jonson Apocrypha." *N&Q* 1 (1954): 243–45.

Main, William W. "Dramaturgical Norms in the Elizabethan Repertory." *SP* 54 (1957): 128–48.

Major, John M. "Milton's View of Rhetoric." *SP* 64 (1967): 685–711.

———. "A Reading of Jonson's 'Epitaph on Elizabeth, L. H.'" *SP* 73 (1976): 62–86.

Manifold, J. S. *The Music in English Drama, from Shakespeare to Purcell.* 1956.

Mark, Jeffrey. "The Jonsonian Masque." *Music & Letters* 3 (1922): 358–71.

Matchett, William. *The Phoenix and the Turtle: Shakespeare's Poem and Chester's "Love's Martyr."* 1965.

Meagher, John C. "The Dance and the Masques of Ben Jonson." *JWCI* 25 (1962): 258–77.

Medine, Peter E. "Object and Intent in Jonson's 'Famous Voyage.'" *SEL* 15 (1975): 97–110.

Meier, T. "The Naming of Characters in Jonson's Comedies." *ESA* 7 (1964): 88–95.

Merchant, Paul. "A Jonson Source for Herrick's 'Upon Julia's Clothes.'" *N&Q* 21 (1974): 93.

Meynell, Alice. *The Wares of Autolycus: Selected Literary Essays of Alice Meynell,* ed. P. M. Fraser. 1965.

Miles, Josephine. *Eras and Modes in English Poetry.* 1957.

———. *Renaissance, Eighteenth-Century, and Modern Language in English Poetry: A Tabular View.* 1960.

Mills, Lloyd L. "Ben Jonson's Poetry: A Caveat and Two Interpretations." *New Laurel Review* 1, no. 1 (1971): 30–34.

Miner, Earl. *The Cavalier Mode from Jonson to Cotton.* 1971.

Morris, Helen. *Elizabethan Literature.* 1957.

Muir, Kenneth. *Introduction to Elizabethan Literature.* 1967.

———, and S. Schoenbaum, eds. *A New Companion to Shakespeare Studies.* 1971.

Murphy, Avon Jack. "The Critical Elegy of Seventeenth-Century England." *Genre* 5 (1972): 75–97.

Murray, W. A. "What Was the Soul of the Apple?" *RES* 10 (1959): 141–55.

Murrin, Michael. "Poetry as Literary Criticism." *MP* 65 (1967–68): 202–7.

N., R. K. "Ben Jonson's 'To Celia.'" *Expl.* 1 (1942–43): query 19.

Nash, Ralph. "Milton, Ben Jonson and Tiberius." *Classical Philology* 41 (1946): 164.

Nethercot, Arthur H. "Milton, Jonson, and the Young Cowley." *MLN* 49 (1934): 158–62.

Neumann, J. H. "Notes on Ben Jonson's English." *PMLA* 54 (1939): 736–63.

Newton, Richard. "'Goe, quit 'hem all': Ben Jonson and Formal Verse Satire." *SEL* 16 (1976): 105–16.

Nicoll, Allardyce. *British Drama.* 1925; 5th ed., 1962.

———. *Stuart Masques and the Renaissance Stage.* 1937.

———. *World Drama from Aeschylus to Anouilh.* 1949.

———. "Shakespeare and the Court Masque. *SJ* 94 (1958): 51–62.

Nicolson, Marjorie Hope. *Voyages to the Moon.* 1948.

Norman, Arthur M. F. "Source Material in *Antony and Cleopatra.*" *N&Q* 3 (1956): 59–61.

Noyes, Robert Gale. "Ben Jonson's Masques in the Eighteenth Century." *SP* 33 (1936): 427–36.

Oates, Mary I. "Jonson's 'Ode Pindarick' and the Doctrine of Imitation." *Papers in Language and Literature* 11 (1975): 126–48.

O'Donnell, Norbert F. "A Lost Jacobean *Phoenissae?*" *MLN* 69 (1954): 163-64.

Ogburn, Dorothy and Charlton. *This Star of England.* 1952. [Oxfordian heresy]

Oliver, Edith. "O Quite Well-Done Ben Jonson!" *New Yorker,* 26 Sept. 1964, pp. 160–63.

Ono, Kyoichi, "A Turning Point of Ben Jonson." *Eibungaku-kenkyu* 27 (1950): 61–74.

Oras, Ants. *Pause Patterns in Elizabethan and Jacobean Drama: An Experiment in Prosody.* UFMH, no. 3 (1960).

Orgel, Stephen. "To Make Boards to Speak: Inigo Jones's Stage and the Jonsonian Masque." *RenD* 1 (1968): 121–52.

————. "The Poetics of Spectacle." *New Literary History* 2 (1971): 367–89.

————, and Roy C. Strong. *Inigo Jones: Theatre of the Stuart Court.* 2 vols. 1973.

Osborn, Louise Brown. *The Life, Letters, and Writings of John Hoskyns.* 1937.

Palme, Per. *The Triumph of Peace: A Study of the Whitehall Banqueting House.* 1957.

Palmer, Ralph Graham. *Seneca's "De Remediis Fortuitorum" and the Elizabethans.* 1953.

Papajewski, Helmut. "Ben Jonsons Laudatio auf Shakespeare: Kategorien des literarischen Urteils in der Renaissance." *Poetica* 1 (1967): 483–507.

Parfitt, George A. E. "The Poetry of Thomas Carew." *RMS* (1968): 56–67.

Parrott, T. M. "Comedy in the Court Masque: A Study of Ben Jonson's Contribution." In *Renaissance Studies in Honor of Hardin Craig,* ed. Baldwin Maxwell et al. (1941), pp. 236–49, and *PQ* 20 (1941): 428–41.

————, and Robert Hamilton Ball. *A Short View of English Drama.* 1943.

Parsons, D. S. J. "The Odes of Drayton and Jonson." *QQ* 75 (1968): 675–84.

Partridge, A. C. "The Periphrastic Auxiliary Verb 'Do' and Its Use in the Plays of Ben Jonson." *MLR* 43 (1948): 26–33.

————. *Orthography in Shakespeare and Elizabethan Drama.* 1964.

Partridge, Edward B. "Ben Jonson: The Makings of the Dramatist (1596-1602)." In *Elizabethan Theatre,* SuAS, vol. 9 (1966), pp. 220–44.

————. "Jonson's *Epigrammes:* The Named and the Nameless." In *Ben Jonson: Quadricentennial Essays,* ed. Mary Olive Thomas. Special ed. of *Studies in the Literary Imagination* 6, no. 1 (1973): 153–98.

Pellegrini, G. "Symbols and Significance." *ShS* 17 (1964): 180–87, 260–61.

Peltz, Catharine. "Thomas Campion, an Elizabethan Neo-Classicist." *MLQ* 11 (1950): 3–6.

Pennanen, Esko V. *Notes on the Grammar in Ben Jonson's Dramatic Works.* Annales Universitatis Turkuensis, Ser. B, 39 (1951).

Perkinson, Richard H. "Topographical Comedy in the Seventeenth Century." *ELH* 3 (1936): 270–90.

Perry, H. T. E. *Masters of Dramatic Comedy and Their Social Themes.* 1939.

Peter, John. *Complaint and Satire in Early English Literature.* 1956.

Peterson, Douglas L. *The English Lyric from Wyatt to Donne: A History of the Plain and Eloquent Styles.* 1967.

Piper, William B. "The Inception of the Closed Heroic Couplet." *MP* 66 (1969): 306-21.

Plumstead, A. W. "Satirical Parody in *Roister Doister*: A Reinterpretation." *SP* 60 (1963): 141-54.

Pohl, Frederick J. "Is This the Face of Shakespeare? " *The Pictou Advocate* (Nova Scotia), 17 Oct. 1957, pp. 7-8.

Potgieter, J. T. "Ben Jonson en die leser." *Tydskrif vir letterkunde* 6, no. 3 (1956): 14-23.

Potts, Leonard J. "Ben Jonson and the Seventeenth Century." *E&S* 2 (1949): 7-24.

————. *Comedy.* 1949.

Prior, Mood E. *The Language of Tragedy.* 1947.

————. "Poetic Drama: An Analysis and a Suggestion." *English Institute Essays, 1949* (1950), pp. 3-32. [*Volpone, Alchemist*]

Pritchard, Allan. "From These Uncouth Shores: Seventeenth-Century Literature of Newfoundland." *Canadian Literature* 14 (1962): 5-20.

Proestler, Mary. "Caesar Did Never Wrong But With Just Cause." *PQ* 7 (1928): 91-92.

Putney, Rufus. "What 'Praise to Give?' Jonson vs. Stoll." *PQ* 23 (1944): 307-19.

Race, Sydney. "Harleian MS 6395 and Its Editor." *N&Q* (1957): 77-79.

Ramsey, Stanley C. *Inigo Jones.* 1924.

Ransom, John C. *The New Criticism.* 1941.

Reddaway, T. F. "London and the Court." *ShS* 17 (1964): 3-12, 241.

Redding, David C. "A Note on Jonson Attribution." *N&Q* 7 (1960): 52-53. [A joke attributed to Jonson]

Reed, Robert Rentoul, Jr. *Bedlam on the Jacobean Stage.* 1952.

————. *The Occult on the Tudor and Stuart Stage.* 1965.

Rendall, Gerald H. *Ben Jonson and the First Folio Edition of Shakespeare's Plays.* 1939. [Questions authorship]

Rexroth, Kenneth. "The Works of Ben Jonson." *Saturday Review,* 17 Dec. 1966, p. 25.

Reynolds, George Fullmer. *The Staging of Elizabethan Plays.* 1940.

————. "The Dramatic Quality of Jonson's Masques." *PQ* 22 (1943): 230-38.

Ribner, Irving. *The English History Play in the Age of Shakespeare.* 1957; rev. ed. 1965.

Richmond, H. M. *The School of Love: The Evolution of the Stuart Love Lyric.* 1964.

Riddell, James. "Some Actors in Ben Jonson's Plays." *ShakS* 5 (1969): 285-98.

Robin, Percy A. *Animal Lore in English Literature.* 1932.

Rodway, Allan. *English Comedy: Its Role and Nature from Chaucer to the Present Day.* 1975.

Røstvig, Maren-Sofie. *The Happy Man: Studies in the Metamorphoses of a Classical Ideal, 1600-1700.* 1954. 2nd ed., 1962.

Rossky, William. "Imagination in the English Renaissance: Psychology and Poetic." *SRen* 5 (1958): 49-73.

Rulfs, Donald J. "Reception of the Elizabethan Playwrights on the London Stage, 1776-1833." *SP* 46 (1949): 54-69.

Sabol, Andrew J., ed. *Songs and Dances for the Stuart Masque: An Edition of Sixty-three Items of Music for the English Court Masque from 1604 to 1641.* 1959.

Sackton, Alexander. "The Paradoxical Encomium in Elizabethan Drama." *Studies in English* (Univ. of Texas) 28 (1949): 83–104.

Saintsbury, George E. B. *A Last Vintage: Essays and Papers,* ed. John W. Oliver et al. 1950.

Saleski, R. E. "Supernatural Agents in Christian Imagery: Word Studies in Elizabethan Dramatists." *JEGP* 38 (1939): 431–39.

Salmon, J. H. M. *The French Religious Wars in English Political Thought.* 1959. [Jonson on Bodin]

Sasayama, Takashi. "Kiritsu to Honno no aida." *Eigo Seinen* 116 (1970): 632–34. [Jonson's imagination]

Savage, James E. "Ben Jonson in Ben Jonson's Plays." *UMSE* 3 (1962): 1–17.

———, ed. *The "Conceited Newes" of Sir Thomas Overbury and His Friends: Facsimile of "Sir Thomas Overbury His Wife" (1616).* 1968.

———. "The Formal Choruses in the Comedies of Ben Jonson." *UMSE* 11 (1971): 11–21.

Schlösser, Anselm. "Ben Jonson und Shakespeare." *SJW* 109 (1973): 22–39.

Schlüter, Kurt von. *Die englische Ode.* 1964.

Schmidtchen, Paul W. "O Rare Ben Jonson." *Hobbies* 69 (Feb. 1965): 106 [For children]

Schoenbaum, Samuel. "Shakespeare and Jonson: Fact and Myth." In *The Elizabethan Theatre, II,* ed. David Galloway (1970), pp. 1–19.

———. *Shakespeare's Lives.* 1970.

———. *William Shakespeare: A Documentary Life.* 1975.

Schücking, Levin Ludwig. *The Baroque Character of the Elizabethan Tragic Hero.* 1939.

———. *Shakespeare und der Tragödienstil seiner Zeit.* 1948.

Sells, Arthur Lytton. *The Italian Influence in English Poetry from Chaucer to Southwell.* 1955.

Sharpe, Robert Boies. "Jonson's 'Execration' and Chapman's 'Invective': Their Place in Their Authors' Rivalry." In *Studies in Language and Literature,* ed. George R. Coffman (1955), pp. 177–85; special issue of *SP* 42 (1945).

———. *Irony in the Drama: An Essay on Impersonation, Shock, and Catharsis.* 1959.

Shillinglaw, Arthur T. "Hobbes and Ben Jonson." *TLS,* 18 April 1936, p. 336.

———. "New Light on Ben Jonson's *Discoveries.*" *Englische Studien* 71 (1936–37): 356–59.

Short, R. W. "Jonson's Sanguine Rival." *RES* 15 (1939): 315–17.

———. "Ben Jonson in Drayton's Poems." *RES* 16 (1940): 149–58.

Silvette, Herbert. *The Doctor on the Stage: Medicine and Medical Men in Seventeenth-Century England,* ed. Francelia Butler. 1967.

Simmonds, James. *Masques of God: Form and Theme in the Poetry of Henry Vaughan.* 1972.

Simpson, Evelyn M. "Ben Jonson's *A New-Yeares Gift.*" *RES* 14 (1938): 175–78.

———. "Jonson and Donne: The Problem of Authorship." *RES* 15 (1939): 274–82.

———. "Jonson's Masques: A Rejoinder." *RES* 18 (1942): 291–300.

———. "Jonson and Dickens: A Study in the Comic Genius of London." *E&S* 29 (1943): 82–92.

Simpson, Percy. "Ben Jonson and Richard Greneway." *TLS*, 14 June 1928, p. 450.
———. "Ben Jonson and Cecilia Bulstrode." *TLS*, 6 March 1930, p. 187.
———. "Ben Jonson on Chapman." *TLS*, 3 March 1932, p. 155.
———. "Lucy Countess of Bedford." *TLS*, 8 Oct. 1938, pp. 643–44.
———. "Ben Jonson and the Devil Tavern." *MLR* 34 (1939): 367–73.
———. "'Ben Jonson in Drayton's Poems.'" *RES* 16 (1940): 303–5.
———. "The Problem of Authorship of *Eastward Ho!*" *PMLA* 59 (1944): 715–25.
———. "The Castle of the Rosy Cross: Ben Jonson and Theophilus Schweighardt." *MLR* 41 (1946): 206–7.
Simpson, Percy, and C. F. Bell. *Designs by Inigo Jones for Masques and Plays at Court.* 1924.
Sloan, Thomas O. "A Renaissance Controversialist on Rhetoric: Thomas Wright's *Passions of the Mind in Generall.*" *Speech Monographs* 36 (1969): 38–54.
Smet, Robert de [Romain Sanvic]. *Le théâtre élizabéthain.* 1955.
Smith, Bruce R. "Ben Jonson's *Epigrammes:* Portrait-Gallery, Theater, Commonwealth." *SEL* 14 (1974): 91–109.
Sorelius, Gunnar. *"The Giant Race Before the Flood": Pre-Restoration Drama on the Stage and in the Criticism of the Restoration.* 1966.
Spencer, Theodore. *Death and Elizabethan Tragedy: A Study of Convention and Opinion in the Elizabethan Drama.* 1936.
Starnes, D. T. "Shakespeare and Apuleius." *PMLA* 60 (1945): 1021–50.
———. "The Figure Genius in the Renaissance." *SRen* 11 (1964): 234–44.
Starr, G. A. "Caesar's Just Cause." *SQ* 17 (1966): 77–79.
Stein, Arnold. "Plain Style, Plain Criticism, Plain Dealing, and Ben Jonson." *ELH* 30 (1963): 306–16.
Stoll, E. E. *Poets and Playwrights.* 1930.
Strachan, Michael. *The Life and Adventures of Thomas Coryate.* 1962. [Biography]
Stratman, Carl J. "A Survey of the Huntington Library's Holdings in the Field of English Printed Drama." *HLQ* 24 (1961): 171–73.
Stroup, Thomas B. *Microcosmos: The Shape of the Elizabethan Play.* 1965.
Summers, Joseph H. "The Heritage of Donne and Jonson." *UTQ* 39 (1970): 107–26.
Tabachnick, Stephen E. "Jonson's 'Epitaph on Elizabeth, L. H.'" *Expl* 29 (1971): item 77. [Elizabeth died in pregnancy with an illegitimate child.]
Talbert, Ernest William. "New Light on Ben Jonson's Workmanship." *SP* 40 (1943): 154–85.
Tanner, Lawrence E. "Ben Jonson's Stepfather." *TLS*, 1 April 1926, p. 249.
Tayler, Edward William. *Nature and Art in Renaissance Literature.* 1964.
Taylor, W. "Arabic Words in Ben Jonson." *Leeds Studies in English* 3 (1934): 33–50.
Ten Hoor, George John. "Ben Jonson's Reception in Germany." *PQ* 14 (1935): 327–43.
Thompson, Alan R. *The Dry Mock: A Study of Irony in Drama.* 1948.
Thomson, J. A. K. *The Classical Background of English Literature.* 1948.
———. *Classical Influences on English Poetry.* 1951.
Tillotson, Geoffrey. "*Othello* and *The Alchemist* at Oxford in 1610." *TLS*, 20 July 1933, p. 494.
———. *Essays in Criticism and Research.* 1942.

Tillotson, Kathleen. "'Ben Jonson in Drayton's Poems.'" *RES* 16 (1940): 305–6.

Tomlinson, T. B. *A Study of Elizabethan and Jacobean Tragedy.* 1964.

Tucker, Martin, ed. *The Critical Temper: A Survey of Modern Criticism on English and American Literature from the Beginnings to the Twentieth Century.* Vol. 1. 1969.

Tuve, Rosemond. *Elizabethan and Metaphysical Imagery: Renaissance Poetic and Twentieth-Century Critics.* 1947.

Ure, Peter. "Shakespeare and the Drama of His Time: IV: Jonson and the Satirists." In *A New Companion to Shakespeare Studies,* ed. Kenneth Muir and S. Schoenbaum (1971), pp. 216–18.

Van Den Berg, Sara. "The Play of Wit and Love: Demetrius' *On Style* and Jonson's 'A Celebration of Charis.'" *ELH* 41 (1974): 26–36.

Veevers, E. E. "Sources of Inigo Jones's Masquing Designs." *JWCI* 22 (1959): 373–74.

Velz, John. "Clemency, Will, and Just Cause in *Julius Caesar.*" *ShS* 22 (1969): 109–18.

Venezky, Alice S. *Pageantry on the Shakespearean Stage.* 1951. [Also issued under Griffin, Alice V.]

Wada, Yuichi. *Ben Jonson.* 1963.

Wagner, Bernard M. "A Jonson Allusion, and Others." *PQ* 7 (1928): 306–8.

Waith, Eugene M. *Ideas of Greatness: Heroic Drama in England.* 1971.

Walker, Ralph S. "Ben Jonson's Lyric Poetry." *Criterion* 13 (1934): 430–48.

Wallerstein, Ruth. *Studies in Seventeenth-Century Poetic.* 1950.

Walls, Peter. "Jonson's Borrowing." *Theatre Notebook* 28 (1974): 80–81.

Watson, George. "Ramus, Miss Tuve, and the New Petromachia." *MP* 55 (1958): 259–62.

Wedgwood, Cicely V. *Poetry and Politics under the Stuarts.* 1964.

Wells, Stanley. *Literature and Drama with Special Reference to Shakespeare and His Contemporaries.* 1970.

Welsford, Enid. *The Court Masque: A Study of the Relationship between Poetry and the Revels.* 1927.

―――. *The Fool: His Social and Literary History.* 1935.

Whitaker, Virgil K. *The Mirror up to Nature: The Technique of Shakespeare's Tragedies.* 1965.

White, Harold Ogden. *Plagiarism and Imitation during the English Renaissance.* 1935.

Wickham, Glynne. "Contribution de Ben Jonson et de Dekker aux fêtes du couronnement de Jacques Ier." In *Les fêtes de la renaissance,* ed. Jean Jacquot, vol. 1 (1956), pp. 279–83.

―――. *Early English Stages, 1300–1660.* 2 vols. 1959–72.

Wilder, Malcolm L. "Did Jonson Write 'The Expostulation' Attributed to Donne?" *MLR* 21 (1926): 431–35.

Wilding, Michael. "Jonson, Sin and Milton." *N&Q* 17 (1970): 415.

Williams, Franklin B., Jr. *Index of Dedications and Commendatory Verses.* 1962. [Jonson is indexed s. v. "Johnson"]

Williams, Raymond. "Pastoral and Counter-Pastoral." *CritQ* 10 (1967): 277–90.

Williamson, George. *Seventeenth-Century Contexts.* 1960.

Wilson, Edmund. "A Definitive Edition of Ben Jonson." *New Yorker,* 6 Nov. 1948, pp. 252–54.

Wilson, F. P. "Ben Jonson and Ralph Crane." *TLS*, 8 Nov. 1941, p. 555.
————. *Elizabethan and Jacobean*. 1945.
Wilson, John Dover. "Shakespeare's 'Small Latin'—How Much?" *ShS* 10 (1957): 12–26.
Winters, Yvor. *Forms of Discovery*. 1967.
Young, R. V., Jr. "Style and Structure in Jonson's *Epigrams.*" *Criticism* 17 (1975): 201–22.
Young, Steven C. "A Check List of Tudor and Stuart Induction Plays." *PQ* 48 (1969): 131–34.
Zwager, N. H. M. *Glimpses of Ben Jonson's London*. 1926.

B. INDIVIDUAL PLAYS

The Alchemist

Boas, F. S. "*Othello* and *The Alchemist* at Oxford in 1610." *TLS*, 31 Aug. 1933, p. 576.
Dircks, Richard. "Garrick and Gentleman: Two Interpretations of Abel Drugger," *Restoration and 18th Century Theatre Research* 7, no. 2 (1968): 48–55.
Duncan, Edgar H. "Jonson's Use of Arnald of Villa Nova's *Rosarium.*" *PQ* 21 (1942): 435–38.
Empson, William. "*The Alchemist.*" *Hudson Review* 22 (1969): 595–608.
Hussey, Maurice. "An Oath in *The Alchemist.*" *N&Q* 196 (1951): 433–34.
Leech, Clifford. "Caroline Echoes of *The Alchemist.*" *RES* 16 (1940): 432–38.
Sisson, C. J. "The Magic of Prospero." *ShS* 11 (1958): 70–77.
Summers, Montague. "*The Alchemist* at Oxford." *TLS*, 7 Sept. 1933, p. 592.

Bartholomew Fair

Bennewitz, Fritz. "Der *Bartholomäusmarkt* am Deutschen Nationaltheater Weimar." *SJW* 109 (1973): 40–46.
Symons, Julian, "Ben Jonson as a Social Realist: *Bartholomew Fair.*" *Southern Review* 6 (1940–41): 375–86.
Worsley, T. C. "*Bartholomew Fair.*" *New Statesman and Nation*, 30 Dec. 1950, p. 676.

Epicoene

Boughner, Daniel C. "*Clizia* and *Epicoene.*" *PQ* 19 (1940): 89–91.
D[avenport], A[rnold]. "The Genesis of Jonson's *Epicoene.*" *N&Q* 193 (1948): 55–56.
Sawin, Lewis. "The Earliest Use of 'Autumnal.'" *MLN* 69 (1954): 558–59. [I.i.83–85]

Every Man In and *Every Man Out*

Dutton, A. Richard. "The Significance of Jonson's Revision of *Every Man in His Humour.*" *MLR* 69 (1974): 241–49.

Eliot, S. A. "The Lord Chamberlain's Company as Portrayed in *Every Man out of His Humour." Smith College Studies in Modern Languages* 21 (1940): 64-80.

Sewell, Sallie. "The Relation Between *The Merry Wives of Windsor* and Jonson's *Every Man in His Humour." SAB* 16 (1941): 175-89.

Snuggs, H. L. "Fynes Moryson and Jonson's Puntarvolo." *MLN* 51 (1936): 230-34. [*Every Man Out*]

The New Inn

Frye, Northrop. *A Natural Perspective: The Development of Shakespearean Comedy and Romance.* 1965.

Levin, Richard. "The New *New Inn* and the Proliferation of Good Bad Drama." *Essays in Criticism* 22 (1972): 41-47.

Manwell, B. "The Date of *Love's Pilgrimage* and Its Relation to *The New Inn." SP* 28 (1931): 702-9.

Poetaster

Campbell, Oscar James. "The Dramatic Construction of *Poetaster." Huntington Library Bulletin* 9 (1936): 37-62.

King, A. N. "A Note on the Virgil Translation in *Poetaster* V.ii." *ES* 23 (1941): 75-80.

Zender, Karl F. "The Function of Propertius in Jonson's *Poetaster." Papers on Language and Literature* 11 (1975): 308-12.

Sejanus

Korninger, Siegfried. "Zu Ben Jonson Roemerdrama *Sejanus." Innsbrucker Beitraege zur Kulturwissenschaft* 4 (1955-56): 99-109.

Law, Richard. "*Sejanus* in 'the wolves black jaw.'" *Pennsylvania Council of Teachers of English Bulletin,* 15 (1967), pp. 27-40.

Maxwell, J. C. "The Poems of Herrick?" *N&Q* 2 (1955): 500.

Vawter, Marvin L. "The Seeds of Virtue: Political Imperatives in Jonson's *Sejanus.*" In *Ben Jonson: Quadricentennial Essays,* ed. Mary Olive Thomas; special ed. of *Studies in the Literary Imagination* 6, no. 1 (1973): 41-60.

Staple of News

Goldsworthy, William Lansdown. *Ben Jonson and the First Folio.* 1931. [*Staple of News* and the Baconian heresy]

Jones, Robert C. "Jonson's *Staple of News* Gossips and Fulwell's *Like Will to Like:* 'The Old Way' in a 'New' Morality Play." *Yearbook of English Studies* 3 (1973): 74-77.

Kifer, Devra Rowland. "Too Many Cookes: An Addition to the Printed Version of Jonson's *Staple of Newes." ELN* 11 (1974): 264-71.

McKenzie, D. F. "*The Staple of News* and the Late Plays." In *A Celebration of Ben Jonson,* ed. William Blissett et al. (1973), pp. 83-128.

Parr, Johnstone. "A Note on Jonson's *The Staple of News." MLN* 60 (1945): 117.

Volpone

Anderson, Mark. "Structure and Response in *Volpone.*" *RMS* 19 (1975): 47-71.

Avery, Emmet L. "Two Early London Playbills." *N&Q* 195 (1950): 99.

Aylward, J. D. "*Volpone* at Drury Lane." *N&Q* 195 (1950): 173.

Creaser, John, "The Popularity of Jonson's Tortoise." *RES* 27 (1976): 38-46.

Deniz, Jose A. G. "Aspectos del humor en *Volpone*, de Ben Jonson." *Filologia Moderna* 12 (1972): 281-97.

Drew, David. "*Volpone* Above-Board." *New Statesman*, 28 April 1961, pp. 681-82.

Fizdale, Tay. "Jonson's *Volpone* and the 'Real' Antinous." *Renaissance Quarterly* 26 (1973): 454-59.

Gagen, Jean. *The New Woman: Her Emergence in English Drama, 1600-1730.* 1954.

Hoffmann, Gerhard. "Zur Form der satirischen Komödie: Ben Jonsons *Volpone.*" *Deutsche Vierteljahrsschrift für Literaturwissenschaft und Geistesgeschichte* 46 (1972): 1-27.

Levin, Richard. "Some Second Thoughts on Central Themes." *MLR* 67 (1972): 1-10.

Lyle, Alexander. "Volpone's Two Worlds." *Yearbook of English Studies* 4 (1974): 70-76.

Miller, Joyce. "*Volpone*: A Study of Dramatic Ambiguity." In *Studies in English Language and Literature*, ed. Alice Shalvi and A. A. Mendilow, Scripta Hieroslymitana, Publications of the Hebrew University 17 (1966): pp. 35-95.

Noyes, Robert Gale. "*Volpone; or, The Fox*—The Evolution of a Nickname." *Harvard Studies and Notes in Philology and Literature* 16 (1934): 161-75.

Ornstein, Robert. "The Ethical Design of *The Revenger's Tragedy.*" *ELH* 21 (1954): 81-93.

Parfitt, George A. E. "Some Notes on the Classical Borrowings in *Volpone.*" *ES* 55 (1974): 127-32.

Perkinson, Richard H. "*Volpone* and the Reputation of Venetian Justice." *MLR* 35 (1940): 11-18.

Whiting, George W. "*Volpone*, Herr Von Fuchs and *Les Heritiers Rabourdin.*" *PMLA* 46 (1931): 605-7.

Others

Bennett, Josephine Waters. "Britain among the Fortunate Isles." *SP* 53 (1956): 114-40. [*The Fortunate Isles and their Union*]

Bergeron, David M. "Harrison, Jonson and Dekker: The Magnificent Entertainment for King James (1604)." *JWCI* 31 (1968): 445-48.

Blair, F. G. "The Costume of Gypsies in the Masque." *Journal of the Gypsy Lore Society* 33 (1954): 74-75. [*The Gypsies Metamorphosed*]

Boddy, Margaret. "A Reading in Jonson's *Oberon.*" *M&Q* 18 (1971): 29.

Chan, Mary. "*Cynthia's Revels* and Music for a Choir School: Christ Church Manuscript Mus 439." *SRen* 18 (1971): 134-72.

Duncan, Edgar H. "The Alchemy in Jonson's *Mercury Vindicated.*" *SP* 39 (1942): 625-37.

Fabian, Bernhard. "'Cynthia' in the O.E.D." *N&Q* 6 (1959): 356.

Falls, Cyril. "Penelope Rich and the Poets: Philip Sidney to John Ford." EDH 28 (1956): 123–37. [*Mask of Blackness*]

Gilbert, Allan H. "The Function of the Masques in *Cynthia's Revels*." *PQ* 22 (1943): 211–30.

Horwich, Richard. "*Hamlet* and *Eastward Ho*." *SEL* 11 (1971): 223–33.

Lambrechts, Guy. "*Love's Labour's Lost* et *The Case Is Altered*." *Recherches Anglaises et Américaines* 4 (1971): 130–40.

Mackin, Cooper. "The Satiric Technique of John Oldham's *Satyrs upon the Jesuits*." *SP* 62 (1965): 78–90. [*Catiline*]

Mills, Laurens J. *One Soul in Bodies Twain: Friendship in Tudor Literature and Stuart Drama.* 1937. [*The Case Is Altered*]

Nevo, Ruth. "The Masque of Greatness." *Shakespeare Studies* 3 (1967): 111–28. [*Hymenaei*]

O'Donnell, Norbert F. "The Authorship of *The Careless Shepherdess*." *PQ* 33 (1954): 43–47. [*The Sad Shepherd*]

Potter, Russell. "Three Jacobean Devil Plays." *SP* 28 (1931): 730–36. [*Devil Is an Ass*]

Sheringham, G. *Design in the Theatre.* 1927. [*Devil Is an Ass*]

Tannenbaum, Samuel A. "A Note on *The Gypsies Metamorphosed*." *PMLA* 47 (1932): 909–10.

Thompson, W. L. "The Sources of the Flower Passage in *Lycidas*." *N&Q* 197 (1952): 97–99. [*Pan's Anniversary*]

Urban, Raymond. "The Somerset Affair, the Belvoir Witches, and Jonson's Pastoral Comedies." *Harvard Library Bulletin* 23 (1975): 295–323. [*The Sad Shepherd*]

Whistler, Laurence. *The Masque of Christmas: Dramatic Joys of the Festival.* 1947. [*Christmas His Masque*]

C. TEXTUAL STUDIES

Bowers, Fredson T. *On Editing Shakespeare and the Elizabethan Dramatists.* 1955.

Brettle, R. E. "*Eastward Ho*, 1605, by Chapman, Jonson, and Marston: Bibliography, and Circumstances of Production." *Library* 9 (1928–29): 287–302, with a Note by W. W. Greg, pp. 303–4.

Davis, Herbert. "Note on a Cancel in *The Alchemist*, 1612." *Library* 13 (1958): 278–80.

Davis, Tom. "Ben Jonson's 'Ode to Himself': An Early Version." *PQ* 51 (1972): 410–21.

DeVocht, Henry. *Comments on the Text of Ben Jonson's "Every Man Ovt of His Hvmovr."* 1937.

Feather, John. "Some Notes on the Setting of Quarto Plays." *Library* 27 (1972): 237–44.

Ford, H. L. *Collation of the Ben Jonson Folios, 1616-31–1642.* 1932.

Greg, W. W. "The Riddle of Ben Jonson's Chronology." *Library* 6 (1926): 340–47.

———. "Thomas Walkley and the Ben Jonson *Works* of 1640." *Library* 11 (1931): 461–65.

———. "Text of *The Gypsies Metamorphosed*." *PMLA* 49 (1934): 963.

———. *The Editorial Problem in Shakespeare.* 1942.

Howard-Hill, T. H. "Towards a Jonson Concordance: A Discussion of Texts and Problems." *RORD* 15-16 (1972-73): 17-32.

Hunter, G. K. "The Marking of *Sententiae* in Elizabethan Printed Plays, Poems, and Romances." *Library* 6 (1951): 171-88.

Jewkes, Wilfred T. *Act Division in Elizabethan and Jacobean Plays, 1583-1616.* 1958.

Maas, P. "Notes on the Text of Jonson's Masques." *RES* 18 (1942): 464-65.

McAvoy, William C. "The Year's Contribution to English Renaissance Textual Study." *Manuscripta* 13 (1969): 12-31. [*Epicoene*]

McIlwraith, A. K. "The Press-Corrections in Jonson's *The King's Entertainment.*" *Library* 24 (1944): 181-86.

Marcham, Frank. "Thomas Walkley and the Ben Jonson *Works* of 1640." *Library* 11 (1931): 225-29.

Merchant, Paul. "Another Misprint in *Epicoene?*" *Library* 27 (1972): 326.

Simpson, Evelyn. "The Folio Text of Ben Jonson's *Sejanus.*" *Anglia* 49 (1937): 398-415.

Whiting, George W. "The Hoe-Huntington Folio of Jonson." *MLN* 48 (1933): 537-38.

D. EDITIONS

Single-Work Editions

Alston, R. C., ed. *The English Grammar (From "The Works"), 1640.* 1972.

Bamborough, J. B., ed. *The Alchemist.* 1967.

Brockbank, Philip, ed. *Volpone.* 1968.

Donaldson, Ian, ed. *Ben Jonson: Poems.* 1975.

Duncan, Ronald, ed. *Poems by Ben Jonson.* 1949.

Friesel, Uwe, trans. *Volpone.* 1971.

Kingsford, R. J. L., ed. *The Alchemist.* 1958.

Knox, R. S., ed. *Every Man in His Humour.* 2nd ed. 1965.

Levin, Harry, ed. *Ben Jonson: Selected Works.* 1939.

McCollum, John I., Jr. *The Alchemist.* 1965.

Moussy, Marcel, adapter. *L'alchimiste: comedie en cinq actes.* 1962.

Parfitt, George A. E., ed. *Ben Jonson: Complete Poems.* 1976.

Petter, C. G., ed. *Eastward Ho!* 1973.

Praz, Mario, trans. *Volpone.* 1943.

Romains, Jules, and Stefan Zweig, adapters. *Volpone, d'après Ben Jonson.* 1965.

Sale, Arthur, ed. *Every Man in His Humour.* 3rd ed., rev., 1968.

———, ed. *The Alchemist.* 1969.

Tasis, Rafael, adapter. *Volpone.* 1957.

Zweig, Stefan, adapter. *Ben Jonsons "Volpone": Eine lieblose Komödie in drei Akten.* 1950.

Anthologies

Bald, R. C., ed. *Six Elizabethan Plays (1585-1635).* 1963. [*Epicoene*]

Baker, Herschel, ed. *The Later Renaissance in England: Nondramatic Verse and Prose, 1600-1660.* 1975.

Baskervill, Charles R., et al. *Elizabethan and Stuart Plays.* 1934. [*The Alchemist, Every Man In, The Sad Shepherd, Sejanus, Volpone*]

Gassner, John, ed. *Four Great Elizabethan Plays.* 1960. [*Volpone*]

Harrier, Richard C., ed. *Jacobean Drama: An Anthology.* Vol. 1, 1963. [*Every Man In*]

Hogan, Robert, and Sven Eric Molin, eds. *Drama: The Major Genres.* 1962. [*Epicoene*]

Hussey, Maurice, ed. *Jonson and the Cavaliers.* 1964.

Huston, J. Dennis, and Alvin B. Kernan, eds. *Classics of the Renaissance Theater.* 1969. [*Volpone*]

Kenner, Hugh, ed. *Seventeenth-Century Poetry: The Schools of Donne and Jonson.* 1964.

Maclean, Hugh, ed. *Ben Jonson and the Cavalier Poets: Authoritative Texts, Criticism, Selections.* 1975.

Messiaen, Pierre, trans. *Théâtre anglais, moyen âge et XVIe siècle: Anonymes, Marlowe, Dekker, Heywood, Ben Jonson, Webster, Tourneur.* 1948.

Morrell, Janet M., ed. *Four English Comedies.* 1950. [*Volpone*]

Nethercot, Arthur, et al., eds. *Stuart Plays.* 1971. [*Every Man In, Sejanus, Volpone, The Alchemist, The Sad Shepherd, The Hue and Cry after Cupid*]

Ornstein, Robert, and Hazelton Spencer, eds. *Elizabethan and Jacobean Comedy: An Anthology.* 1966 [*Every Man In, The Alchemist*]

Praz, Mario, ed. *Teatro Elisabettiano: Kyd, Marlowe, Heywood, Marston, Jonson, Webster, Tourneur, Ford.* 1948.

Salgādo, Gāmini, ed. *Four Jacobean City Comedies.* 1975. [*The Devil Is an Ass*]

Schelling, Felix, ed. *Five Plays by Ben Jonson.* World's Classics. 1953.

Szenczi, Miklós József, ed. *Angol Reneszánsz Drámák.* 1961. [*Volpone, Bartholomew Fair*]

Weimann, Robert, ed. *Dramen der Shakespearezeit.* 1964. [*Volpone*]

Wine, M. L., ed. *Drama of the English Renaissance.* 1969. [*Volpone, The Mask of Blackness*]

GEORGE CHAPMAN

Terence P. Logan

The standard edition of the comedies is *The Plays of George Chapman: The Comedies*, Allan Holaday general editor (1970). When completed this will replace the earlier standard, Thomas Marc Parrott's *The Plays of George Chapman: The Tragedies*, 2 vols. (1910), and *The Comedies*, 2 vols. (1913). Phyllis Brooks Bartlett, ed., *The Poems of George Chapman* (1941), and Allardyce Nicoll, ed., *Chapman's Homer*, 2 vols. (1956), are standard for the nondramatic works.

I. GENERAL

A. BIOGRAPHICAL

The first two chapters of Millar MacLure's *George Chapman: A Critical Study* (1966) summarize the known facts of Chapman's life and trace his early intellectual development. There is no firm evidence of Chapman having attended a university. His early manhood probably included service in Sir Ralph Sadler's household and with the army in the Low Countries. The dedication of his first poem, *The Shadow of Night* (1594), to Matthew Royden and possible allusions in other works have resulted in attempts to link Chapman to the Raleigh faction. MacLure concludes there is "no satisfying substance" to these conjectures. After working for Henslowe, Chapman became an independent playwright; the Chapel, Paul's and Queen's Revels companies performed his plays. An appointment as tutor to Prince Henry gave Chapman the means and leisure to start translating Homer; the Prince's death, on 12 November 1612, ended the only period of financial security in Chapman's life. The few records of his later years are all concerned with legal and financial problems. MacLure sees Chapman as an eccentric, a great melancholic, and especially as a man who "did not deserve his difficulties."

The presentation of the life in Jean Jacquot's *George Chapman (1559-1634): Sa vie, sa poésie, son théâtre, sa pensée* (1951) is more detailed than that in MacLure. Jacquot includes extensive material about Chapman's family, his connections with contemporary writers and court figures, and a full list of contemporary allusions to Chapman. The footnotes indicate virtually all of the available material, including legends and pseudo-scholarship. The accounts of Chapman's relations with the Grimeston family and his sources of French history are especially authoritative. The TEAS *George Chapman* (1967), by Charlotte Spivack, and Havelock Ellis's book of the same title (1934) are general surveys which include biographies.

In "Chapman's Early Years," *SP* 43 (1946): 176-93, Mark Eccles reconfirms Chapman's early connection with Sir Ralph Sadler, gives evidence of a trip abroad in 1585, and outlines dealings with the usurer John Wolfall which led to Chapman's arrest in 1600. Jean Robertson, "The Early Life of George Chapman," *MLR* 40 (1945): 157-65, adds information about the Sadler and Wolfall connections and advances a conjecture on Chapman's education. Chapman's legal involvements with the heirs of his sometime benefactor Henry Jones and the related Chancery actions are discussed by C. J. Sisson and Robert Butman in "George Chapman, 1612-1622: Some New Facts," *MLR* 46 (1951): 85-90. These court actions may have forced Chapman to retire to Hitchin from 1614 until 1619 and thus obliged him to stop writing for the theaters. Sisson describes other legal actions involving Chapman in connection with his reconstruction of *The Old Joiner of Aldgate* in *Lost Plays of Shakespeare's Age* (1936).

There is extensive conjecture about Chapman's possible relations with Shakespeare. In *Shakespeare and the Rival Poet* (1903) and *Shakespeare's Sonnet Story* (1922), Arthur Acheson advances a case for Chapman as the rival poet of Shakespeare's sonnets. In contrast, G. Legman, "'Ever or Never,'" *N&Q* 2 (1955): 361, sees Chapman as a member of an anti-Shakespeare cabal with his title as its motto. G. Wilson Knight, *The Mutual Flame* (1955) and "Shakespeare's Sonnets," *TLS*, 26 Dec. 1963, p. 1072, reads selected works as proof of a homosexual involvement between Chapman and Shakespeare. In *An Introduction to the Sonnets of Shakespeare* (1964), John Dover Wilson, admitting that the evidence is only circumstantial, concludes that Chapman is clearly the rival poet. Marlow's claims are advanced and Chapman's rejected by Lawrence Durrell in "The Rival Poet," *TLS*, 5

Jan. 1951, p. 7; under the same title, *TLS*, 2 Feb. 1951, p. 69, Clara Longworth de Chambrun rejects some of Durrell's evidence but supports his conclusion. Henry David Gray, "Shakespeare's Rival Poet," *JEGP* 47 (1948): 365-73, dismisses Chapman's claims in favor of Spenser's. Selected lines in *Love's Labour's Lost* and Shakespeare's nondramatic poems parallel Chapman's *School of Night* and reveal Shakespeare's continuing resentment of his fellow poet, according to W. Schrickx, "Shakespeare and the School of Night: An Estimate and Further Interpretation," *Neophil* 34 (1950): 35-44. The supposed allusions in *Love's Labour's Lost*, which are central to Schrickx's argument, are dismissed in an earlier essay by E. A. Strathmann, "Textual Evidence for 'The School of Night,'" *MLN* 56 (1941): 176-86; there probably was no school. While there is no solid evidence of Chapman's connections with Shakespeare, the frequent conjectures have resulted in Chapman receiving at least passing attention in discussions of Shakespeare's life and sonnets.

M. C. Bradbrook discusses Chapman's possible relations with Raleigh in *The School of Night* (1936). Her readings, especially of the nondramatic poetry, add levels of political allegory. Chapman's less elusive ties with Ben Jonson are the subject of Robert Boies Sharpe's "Jonson's 'Execration' and Chapman's 'Invective': Their Place in Their Authors' Rivalry," *SP* 42 (1945): 555-63. Sharpe rejects Phyllis Bartlett's suggestion (in the notes to her edition of the poems) that Chapman's discovery of Jonson's marginal criticisms in a copy of *The Whole Works of Homer* was directly responsible for the satire of the "Invective"; time, and Chapman's sense of failure in his professional rivalry with Jonson, resulted in a gradual ending of their friendship. H. W. Crundell, "Chapman and the Grevilles," *N&Q* 185 (1943): 137, and 189 (1945): 213, discusses Chapman's possible acquaintance with a son of Katherine Greville Reed. Allardyce Nicoll's "The Dramatic Portrait of George Chapman," *PQ* 41 (1962): 215-28, finds Bellamont in Dekker and Webster's *Northward Ho* "a full-length portrait" of Chapman; there are also clear allusions to Chapman's *Old Joiner of Aldgate, Caesar and Pompey, All Fools*, the Byron plays, and a lost play about Astynax. Fleay's hesitation when he originally made the identification was unwarranted; "its certainty is beyond question." In articles dating the canon (III, A), Elias Schwartz and Robert Ornstein respectively accept and reject the Bellamont identification.

B. GENERAL STUDIES OF THE PLAYS

Millar MacLure's *George Chapman* (1966) is the best comprehensive consideration. MacLure presents Chapman as "a divided man" whose thought and art develop along irregular lines. Ennis Rees and others who force the Chapman corpus into a single schema "have made a falsely homogeneous and sad hash of him." The early works characteristically combine Chapman's "capacity of seeing both sides" with his "incapacity in forming a synthesis of the elements of his divided imagination." The poetry and the plays are not as consistent as most earlier criticism assumes; "all of Chapman's critical data are occasional" and therefore of limited value for explication. More attention should be given to Chapman's experimentation with forms and his exploitation of popular interests in his selection of subject matter. His notorious obscurity reflects "the complexity of imperfection rather than of profundity." Within these limits, Chapman holds a personal philosophy. *Tears of Peace* is "the centre of Chapman's thought and the clue to his inner life"; his definition of learning as "soul-craft, self-making, not an infusion of grace" is found there. *Tears* also "undoubtedly marks the transition from Chapman's admiration of the Achillean virtues to his glorification of the inward powers in Odysseus, or from Bussy and Byron to Clermont, or from wisdom as the initiation into *mysteria* to wisdom as the *habit* of self-discipline and virtue." This transition, however, was gradual and complicated; there is no "clear line of development passing comfortably from the Achillean to the Ulyssean ideal."

MacLure's assessment of the plays is consistent with his larger impressions of Chapman. The comedies contain "no vision of a total social harmony." While often poorly structured, they have genuine stylistic grace and the humor can be extremely effective. "Chapman's tragedies are not just political moralities"; they are eminently dramatic in conception and often experiment with popular forms and conventions. However, they are frequently impaired by a "pedantic insistence upon preconceived propositions . . . at war with an imagination which responds to all magnificence, and to the paradoxes of human power and knowledge." Chapman is an "orator and emblemist" who gradually became "a minor prophet, narrow and intense, with an unresonant message." The corpus develops an increasing constriction of imaginative power, a related movement toward intolerance, and a preoccupation "with his integrity as an end in itself." Chapman's typical style involves "the 'evincing' of a limited number of propositions, by a rhetorical elaboration designed to image them as monumental, in their true magnitude and 'composure,' which is an 'outward' or affirmatory process, and the 'inward' wrestling with images marking the 'struggle for birth' of the 'genuine formes' of the poet's 'hid soule,' 'under the clawes of this fowle Panther earth.'" MacLure closes his study by observing that he is himself struck "by how much of it is qualification, reduction."

Jean Jacquot, in *George Chapman* (1951), sees a much closer relationship between Chapman's philosophy and his writing than does MacLure. Jacquot presents detailed formulations of Chapman's Neoplatonism, Stoicism, and humanism, including discussions of the likely sources. Chapman is seen as a frequent partisan and polemicist of court factions; much of his work can be read, at least in part, as contemporary political allegory. The tragedies receive respectful treatment but "Chapman est un auteur comique de second plan." The sections concerned with Chapman's knowledge of French history and his use of it in the tragedies are especially authoritative. Jacquot allows for changes and a gradual evolution of Chapman's thought; as a dramatist, Chapman ranks just below Marlowe in accomplishment. Appendixes argue for the inclusion of *Charlemagne* and at least a first draft of *Histriomastix* in the canon. There is also a useful historical survey of Chapman's critical reputation, and a bibliography.

George Chapman (1967), by Charlotte Spivack, is directed to less specialized readers. The survey of Chapman's thought is less detailed than those in MacLure and Jacquot. Her critical estimation is usually markedly more favorable. Chapman's "plays—particularly the comedies—seem written by natural instinct rather than by will" and he is "one of the real masters of dramatic craftsmanship." The comedies equal those of Jonson and Middleton; the tragedies compare equally well with others of the period. The nondramatic poems are absolved of the customary charge of obscurity; rather, they have "exceptional clarity" and any apparent difficulty is simply the result of the passage of time. In contrast to MacLure's "qualification, reduction," Spivack rates Chapman a consistent philosopher, an important poet, and an Elizabethan playwright "who would have been great even if Shakespeare had never lived."

Forme e motivi nelle poesie e nelle tragedie di George Chapman (1957), by Marcello Pagnini, places Chapman in the metaphysical tradition. Chapman's unique contribution to Elizabethan drama was his incorporation of the "gusto del poema epico" in his tragedies. The influence of the Homerica and of humanistic philosophy on the tragedies is outlined. A stylistic analysis concludes that obvious energy is the dominant characteristic. The bibliography includes theses. Franck L. Schoell's *Études sur l'humanisme continental en Angleterre* (1926) traces Chapman's debts to the humanists, especially Ficino, Comes, Gyraldus, Erasmus, Spondanus, and Hieronymous Wolfius. The conclusions give insights into Chapman's methods of composition. Three earlier articles by Schoell—"George Chapman and the Italian Neo-Latinists of the Quattrocento," *MP* 13 (1915): 215-38; "G. Chapman's 'Commonplace Book,'" *MP* 17 (1919): 199-218; and "Les emprunts de George Chapman à Marsile Ficin," *RLC* 3 (1923): 17-35—contain material developed more fully in the book. A more conservative estimate of Chapman's use of Ficino is given by Roderick S. Wallace in "Chapman's Debt to Ficino," *N&Q* 17 (1970): 402-3.

Chapman's artistic accomplishment is reassessed, on the basis of a balanced view of the entire corpus, by Robert K. Presson in "Wrestling with This World: A View of George Chapman," *PMLA* 84 (1969): 44-50. In all the works there is a pervasive faith and "a kind of optimism. . . . Chapman never fails to assert the necessity to be good." Emil Koeppel's *Quellen-studien zu Dramen George Chapmans, Philip Massingers, und John Fords* (1897) considers problems of canon, dating, and sources; sections are abstracted in the Parrott edition's introductions to individual plays. "'Übermensch und treue,' zur unstrittenen Entwicklung von George Chapmans Drama," by Richard Gerber, *Anglia* 76 (1958): 510-35, traces patterns of intellectual development revealed in the corpus. There is a striking transition from amoral cynicism in the early plays to the pervasive, bitter, moral cynicism of the later ones. Wilfred T. Jewkes, *Act Division in Elizabethan and Jacobean Plays, 1583-1616* (1958), surveys Chapman's structural practice. Thomas B. Stroup considers the structure and aims of the plays in *Microcosmos* (1965). An earlier appreciative study, Algernon Charles Swinburne's *George Chapman* (1875), accuses Chapman of attempting "to bring to perfection the qualities of crabbed turgidity and barbarous bombast"; the "pure and lucid style" of the better comedies is Chapman's greatest strength.

The Tragedies of George Chapman: Renaissance Ethics in Action (1954), by Ennis Rees, maintains as its central thesis that the "poems, plays, and translations written over a period of thirty years are nothing if not consistent in doctrine and intention." In the nondramatic poetry, without the constricting influence of dramatic conventions, Chapman "felt free to give his ideas their most explicit and analytic expression."

Three central concepts—Chapman's definition of learning and his related sense of a conflict between reason and passion, Neoplatonism and its philosophy of love, and the opposition of justice and policy—are the keys to reading Chapman. His moral vision was also deeply influenced by his work of translating Homer. Later chapters trace the effects of these elements on the tragedies. Bussy and Byron are "Achillean protagonists" who demonstrate the tragic limitations of greatness without virtue; Chapman has only limited sympathy for them. Clermont, Cato, and Chabot possess Chapman's ideal virtue which is "largely dependent upon the degree of unworldliness in a man." The heroes of the tragedies are either monitory or exemplary types and the didactic method of each play is determined by the type of its protagonist. The tragedies "represent a fine poetic effort to embody a philosophic ideal in art that would outlast brass and marble." Rees regularly invokes "irony" to resolve cruxes which threaten the pattern; he presents Chapman as an ethical philosopher who uses literature to gain converts.

Much subsequent scholarship qualifies and redirects Rees's arguments. Robert Ornstein, *The Moral Vision of Jacobean Tragedy* (1960), accuses Rees of oversimplifying. Ornstein offers a significantly less unified Chapman who is "intellectual in his ethics but anti-intellectual in his religion." The tragedies are more concerned with political philosophy than with individual morality; they can all be read as variations on the single theme of the conflict between a virtuous and at least potentially noble hero and a corrupt society. Chapman was intrigued by the ethical implications of Machiavelli's vision of man and society which had obvious relations to his own belief in the progressive decay of natural man in an artificial and hostile social environment. The tragedies look backward to "ancient moral values" and bemoan the perils of attempting to preserve them in modern states where policy has absolute dominance. All the tragedies "attempt to integrate melodrama and moral intention." The latter becomes progressively more important and the "last plays are upright Moralities, noble in thought and sentiment, but only incidently or coincidently dramatic in conception." His ethical bias was Chapman's chief limitation as a dramatist; "because he had more integrity and independence of purpose than creative sense of the theatre, other Jacobeans could respect and admire his plays but learn or borrow little from them." The tragic corpus should be "studied as a continuum" to understand the gradual evolution of Chapman's ethical ideals.

In *Jacobean Tragedy: The Quest for Moral Order* (1962), Irving Ribner rates Chapman "the most deliberately didactic tragedian of his age." His heroes personify various allegorical values; these are often multiple, with frequent shifts of emphasis. Characters are also used as dramatically neutral choric commentators. The several functions of the *personae* are not always consistent and the reader has to shift to accommodate the various levels of meaning. Ribner agrees with Elias Schwartz (III,A, *Byron*) that Chapman's ethical allegory is not consistent through the corpus; a distinct change in his thinking occurs around the time of the Byron plays. Ethical purpose, which creates artistic problems, is central to all of the tragedies; Chapman "found it difficult to adapt his concept of the dramatist's high philosophical mission to the requirements of the popular stage."

Jean Jacquot's book (I,A) sees a conflict between spirit and matter as the central theme of all the tragedies. Chapman defends royal authority, national unity, and interior peace; at the same time, he stresses the obligations of the monarch to the subject and the individual's freedom of conscience. Their protagonists shaped by these theses, the plays are more learned than popular. Jacquot again considers Chapman's tragedies in "Les tragédies de Sénèque et le théâtre élisabéthain," *EA* 14 (1961): 343-44. MacLure's responses are more guarded: the tragedies are artificial, but they reflect a strong imaginative vision. Chapman never realized "that the tragic experience is rooted in the rhythms of nature"; his tragedies, instead, move "to the rhythms, sometimes in harmony, sometimes in discord, of dialectic and vision." Charlotte Spivack finds that the heroes of the tragedies are either "Herculean Heroes" or "Senecal Saints." The shift in the conception of the protagonists is paralleled by a shift in technical emphasis; in the latter group "plot develops vertically through illustration rather than horizontally through complication."

Peter Ure, "Chapman's Tragedies," in *Jacobean Theatre*, SuAS, vol. 1 (1960), pp. 226-47, holds that there is more in the tragedies "than meets the eye of the moralist and ironist." The paradoxes apparent in several protagonists, especially Bussy, are resolved by postulating double vision and deliberate ambivalence on Chapman's part. Chapman's unit of composition is the long speech which is often "a complete 'poem' in itself"; he has, however, a keen awareness of the requirements of the stage and his plot structures are especially solid. Considering the full corpus, "the effect as of a long *decrescendo* cannot be overcome." There is a shift from an early emphasis on character to a greater stress on heroic ideals. "The final impression left by these tragedies might be that they are the work of a man who grew to be one of nature's academicians, resisting his age more than he explored it; and it is true that Chapman, although unusually learned, did not resemble Donne or Bacon in being unusually intelligent as well." Ure's "Chapman as Translator and Tragic Playwright," in *The Age of Shakespeare* (1955; vol. 2 of the Pelican *Guide to English Literature*, ed. Boris Ford), pp. 318-33, is a more general treatment.

George Chapman: The Effect of Stoicism upon His Tragedies, by John W. Wieler (1949), treats the sources of Chapman's Stoicism and its increasing importance in the tragedies. *Bussy* contains little that is distinctly Stoic; by the time of *The Revenge*, however, Chapman has a "thoroughgoing comprehension of Stoic doctine," and "Stoicism continued as a living and growing force upon Chapman's art until finally the artist and the philosophy of Stoicism often seemed to become one." Since the influence increased in a regular pattern, the quantity and sophistication of Stoic elements can be used to determine the composition dates of most of the tragedies; they are also valid tests to resolve questions of uncertain authorship. Unfortunately, the Stoic influence was not entirely positive: "As the playwright adapts Stoicism more and more to his dramatic purposes, his art exhibits a proportionate decline in tragic power that results finally in the negation of tragedy." Two articles by Michael Higgins supplement Wieler. "Chapman's 'Senecal Man,'" *RES* 21 (1945): 183-91, finds the tragedies considering large problems of fundamental justice in a manner determined by "the spirit of classical republicanism." Chapman uses Stoic, particularly Senecan, principles to resolve moral issues. In the process, he fully reveals "the defects of the Stoic system of moral psychology." His Stoic heroes, especially Clermont, are proud, indifferent, essentially inhuman, and rarely credible. Higgins's "The Development of the 'Senecal Man,'" *RES* 23 (1947): 24-33, traces the blending of Christian and Senecan elements in a character type which first appears in George Buchanan's *Jephthes* (1542); Chapman is experimenting with the type as early as *The Gentleman Usher*.

Roy Battenhouse, "Chapman and the Nature of Man," *ELH* 12 (1945): 87-107; rpt. in *Elizabethan Drama: Modern Essays in Criticism*, ed. Ralph J. Kaufmann (1961), pp. 104-12, describes Chapman as "a syncretist of classical and Christian thought, assimilating the two in such a way as generally to blur over historical and theological distinctions." Chapman's view of man is Hellenistic, rather than Christian. His heroes, often based on mythological prototypes, are all "either slaves of passion or exemplars of calm." Man has both a secular or natural life under the sway of fate and a divine life under Providence. Finally, Chapman "believes man sure to be outwardly beaten, since world calamity is irresistible and inescapable." *Die philosophisch-poetische Entwicklung George Chapmans: Ein Versuch zur Interpretation seines Werkes* (1939), by Nancy von Pogrell, traces the transition from Chapman's early Platonism to the Stoicism of the later works. Peter Ure's "On Some Differences between Senecan and Elizabethan Tragedy," *DUJ* 10 (1948): 17-23, describes Chapman's experiments with Stoicism and the Senecan mode. In "Chapman's Stoicism," *LHR* 9 (1967): 8-15, Marvin J. LaHood decides that "Chapman's Stoicism was Senecan" and offers a pattern of its development. Hardin Craig, "Ethics in the Jacobean Drama: The Case of Chapman," in *Essays in Dramatic Literature: The Parrott Presentation Volume*, ed. Hardin Craig (1935), pp. 25-46, and in *The Enchanted Glass* (1936), ranks Chapman as "one of the leaders of the metaphysical school of poets"; the essay sees him as "the first great writer of the tragedy of passion, of psychological titanism."

Chapman's political thought is the subject of K. M. Burton's "The Political Tragedies of Chapman and Ben Jonson," *Essays in Criticism* 2 (1952): 397-412. Neither writes Aristotelian tragedy; they are, instead, "concerned with the tragic flaw *within the social order*, not within the individual." Chapman holds the moral failures of kings responsible for universal decay; in most of his tragedies "a king is depicted as the propagator of evil through society." This failure at the top results in a world which is hostile to true nobility, and men of worth must be either corrupted or destroyed. Charles Kennedy, "Political Theory in the Plays of George Chapman," in *Essays in Dramatic Literature*, ed. Hardin Craig (1935), pp. 73-86, finds political theory is the chief interest of the later plays. "We have nowhere in Jacobean Drama any expression of political philosophy as definite as Chapman's, and nowhere outside the drama any movement of which he may be considered the exponent." There are four areas of special concern: "the nature of a true ruler, the nature of an upright citizen, the obligation of a prince to his people, and the duties of a subject to his prince." The "inherent injustice of men" makes government necessary. Chapman, with an obvious debt to *The Republic*, maintains that the ideal citizen has a divided loyalty, "first to justice and honor, then to sovereign." Chapman's sophisticated sense of history is analyzed by G. R. Hibbard, "George Chapman: Tragedy and the Providential View of History," *ShS* 20 (1967): 27-31. Shakespeare and Chapman, alone of the dramatists of the period, share a sense that "many of the great conflicts of history arise, not out of the clash of right with wrong, but of right with right." Also, Chapman's fundamental Neoplatonism enabled him "to transcend the limitations that his adoption of the providential view of history would otherwise have set to his tragic writings."

Several recent studies reject the use of philosophical systems to explicate the tragedies. Edwin Muir's "'Royal Man,' Notes on the Tragedies of George Chapman," *Orion* 2 (1945): 95-100; rpt. in his *Essays on Literature and Society* (1949; rev. ed. 1965), pp. 22-32, suggests that Chapman is "an erratic moralist"; frequently, "we cannot even guess at the standard by which he judges the action." His heroes are Marlovian and move in pre-lapsarian worlds. Chapman values greatness in states of crisis and "pays little attention to goodness." In *A Study of Elizabethan and Jacobean Tragedy* (1964), T. B. Tomlinson charges Chapman with mesmerizing critics with pretensions of "both complexity and depth of meaning." His intellectual claims rest on nothing more than his syntactical indirectness, "academic philosophizing," and vague ideals. Stripped of surface ornament, the plays are simple and Chapman is exposed as "merely a well-intentioned bore." G. R. Hibbard, "Goodness and Greatness: An Essay on the Tragedies of Ben Jonson and George Chapman," *RMS* 11 (1967): 5-54, finds that there is an increasingly imperfect understanding of the genre on the part of both playwrights; "Chapman never wrote a single tragedy which is an unqualified artistic success." Another comparative study, "Chapman and Marlowe: The Paradoxical Hero and the Divided Response," *JEGP* 68 (1969): 391-406, by Sidney R. Homan, contends that the two critical terms in its title "most clearly apply" to Chapman's work, not Marlowe's.

Alfred Harbage, in *Shakespeare and the Rival Traditions* (1952), sees little specifically Christian morality in the plays. Some of the critical confusion about Chapman results from a failure to see that he is capable of feeling strong admiration "for passions bred in the blood" when he is not consciously moralizing. In *Ideas of Greatness: Heroic Drama in England* (1971), Eugene M. Waith studies the tragedies as "attempts to dramatize various heroic ideals." *The Golden Labyrinth* (1962), by G. Wilson Knight, restates his contention (I,A) that there is "a homosexual strain" in Chapman's work; further, it argues that Chapman's view of human nature is ultimately optimistic. Frederic de Heeckeren traces Chapman's development of the ideal man who is his own king through the five tragedies based on French history in

"Chapman et les pieces d'actualité francaise," in *Le théâtre élizabé-thain* (a special issue of *CS* 10 [1933] : 175-82; rpt. with additions 1940, pp. 226-35). There is a short, but suggestive, discussion of the tragedies in Madeleine Doran's *Endeavors of Art: A Study of Form in Elizabethan Drama* (1954), and Chapman's influence on Webster is studied in the first chapter of Travis Bogard's *The Tragic Satire of John Webster* (1955). Allen Bergson, "The Ironic Tragedies of Marston and Chapman: Notes on Jacobean Tragic Form," *JEGP* 69 (1970): 613-30, classifies Chapman's early tragedies as "ironic"; "it seems a major assumption of ironic tragedy that any involvement in the world means involvement in limiting or corrupting activity." Chapman was a polem-icist for a decadent court and his plays express "a massive negativism in rational terms in order to show the complete futility of attempting to do anything at all," according to Leonard Goldstein, "George Chapman and the Decadence in Early Seventeenth-Century Drama," *Science and Society* 27 (1963): 23-48. Louis C. Stagg surveys image patterns on a model suggested by Caroline Spurgeon's *Shakespeare's Imagery and What It Tells Us* (1935) in *An Index to the Figurative Language of George Chapman's Tragedies* (1970). A possible connec-tion between Chapman's political thought and the legal works of Bracton and Fortesque is revealed by Lilian Haddakin in "A Note on Chapman and Two Medieval Jurists," *MLR* 47 (1952): 550-53.

Thomas Mark Grant, *The Comedies of George Chapman: A Study in Development* (1972), develops a consistently high estimate of Chapman's comic achievement. Grant's arguments in behalf of the neglected comedies are often made at the direct expense of works which have been traditionally better received; "the progressive decline of Chapman's later plays puts in bold relief the high achievement of his comedies. These plays represent . . . Chapman's only truly *creative* work." The only other book-length study, Paul Kreider's *Elizabethan Comic Character Conventions as Revealed in the Comedies of George Chapman* (1935), notes an "almost complete lack of originality" in Chapman's comedies and uses them merely as a point of departure "to codify the conventions observed by all Elizabethan comic drama-tists." The chapters on the comedies in the Jacquot and MacLure books (I,A) are more responsive than Kreider but significantly more qualified than Grant. Charlotte Spivack (I,A) finds that the comedies have a "remarkable Elizabethan gift for theatricality at its liveliest"; Chap-man's comedies "rank easily with the productions of Middleton, Marston, and Jonson." The comedies are "a far from negligible part of his work" in which he often attains "genuine verve and comic life," according to Louis Cazamian, *The Development of English Humor* (1952). The disguise plots of the comedies are briefly outlined in John V. Curry's *Deception in Elizabethan Comedy* (1955).

C. THE WORKS AT LARGE

Raymond B. Waddington's *The Mind's Empire: Myth and Form in George Chapman's Narrative Poems* (1974) achieves a much needed synthesis of the scholarship on the especially complicated nondramatic corpus. Waddington advances a holistic view of Chapman's theory of poetry and his accomplishment; "essentially the poet remains for Chapman the Orphic civilizer described in *Hymnus in Noctem*; his function is the reformation of reluctant mankind by restoring the memory of the good that once was." Chapman is a vatic, public, and ceremonious poet who can be more appropriately compared to Spenser than to Donne. The readings stress the importance of the mythic and allegorical levels of meaning. The chapters on the nondramatic poetry in the books by MacLure, Jacquot, and Spivack (I,A) and the early chapters of the Rees and Wieler books on the tragedies (I,B), supplement the material which follows. Douglas Bush devotes a full chapter of *Mythology and the Renaissance Tradition* (1932; rev. ed. 1963) to Chapman's poems. Chapman has "a high philosophic belief in order" but the "tangential quality of his intellect" and his deliberate obscurity often prevent the coherent articulation of his vision. In *English Literature in the Earlier Seventeenth Century* (1945; rev. ed. 1961), Bush praises the occasional "lucid gnomic strain" found in the poems but finds that their "characteristic texture is tough and knotted with emblematic images and symbols sought for their philosophical and functional expressiveness." C. S. Lewis offers a less enthusiastic overview in *English Literature in the Sixteenth Century* (1954); he excepts the continuation of *Hero and Leander* from his generally negative conclusions.

Charles Kendrick Cannon, "Chapman on the Unity of Style and Meaning," *JEGP* 68 (1969): 245-64, holds that Chapman's poetic obscurity was intentional. Like Ezra Pound, Chapman employs a difficult idiom to challenge intelligent readers; his strangeness "has the aesthetic value of exciting wonder." Spartico Gamberini considers sources and baroque stylistic elements in *Poeti metafisici e cavalieri in Inghilterra* (1959). Chapman's "philosophical theology" is defined in Roy Battenhouse's *Marlowe's "Tamburlaine": A Study in Renaissance Moral Philosophy* (1941); the poetry views the world as a school and regards man's salvation "as a rational process within a cosmic framework." "Chapman's *The Shadow of Night*: An Interpretation," *SP* 38 (1941): 584-608, also by Battenhouse, traces the "logical plan" and "consecutive argument" which join the two parts of the poem together as "a religious service." Janet Spens considers Chapman's borrowings from Cicero and his definition of learning in "Chapman's Ethical Thought," *E&S* 11 (1925): 145-69. Other debts are traced in W. Schrickx's "George Chapman's Borrowing from Natali Conti, Some Hitherto Unnoted Passages," *ES* 32 (1951): 107-12.

Peter Ure cites a special negative connotation in "A Note on 'Opinion' in Daniel, Greville and Chapman," *MLR* 46 (1951): 331-38. The use of sonnet form and rhythm is detailed by Arnold Stein, "Sonnet Structure in Chapman's Blank Verse," *MLN* 59 (1944): 397-403. Allusions to Chapman's poetry by other poets are identified in: Mary Ellen Rickey, "Chapman and Crashaw," *N&Q* 3 (1956): 472-73; J. H. Walter, "'In a Little Room': Shakespeare and Chapman," *N&Q* 12 (1965): 95-96; and S. K. Heninger, Jr., "Chapman's *Hymnus in Noctem*, 376-377, and Shakespeare's *Love's Labour's Lost*, IV, iii, 346-347," *Expl* 16 (1958): item 49. Heninger also has two notes on the sources of *Eugenia*: "The Tempestatis Praesagia in Chapman's *Eugenia*," *MLN* 70 (1955): 478-84, and "Chapman's Plagiarism of Poliziano's *Rusticus*," *MLN* 73 (1958): 6-8. An allusion to Spenser is pointed out by Richard H. Perkinson in "The Body as a Triangular Structure in Spenser and Chapman," *MLN* 64 (1949): 520-22. Maren-Sophie Røstvig compares Spenser and Chapman, with special attention to their use of numerological symbolism, in "George Chapman and Edmund Spenser," in *The Hidden Sense and Other Essays*, Norwegian Studies in English 9 (1963), pp. 71-92. Raymond B. Waddington, "The Iconography of Silence and Chapman's Hercules," *JWCI* 33 (1970): 248-63, gives the mythological sources behind the personification of silence as "Herculean" in *Tears of Peace*.

The continuation of *Hero and Leander* is warmly championed in C. S. Lewis's "*Hero and Leander*," *PBA* 38 (1952): 23-37; rpt. in *Selected Literary Essays* (1969), pp. 58-73, and in *Elizabethan Poetry: Modern Essays in Criticism*, ed. Paul J. Alpers (1967), pp. 235-50: Chapman's contribution is "the product of serious thought" and fully consistent with Marlowe's beginning. Veselin Kostič, "Marlowe's *Hero and Leander* and Chapman's Continuation," in *Renaissance and Modern Essays Presented to Vivian de Sola Pinto*, ed. G. R. Hibbard (1966), pp.

25-34, judges the continuation "a rather unsuitable sequel"; Chapman destroys Marlowe's special unworldly context and reduces the lovers by surrounding them "with limiting contexts." "Chapman's *Hero and Leander*," by D. J. Gordon, *EM* 5 (1954): 41-94, considers the antecedents and significance of Ceremony. Chapman's attitude toward the lovers is seen as subtly ambivalent and the continuation is a fit completion. Gordon treats a source influence in "Chapman's Use of Catari in the Fifth Sestiad of *Hero and Leander*," *MLR* 39 (1944): 280-85. M. C. Bradbrook, *Shakespeare and Elizabethan Poetry* (1951), finds Chapman's share merely "a series of emblems, a gorgeous gallery of gallant inventions strung together by a very slender thread." In "Lucan–Marlow?–Chapman," *RES* 24 (1948): 317-21, L. C. Martin proposes that Chapman completely revised Marlow's translation of the first book of Lucan in connection with its 1600 publication in the same volume as *Hero and Leander*.

Frank Kermode's "The Banquet of Sense," *BJRL* 44 (1961): 68-99; rpt. in his *Shakespeare, Spenser, Donne: Renaissance Essays* (1971), pp. 84-115, considers the sources, analogues, and meaning of *Ovid's Banquet of Sense*: "Chapman's use of the theme is perhaps intended as an ironical comment on erotic poets (notably Shakespeare) whose works in his view have dishonest moral pretensions." Support is given Kermode's ironic reading in "Chapman and Persius: The Epigraph to *Ovid's Banquet of Sence*," *RES* 19 (1968): 158-62, by Raymond B. Waddington; "the content of the epigraph serves to direct the audience of initiates to a satiric reading of an erotic poem." Waddington advances a more complex and less derivative reading in his book (above): "As a 'perspective poem,' then, *Ovids Banquet* can be interpreted in more than one way; the problem for the reader is to find the vantage point determining the right perspective." In "'This Curious Frame': Chapman's *Ovid's Banquet of Sense*," *SP* 65 (1968): 192-206, James Phares Myers, Jr., also drawing on Kermode, suggests that the *Coronet for His Mistress Philosophy*, published in the same volume as the *Ovid*, offers "an amplification of the description of intellectual love" and, with an important digression in the *Ovid*, effectively censures the sensual love of the *Ovid's* main body. Phyllis Brooks Bartlett, "Ovid's 'Banquet of Sense'?" *N&Q* 197 (1952): 46-47, strengthens her contention, in a note in her edition of the poetry, that Ovid never wrote on this topic: "the title, design, and development of Chapman's poem must be considered as original inventions." That the *Ovid* and

other Chapman poems are "essentially emblematic" is Rhoda M.
Ribner's contention in "The Compasse of This Curious Frame: Chapman's *Ovids Banquet of Sence* and the Emblematic Tradition," *SRen*
17 (1970): 233-58. Parallels in Chapman's and Peele's use of Ovid are
shown by Inga-Stina [Ekeblad] Ewbank, *"The Love of King David and
Fair Bethsabe*: A Note on George Peele's Biblical Drama," *ES* 39
(1958): 57-62; despite the frequent parallels, Peele's play was probably
not a direct influence on Chapman. Waddington's "Chapman's
Andromeda Liberata: Mythology and Meaning," *PMLA* 81 (1966): 34-
44, describes that poem's occasion, sources, mythological antecedents,
and allegory; the poem may have been sponsored by the Howard
faction.

George deF. Lord provides a generously complete study of the
Homerica in *Homeric Renaissance: The "Odyssey" of George Chapman*
(1956). Chapman's major innovation is a heightened moral tone and his
"emphatic allegorical treatment penetrates to central themes which
Homer presents suggestively, obliquely and subtly." MacLure's discussion is less sympathetic. Chapman is often insensitive to his original
and he "expands and contracts the *Iliad* like an accordion to play his
own tune upon it." In the *Odyssey* the hero becomes the translator's
mouthpiece expressing sentiments "worthy of Milton's Raphael."
MacLure's chapter on the non-Homerica is a revision of his "The Minor
Translations of George Chapman," *MP* 60 (1963): 172-82. Chapman's
alterations of the original to stress what he believed was Homer's ethical
vision is detailed by Donald Smalley in "The Ethical Bias of Chapman's
Homer," *SP* 36 (1939): 169-91. The English text is a "free and periphrastic translation" according to Phyllis Brooks Bartlett, "Stylistic
Devices in Chapman's *Iliad*," *PMLA* 57 (1942): 661-75. *Homer und die
englische Humanität: Chapmans und Popes Übersetzungkunst*, by
Rudolph Sühnel (1958), compares Chapman's standards with Pope's.
The two relevant Oxford histories (above) offer an interesting difference of opinion on the merits of the Homer translations. Lewis
chides Chapman for reducing Homer to "a cryptic wiseacre on the
model of Chapman himself"; Bush praises him as "the greatest of poetic
translators" and Homer's "truest son." Jacquot's book (I,A) and Ure's
essay in the Pelican *Guide* (I,B) include balanced general treatments.

Jack E. Reese traces the reception of the Homerica from 1800-1900
and its influence in "Keats and Others on Chapman's Homer," *Cithara*
4 (1965): 32-42. G. S. Rousseau's "Seven Types of *Iliad*," *EM* 16
(1965): 143-67, compares various translations. Schoell's treatment of

sources and influences in *Etudes sur l'humanisme* (I,B) is expanded and slightly amended by Edward Phinney, Jr., in "Continental Humanists and Chapman's *Iliads*," *SRen* 12 (1965): 218-26; this item also supplies omissions in the notes to Nicoll's edition and qualifies Lord's critical estimate, H. C. Fay further supplements Schoell in "Chapman's Materials for His Translation of Homer," *RES* 2 (1951): 121-28; Valla's Latin prose version was an influence. Fay writes about Chapman's attitude toward Homer and his corrections of the text, respectively, in "Poetry, Pedantry, and Life in Chapman's *Iliads*," *RES* 4 (1953): 13-25 and in "Chapman's Text Corrections in His *Iliads*," *Library* 7 (1952): 275-81. "Critical Marks in a Copy of Chapman's *Twelve Bookes of Homers Iliades*," *Library* 8 (1953): 117-21, by Fay, maintains that the marginalia in the Trinity College, Cambridge, copy are in Ben Jonson's hand and that Jonson may be the critic referred to in the 1611 preface. Changes in the translation are identified by Phyllis Brooks Bartlett, "Chapman's Revisions in His *Iliads*," *ELH* 2 (1935): 92-119. For the bibliographical history of the 1616 edition see Paul S. Durkin, *"The Whole Works of Homer,"* *PBSA* 40 (1946): 230-31. T. J. B. Spencer, "Longinus in English Criticism: Influences Before Milton," *RES* 8 (1957): 137-43, observes that Chapman's reference in the dedicatory epistle of the *Odyssey* translation antedates *Of Education* and may be the first in English literature. In "Chapman and Shakespeare," *N&Q* 5 (1958): 99-100, J. W. Lever sees an allusion to Shakespeare's Sonnet 55 in the verses prefacing the *Homer*. William Carlos Williams, "Chapman Still Heard," *Poetry* 91 (1957): 60-64, defends Chapman as a poet and translator whose merits are too often undervalued because he was a contemporary of Shakespeare. A classic negative assessment of Chapman as translator is given in Matthew Arnold's *On Translating Homer* (1861).

George Chapman (A Concise Bibliography) by Samuel A. Tannenbaum and the *Supplement*, compiled with Dorothy R. Tannenbaum, were published in 1938 and 1946, respectively; these are reprinted in *Elizabethan Bibliographies*, vol. 1 (1967). *Elizabethan Bibliographies Supplements*, vol. 4 (1968), compiled by Charles A. Pennel and William P. Williams, has a chronological listing of Chapman material published between 1937 and 1965. Akihiro Yamada, "George Chapman: A Checklist of Editions, Biography, and Criticism, 1946-1965," and an "Addenda" by George W. Ray appeared, respectively, in *RORD* 10 (1967): 75-86, and 11 (1968): 55-58. Yamada and Ray include some theses and reviews. In the Goldentree series, Irving Ribner's *Tudor and*

Stuart Drama (1966) and John L. Lievsay's *The Sixteenth Century: Skelton through Hooker* (1968) give selected titles.

II. CRITICISM OF INDIVIDUAL PLAYS AND STATE OF SCHOLARSHIP

A. INDIVIDUAL PLAYS

The discussions in the MacLure, Jacquot, and Spivack books (I,A) and Parrott's introductions supplement the material below.

Bussy D'Ambois

Ennis Rees, *The Tragedies of George Chapman* (I,B), gives a reading which has influenced, often in negative or qualified fashions, much subsequent criticism. Rees stresses Bussy's ambivalence; he is potentially great but actually uncontrolled. The characterization is an ironic variation of the Marlovian superman type. It illustrates the tragic emptiness of *virtú* without virtue. Ornstein (I,B) labels Rees's definition of Bussy as a cautionary hero "morally absurd"; his role is determined by the play's philosophic purpose which is to show "an isolated virtuous man" destroyed by a corrupt society. In *Jacobean Tragedy* (I,B) Ribner postulates a shifting tripartite Bussy. He is "a dramatic symbol of humanity, faced with a problem which all mankind must face," a natural pre-lapsarian man, and an objective choral commentator. Ribner has an earlier version of this triple Bussy in "Character and Theme in Chapman's *Bussy D'Ambois*," *ELH* 26 (1959): 482–96; Tamyra is here described as "a symbol of the natural force which man cannot evade and of the conflict between the demands of this force and those of social order." Wieler's book (I,B) reduces Bussy to a mere "slave of passion" of limited interest. Peter Ure's SuAS essay (I,B) concludes: "The evidence suggests that in *Bussy D'Ambois* something not perfectly within the moralist's control came up from below the threshold of his mind, and . . . transformed a moral spectacle into a piece of tragic theatre." In a full chapter on *Bussy* in *The Mind's Empire* (I,C), Raymond Waddington suggests that the play consistently maintains two levels of meaning: "Superficially, it presents engrossing sensational melodrama . . . but 'inwardly' the mythic form heightens the story to something far more meaningful for the initiates." Jacquot (I,A) adds a useful treatment of sources and an in-depth study of Tamyra. MacLure

(I,A) deemphasizes the philosophic content and stresses theatrical effectiveness. In *The Herculean Hero in Marlowe, Chapman, Shakespeare, and Dryden* (1962), Eugene M. Waith notes parallels between *Bussy* and *Hercules Oetaeus*. Bussy is both "the historical figure" and "a mythic figure, a Hercules disguised as Bussy." Chapman respects his virtuous hero; fate and policy join to destroy this "unspoiled man."

William G. McCollom traces the influence of a more contemporary type in "The Tragic Hero and Chapman's *Bussy D'Ambois*," *UTQ* 18 (1949): 227–33. Bussy represents "the Marlovian superman transferred from the battlefield to the court." He is primarily "a man of spirit . . . who characteristically follows his lower nature," and his death is consistent with the demands of Chapman's Neoplatonic ethics. Elias Schwartz's "Seneca, Homer, and Chapman's *Bussy D'Ambois*," *JEGP* 56 (1957): 163–76, sees Bussy as "a wholly virtuous man . . . who finds himself in a disordered world" and becomes its victim. This interpretation is extended in Raymond B. Waddington's "Prometheus and Hercules: The Dialectic of *Bussy D'Ambois*," *ELH* 34 (1967): 21–48. The myths of Prometheus, Orpheus, and Hercules determine the play's action. Chapman gradually transforms Bussy "from a Prometheus to a Hercules" and he dies as a Christian Hercules, a "heroic man patiently enduring his suffering through Christian fortitude." Tamyra's role is crucial and there is an unorthodox use of light and dark imagery. Traces of the Proteus and Phaeton myths are outlined by W. Schrickx in "Mythological Patterns in Chapman's *Bussy D'Ambois*: Their Interpretative Value," *RLV* 18 (1952): 279–86.

The use of light is again considered by Peter Bement, "The Imagery of Darkness and Light in Chapman's *Bussy D'Ambois*," *SP* 64 (1967): 187–98; the radical shift between the use of dark images to suggest contemplation in the first act and the false night context employed in later acts "provides a well-defined symbol of the moral confusion of Bussy's career as a man of action." The image of a torch of beauty which extinguishes the love it feeds, used by both Chapman and Grimeston, is traced by Albert R. Braunmuller, "The Natural Course of Light Inverted: An *Impressa* in Chapman's *Bussy D'Ambois*," *JWCI* 34 (1971): 356–60; there are possible common sources and Chapman's use of it may be independent of Grimeston. Bird imagery in the play is noted in Adrian B. Weiss's "Chapman's *Bussy D'Ambois*, Act III, Scene ii," *Expl* 27 (1969): item 56.

"Chapman's *Bussy D'Ambois*: A 'Metaphysical' Drama," is the common title of a series of short articles by S. Kandaswami in *Mother India*

12 and 13 (1960, 1961): Sept., pp. 55-58; Oct., pp. 60-63; Dec., pp. 107-11; Jan., pp. 75-76. Bussy is a character who, like Falstaff, escapes his creator; the play is "metaphysical" by reason of "the dramatist's hovering between two equally strong but opposed attitudes." The hero's ambivalence is again prominent in Roger T. Burbridge's reading in "Speech and Action in Chapman's *Bussy D'Ambois*," *TSL* 17 (1972): 59-65; a "radical split between what Bussy says and what he does is the most significant feature of the play." C. L. Barber, "The Ambivalence of Bussy D'Ambois," *REL* 2 (1961): 38-44, finds the hero "an early dramatic example of the Man of Honour," a type of considerable importance in the Restoration theater. Bussy as "une sorte de caméléon supérieur" and a "coq de village" is the topic of Roger Decap's "Bussy d'Amboise héros tragique: Sur le *Bussy d'Amboise* de George Chapman," *Caliban* 3 (1966): 97-114.

Jean Jacquot, "*Bussy D'Ambois* and Chapman's Conception of Tragedy," *English Studies Today* 2 (1961): 129-41; rpt. in *Shakespeare's Contemporaries: Modern Studies in English Renaissance Drama*, ed. Max Bluestone and Norman Rabkin (2nd ed., 1970), pp. 292-306, identifies Pierre de Dampmartin's *Du bon-heur de la cour* as the source of most of Bussy's remarks in the first scene. Sources, including Dampmartin, are also identified by Claire-Elaine Engel, "Les sources du *Bussy D'Amboise* de Chapman," *RLC* 12 (1932): 587-95. In "Chapman's 'Friar Camolet,'" *N&Q* 15 (1968): 250-52, N. W. Bawcutt establishes some historical allusions; the friar's name is that of "an actual French Jesuit priest who preached sermons encouraging the assassination of the French King Henry IV." Charles R. Forker discusses possible allusions in this play and in the translations in "*A Midsummer Night's Dream* and Chapman's *Homer*," *N&Q* 5 (1958): 524.

In "*The Atheist's Tragedy* as a Dramatic Comment on Chapman's *Bussy* Plays," *JEGP* 52 (1953): 525-30, Clifford Leech holds that Tourneur's "initial purpose seems to have been to retort to Chapman's *Bussy* plays." *The Revenger's Tragedy* is compared to the *Bussy* plays by Henry Hitch Adams, "Cyril Tourneur on Revenge," *JEGP* 48 (1949): 72-87.

Robert P. Adams, "Critical Myths and Chapman's Original *Bussy D'Ambois*," *RenD* 9 (1966): 141-61, maintains that the 1607 and 1641 versions "are not textually interchangeable"; the earlier text is Chapman's sole great tragedy and a number of critical misconceptions arise from reliance on the later version. *The Rhetoric of Tragedy*

(1966), by Charles Osborne McDonald, includes an outline of "rhetorical patterns of structure" in *Bussy*. Thomas D'Urfey revised the play as *Bussy D'Ambois, or the Husband's Revenge* in 1691.

The Revenge of Bussy D'Ambois

MacLure (I,A) stresses the "fundamental continuity between the two plays" and regards the second as a partial retraction of some of the ideas of the first. Close continuity is also argued by Albert H. Tricomi, "The Revised *Bussy D'Ambois* and *The Revenge of Bussy D'Ambois*: Joint Performance in Thematic Counterpoint," *ELN* 9 (1972): 253-62. Chapman could have revised *Bussy* in 1604 for a planned joint performance with the *Revenge* at Whitefriars. The *Revenge* is "a confutation of the original" and "realizes most completely its dramatic potential and its ethical impact only when the revised version of *Bussy D'Ambois* has been played before it." Jacquot (I,A) attributes the shift in the characterization of the Guise to a change in the English attitude toward French Catholicism following the accession of James; Baligny may have been intended to offer a deliberate parody of James's views on royal absolutism. Ornstein (I,B) finds Clermont "an impossible protagonist" whose death is "almost ludicrous"; Rees (I,B) is more sympathetic and believes Clermont embodies Chapman's personal ideals. Peter Ure (SuAS essay, I,B) concludes that the play's chief interest is as a document of cultural history: "it is the most complete and whole-hearted of a number of attempts by previous dramatists to show us the Stoic Wise Man in a world of Neronian equivocation." Spivack (I,A) excepts the *Revenge* from her generally favorable response to the plays; "this one play seems to justify the traditional disparagement of Chapman's theatricality."

"Nature and the Tragic Hero in Chapman's *Bussy* Plays," *MLQ* 3 (1942): 263-85, by Richard H. Perkinson, finds the plays an experiment with two fashionable dramatic types. *Bussy* attempts "to fit the super-man into the mould of Senecan tragedy"; in the *Revenge* "the Stoic pantheistic Nature, with which Clermont identifies himself, is the real protagonist." Clermont exemplifies "the doctrine of 'adiaphora' or 'indifferent things,'" according to Michael Higgins, "Chapman's 'Senecal Man,'" *RES* 21 (1945): 183-91; the characterisation is striking evidence of the limitations of the Stoic system. In contrast, Geoffrey Aggeler, "The Unity of Chapman's *The Revenge of Bussy D'Ambois*," *Pacific Coast Philology* 4 (1969): 5-19, sees

Clermont facing a suspenseful challenge to his Christian Stoic ethics; he "must either simply disregard explicitly stated principles of his ethical credo and his moral purpose altogether, or he must find sanctions for vengeance transcending them." Peter Bement, "The Stoicism of Chapman's Clermont d'Ambois," *SEL* 12 (1972): 345-57, also defends Clermont from critical charges of indifference or priggishness; Clermont moves through a hopelessly corrupt world as "a scourge with a supernatural mandate to right the dreadful injustice symbolized by his brother's death, the restitution of natural law in a lawless world." Bement concludes, "The cold remoteness of the stage hero is the paradigm of his creator's high moral idealism." A similar rebuttal of negative criticism of the hero is given by Ronald Broude, "George Chapman's Stoic-Christian Revenger," *SP* 70 (1973): 51-61; "ironically, critical confusion has resulted from Clermont's failure to conform to expectations aroused by the very revengers with whom he was meant to contrast. Viewed within the context of Chapman's Christian Stoicism, however, Clermont's revenge is both philosophically consistent and dramatically effective." J. W. Lever, "Chapman: The *Bussy* Plays," in *The Tragedy of State* (1971), pp. 37-58, sees Clermont as neither an "abstract Senecal man" nor a conventional revenge hero; rather, he is "a complete and suffering human being."

The account of D'Auvergne in Grimeston and Chapman's experiment with him as a minor character in the Byron plays are the "key to the genesis of *The Revenge*," according to E. E. Wilson, Jr., "The Genesis of Chapman's *The Revenge of Bussy D'Ambois*," *MLN* 71 (1956): 567-69. In *Elizabethan Revenge Tragedy* (1940), Fredson Bowers finds "the fevered action of the revenge play" not consistent with Chapman's highly moral conception of tragedy; the play reflects its author's obvious dissatisfaction with the requirements of the genre. Percy Simpson, "The Theme of Revenge in Elizabethan Tragedy," in *Studies in Elizabethan Drama* (1955), pp. 138-78, treats Chapman as the last writer of revenge tragedy "in the classical tradition." Several allusions and adaptations are noted in Bertram Jerome Cohon's "A Catulian Echo in George Chapman's *The Revenge of Bussy D'Ambois*," *MLN* 60 (1954): 29-33.

The Conspiracy and Tragedy of Charles Duke of Byron

Ennis Rees (I,B) holds that Chapman here "more or less rewrote the story of Achilles in terms of Christian ethics and the Elizabethan stage." Byron, like Bussy, is a "cautionary example" and the object of heavy irony within the play; Henry IV is Chapman's "most complete portrait of the ideal king." The plays offer "the tragedy of egoism incarnate." Ornstein's *Moral Vision* finds no unity between the two; their value is primarily as signals of an important unfortunate turn in Chapman's development as a dramatist: "The long, even-tempered, sententious passages already signal a pyrrhic victory of moralizing intellect over dramatic instinct." Peter Ure (SuAS essay, I,B) regards the hero as "a wildfire without a centre." "The paradox of his fall is that his theory of self-sufficiency, which helped him to cut loose from the 'natural clime' of his society and to try to become a 'lonely dragon' like Shakespeare's Coriolanus, blinds him to the extent to which he has in reality given hostages to that society and put himself wholly in its power." MacLure finds these plays "a secular oratorio" in which Chapman, for the first and last time, realized his personal dramatic form. Elias Schwartz takes exception to Rees's treatment of Byron as merely a cautionary hero and offers his own interpretation in "Chapman's Renaissance Man: Byron Reconsidered," *JEGP* 58 (1959): 613–26. Chapman's thought has yet to reach its final shape and his attitude toward this Achillean hero is ambivalent. The political issues are of only secondary interest; "the action of the play involves the attempt of an immensely egotistical nature to transcend the limitations of its own being, the catastrophic failure of this attempt, and the reaction to this failure." When compared to the Bussy plays, the Byron plays reveal "a radical change in Chapman's ethical outlook."

Peter Ure, "The Main Outlines of Chapman's Byron," *SP* 47 (1950): 568–88; rpt. in his *Elizabethan and Jacobean Drama*, ed. J. C. Maxwell (1974), pp. 123–44, discusses sources, mythic parallels, and themes. There is "a shifting of viewpoint and change of tone" between the two plays. In "James I and Chapman's Byron Plays," *JEGP* 64 (1965): 677–90, Edward D. Kennedy finds the plays an allegorical treatment of issues and events in Jacobean England; "Chapman used James's work as a source for the political theories of the Byron plays." Political pressures led to severe mutilation of the extant text according to John B. Gabel in "The Original Version of Chapman's *Tragedy of Byron*," *JEGP* 63 (1964): 433–40. He gives a conjectural reconstruction of the uncensored text and regards the mask in II.i as an interpolation by another hand meant to fill the blue pencil gap. "The Stage Furnishings of George Chapman's *The Tragedy of Charles, Duke of Byron*," *Theatre Notebook* 16 (1962): 113–17, Marion Jones and Glynne Wickham, discusses mounting problems, sees the two plays as an allegory of the fall of Essex, and advances tentative dates of original composition and revision. The meaning of an astrological forecast in *The Conspiracy* is explained by Johnstone Parr, "The Duke of Byron's Malignant *Caput Algol*," *SP* 43 (1946): 194-202; rpt. under the title "The Duke of Byron's Malignant Nativity," in Parr's *Tambourlaine's Malady and Other Essays on Astrology in Elizabethan Drama* (1953), pp. 85-93. A letter by Chapman is used to confirm that a censor stayed publication of the Byron plays for political reasons in Elias Schwartz's "Sir George Buc's Authority as Licenser for the Press," *SQ* 12 (1961): 467-68. M. C. Bradbrook, "Chapman and Webster: Some Parallels between *The Conspiracy and Tragedy of Byron* and *The Duchess of Malfi*" (part II of "Two Notes upon Webster"), *MLR* 42 (1947): 291-94, cites allusions to Chapman and evaluates his influence on Webster. Further parallels to the Byron plays are noted by G. K. Hunter, "Notes on Webster's Tragedies," *N&Q* 4 (1957): 53-55. In *"Henry IV* and the Elizabethan Two-Part Play," *RES* 5 (1954): 236-48, Hunter compares the Byron plays to plays by Shakespeare and Marlowe and suggests Chapman employs a "method of parallelism" to attain unity of effect.

Caesar and Pompey

MacLure rates this "a dull piece of work"; Ribner finds it merely "a series of dull moralistic speeches"; Jacquot is equally negative. J. W. Lever, "Roman Tragedy: *Sejanus, Caesar and Pompey*," in *The Tragedy of State* (1971), pp. 59-77, suggests that the play "suffers from a diversity of methods and artistic aims." It "appeals on many levels but fails to make a unified impact." Ennis Rees (I,B) makes a more favorable case for what he considers "one of Chapman's first attempts at tragedy." His reading has Cato representing Chapman's personal philosophy and the play's real hero. Wieler (I,B) concludes the opposite. The play is the most complete expression of Chapman's Stoicism and, therefore, probably his last tragedy. Cato is too static to be the hero; the real interests of the play are Caesar's "heroic stature" and Pompey's gradual intellectual growth. In "A Neglected Play by Chapman," *SP* 58 (1961): 140-59, Elias Schwartz finds that the critical hostility depends on two claims: "that the play is disunified and . . . that Pompey is inconsistently characterized." Pompey is the real protagonist and his complex characterization is effected by the manipulation of a polarity of values represented by Caesar and Cato. Pompey is torn between the claims of expedience and the maintenance of right; his characterization rivals those of Shakespeare and Middleton in its "depiction of change and growth." Derek Crawley's "Decision and Character in Chapman's *The Tragedy of Caesar and Pompey*," *SEL* 7 (1967): 277-99, is equally sympathetic. Cato is "the touchstone rather than the 'central figure'"; Caesar vacillates between Roman nobility and Machiavellianism. Pompey is the most humanized of all Chapman's heroes.

Charlotte Spivack (I,A) praises this as "an introspective play with integrity and clarity of meaning." John Russell Brown in "Chapman's *Caesar and Pompey*: An Unperformed Play," *MLR* 49 (1954): 466-69, dismisses the title-page line "Acted at the Black-Fryers" as a publisher's puff. Hardin Craig argues that it was publicly performed, possibly with Shakespeare in the cast, and that an early version may have influenced the allusions in *Julius Caesar* and *Antony and Cleopatra*, in "The Shadow of Pompey the Great," *Topic* 7 (1964): 5-11. Peter Ure's "Chapman's Use of North's Plutarch in *Caesar and Pompey*," *RES* 9 (1958): 281-84, suggests the main source was read in translation, not the original. Some thirty lines indicate that Chapman also used Lucan's *Pharsalia*, according to J. E. Ingledew in "Chapman's Use of Lucan in *Caesar and Pompey*," *RES* 13 (1962): 283-88. A source for Ophioneus in II.i is identified by Lilian Haddakin, "Chapman's Use of Origen's *Contra Celsum* in *The Tragedy of Caesar and Pompey*," *N&Q* 198 (1953): 147-48. Adolph Kern considers sources and gives a detailed commentary on the text in *George Chapmans Trägodie "Caesar and Pompey" und ihre Quellen* (1901).

The Tragedy of Chabot Admiral of France (revised by Shirley)

Norma Dobie Solve's *Stuart Politics in Chapman's "Tragedy of Chabot"* (1928) interprets the play as a topical allegory of the career of Robert Carr, Earl of Somerset. Allegre reveals Chapman's personal devotion to Carr; other characters represent Bacon, Villiers, James I, and Edward Coke. Solve provides an extensive bibliography. Irving Ribner cautions against overstressing the topical element in "The Meaning of Chapman's *Tragedy of Chabot*," *MLR* 55 (1960): 321-31, and in *Jacobean Tragedy* (1962). The article contends that the characters "were shaped primarily as symbols of various moral positions" and the play "was conceived without regard to the affairs of Somerset or Bacon and probably is anterior to them, the contemporary allegorical significance having been added in a later revision." Chabot, like

Coriolanus, is guilty of pride and of attempting to deny his common humanity. The book develops a similar interpretation: Chapman believes that "involvement in living must be an involvement in sin"; Chabot dies because he failed to accept this first principle of Christian life. Thelma Herring finds Ribner's reading too Christian in "Chapman and an Aspect of Modern Criticism," *RenD* 8 (1965): 153-79. Chapman is more Stoic than Christian and "the stress falls . . . not on the Christian conception of the fall of man but on the Stoic belief that even now the truly virtuous man is a law unto himself." Chabot is not guilty of pride, and any irony in the play is directed at the limitations of the king. The foundation for some of Miss Herring's conclusions is found in John Wieler's *George Chapman* (1949).

Albert R. Braunmuller, "'A Greater Wound': Corruption and Human Frailty in Chapman's *Chabot, Admiral of France*," *MLR* 70 (1975): 241-59, finds the play, especially the ending, "remarkably dim." Its emptiness and negative qualities are elements "Chapman himself faced and sought to emphasize through the extraordinary manner of Chabot's death and the barren comments upon it." Takashi Sasayama's "*Chabot, Admiral of France*," *Shakespeare Studies* (Tokyo) 1 (1962-63): 15-32, suggests that Chapman here departs from his usual practice and writes "a *human* tragedy instead of a *political* one." *Chabot* is "a masterpiece which for the singleness and purity of interest is almost unrivalled." Peter Ure's SuAS essay (I,B) rates the play considerably lower. Its "historical hurly-burly never achieves full form or meaning"; it is of limited interest as a study of "a wrong done to a soul." MacLure's interpretation is partly determined by his acceptance of Solve's reading. Jacquot, again, is especially helpful on the relevant French history and the sources.

The Widow's Tears

Thomas Mark Grant, *The Comedies of George Chapman* (I,B), regards this as "the most provocative and the most paradoxical of any of his dramatic works." It also marks a breakdown of the personal and artistic balance found in Chapman's best comedies. "It is a sad irony, the sadder if intended, that this, the last comedy of a visionary humanist, should end with a vision . . . of an island paradise of glorious Chaos (England?), an Imposter's utopian dream of 'golden' misrule." Samuel Schoenbaum's "*The Widow's Tears* and the Other Chapman," *HLQ* 23 (1960): 321-28, describes the play as "the most mature of

Chapman's comedies, the most serious of purpose, and certainly the most striking." Chapman is not a systematic philosopher; "his primary concern is not with doctrine but with his art." *Tears* is a well-constructed, sophisticated comedy, remarkably free of the intellectual and rhetorical pretensions of the tragedies. A reading fully consistent with Chapman's Stoic and Neoplatonic philosophy is given by Henry M. Weidner, "Homer and the Fallen World: Focus of Satire in George Chapman's *The Widow's Tears*," *JEGP* 62 (1963): 518–32. Tharsalio is a "fallen Ulysses" bent on destroying all the values Chapman usually upholds. "The play is a horrendous climactic statement in Chapman's increasingly embittered dialectic between Homeric virtue and modern corruption." Most of the comedies follow a similar pattern. Thelma Herring, with an acknowledged debt to Schoenbaum, rebuts Weidner in "Chapman and an Aspect of Modern Criticism," *RenD* 8 (1965): 153–79. This and other doctrinaire approaches "underestimate the vivacity of *The Widow's Tears*."

Tears is Chapman's "most powerful play this side of tragedy" in the opinion of Charlotte Spivack (I,A). In sharp contrast, Jackson I. Cope, *The Theater and the Dream* (I,B), finds the play "a bad joke, an outrageous joke" in which "man willfully misinterprets his own myths and acts out an ironic role in the pseudo-philosophic puppet plays through which he tries to locate absolutes in a shadow world." Another strongly qualified interpretation, Albert H. Tricomi, "The Social Disorder of Chapman's *The Widow's Tears*," *JEGP* (1973): 350–59, finds the theme to be "that religious and ethical values exist everywhere only in illusion and hypocrisy." Tharsalio is neither Chapman's spokesman nor the play's hero and his "triumph represents the victory of all inverted values." Marilyn Williamson's "Matter of More Mirth," *RenP*, 1956, pp. 34–41, notes that alterations of Petronius's plot result in a greatly increased comic effect. Analogues from early folk literature to the present are listed in Peter Ure's "The Widow of Ephesus: Some Reflections on an International Comic Theme," *DUJ* 18 (1956): 1–9; Chapman's version is "the first known dramatization of the subject." The RRDS edition by Ethel Smeak (III,D) has a useful general introduction.

All Fools

The introduction to Frank Manley's RRDS edition (1968) has a brief critical appraisal which concludes that *All Fools* is "not only Chapman's most flawless, perfectly balanced play, it is also his most human and large-minded." Elizabeth Woodbridge, "An Unnoted Source of Chapman's *All Fools*," *JEGP* 1 (1897): 338–41, agreeing with Koeppel (I,B) that Terence's *Heautontimorumenos* is the main source, identifies the *Adelphi* as the model for the Gostanzo-Valerio plot. Leonard Goldstein submits the play to Marxian analysis in "Some Aspects of Marriage and Inheritance in Shakespeare's *The Merry Wives of Windsor* and Chapman's *All Fools*," *ZAA* 12 (1964): 375–86. W. Schrickx's "Notes on the So-Called Collier Forgery of the Dedication to Chapman's *All Fools*," *RBPH* 28 (1950): 142–46, considers the sonnet in question to be authentic. The play is tentatively identified with the earlier (1599) lost *The World Runs on Wheels*, by S. Y. E., "Chapman's *All Fools*," *N&Q* 194 (1949): 534.

The Gentleman Usher

In "The Dramatic Uses of Homeric Idealism: The Significance of Theme and Design in George Chapman's *The Gentleman Usher*," *ELH* 28 (1961): 121–36, Harry M. Weidner traces the influence of Homer on the ideals expressed in the play. This comedy marks a critical point in Chapman's artistic and philosophic development: "Beginning with *The Gentleman Usher*, in each of his later plays Chapman attempts to 'solve' the problem of the confrontation and interaction of the Homeric ideal with modern life as he saw it; in none but *The Gentleman Usher* is there both a rich and complete artistic triumph and the hopeful, self-aware triumph of moral man." Jackson I. Cope (I,B) finds *Usher* "an unexpected *commedia divina*" in which Strozza "becomes not merely a modern Hercules, but imitator of that imitator of the great epileptic of myth, an icon for Ficino himself." Thomas Marc Grant's analysis (I,B) finds the play dramatizing "an action which is itself ceremonial, *emblematic*, and which is not properly a saturnalian movement . . . ." "The Genesis of the Strozza Subplot in George Chapman's *The Gentleman Usher*," *PMLA* 88 (1968): 1448–53, by John H. Smith, details Chapman's use of a medical treatise by Antonio Benivieni; Chapman transforms this dry narrative "with striking images and with fine poetry that have no counterpart in Benivieni." In "The 'Deformed Mistress' Theme and Chapman's *Gentleman Usher*," *N&Q* 7 (1960): 22–24, Samuel Schoenbaum finds Margaret the "most striking early manifestation" of a character type popular in later drama.

The Memorable Mask of the Middle Temple and Lincoln's Inn

A full discussion of sources, themes, allegory, and aesthetic quality is given in D. J. Gordon's "Le 'masque mémorable' de Chapman," in *Les fêtes de la renaissance,* ed. Jean Jacquot (1956), vol. 1, pp. 305–17. Gordon gives an impressive survey of the moral allegory and suggests a topical allegory in which "les projets de colonization et les idées politiques de l'entourage de Raleigh sont présentés." In "Unity in Chapman's *Masque of the Middle Temple and Lincoln's Inn,*" SEL 4 (1964): 291–305, Jack E. Reese considers mythological prototypes, the influence of Ripa's *Iconologia,* and concludes that the mask is "a work of art so closely unified that it could in itself stand as a testament to the grand unity underlying all creation." MacLure devotes an appendix to this mask.

The Blind Beggar of Alexandria

Helen Andrews Kaufman, "*The Blind Beggar of Alexandria*: A Reappraisal," *PQ* 38 (1959): 101–6, takes exception to the negative findings of many earlier critics. The play is "Chapman's version of an actual *commedia dell' arte,*" probably seen on a trip to Italy, and it would succeed on stage. The incomplete remains of a romance plot are probably the result of cuts already made in the source. Folk tale analogues suggest to Jack E. Reese, "'Potiphar's Wife' and Other Folk Tales in Chapman's *Blind Beggar of Alexandria,*" *TSL* 18 (1973): 33–48, that Elizabethan audiences did not consider Cleanthes a mere rogue. He is, rather, "a dramatic spokesman expressing a significant view of life not normally allowed the author." Ennis Rees, in "Chapman's *Blind Beggar* and the Marlovian Hero," *JEGP* 57 (1958): 60–63, sees the hero as "essentially a burlesque of the Marlovian hero," and he finds the sexual intrigue a "deliberate parody of the erotic element in Marlovian poems and drama." Grant (I,B) notes parallels with the Homerica; Irus is the "perfect avenging Hercules" and Cleanthes is an "Odyssean patriarch."

Sir Giles Goosecap

Grant summarizes it as a "rarefied, pedantic neo-platonic allegory . . . set down in the midst of farcical action of gulled knights and waggish servants." In "A New Source of *Sir Gyles Goosecappe,*" *MP* 11 (1914):

547-48, Franck L. Schoell suggests that the play is a modern dress
version of the Troilus story, based primarily on Chaucer's account and
on Estienne Tabourot's *Les apophtegnes du sieur Gaulard*. The possibility that *Giles* is a later version of a lost play is raised by G. A. Wilkes,
"Chapman's 'Lost' Play, *The Fount of New Fashions*," *JEGP* 62
(1963): 77-81.

Eastward Ho (with Jonson and Marston)

Joseph Q. Adams, "*Eastward Hoe* and Its Satire against the Scots,"
SP 28 (1931): 689-701, considers the play's notoriety and the likely
differences between the printed text and the acting version; "the
printed play—even the first issue of the first edition—did not reproduce
Eastward Hoe in the full form in which it was acted on the stage of the
Blackfriars." Richard Horwich, "*Hamlet* and *Eastward Ho*," *SEL* 11
(1971): 223-33, cites a large number of borrowings from *Tamburlaine,
The Spanish Tragedy*, and, especially, *Hamlet*; the authors intend these
to be noticed and *Eastward Ho* is meant as "a parody of *Hamlet*."
Nahum Tate adapted it as *Cuckhold's Haven, or an Alderman No
Conjurer* (1685). Much of the criticism is significantly concerned with
the attribution of specific shares of authorship (III,A).

Monsieur D'Olive

A. P. Hogan, "Thematic Unity in Chapman's *Monsieur D'Olive*,"
SEL 11 (1971): 295-306, traces the influence of Ficino and Neo-
platonism in general on the play. Aside from this source interest, the
play is sterile; Chapman never manages to bring his plots together.
Thomas Mark Grant (I,B) has an equally low opinion of the plot:
"There is a collapse of romance into mechanical intrigue."

May-Day

Grant maintains that much of the play's humor probably derived
from the child actors' interpretations of adult roles. The structure is
best described as "only the pleasant formlessness one expects from light
satirical *revue*." Chapman's use of Piccolomini's *Alessandro* as a source
for much of the plot and dialogue is described by A. L. Stiefel, "George
Chapman und das italienische Drama," *SJ* 35 (1899): 180-213.

B. OVER-ALL STATE OF CRITICISM

The *TLS* review of MacLure's *George Chapman* (28 Sept. 1967, p. 890) found it "the tribute of a fine scholar to a scholar-poet." This first full-length study in English of the entire corpus redeems Chapman from the thesis hawking, forced synthesis, and outright hostility of much earlier criticism. The Chapman corpus is unusually large and diverse, even by Renaissance standards; MacLure, and to an extent, Jacquot, provide comprehensive over-views. Raymond B. Waddington's *The Mind's Empire* (I,C) supplements their work. Chapman's original non-dramatic poetry is generally recognized as important to an understanding of his other works; Waddington's book is the most systematic and comprehensive study of this difficult material. Recent criticism, especially since the publication of MacLure's book, has increasingly responded to Chapman's artistic qualities rather than to his involved philosophic systems. It is even suggested that the systems may be only apparent and that the artist, not the visionary, is in control. Chapman is increasingly seen as more a poet, translator, and dramatist and less a half-coherent seer.

There remain some issues of unresolved canonicity. Parrott's composition dates, despite evidence of errors, tend to be challenged only when they inhibit a given interpretative thesis. Articles by Elias Schwartz and Robert Ornstein (III,A) point toward changes in the chronology. There are other large lacunae; for example, a full study of Chapman's use of Grimeston, first called for in the preface of Frederick S. Boas's 1905 edition of the Bussy plays, has yet to be done. Individual plays, as the preceding section illustrates, have been neglected, as have aspects of the translations and some of the original poems. In the last fifteen years, however, Chapman scholarship has been proliferous and rich. It is an impressive indication of the scholar-poet's appeal to scholars.

III. CANON

A. PLAYS IN CHRONOLOGICAL ORDER

This list follows the preferred first performance dates given in Alfred Harbage, *Annals of English Drama, 975–1700*, rev. S. Schoenbaum (1964), and the *Supplements* by Schoenbaum (1966, 1970). These are

the sources of the dates of first performances (in italics), first editions
(following the semicolons), and type of play. Descriptions of early
quartos are given by W. W. Greg, *A Bibliography of the English Printed
Drama to the Restoration*, 4 vols. (1939–59). Issues of canon and date
are discussed by E. K. Chambers in *The Elizabethan Stage*, 4 vols.
(1923), and by G. E. Bentley in *The Jacobean and Caroline Stage*, 7
vols. (1941–68). S. Schoenbaum reconsiders several disputed ascriptions in *Internal Evidence and Elizabethan Dramatic Authorship: An
Essay in Literary History and Method* (1966) and earlier in "Internal
Evidence and the Attribution of Elizabethan Plays," *BNYPL* 65
(1961): 102–24. The introductions in Parrott's edition also indicate
composition and performance dates and the most important authorship disputes. Parrott's conclusions on canonicity are usually regarded
as definitive; recent evidence suggests his composition dates may
require upward revision. The introductions in the Holaday edition of
the comedies include authoritative surveys of textual issues. The tentative identification of Chapman as the model for Bellamont in *Northward Ho* (I,A) and possible allusions to specific Chapman tragedies in
the Dekker-Webster play have been used by Elias Schwartz, "The Dates
and Order of Chapman's Tragedies," *MP* 57 (1959): 80–82, as the basis
of a full revision of the traditionally accepted dates. Robert Ornstein
rejects the identification and the dependent redating in "The Dates of
Chapman's Tragedies, Once More," *MP* 59 (1961): 61–64. Schwartz
reinforces his dates with additional evidence in later articles on individual tragedies. MacLure agrees with Ornstein and follows the traditional dates. References to Parrott and Schwartz in this section are to
the edition introductions and the *MP* general redating article, respectively, except where otherwise indicated. Relatively few "lost" plays
are associated with Chapman. In most cases there is good evidence of
their temporary existence and they are included in the second part of
this section.

The Blind Beggar of Alexandria, comedy (*1596*; 1598)

Parrott holds that the extant text derives from a stage copy which
was cut to stress the farcical elements at the expense of a once complete Aegiale-Cleanthes romance plot; he provides a partial reconstruction of the missing material. Greg's preface to the Malone Society
edition (1929) accounts for the mutilated condition of the text by
speculating that the copy may have been "surreptitiously obtained."

Helen Andrews Kaufman (II,A, *Beggar*) argues that the cuts had already been made in the *commedia dell' arte* which was Chapman's source. "Bibliographical Studies of George Chapman's *The Blind Beggar of Alexandria* (1598)," *Shakespeare Studies* (Tokyo) 6 (1967-68): 147-65, by Akihiro Yamada, analyzes twelve copies of the first quarto and lists the variants. The printer's copy was probably a cut version and not authorial.

An Humorous Day's Mirth, comedy (*1597*; 1599)

A shop proofreader was especially careful in correcting the first quarto edition according to Akihiro Yamada, "A Proof-Sheet in *An Humorous Day's Mirth* (1599), Printed by Valentine Simmes," *Library* 21 (1966): 155-57. Yamada's "Bibliographical Studies of George Chapman's *An Humourous Day's Mirth* (1599), Printed by Valentine Simmes," *Shakespeare Studies* (Tokyo) 5 (1966-67): 119-49, gives the press variants in fifteen copies, cites five errors in the Malone Society reprint (1937), and concludes that the printer's copy was Chapman's foul papers.

The Gentleman Usher, comedy (*1602*; 1606)

Yamada discusses the nature of the copy behind the quarto and concludes that it was carefully revised author's fair copy, in "Bibliographical Studies of George Chapman's *The Gentleman Usher* (1606), Printed by Valentine Simmes," *Shakespeare Studies* (Tokyo) 2 (1963-64): 82-113.

May-Day, comedy (*1601-2*; 1611)

Parrott holds that an early version of the play was finished by late 1601 or early 1602. Allusions to later works were added in a revision done after 1607. Akihiro Yamada identifies the quarto copy as "autograph manuscript" in "Bibliographical Studies of George Chapman's *May-Day* (1611), Printed by William Stansby," *Journal of the Faculty of Liberal Arts and Sciences, Shinshu University*, 15 (1965): 13-34.

Sir Giles Goosecap, comedy (*1601-3*; 1606)

Parrott gives the evidence for the Chapman ascription in his introduction and, at greater length, in "The Authorship of *Sir Giles Goosecap*," *MP* 4 (1906): 25-37. Franck Schoell accepts the attribution in his unpublished University of Paris thesis, *George Chapman as a Comic Writer* (1911). There has been no serious challenge of its canonicity and Schoenbaum (*Internal Evidence*) concludes that the case for Chapman's authorship is strong but not absolutely certain. On the basis of internal allusions, Parrott dates composition between September 1601 and March 1603. Robert J. Fusillo, "On the Date of *Sir Gyles Goosecap*," *N&Q* 1 (1954): 335-36, also uses internal evidence to suggest the more precise limits of 6 September 1601 to 26 April 1602. Wilkes's article identifying this with the lost *Fount of New Fashions* (II,A, *Giles*) dates the composition of at least a preliminary version as early as 1598.

All Fools, comedy (*1599-1604*; 1605)

Parrott, relying on Henslowe, concludes that the play was completed by July 1599; he also suggests that the quarto copy indicates a subsequent revision. Frank Manley, in his edition (1968), rejects the revision theory held by most critics since Parrott. "What few facts we have seem to me to indicate that Chapman did not revise the play as we have it in any thoroughgoing fashion." S. Y. E. (III,A, *All Fools*) holds that this is identical with the "lost" *The World Runs on Wheels* and that both titles may be alternates for the "lost" *All Fools But the Fool*. The nature of the copy-text (authorial fair copy) and the roles of the compositors of the first quarto are considered by Akihiro Yamada, "Bibliographical Studies of George Chapman's *All Fools* (1605), Printed by George Eld," *Shakespeare Studies* (Tokyo) 3 (1964-65): 73-99.

Bussy D'Ambois, foreign history (*1600-1604*; 1607 or 1608)

Parrott's composition date of 1603-4, with a revision around 1610, is generally accepted. Elias Schwartz advances a 1597-98 date, based on possible allusions in *Northward Ho*, in his article redating the tragedies. Schwartz gives additional evidence from Henslowe and fresh interpretations of internal allusions as support in "The Date of *Bussy D'Ambois*," *MP* 59 (1961): 126-27. Ornstein's rebuttal of Schwartz's original argument is cited at the start of this section. Peter Ure, "The Date of the Revisions of Chapman's *The Tragedy of Bussy D'Ambois*," *N&Q* 197 (1952): 1-2, outlines close parallels between the two Bussy plays and concludes that "there is presumptive evidence not only that the revision of *The Tragedy* is roughly contemporaneous in date with *The Revenge* but also that Chapman was responsible for the revison." This last point is a refutation of Berta Sturman's contention, in "The 1641 Edition of

Chapman's *Bussy D'Ambois*," *HLQ* 14 (1951): 171-201, that the second quarto's revisions "scarcely point to Chapman." Sturman finds no evidence of authorial involvement in the 1641 text; the readings of the 1607 quarto are definitive. In "Chapman's *Tragedy of Bussy D'Ambois*: Problems of the Revised Quarto," *MLR* 48 (1953): 257-67, Ure replies in greater detail. There are 228 variants, including thirty long alterations and additions and five excisions; their extent and tone show a concern only an author could feel. Conclusions similar to Ure's are reached by Albert H. Tricomi in an *MLN* article discussed above (II,A, *The Revenge of Bussy D'Ambois*).

The two texts are "two different works of art" according to Robert P. Adams (II,A); the 1607 version is far superior to the 1641 one. John Freehafer, "The Contention for *Bussy D'Ambois*, 1622-41," *Theatre Notebook* 23 (1968): 61-69, finds the revised quarto entirely Chapman's work and playing a "key part" in a "hitherto unrecognized war of the theatres." Chapman, at William Beeston's request, rewrote the play to give Lady Elizabeth's Men a more theatrical version than the original then in the possession of the King's Men; the rival companies may have simultaneously performed the two versions. Editions published since Sturman's challenge to the authority of the 1641 text (see III,E) are divided on the question. Jacquot and Lordi follow the 1641 quarto. Evans holds that the revisions are by another hand and uses the 1607 text with four emendations from the later quarto. Nicholas Brooke, in his Revels edition (1964), dismisses Sturman's argument as "rashly generalized." The play was "twice revised, by Chapman himself and by someone else," possibly Nathan Field. Brooke's copy-text is the 1607 quarto and he admits three emendations from the 1641 version.

Monsieur D'Olive, comedy (*1604*; 1606)

Parrott dates composition "sometime in the autumn or early winter of 1604-5." Akihiro Yamada discusses the nature of the quarto copy and variants found in twenty-nine copies in "Bibliographical Studies of George Chapman's *Monsieur D'Olive* (1616), Printed by Thomas Creede," *SELit*, English No. (1963): 1-48. Yamada treats more specialized bibliographical concerns in "Press Variants and Emendations in *Monsieur D'Olive* (1606)," *Journal of the Faculty of Liberal Arts and Sciences, Shinshu University*, 13 (1963): 49-70, and, in the same journal issue, "The Printing of Sheet B in the W. A. Clark Library Copy of *Monsieur D'Olive* (1606)," pp. 43-47.

Caesar and Pompey, classical history (*1599-1607*; 1631)

Parrott doubts "whether it is possible to settle, even approximately, the date of composition"; he inclines to a 1612-13 date. A significantly earlier date is advanced by J. E. Ingledew, Jr., "The Date of Composition of Chapman's *Caesar and Pompey*," *RES* 12 (1961): 144-59. Schwartz's reading of allusions to this play in *Northward Ho* and his 1605 composition date are supported by additional internal evidence. Act II, scene i is clearly a later interpolation; it may be a satiric portrait of Edmund Tilney inserted after his death in 1610. Spivack (I,A) regards it "an earlier rather than a later play." The Wieler and Rees books on the tragedies (I,B), respectively, see this as Chapman's last and most Stoic play (1612) and "one of Chapman's first attempts at tragedy" (1602). Ornstein's rejoinder to Schwartz (above) rejects the early date. Thomas L. Berger and Dennis G. Donovan, "A Note on the Text of Chapman's *Caesar and Pompey*," *PBSA* 65 (1971): 267-68, treat the variants in the two states of the title page of the 1631 quarto and the priority of issue.

The Widow's Tears, comedy (*1603-9*; 1612)

This was written between the fall of 1605 and the spring of 1606, according to Parrott; there may have been a revision. The nature of the text is treated by Akihiro Yamada, "Bibliographical Studies of George Chapman's *The Widow's Tears* (1612), Printed by Richard Bradock," *Shakespeare Studies* (Tokyo) 4 (1965-66): 57-83.

Eastward Ho, with Jonson and Marston; comedy (*1605*; 1605)

Parrott assigns the main plot to Marston and the underplot to Chapman; Jonson, except for general advice, "did little more than revise and finish the work of his collaborators." Chapman is given credit for all or most of II.iii, III.i, III.iii, and IV.i. Percy Simpson in "The Problem of Authorship of *Eastward Ho*," *PMLA* 59 (1944): 715-25, and in the commentary on the play in vol. 9 of the Herford and Simpson edition of Jonson (1950), differs slightly in his allocation of specific scenes. The most recent analysis, that by C. G. Petter in his edition (1973), is closer to Simpson than to Parrott. Julia Hamlet Harris, in her edition (1926), claims most of Acts II, III, IV, and V are by Chapman. MacLure (I,A), in contrast, gives the largest share to Marston. Jacquot (I,A) adopts a slight modification of Harris's analysis.

Rinaldo Simonini, Jr., "Ben Jonson and John Florio," *N&Q* 195 (1950): 512-13, assigns authorship of the last act to Jonson. Jackson I. Cope takes exception to most earlier authorship assignments and attributes II.ii to Jonson on the basis of parallels, "*Volpone* and the Authorship of *Eastward Hoe*," *MLN* 72 (1957): 253-56.

The Conspiracy and Tragedy of Charles Duke of Byron, tragedy (*1608*; 1608)

Parrott relies on the publication date of the source to establish composition late in 1607 or early in 1608. The Schwartz and Ornstein general articles on the dates of the tragedies (above) include the Byron plays. In "The Date of Chapman's Byron Plays," *MP* 58 (1961): 201-2, Schwartz rejects the 1602 date he advanced in the general dating article in favor of 1605-6. The later date would allow for Chapman having read Grimeston's *History of France* in manuscript. Schwartz's hypothesis is rejected by John Butler Gabel, "The Date of Chapman's *Conspiracy and Tragedy of Byron*," *MP* 66 (1969): 330-32. Chapman could not have had access to Grimeston's manuscript; the play was written in 1607 after publication of the source. Marion Jones and Glynne Wickham (II,A, *Byron*) advance a date of 1602, with later revisions. Revisions, some of which may be by another playwright, are also suggested by John B. Gabel (II,A, *Byron*). Limitations of Parrott's text of this play are pointed out in Peter Ure's "Chapman's *Tragedy of Byron*, IV, ii, 291-5," *MLR* 54 (1959): 557-58, and in John Butler Gabel's "Some Notable Errors in Parrott's Edition of Chapman's Byron Plays," *PBSA* 58 (1964): 465-68.

The Revenge of Bussy D'Ambois, tragedy (ca. *1601-12*; 1613)

Parrott dates the composition in 1610 or 1611. Schwartz's general redating article advances this to 1602-3. R. J. Lordi, "Proofreading of *The Revenge of Bussy D'Ambois*," *ELN* 10 (1973): 188-97, finds three levels of correction in eighteen copies of the first quarto; the unusual care may indicate that Chapman read the proof himself.

The Memorable Mask of the Middle Temple and Lincoln's Inn, mask (*15 Feb. 1613*; ca. 1613)

Press variants in eighteen copies of the first quarto and seven of the second, the division of work between the compositors, and the nature of the copy-text are considered by Akihiro Yamada, "Bibliographical Studies of George Chapman's *The Memorable Mask of the Middle Temple and Lincoln's Inn* (1613), Printed by George Eld," *Shakespeare Studies* (Tokyo) 7 (1968-69): 81-111.

The Tragedy of Chabot Admiral of France, revised by James Shirley, 1635; tragedy (*1611-22?*; 1639)

The play was written between 1612 and 1613, according to Parrott; there is no substantive evidence, but Chapman likely would have resumed writing plays after the death of Prince Henry to improve his financial situation. Koeppel establishes an outside limit of 1622 in *Quellenstudien* (I,B); Parrott's introduction rejects Koeppel's claim that Chapman had to have used the 1621 edition of Pasquier's *Les recherches de la France*. Koeppel's date is central to Norma Dobie Solve's reading (II,A, *Chabot*) of the play as an allegory of the Somerset scandal. Jacquot, MacLure (I,A), and Rees (I,B) accept her reading and the corollary 1621-24 date. Jacquot offers additional evidence supporting the 1621-24 date in the introduction to his edition of *Bussy* (1960); Ure, reviewing the edition, *RES* 13 (1962): 190-93, disputes Jacquot's acceptance of the later date. Schwartz also accepts the Solve dating. John W. Wieler, in his book on Chapman's Stoicism (I,B), advances 1612 as the date of an original version on the basis of his belief that there was a progressive pattern to Chapman's intellectual development. Irving Ribner, in *Jacobean Tragedy* (1962) and in an earlier article (II,A, *Chabot*), contends that Chapman's version was finished before Field's 1613 merger with Princess Elizabeth's Men. Shirley revised it some time after 1621 and developed the topical level of interest. Chapman may have contributed several minor allusions to the Somerset affair, but the topical allegory is primarily Shirley's.

Most critics accept Parrott's judgment that "collaboration in the proper sense of the word is almost incredible between Chapman and Shirley." It is generally agreed that Shirley's share in the play is limited to a general improvement of its stage effectiveness and possibly the addition of several minor characters. Derek Crawley evaluates the authorship issue, with a review of earlier opinions, in "The Effect of Shirley's Hand on Chapman's *The Tragedy of Chabot Admiral of France*," *SP* 63 (1966): 677-96, and concludes that "Shirley's revision of Chapman's *Chabot* has quite drastically affected the relation of character and action in the play, and critics have been prone to ignore this fact." In particular, "Shirley's interest in emotional scenes has often undermined Chapman's interest in moral teaching." Metrical and vocabulary tests are used to argue that most of the play's cruxes can be resolved if the reader attributes them to Shirley's imperfect understanding of Chapman's intention and relies on Chapman's usual practice. The revision was probably done after Chapman's death. Albert R. Braunmuller, in his *MLR* article on *Chabot* (II,A), holds that the main features, including some of the more sentimental passages, are Chapman's; Shirley's contribution was not central.

B. UNCERTAIN ASCRIPTIONS AND APOCRYPHA

Fedele and Fortunio, by Anthony Munday?; comedy (*1579-84*; 1585)

Richard Hosley's recent studies, especially "Anthony Munday, John Heardson, and the Authorship of *Fedele and Fortunio*," *MLR* 55 (1960): 564-65, and "The Authorship of *Fedele and Fortunio*," *HLQ* 30 (1967): 315-33, consider the internal evidence and earlier scholarship and conclude there is no possibility of Chapman's authorship. See the canon section of the essay on Munday in *The Popular School*.

A Knack to Know an Honest Man, by Anthony Munday?; Thomas Heywood?; tragicomedy (*22 Oct. 1594*; 1596)

Robert Boies Sharpe, *The Real War of the Theaters: Shakespeare's Fellows in Rivalry with the Admiral's Men* (1935), suggests that at least parts of the play are by Chapman. See the discussion in the Anonymous Plays section of *The Popular School*.

The Tragedy of Alphonsus Emperor of Germany, by George Peele?; tragedy (*1594-1604?*, revised ca. *1630*; 1654)

The Stationers' Register (1653) gives Peele as the author; the title page of 1654 quarto carries Chapman's by-line. In his introduction, Parrott notes that there is not "a single parallel to a passage in one of Chapman's undisputed works" and concludes that this "cannot be the work of Chapman." Wieler's *George Chapman* (1949) devotes an appendix to the evidence and rejects the attribution. Negative conclusions are also reached in Herbert F. Schwarz's edition (1913), Schoenbaum's *Internal Evidence* (1966), and vol. 5 of G. E. Bentley's *The Jacobean and Caroline Stage* (1956). Fredson Bowers, "The Date and Composition of *Alphonsus, Emperor of Germany*," *Harvard Studies and Notes in Philology and Literature* 15 (1933): 165–89, agrees that the play is not by Chapman. Bowers also rejects Parrott's theory of a revision and suggests that the play was written between 1594 and 1599. In the same issue of *Harvard Studies*, Taylor Starck's "The German Dialogue in *Alphonsus, Emperor of Germany*, and the Question of Authorship," pp. 147–64, rejects Parrott's tentative attribution to Rudolf Weckherlin; *Alphonsus* was clearly written by an Englishman, perhaps an actor who toured Germany. Sharpe, *The Real War of the Theaters*, suggests that Chapman wrote at least part of the play. Harold M. Dowling presents a case for Chapman's partial authorship in "Peele and Some Doubtful Plays," *N&Q* 164 (1933): 366–70; *Alphonsus* is "an old Peele play revised by Chapman for a special occasion before 1634." Attribution is more fully discussed under the play title in the Anonymous Plays section of *The Popular School*.

Sir Thomas More, by Anthony Munday, Thomas Dekker, Henry Chettle, Thomas Heywood?, William Shakespeare?; history (ca. *1593–*ca. *1601*; MS)

In *Shakespeare, Chapman and "Sir Thomas More"* (1931), Arthur Acheson proposes that Munday and Chapman collaborated on an early version of the text in 1586; Shakespeare revised this ca. 1589–90. See the discussion of authorship in the canon section of the Munday essay in *The Popular School*.

The Fount(ain) of New Fashions, comedy (*16 May–12 Oct. 1598*; lost)

See the Wilkes article on *Sir Giles Goosecap* (II,A).

All Fools But the Fool, comedy (*22 Jan.–2 July 1599*; lost)

See the note by S. Y. E. (III,A, *All Fools*).

The Four Kings, unknown (*licensed 18/22 March 1599*; lost)

Histriomastix, or The Player Whipped, revised by John Marston? and others?; comedy (*1589–99*; 1610)

In "Shakespeare, Chapman et *Sir Thomas More*," *RAA* 3 (1926): 428–34, Franck L. Schoell reviews Arthur Acheson's several attempts to extend the Chapman canon in *Shakespeare and the Rival Poet* (1903), *Mistress Davenant, The Dark Lady of Shakespeare's Sonnets*

(1913), *Shakespeare's Lost Years in London, 1586–1592* (1920), *Shakespeare's Sonnet Story* (1922), and *Shakespeare, Chapman, and "Sir Thomas More"* (1931). Schoell accepts Acheson's attribution of *Histriomastix* to Chapman and supplies fresh supporting evidence. Acheson's attributions of *Fedele and Fortunio*, portions of *Sir Thomas More*, and *The Whole Life and Death of Thomas Lord Cromwell* have had virtually no adherents. The most recent restatement of the case for the *Histriomastix* attribution appears in an appendix to Jacquot's book (I,A).

A Pastoral Tragedy (not completed?), tragedy (*17 July 1599*; lost)

Charlemagne, or the Distracted Emperor, tragedy (*1584*-ca. *1605*; MS)

The preface of Schoell's edition (1920) considers, in detail, the possibility of Chapman's authorship. Jacquot is less convinced, but his book has an appendix listing parallels with works of proven canonicity in support of the attribution. Parrott does not include it in his edition with the more significant apocrypha. Greg rejects Schoell's case in his preface to the Malone Society edition (1937); "the play seems most likely to be the work of an amateur—influenced, possibly, by the work of Chapman." Schoenbaum doubts the assignment in *Internal Evidence* (1966), and MacLure rejects it. See also the Anonymous Plays section of *The Popular School*.

Thomas Lord Cromwell, history (ca. *1599–1602*; 1602)

Arthur Acheson's attribution (in *Shakespeare, Chapman and "Sir Thomas More"* and elsewhere) is referred to in the discussion of *Histriomastix*. See the Anonymous Plays section of *The Popular School*.

Biron, tragedy (?) (*25 Sept.–3 Oct. 1602*; lost)

In the first *Supplement* (1966) Schoenbaum replaces the anonymous attribution given in earlier editions of the *Annals* with "Chapman, G.?" and suggests this lost play may be an earlier version of Chapman's *The Tragedy of Charles Duke of Byron*.

The Old Joiner of Aldgate, comedy (*Feb. 1603*; lost)

C. J. Sisson uses Star Chamber and other court records to reconstruct the play in *Lost Plays of Shakespeare's Age* (1936). The play was perhaps a pointed topical satire which Chapman wrote on a commission from a principal in the legal actions in the background.

The Wit of a Woman, comedy (*1604*; 1604)

June J. Morgan, "Toward a Textual Study of *The Wit of a Woman*," *ESRS* 15 (1966): 8-17, suggests Chapman as a possible author; Munday is her preferred candidate. See the Anonymous Plays section of *The Popular School*.

The Silver Mine, comedy (*Feb.-March 1608*; lost)

Schoenbaum (first *Supplement*) adds "Chapman, G.?" to the *Annals* attribution of "Marston, J.?" and indicates that this may be the same play as *The Conspiracy of Charles Duke of Byron*.

The Second Maiden's Tragedy, tragedy (*licensed 31 Oct. 1611*; MS)

Leonora Leet Brodwin assigns the play to Chapman in "Authorship of *The Second Maiden's Tragedy*: A Reconsideration of the Manuscript Attribution to Chapman," *SP* 63 (1966): 51-77. The MS attribution dates from the seventeenth century and the MS is not in Chapman's holograph. In lieu of any new substantive evidence, Brodwin bases her attribution on "philosophic parallels" between this and *The Revenge of Bussy D'Ambois* and *Caesar and Pompey*. Attribution to Middleton (see, for example, S. Schoenbaum, *Middleton's Tragedies* [1955]; qualified later, in *Internal Evidence*, as "at least doubtful") is rejected on the grounds that Middleton lacked the talent evident here; he may have revised Chapman's original version. A more detailed account appears in the Anonymous Plays section of *The Popular School*.

The Mask of the Twelve Months, mask (*1608-12*; MS [lost?])

Margaret Dean-Smith dates the first performance in the winter of 1611/12 in two *TLS* notes under the common title "A Chapman Masque," 29 Dec. 1950, p. 827, and 26 Jan. 1951, p. 53. Sidney Race questions its authenticity in "John Payne Collier and His Fabrications," *N&Q* 197 (1952): 54-56; "The Masques of *The Twelve Months* and *The Four Seasons*," *N&Q* 197 (1952): 347-49; and "*The Masque of the Twelve Months*," *N&Q* 197 (1952): 525. Kenneth Muir initiated several controversies in "A Chapman Masque?" *TLS*, 15 Dec. 1950, p. 801, in which he accepts the work as Chapman's and advances a 1618 date. Muir replies to Race's forgery charges in "Collier Fabrications," *N&Q* 197 (1952): 150. Race is refuted again, with detailed evidence, by Ralph C. Elsley in two notes under the title *"The Masque of the Twelve Months,"* *N&Q* 197 (1952): 229-32, and, in the same volume, p. 402.

A Yorkshire Gentlewoman and Her Son, tragedy (ca. *1595*-ca. *1613*; lost)

The play is mentioned in the Stationers' Register (1660) and by Warburton.

The Bloody Brother, or *Rollo Duke of Normandy*, by John Fletcher (and Philip Massinger?, Ben Jonson?, and another?); tragedy (*1616-24*; 1639)

William Wells holds Chapman responsible for at least a part in *"The Bloody Brother,"* *N&Q* 154 (1928): 6-9. J. D. Jump extends Wells's argument and assigns parts of III.i and all of IV.iii to Chapman in his edition (1948). The ascription depends on metrical and vocabulary parallels. Cyrus Hoy's consideration in "The Shares of Fletcher and His Collaborators in the Beaumont and Fletcher Canon (VI)," *SB* 14 (1961): 45-61, and more briefly in *SB* 15 (1962): 71-90, carefully evaluates Wells's claim. Hoy finds the linguistic evidence of Chapman's involvement "painfully slight"; he feels, however, that Wells offers "convincing proof" of "Chapman's presence in the play." The involvement of Fletcher and Massinger is certain and Chapman's can be accepted with reservations. The case for Jonson is less certain.

Two Wise Men and All the Rest Fools, dialogues (*1619*; 1619)

Kreider (I,B) includes it in a list of comedies by Chapman. Bentley, *The Jacobean and Caroline Stage*, vol. 3 (1956), dismisses the title-page ascription to Chapman as a publisher's puff.

The Ball, by James Shirley; comedy (*licensed 16 Nov. 1632*; 1639)

Parrott's introduction suggests that Chapman's name was associated with *The Ball* through a printer's error; this was in the same MS as Shirley's revision of *Chabot*. Parrott concludes that "the play is the sole and unaided work of Shirley."

Christianetta, or Marriage and Hanging Go by Destiny, also ascribed to Richard Brome; comedy? (ca. *1623-34*; lost)

The title appears in Abraham Hill's MS catalogue. See *Annals of English Drama*, Supplementary List II, m.

Revenge for Honour, by Henry Glapthorne?; tragedy (*1637-41*; 1654)

Parrott notes that Chapman's name appears on the title page but the Stationers' Register (1653) gives Glapthorne as author. A case for Chapman is advanced by E. E. Stoll, "On the Dates of Some of Chapman's Plays," *MLN* 20 (1905): 206-9. Wieler's *George Chapman* (I,B) reviews critical opinions and concludes "there can be no reason for linking Chapman's name with the writing of this tragedy." That Glapthorne is almost certainly the sole author is D. L. Thomas's finding in "Authorship of *Revenge for Honour*," *MP* 5 (1908): 617-36. Different evidence leads to the same judgment in J. H. Walter's *"Revenge for Honour*: Date, Authorship, and Sources," *RES* 13 (1937): 425-37.

C. CRITIQUE OF THE STANDARD EDITION

In the preface to vol. 1 of his four-volume edition (1910-13), Thomas Marc Parrott indicates that his work is "offered to the general public"; his text represents "a frank attempt to find a middle ground between a slavish retention of the errors of the old texts, and such a radical revision as would dispel the ancient flavour of the work." The limitations of this popular and mildly eclectic standard are obvious in the light of recent advances in editorial practice. Also, Parrott usually collated only readily available copies and he does not provide detailed bibliographical accounts. Recent studies by Peter Ure, John B. Gabel, and Akihiro Yamada (III,A, passim) note specific weaknesses of the Parrott text. The standards of the Parrott edition, however, are generous by the measure of its time. The introductions and notes occasionally reflect the influence of critical commitments but they remain an important source. Parrott's critical decisions still generally obtain. His determinations of canonicity have met with little serious challenge and his dating remains generally accepted.

The Illinois edition (*Comedies*, 1970), under the general editorship of Allan Holaday, follows the more exacting principles established primarily by Fredson Bowers's editions of other Renaissance playwrights. When the Illinois edition of the tragedies is published, the full dramatic corpus will be available in a standard edition textually equal to the better editions available for other Elizabethan and Jacobean playwrights. A major desideratum, at that time, will be a full glossarial apparatus keyed to the Illinois text.

D. TEXTUAL STUDIES

Textual introductions precede the texts of each play in the Illinois edition of the comedies. The Parrott edition has less detailed treatments and other studies are found under individual play headings above (III,A and B).

E. SINGLE-WORK EDITIONS

Of the recent editions of *Bussy D'Ambois*, that by Marcello Pagnini (1959) is primarily of interest for the discussion of Chapman's style in the introduction. Jean Jacquot's edition and French translation (1960) has an introduction which is virtually an independent monograph on Chapman at large, qualifying and extending the arguments of Jacquot's book. There are two valuable supplements to the ideas in the book: a fresh interpretation of Friar Camolet's dealings with spirits and a general analysis of Chapman's views on Fortune, Nature, and Destiny. Nicholas Brooke did the Revels edition (1964); its unique value is its adherence to the series's generous standards of textual and glossarial annotation. Brooke also discusses stage history and argues for a quasi-independent revision by Nathan Field. He suggests that the hero's ambivalence was carefully planned by Chapman. Maurice Evans's edition (New Mermaid, 1966) is decidedly influenced by Brooke, especially his arguments against the authority of the 1641 quarto (III,A, *Bussy*). Evans is impressed by the play's resemblance to Bruno's *Spaccio della bestia trionfante*; the parallels lead to the conclusion "that in *Bussy D'Ambois*, Chapman is writing his own *Spaccio*: he is showing the expulsion of the triumphant beast of the vices and prophesying their replacement by the ancient virtues." The RRDS edition by Robert Lordi (1964) is conservative in editorial practice and critical position. A Scolar Press facsimile of *The Revenge of Bussy D'Ambois* was published in 1968. Ethel Smeak's edition of *The Widow's Tears* (RRDS, 1966) effectively compensates for the general critical neglect of the play in the introduction; the text employs a collation of twenty-one copies of the first quarto. The RRDS *The Gentleman Usher* (1970), ed. John Hazel Smith, offers an introductory critical reading which develops "the dominance of its romantic plot." A text of *Eastward Ho* appears in vol. 4 of the Herford and Simpson *Ben Jonson* (1932). The New Mermaid edition of the same play (1973) is edited by C. G. Petter. His lengthy introduction covers the shares of the several authors, date and sources, and a thorough analysis of textual problems. There is an edition by Julia Hamlet Harris (1926) with full apparatus and a Scolar Press facsimile printing (n.d.). Malone Society texts are W. W. Greg, ed., *The Blind Beggar of Alexandria* (1929), and W. W. Greg, with David Nichol Smith, eds., *An Humorous Day's Mirth* (1937). Frank Manley edited *All Fools* for RRDS (1968); his introduction offers a spirited defense of the play, which he ranks as Chapman's best dramatic work. There is a facsimile of *Sir Giles Goosecap* (1912).

F. NONDRAMATIC WORKS

Phyllis Brooks Bartlett, ed., *The Poems of George Chapman* (1941), is the standard edition; the apparatus is quite full and her readings are definitive. A minor correction of her text of *Tears of Peace* appears in "Chapman's Missing Couplet," *ELN* 11 (1973): 30–33, by Len Krisak. *Chapman's Homer*, 2 vols., ed. Allardyce Nicoll (1956), also exemplifies very high technical and scholarly standards. Chapman's continuation of *Hero and Leander* is included in both *The Poems of Christopher Marlowe*, ed. Millar MacLure (1968), and *Marlowe's Poems*, ed. L. C. Martin (1931); these editions have full notes and critical introductions. The continuation and *Ovid's Banquet of Sense* are included in Elizabeth Story Donno, ed., *Elizabethan Minor Epics* (1963). A French translation of *Hero and Leander*, by Joseph B. Fort (1950), has an introduction and annotation which occasionally supplement Bartlett. There are facsimile texts of *Hero and Leander* (1970), *The Iliads of Homer* (1969), *Ovid's Banquet of Sense (and Other Poems)* (1970), and *The Georgics of Hesiod* (1971).

IV. SEE ALSO

A. GENERAL

Biographical

Allen, Percy. "Shakespeare and Chapman." *TLS*, 12 Sept. 1929, p. 704, and 26 Sept. 1929, p. 747.

Bartlett, Henrietta C. "Extant Autograph Material by Shakespeare's Fellow Dramatists." *Library* 10 (1929): 308–12.

Bullen, A. H. "G. C." In *Elizabethans* (1924), pp. 49–69.

Crundell, H. W. "George Chapman and the Grevilles." *N&Q* 185 (1943): 137.

Dodds, M. Hope. "George Chapman and Holofernes." *N&Q* 172 (1937): 286–87.

Douglas, Alfred. "G. C. and 'the Rival Poet.'" *TLS*, 11 June 1938, p. 402.

Ferguson, A. S. "Shakespeare and Chapman." *TLS*, 17 Sept. 1929, p. 723.

Gaselee, S. "George Chapman." *The Observer* (London), 13 May 1934, p. 10.

Hine, Reginald L. "George Chapman." In *Hitchins Worthies: Four Centuries of English Life* (1932), pp. 48–69.

Loane, George G. "George Chapman as Holofernes." *N&Q* 172 (1937): 7.

———. "Chapman the Rival Poet." *TLS*, 11 June 1938, p. 402.

"Memorabilia." *N&Q* 166 (1934): 325.

Parsons, Robert D. "Chapman's Letter to Mr. Sares: A *Hamlet* Parallel." *N&Q* 16 (1969): 137.

Simpson, Percy. "Ben Jonson on Chapman." *TLS*, 5 March 1932, p. 155.

T., D. G. "George Chapman." *RES* 1 (1925): 350.

General Studies of the Plays

Adams, Joseph Q. "Another Fragment from Henslowe's Diary." *Library* 20 (1939): 154–58.

Albright, Evelyn May. *Dramatic Publication in England: A Study of Conditions Affecting the Content and Form of Drama*. 1927.

Allen, Percy. *Shakespeare and Chapman as Topical Dramatists*. 1929.

———. *The Plays of Shakespeare and George Chapman in Relation to French History*. 1933.

Anderson, Donald K., Jr. "The Banquet of Love in English Drama (1595–1642)." *JEGP* 63 (1964): 422–32.

Armstrong, W. A. "The Elizabethan Conception of the Tyrant." *RES* 22 (1946): 161–81.

Aronstein, Philipp. *Das englische Renaissancedrama*. 1929.

Babb, Lawrence. *The Elizabethan Malady: A Study of Melancholia in English Literature from 1580 to 1642*. 1951.

Bakeless, John. *The Tragicall History of Christopher Marlowe*. 2 vols. 1942.

Baldwin, T. W. *Shakespeare's Small Latine and Lesse Greeke*. 2 vols. 1944.

Barber, C. L. *The Idea of Honour in the English Drama, 1591–1700*. 1957.

Beckingham, C. F. "Seneca's Fatalism and Elizabethan Tragedy." *MLR* 32 (1937): 434–38.

Bentley, Gerald Eades. "John Cotgrave's *English Treasury of Wit and Language* and the Elizabethan Drama." *SP* 40 (1943): 186–203.

Bethel, S. L. *The Cultural Revolution of the Seventeenth Century*. 1952.

Bevington, David. *Tudor Drama and Politics: A Critical Approach to Topical Meaning*. 1968.

Boas, Frederick S. *An Introduction to Tudor Drama*. 1933.

———. *An Introduction to Stuart Drama*. 1946.

Bowden, William R. *The English Dramatic Lyric 1603–42: A Study in Stuart Dramatic Technique*. 1951.

Bradbrook, M. C. *Themes and Conventions of Elizabethan Tragedy*. 1935.
————. *The Growth and Structure of Elizabethan Comedy*. 1955.
————. *English Dramatic Form: A History of Its Development*. 1965.
Briggs, K. M. *The Anatomy of Puck: An Examination of Fairy Beliefs among Shakespeare's Contemporaries and Successors*. 1959.
Cazamian, Louis. *The Development of English Humor*. 1952.
Chambers, E. K. *The Shakspeare Allusion-Book*. 1932.
Clarkson, Paul S., and Clyde T. Warren. *The Law of Property in Shakespeare and Elizabethan Drama*. 1942.
Cunningham, John E. *Elizabethan and Early Stuart Drama*. 1965.
Ellis-Fermor, Una M. *The Jacobean Drama: An Interpretation*. 1936.
Farnham, Willard. *The Medieval Heritage of Elizabethan Tragedy*. 1936.
————. *Shakespeare's Tragic Frontier*. 1950.
Frost, David L. *The School of Shakespeare*. 1970.
Gentili, Vanna. *La figure della pazzi nel teatro elisabettiano*. N.d.
Granville-Barker, Harley, and G. B. Harrison, eds. *A Companion to Shakespeare Studies*. 1934.
Greaves, Margaret. *The Blazon of Honour: A Study in Renaissance Literature*. 1964.
Greg, W. W. "A Fragment from Henslowe's Diary." *Library* 19 (1939): 180–84.
Harrison, G. B. *Shakespeare's Fellows; Being a Brief Chronicle of the Shakespearean Age*. 1923.
————. *The Elizabethan Journals; Being a Record of Those Things Most Talked of during the Years 1591–1603*. 1939.
————. *Elizabethan Plays and Players*. 1940.
Haydn, Hiram. *The Counter-Renaissance*. 1950.
Heninger, S. K., Jr. *A Handbook to Renaissance Meteorology, with Particular Reference to Elizabethan and Jacobean Literature*. 1960.
Herrick, Marvin T. *Tragicomedy: Its Origins and Development in Italy, France, and England*. 1955.
————. *Italian Comedy in the Renaissance*. 1960.
Hibernicus. "Ianthe." *N&Q* 184 (1943): 76.
Holzknecht, Karl J. *Outlines of Tudor and Stuart Plays, 1497–1642*. 1947. [*All Fools, Bussy D'Ambois, The Revenge of Bussy D'Ambois, Eastward Ho*]
Howarth, R. G. *Literature of the Theatre: Marlowe to Shirley*. 1953.
Hoy, Cyrus. *The Hyacinth Room: An Investigation into the Nature of Comedy, Tragedy, and Tragicomedy*. 1964.
Hyde, Mary Crapo. *Playwriting for Elizabethans, 1600–1605*. 1949.
Kaufman, Helen. "The Influence of Italian Drama on Pre-Restoration English Comedy." *Italica* 31 (1954): 9–23.
Klein, David. *The Elizabethan Dramatists as Critics*. 1963.
Koskenniemi, Inna. *Studies in the Vocabulary of English Drama, 1550–1600, Excluding Shakespeare and Ben Jonson*. 1962.
Lawrence, William J. *Pre-Restoration Stage Studies*. 1927.
Leech, Clifford. *Shakespeare's Tragedies and Other Studies in Seventeenth Century Drama*. 1950.

Loane, George G. "Notes on Chapman's Plays." *MLR* 33 (1938): 248-54.

————. "More Notes on Chapman's Plays." *MLR* 38 (1943): 340-47.

McCollom, William G. *Tragedy.* 1957.

Manifold, J. S. *The Music in English Drama: From Shakespeare to Purcell.* 1956.

Muir, Kenneth, and S. Schoenbaum, eds. *A New Companion to Shakespeare Studies,* 1971.

Oras, Ants. *Pause Patterns in Elizabethan and Jacobean Drama: An Experiment in Prosody.* UFMH, no. 3 (1960).

Parrott, Thomas Marc, and Robert Hamilton Ball. *A Short View of Elizabethan Drama.* 1943.

Praz, Mario. "Machiavelli and the Elizabethans." *PBA* 14 (1928): 49-97.

Prior, Moody E. *The Language of Tragedy.* 1947.

Rébora, Piero. *L'Italia nel drama inglese (1558-1642).* 1925.

Reul, Paul de. *Présentation du théâtre jacobéen de Marston à Beaumont et Fletcher (1600-1625).* N. d.

Schelling, Felix E. *Foreign Influences in Elizabethan Plays.* 1924.

————. *Elizabethan Playwrights: A Short History of the English Drama from Medieval Times to the Closing of the Theatres in 1642.* 1925.

Schücking, Levin Ludwig. "The Baroque Character of the Elizabethan Tragic Hero." *PBA* 24 (1938): 85-112.

Shalvi, Alice. *The Relationship of Renaissance Concepts of Honour to Shakespeare's Problem Plays.* 1972.

Sisson, Charles J. *Le goût public et le théâtre élisabéthain jusqu'à la mort de Shakespeare.* 1922.

Smet, Robert de [Romain Sanvic]. *Le théâtre élisabéthain.* 1955.

Smith, James, "Revaluations (VII), George Chapman." *Scrutiny* 3 (1934-35): 339-50, and 4 (1935-36): 45-61.

Spencer, Theodore. *Death and Elizabethan Tragedy: A Study of Convention and Opinion in the Elizabethan Drama.* 1936.

Stagg, Louis C. "Characterization through Nature Imagery in the Tragedies of George Chapman." *Ball State University Forum* 9 (1968): 39-43.

Sugden, E. H. *A Topographical Dictionary to the Works of Shakespeare and His Fellow Dramatists.* 1925.

Sykes, H. Dugdale. *Sidelights on Elizabethan Drama: A Series of Studies Dealing with the Authorship of Sixteenth and Seventeenth Century Plays.* 1924.

Thorp, Willard. *The Triumph of Realism in Elizabethan Drama, 1558-1612.* 1928.

Wallis, Lawrence B. *Fletcher, Beaumont, and Company.* 1947.

Wells, Henry W. *Elizabethan and Jacobean Playwrights.* 1939.

————. *A Chronological List of Plays Produced in or about London, 1581-1642.* 1940.

West, Robert Hunter. *The Invisible World: A Study of Pneumatology in Elizabethan Drama.* 1939.

Wickham, Glynne. *Early English Stages, 1300-1660.* 2 vols. 1959-72.

Wilson, F. P. *Elizabethan and Jacobean.* 1945.

Studies of the Poetry and Translations
Bartlett, Phyllis Brooks, "Chapman and Phaer." *MLN* 56 (1941): 599-601.

————. "The Heroes of Chapman's Homer." *RES* 17 (1941): 257–80.

Bensly, Edward. "Chapman and Epigrams Attributed to Virgil." *N&Q* 162 (1932): 373, 407.

Bottrall, Margaret. "George Chapman's Defence of Difficulty in Poetry." *Criterion* 16 (1937): 638–54.

Braunmuller, Albert H. "The 'Hot Low Countries' in Chapman's *Hero and Leander*." *ELN* 8 (1970): 97–99.

Campbell, Oscar J. *Comicall Satyre and Shakespeare's "Troilus and Cressida."* 1938. [*Homer*]

Delattre, F. "Keats's Sonnet on George Chapman's *Homer*." *N&Q* 175 (1938): 285–86.

Dodds, M. Hope. "A Possible New Source of Keats's Sonnet on Chapman's *Homer*." *N&Q* 175 (1938): 248–49.

Eade, Christopher. "Some English Iliads: Chapman to Dryden." *Arion* 6 (1967): 336–45.

Edwards, H. L. R. "Chapman and Florio." *TLS*, 20 June 1935, p. 399. [*The Shadow of the Night*]

Ellrodt, Robert. *Les poètes métaphysiques anglais.* Part 2. 1960.

Evans, B. Ifor. "Keats's Approach to the Chapman Sonnet." *E&S* 16 (1930): 26–52.

Fay, H. C. "George Chapman's Translation of Homer's *Iliad*." *Greece and Rome* 21 (1952): 104–11.

Fraser, Russell A. "The Art of *Hero and Leander*." *JEGP* 57 (1958): 743–54.

Gilbert, Allan H. "Philosophical Conceits in Shakespeare and Chapman." *ES* 54 (1973): 118–21. [*Ovid's Banquet of Sense*]

Greg, W. W. "The Copyright of *Hero and Leander*." *Library* 24 (1944): 165–74.

Herzing, Thomas W. "George Chapman: The Doctrine of Functional Obscurity." *English Notes* 3 (1969): 15–32.

Hibernicus. "Milton: Two Verbal Parallels: 'Autumnal Leaves.'" *N&Q* 184 (1943): 85. [*Homer*]

Hobsbaum, Philip. "Elizabethan Poetry." *Poetry Review* 56 (1965): 80–97.

Holmes, Elizabeth. *Aspects of Elizabethan Imagery.* 1929.

Howarth, R. G. "Notes on Chapman." *N&Q* 192 (1949): 70–72.

Janish, W. "Die erste englische Übersetzung der sogenannten homerischen hymnen [by Chapman]." *Mitt d. vereins klassichen Philologen in Wien* 8 (1933): 74–88.

K. "Chapman and Epigrams Attributed to Virgil." *N&Q* 162 (1932): 430.

Landrum, Grace Warren. "More Concerning Chapman's Homer and Keats." *PMLA* 42 (1927): 986–1009.

Lathrop, Henry Burrowes. *Translations from the Classics into English from Caxton to Chapman, 1477–1620.* 1933.

Leech, Clifford. "Venus and Her Nun: Portraits of Women in Love by Shakespeare and Marlowe." *SEL* 5 (1965): 247–68. [*Hero and Leander*]

Lewalski, Barbara K. "Hero's Name—and Namesake—in *Much Ado about Nothing*." *ELN* 7 (1969): 175–79. [*Hero and Leander*]

Loane, George G. "Chapman's Homer." *TLS*, 5 Sept. 1935, p. 552.

————. "Perfuming Pea-soup." *TLS*, 21 Feb. 1935, p. 108.

————. "Chapman's Homer Again." *TLS*, 21 Dec. 1935, p. 879.

————. "A Cause of Corruption?" *TLS*, 28 Nov. 1936, p. 996. [Homer]

————. "Chapman's Greek." *N&Q* 171 (1936): 94.

————. "Queries from Chapman's *Iliad.*" *N&Q* 171 (1936): 261-62.

————. "Queries from Chapman's *Odyssey.*" *N&Q* 171 (1936): 330-31.

————. "The Text of Chapman's *Homer.*" *TLS*, 18 April 1936, p. 336.

————. "Chapman's Homer." *Cornhill* 156 (1937): 637-44.

————. "Chapman's Method." *TLS*, 24 July 1937, p. 544.

————. "Misprints in Chapman's Homer." *N&Q* 173 (1937): 398-402, 453-55.

————. "Chapman and Hierocles." *N&Q* 174 (1938): 119-20. ["A Hymne to Our Saviour"]

————. "Final S in Rhyme." *TLS*, 15 Jan. 1938, p. 44.

————. "Milton and Chapman." *N&Q* 175 (1938): 456-57.

————. "Misprints in Chapman's Homer." *N&Q* 174 (1938): 367; 175 (1938): 331-32.

————. "'Thick as Autumnal Leaves': Chapman's *Iliad.*" *N&Q* 175 (1938): 116.

————. "Chapman and Scapula." *N&Q* 176 (1939): 405-6. [Homer]

————. "Chapman's Compounds in *N. E. D.*" *N&Q* 181 (1941): 130-31.

————. "'Man-making Gold.'" *N&Q* 181 (1941): 146. [Homer]

————. "Some Notes on Chapman's Poems." *N&Q* 183 (1942): 272-76, 332-33.

M. M. "Andromeda's Rescue." *More Books: Bulletin of the Boston Public Library* 13 (1938): 159.

McClennen, Joshua. *On the Function and Meaning of Allegory in the English Renaissance.* 1947.

Murry, J. Middleton. "On First Looking into George Chapman's Homer." *Studies in Keats* (1930), pp. 15-33.

————. "Chapman the Rival Poet." *TLS*, 4 June 1938, pp. 385-86.

Pfeiffer, Karl G. "A Possible New Source of Keats's Sonnet on Chapman's *Homer.*" *N&Q* 175 (1938): 203-4.

"The Poems of George Chapman." *TLS*, 3 Oct. 1942, p. 486.

Praz, Mario. *La poesia metafisica inglese de seicento.* 1945.

————. *Studi sul concettismo.* 1946.

Robertson, Jean. "Some Additional Poems by George Chapman." *Library* 22 (1941): 168-76.

S. "Chapman and Epigrams Attributed to Virgil." *N&Q* 162 (1932): 317.

Samuel, Howard. "Chapman's *Iliad.*" *TLS*, 31 March 1932, p. 229.

Savage, James E. "*Troilus and Cressida* and Elizabethan Court Factions." *UMSE* 5 (1964): 43-66. [Homer]

Sayer, "Chapman's Compounds in *N. E. D.*" *N&Q* 181 (1941): 161.

Schaus, Hermann. "The Relationship of *Comus* to *Hero and Leander* and *Venus and Adonis.*" *Studies in English* (Univ. of Texas), (1945-46), pp. 129-41.

Seronsy, Cecil C. "Chapman and Dryden." *N&Q* 3 (1956): 64. [*Hero and Leander*]

Sjögren, Gunnar. "'Take This from This': Polonius and Ulysses." *N&Q* 15 (1968): 139.

Slote, Bernice. "Of Chapman's Homer and Other Books." *CE* 23 (1961): 256-60.

Smith, Hallett. *Elizabethan Poetry: A Study in Conventions, Meaning, and Expression,* 1952.

Stanford, W. B. "Studies in the Characterization of Ulysses—VII." *Hermathena* 81 (1953): 41–58.

Starnes, De Witt T., and Ernest W. Talbert. *Classical Myth and Legend in Renaissance Dictionaries.* 1955.

Sturman, Berta. "Chapman in the *O. E. D.*" *N&Q* 194 (1949): 442–43.

Thompson, J. A. K. *Classical Influences on English Poetry.* 1951. [Esp. Homer]

Tilley, Morris P. "A Variant of Homer's Study of Ulysses and the Sirens." *Classical Philology* 21 (1927): 162–64.

Tuve, Rosemond. *Elizabethan and Metaphysical Imagery.* 1947.

Wagenblass, J. H. "J. Keats' Sonnet on George Chapman." *TLS*, 25 Jan. 1936, p. 75.

Wallerstein, Ruth. *Studies in Seventeenth-Century Poetic.* 1950.

Weevers, Th. "Coornhert's and Chapman's *Odysseys*, an Early and a Late Renaissance Homer." *ES* 18 (1936): 145–52.

Williams, William Carlos. "Measure—A Loosely Assembled Essay on Poetic Measure." *Spectrum* 3 (1959): 131–57.

Zocca, Louis R. *Elizabethan Narrative Poetry.* 1950.

B. INDIVIDUAL PLAYS

Bussy D'Ambois

Atkins, Nelson F. "A Borrowing of Lowell from George Chapman." *American Literature* 5 (1933): 172–75.

Dean, William. "Chapman's *Bussy D'Ambois*: A Case for the Aesthetic and Moral Priority of the 1607 Version." *AUMLA* 38 (1971): 159–76. [Not seen]

Gilbert, Allan H. "Chapman's Fortune with Winged Hands." *MLN* 52 (1937): 190–92.

———. "Chapman's Fortune with Winged Hands: Supplementary." *MLN* 54 (1939): 201.

Graves, T. S. "The 'Third Man' in the Prologue to *Bussy D'Ambois*." *MP* 23 (1925): 3–5.

Howarth, R. G. "The Date of *Bussy D'Ambois*." *N&Q* 177 (1939): 25.

Inglis, Fred. "Classicism and Poetic Drama." *Essays in Criticism* 16 (1966): 154–69.

Loane, George. "Bussy D'Ambois's Dying Words." *TLS*, 1 March 1923, p. 143.

Orange, Linwood E. "*Bussy D'Ambois*: The Web of Pretence." *Southern Quarterly* 8 (1969): 37–56.

Reed, Robert Rentoul, Jr. *The Occult on the Tudor and Stuart Stage.* 1965. [And *The Revenge*]

Sprinchorn, Evert. "Wrapt in a Canapi." *Theatre Notebook* 24 (1969): 36–37.

Tamaizumi, Yasuo. "Guise and Elizabethan Dramatists." *SELit*, English No. (1971): 201–2.

Vaganay, Hughes. "Les vers de Pibrac sur la mort de Bussy D'Amboise." *RLC* 13 (1933): 336.

Viebrock, Helmut. "'Thus': das demonstrative Adverb als verbales Signal fur klimaktische dramatische Gesten, aufgezeigt an Beispielen aus dem V Akt von

George Chapmans *Bussy D'Ambois*." In *Festschrift Rudolph Stamm*, ed. Eduard Kolb and Jorg Hasler (1969), pp. 155-61.

Yamada, Akihiro. "Seneca—Chapman—Eliot." *N&Q* 17 (1970): 457-58.

The Revenge of Bussy D'Ambois

Lawlor, J. J. "The Tragic Conflict in *Hamlet*." *RES* 1 (1950): 97-113.

Waggoner, G. R. "An Elizabethan Attitude toward Peace and War." *PQ* 33 (1954): 20-33.

The Tragedy of Charles Duke of Byron

Braunmuller, Albert R. "Chapman's Use of Plutarch's *De Fortuna Romanorum* in *The Tragedy of Charles, Duke of Byron*." *RES* 23 (1972): 178-79.

Jump, J. D. "The Anonymous Masque in MS Egerton 1994." *RES* 11 (1935): 186-91.

Kennedy, Milton Boone. *The Oration in Shakespeare*. 1942.

Caesar and Pompey

Blissett, William. "Lucan's Caesar and the Elizabethan Villain." *SP* 53 (1956): 553-75.

Loane, George. "A Lion Simile of Chapman's." *N&Q* 184 (1943): 16.

The Tragedy of Chabot Admiral of France

Ferguson, A. S. "Chapman, *The Tragedy of Chabot*, Act III, sc. ii." *MLR* 23 (1928): 46.

King, T. J. "Staging of Plays at the Phoenix in Drury Lane, 1617-42." *Theatre Notebook* 19 (1965): 146-66.

The Gentleman Usher

Mustard, W. P. "Hypocrates' Twins." *MLN* 41 (1927): 50.

The Memorable Mask of the Middle Temple and Lincoln's Inn

Linthicum, M. Channing. "Oes." *RES* 7 (1931): 198-200.

The Blind Beggar of Alexandria

Orsini, N. "'Policy' or the Language of Elizabethan Machiavellianism." *JWCI* 9 (1946): 122-34.

Sir Giles Goosecap

Ferguson, A. S. "Chapman and Mary Stewart." *TLS*, 28 May 1925, p. 368.

Eastward Ho

Brettle, R. E. "*Eastward Ho*, 1605, by Chapman, Jonson, and Marston. Bibliography and Circumstances of Production." *Library* 9 (1928): 287–304.

Cooper, Lane. "A Note on *Eastward Ho*, I, ii, 178." *MLN* 43 (1928): 324–25.

Farmer, A. J. "Une source de *Eastward Hoe*: Rabelais." *EA* 1 (1938): 325.

Peery, William. "*Eastward Ho!* and *A Woman is a Weathercock*." *MLN* 62 (1947): 131–32.

Small, Miriam Rossiter. *Charlotte Ramsay Lennox: An Eighteenth Century Lady of Letters*. 1935.

Withington, Robert. "A Note on *Eastward Ho*, I, ii, 178." *MLN* 43 (1928): 28–29.

An Humorous Day's Mirth

Campbell, Oscar James. "Jaques." *Huntington Library Bulletin* 8 (1935): 71–102.

Young, G. M. "Pretty and Pathetical." *TLS*, 26 April 1947, p. 197.

C. UNCERTAIN ASCRIPTIONS, BORROWINGS, INFLUENCE, APOCRYPHA

Beckingham, C. F. "*Othello* and *Revenge for Honour*." *RES* 11 (1935): 198–200.

Bowers, Fredson Thayer. "*Alphonsus, Emperor of Germany*, and the *Ur-Hamlet*." *MLN* 48 (1933): 101–8.

———. "The Date of *Revenge for Honour*." *MLN* 52 (1937): 192–96.

———. "Correspondence on *Revenge for Honour*." *RES* 14 (1938): 329–30.

Robertson, J. M. *The Shakespeare Canon*. Part 2. 1923.

———. *An Introduction to the Study of the Shakespeare Canon*. 1924.

———. *The Shakespeare Canon*. Part 3. 1925.

Shaver, Chester L. "The Date of *Revenge for Honour*." *MLN* 53 (1938): 96–98.

Wells, William. "*Alphonsus, Emperor of Germany*." *N&Q* 179 (1940): 218–23, 236–40.

D. TEXTUAL STUDIES

Greg, W. W. "A Proof-Sheet of 1606." *Library* 17 (1937): 454–57. [*Monsieur D'Olive*]

Stratman, Carl J. *Bibliography of English Printed Tragedy, 1565–1900*. 1966.

Yamada, Akihiro. "Emendations in *The Gentleman Usher* [1606]." *Journal of the Faculty of Arts and Sciences, Shinshu University*. 1966, pp. 19–26. [Not seen]

E. EDITIONS OF THE POETRY AND TRANSLATIONS

Chapman, George. *The Iliad and the Odyssey*. Ed. Richard Herne Shepherd. 1924.

———. *The Whole Works of Homer Prince of Poetts, in His Iliads and Odysses*. 5 vols. 1931.

———. *Hero and Leander, The Divine Poem of Musaeus*. 1936.

JOHN MARSTON

Cecil M. McCulley

The Plays of John Marston has been edited by H. Harvey Wood, 3 vols. (1934-39).

I. GENERAL

A. BIOGRAPHICAL

Convenient gatherings of biographical information have appeared in Anthony Caputi, *John Marston, Satirist* (1961); A. José Axelrad, *Un malcontent élizabéthain: John Marston (1576-1634)* (1955); Philip J. Finkelpearl, *John Marston of the Middle Temple: An Elizabethan Dramatist in His Social Setting* (1969); and Giuliano Pellegrini, *Il teatro di John Marston* (1952).

Several articles by R. E. Brettle provide biographical details. "Marston Born in Oxfordshire," *MLR* 22 (1927): 317-19, establishes the place of birth and the approximate date—a few weeks before 7 October, 1576—as well as giving facts about the marriage of Marston's parents and some property in Oxfordshire later inherited by the play-wright. "John Marston, Dramatist, at Oxford, 1591(?)-1594, 1609," *RES* 3 (1927): 398-405, suggests that the residence at Brasenose College began with Trinity Term 1591, although Marston did not "subscribe and matriculate" until February 1591-92; details of his clerical career are listed. "John Marston, Dramatist: Some New Facts about His Life," *MLR* 22 (1927): 7-14, deals first with the residence at the Middle Temple, but also covers the return to Oxford, probably in 1609. In "Bibliographical Notes on Some Marston Quartos and Early Collected Editions," *Library* 8 (1927-28): 336-48, Brettle suggests that perhaps from about 1609 on Marston would not willingly lend his name to a "play-quarto or collection." "The 'Poet Marston' Letter to Sir Gervase Clifton, 1607," *RES* 4 (1928): 212-14, concerns text and date.

Brettle's "Notes on John Marston," *RES* 13 (1962): 390-93, describes seven known examples of Marston's handwriting and signature, and discusses probate documents relating to his father-in-law, Dr. William Wilkes, the most significant suggestion being the dating of the marriage in 1605. A family connection between the poet and his fellow satirist Everard Guilpin, first indicated by Philip J. Finkelpearl in "Donne and Everard Gilpin: Additions, Corrections, and Conjectures," *RES* 14 (1963): 164-67, is strengthened with new evidence by Brettle in "Everard Guilpin and John Marston (1576-1634)," *RES* 16 (1965): 396-99. Brettle's "John Marston and the Duke of Buckingham, 1627-1628," *N&Q* 14 (1967): 326-30, examines the evidence that during his priestly service in Hampshire in 1627-28 Marston wrote two satirical poems on the Isle of Rhé expedition of the Duke of Buckingham and a chronogram and couplet also attacking the duke.

In "The Commencement of Marton's Career as a Dramatist," *RES* 22 (1971): 442-45, David G. O'Neill cites a canceled passage from the father's will, of late October 1599, on the likelihood that his "willfull disobedyent sonne" will sell the inherited law books, and on the younger man's "delighte in playes vayne studdyes and fooleryes." O'Neill interprets this as evidence that Marston may have begun writing plays, perhaps late in 1598 or early the following year.

Philip J. Finkelpearl in "Henry Walley of the Stationers' Company and John Marston," *PBSA* 56 (1962): 366-68, suggests that Marston used his friend Walley, at that time Clerk of the Stationers' Company, to bring pressure on William Sheares to remove the author's name from the reissue of the *Works* in 1633 as *Tragedies and Comedies*. In "A New Date for *Antonio's Revenge*," *PMLA* 53 (1938): 129-37, Donald J. McGinn advises scepticism about a reference to Marston in the phrase "mr maxton the new poete" in Henslowe's *Diary*. In their edition of the *Diary* (1961), however, R. A. Foakes and R. T. Rickert believe the interlined addition "mr mastone" to be Henslowe's. Arnold Davenport, ed., *The Poems of John Marston* (1961), notes news and gossip of the playhouses in *Certain Satires* and *The Scourge of Villainy* which suggest that as early as 1598 Marston "was already in touch with the world of the theatre." Irwin Smith, *Shakespeare's Blackfriars Playhouse: Its History and Its Design* (1964), reprints documents from a suit in the Court of Requests in 1610 relating to Marston's one-sixth share in the Blackfriars company.

In *John Marston*, Finkelpearl points out further implications of known facts about the dramatist. The entertainment expenses involved in acceptance of the office of Reader at the Middle Temple indicate that the elder Marston was well off; therefore upon his father's death in 1599 the son must have been "relatively wealthy." The connection with Henry Walley reveals that Marston's friendships extended beyond class barriers. Several references from 1600 on indicate recognition of the poet as an important writer; and a passage from the revels of 1635-36, pairing Shakespeare with Marston, implies that at the Middle Temple he was "still something of a hero." Legal allusions in the works suggest that Marston did study some law.

The remaining biographical material, less central, relates to three episodes: quarrels involved in Marston's early verse satires, the Poetomachia, and the *Eastward Ho* affair. In "The Quarrel of the Satirists," *MLR* 37 (1942): 123-30, Arnold Davenport discusses Hall and Marston and related events in the "series of interlocked quarrels," which he considers separate from the Poetomachia. In his edition of the *Collected Poems of Joseph Hall* (1949), Davenport judges the attack on Hall unprovoked, and suggests a chronology postulating an early edition of the *Metamorphosis of Pygmalion's Image*. In "John Weever's *Epigrammes* and the Hall-Marston Quarrel," *RES* 11 (1935): 66-68, Davenport looks at another who aided Marston by attacking Hall, and in his edition of Marston's poetry he speculates that Mastigophoros in *Certain Satires* refers to Hall and Curio to Davies. Anthony Caputi, in "'Certain Satires' and the Hall-Marston Quarrel," *N&Q* 1 (1954): 235-36, suggests a possible additional motive for Marston: he objected that Hall presumed to write about London without, like himself, knowing it well. In *Complaint and Satire in Early English Literature* (1956), John Peter thinks that Marston may have concluded from acquaintance with the Greene-Nashe quarrel that a similar one would increase sales of his satires. J. B. Leishman, editing *The Three Parnassus Plays (1598-1601)* (1949), offers evidence for his contention that the impact of the dispute of the satirists as well as Jonson's criticism of Marston is reflected in 2 *Return from Parnassus* in Furor Poeticus, who, though not a "satirical portrait of Marston, . . . was certainly intended as a vehicle for the parody of Marston's style." Bernard Harris in "Men Like Satyrs," *Elizabethan Poetry*, SuAS, vol. 2 (1960), pp. 174-201, also sees Furor Poeticus as Marston; but Marjorie L. Reyburn in "New Facts and Theories about the Parnassus Plays," *PMLA* 74 (1959): 325-35, views him as a "composite figure" parodying Jonson and Marston, and even Marlowe. Finkelpearl, *John Marston* (above), cites further evidence from the satires suggesting that Ruscus is meant to be Sir John

Davies. In "The Portraiture of Gabriel Harvey in the Parnassus Plays and John Marston," *Neophil* 36 (1952): 225-34, W. Schrickx argues that Harvey is the target of much of the satire in *The Scourge of Villainy*.

Several general treatments of the Poetomachia discount the quarrel: W. L. Halstead, "What 'War of the Theatres'?" *CE* 9 (1947-48): 424-26; Robert Withington, in an article with the same title in *CE* 10 (1948-49): 163-64; Bernard Harris, ed., *The Malcontent* (1967); and John J. Enck, *Jonson and the Comic Truth* (1957). On the other hand, Henryk Zbierski in *Shakespeare and the "War of the Theatres"* (1957) sees the struggle opposing two types of theater, the "private" and the "open" stages. In "La compagnie des enfants de St. Paul, Londres (1599-1606)," in *Dramaturgie et société: rapports entre l'oeuvre théâtrale, son interprétation, et son public aux 16. et 17. siècles*, ed. Jean Jacquot et al., 2 vols. (1968), 2: 655-74, W. R. Gair proposes that the Poetomachia had three underlying causes: the increase of topical allusions in the late moralities, the public predilection for discovering hidden references in literary works, and the "littérature contemporaine d'invective."

Esther Cloudman Dunn in *Ben Jonson's Art* (1925), following earlier criticism, suggests that Marston satirized Jonson as early as 1598 in the preface to *The Scourge of Villainy*; H. Harvey Wood in his edition of the *Plays* agrees, as does M. T. Jones-Davies in *Un peintre de la vie londonienne: Thomas Dekker (circa 1572-1632)*, 2 vols. (1958). Others, however, examine *Histriomastix* as the beginning of the quarrel. C. H. Herford and Percy and Evelyn Simpson, eds., *Ben Jonson*, 11 vols. (1925-52), vol. 1, find that Chrisoganus is intended to be a flattering picture of Jonson, but Marston evokes Jonson's tirades so badly that he seems to parody: "to modern eyes, and quite probably to those of contemporaries, it reads like caricature." Others also believe Chrisoganus designed as a complimentary portrait: John Peter and J. B. Leishman; Eduard Eckhardt, *Das englische Drama der Spätrenaissance* (1929); and Ralph W. Berringer, "Jonson's *Cynthia's Revels* and the War of the Theatres," *PQ* 22 (1943): 1-22. Chrisoganus may be Jonson, agrees Finkelpearl in *John Marston*, and is intended as a "totally admirable figure"; nevertheless, some of his speeches echoing the manner of *The Scourge of Villainy* might have annoyed Jonson. Harold Ogden White in *Plagiarism and Imitation during the English Renaissance* (1935), however, sees in the character an attack on Jonson for excessive closeness in imitation of the classics, amounting to simple translation.

Oscar James Campbell, "The Dramatic Construction of *Poetaster*," *Huntington Library Bulletin* 9 (1936): 37–62, finds a sign that Jonson took offense at Chrisoganus: Horace is partly "Jonson's own redrawing of those lineaments in that portrait which he did not consider flattering." In his edition of *The Malcontent* (1933), G. B. Harrison suggests that Chrisoganus is too close an imitation of Macilente in *Every Man Out of His Humour*, so that Jonson added a parody of Marston's vocabulary to the published edition of that play. Finally, David Bevington, *Tudor Drama and Politics: A Critical Approach to Topical Meaning* (1968), doubts that Chrisoganus can be identified with Jonson: like Posthaste, the character is a social type joined with such abstractions as Peace, Plenty, and Pride; and to Gair (above), no matter what Jonson thought, Chrisoganus is a "portrait amplifié de Marston satiriste."

Reflections on Jonson in *Antonio and Mellida* also have been suggested. In his edition of Kyd's *Spanish Tragedy* for the Revels Plays (1959), Philip Edwards says that the parodies seemingly directed at the painter scene in the 1602 additions to Kyd's play may have been inserted in Marston's work after the first productions, to mock Jonson. G. B. Harrison in *Shakespeare's Fellows* (1923) thinks Feliche a parody of Jonson's Crites in *Cynthia's Revels*.

As to *Jack Drum's Entertainment*, Herford and Simpson, vol. 1, believe that Brabant Senior caricatures Jonson, but too ambiguously to represent much of an attack. Harold Ogden White, John Peter, and W. R. Gair find that the character satirizes Jonson; Peter calls Brabant an "unsympathetic portrait." Tucker Brooke, *The Renaissance (1500–1660)*, in *A Literary History of England*, ed. Albert C. Baugh (1948; 2nd ed. 1967), thinks the identification probable. J. B. Leishman inclines to believe Brabant Senior a "savage caricature" of Jonson; David Bevington, while not sure that the matter contributes directly to the Poetomachia, finds in the character a lampoon of "self-appointed literary dictators" scanting rivals and being overly harsh on court pleasures. But Berringer judges that there is no convincing evidence for the identification of Brabant Senior; and Finkelpearl in *John Marston* calls the identification "utterly groundless." Oscar James Campbell in *Comicall Satyre and Shakespeare's Troilus and Cressida* (1938) sees Brabant as indicative of annoyance at Jonson's faults, but not identifiable as the man.

The role of *What You Will* in the Poetomachia has been variously estimated. Although it is uncertain whether this play preceded or followed Jonson's *Poetaster* in 1601, Herford and Simpson, vol. 9, suggest that Marston's play, with a satiric portrait of Jonson as Lampatho Doria, came first; in III.ii Lampatho parodies the manner of Asper in Jonson's *Every Man Out*. Berringer sees in Lampatho thrusts at both *Every Man Out* and *Cynthia's Revels* and a probable caricature of Jonson; in this work Marston may well have "detonated" the Poetomachia. Leishman considers Lampatho a "more elaborate but less savage portrait of Jonson" than Brabant Senior; Quadratus, in turn, may be an "idealized self-portrait of Marston, or of Marston's point of view." Bevington sees in *What You Will* another attack on the self-righteous literary tyrant like that already put forth in *Jack Drum's Entertainment*; if not a vital part of the War, these sketches at least show why Marston encouraged *Satiromastix*. John Peter, while seeing Lampatho as Jonson, judges him too volatile in manner to be very persuasive; in addition, Quadratus is an attractive self-portrait by Marston. Bernard Harris in his edition of the *Malcontent* (1967) views *What You Will* instead as Marston's finale in the War of the Theaters. O. J. Campbell, *Comicall Satyre*, finds Lampatho not literally Jonson, though used as an instrument to criticize the man; the character at times also apparently mocks the violence of Marston's own verse satires. On the other hand, Finkelpearl in his book sees Lampatho as hardly at all like Jonson and much more like Marston himself—though as representing some traits, not constituting a self-portrait. G. B. Harrison, in the "Essay on Elizabethan Melancholy" accompanying his edition of Nicholas Breton's *Melancholike Humours* (1929), pp. 49–89, suspects that Lampatho is indeed a self-portrait.

There is some weighing of Shakespeare's possible role in the quarrel as regards Marston. Henryk Zbierski considers not only that Marston may be attacking Shakespeare in *The Metamorphosis of Pygmalion's Image* and *The Scourge of Villainy,* but that Thersites in *Troilus and Cressida* represents Marston. Alfred Harbage in *Shakespeare and the Rival Traditions* (1952) had suggested earlier that a common "gleeful morbidity" in particular would have made contemporaries inevitably relate Thersites to Marston. G. B. Harrison, ed., *The Scourge of Villainy, 1599* (1925), thinks it "not improbable" that Jaques in *As You Like It* gently satirizes Marston; but Oscar James Campbell in "Jaques," *Huntington Library Bulletin* 8 (1935): 71–102, finds a particular reference unlikely because of the conventional quality in the construction of both Marston's satire and Shakespeare's play.

Finally, Marston's part in calling down the royal wrath upon *Eastward Ho* in 1605 has received comment. E. K. Chambers, in *The Elizabethan Stage*, 4 vols. (1923), vols. 2 and 3, considers Marston "mainly responsible" for the incident, although he avoided imprisonment by flight. Since the scene which Chambers believes caused the scandal (III.iii) is generally attributed to Chapman, Marston must have interpolated the offending passage. G. B. Harrison, on the other hand, in *Shakespeare's Fellows*, supposes that Chapman wrote the provocative passage. R. E. Brettle in *"Eastward Ho*, 1605, by Chapman, Jonson, and Marston, Bibliography and Circumstances of Production," *Library* 9 (1928-29): 287-302, finds room for doubt that the published version of the play caused trouble; more likely the first production fell between 16 July and 31 August or a little later in 1605, when the Lord Chamberlain was away on the royal progress to Oxford, hence without regular approval. Marston may have fled, may have already been out of town, or may have been imprisoned but not with Jonson or Chapman or not for so long. Jean Jacquot, *George Chapman (1559-1634), sa vie, sa poésie, son théâtre, sa pensée* (1951), finds it unlikely that Marston would have retouched a Chapman scene and thus produced the offense; if it happened, Chapman certainly knew what was going on and was partly responsible.

B. GENERAL STUDIES OF THE PLAYS

Of the five full-scale recent studies of the drama, the most extensive is A. José Axelrad's *Un malcontent élizabéthain: John Marston (1576-1634)* (1955). After preliminary treatment of the satires, Axelrad analyzes the plays in terms of action, influences, dramatic technique, characters (including spokesmen of the author), style, and the author's personality and literary position. Marston emerges as preeminently a man of his time, a satirist concentrating on the double theme of sex and hypocrisy, perhaps "un obsédé sexuel." While generally criticizing women, he is fascinated by them. He is effective in the "scène frappante," in the appeal of secondary characters, and in dramatic prose rather than poetry. His spokesmen are malcontents; "Il n'est pas exagéré de dire que ce caractère domine toute l'oeuvre de Marston." Appropriately, *The Malcontent* is his best play.

Anthony Caputi's *John Marston, Satirist* (1961) announces itself as a "formal study of his work as a continuous experiment in satiricomic forms." While the tragedies receive less emphasis, the verse satires are treated substantially as evidence of Marston's world view—Stoic, Neo-Stoic, and Christian—but the technique painstakingly developed through the dramas is also a distinct topic. He goes from "structures of thesis such as are found in the satires and *Histriomastix* toward imitative structures." Caputi stresses Marston's positive use of the inherent power of child actors to burlesque adults, with the converse suggestion that adults are like children; he notes the development of a strong comic element in the satirical plays. The best of Marston's satirical comedies, headed by *The Malcontent*, exploit the disguise plot.

Philip J. Finkelpearl's innovative *John Marston of the Middle Temple* (1969) studies the works with particular emphasis upon the possible influence of the dramatic customs and intellectual audience of the Inns of Court. A substantial first part explores this institution. Marston's verse satires generally expose the vices of young gallants such as his fellow law students, yet he espouses their Ovidian, anti-Petrarchan attitudes toward love. In Calvinist severity, however, he does not allow his sinners freedom to reform; and the vituperative satirical persona he adopts makes rapport with the audience impossible. Hence before the bishops' opposition he gave up verse satire. In the plays gallants and their "linguistic mannerisms" are again prime targets, but Marston learns to suppress the arrogant satiric commentator, and acquires a sensitivity to human suffering and a dark sense of man's fate. *The Malcontent* successfully combines satire and characterization, but moves into the dangerous realm of political relevance. That Montaigne influenced Marston is evident in *The Dutch Courtesan*; a young man's lust is natural if brutish, and one may learn from experience. *The Fawn* draws heavily on the Middle Temple Christmas revels, but may also in Gonzago contain a full-scale satiric portrait of King James. *Sophonisba* seeks to embody an old ideal of Marston's, a woman good, true, and beautiful; the heroine is the dramatist's one real Stoic, but as a virgin martyr she shows how unlikely the role is for most people. In this, his one dramatic poem and would-be masterpiece, Marston follows in the line of Sidney in expressing "avant-garde taste for an abstract, stylized drama like that of France and Italy." After a course of drama of gloom and irony, Marston comes to believe in the survival of virtue, even a generous virtue which should be a fitting goal for an audience of gallants.

In *John Marston's Theatrical Drama* (1974), John Scott Colley stresses the playwright's satiric purpose, which produces separate "scenic units" rather than an integrated design for the whole, and the importance of stage action over dialogue. Marston's "staunch Christian consciousness" has absolute standards; he rejects optimism and the Stoic formula. His dramas present reactions, undifferentiated as to moral or aesthetic, against the great plays of the 1590s. While concerned about stage success and continually experimenting to that end, as in his adaptation of Jonsonian method in the middle plays, he also uses theatricality to make the "audience view his drama with both detachment and concern."

Giuliano Pellegrini's less-known *Il teatro di John Marston* (1952) sees the plays as representing a higher regard for the artistic values of the genre than perhaps is found among Marston's contemporaries. Though the characters are somewhat distorted—a heritage of his previous work in verse satire—the plays contain such compensation as conscious valuation of imagery. After inconclusive experiment in the two parts of *Antonio and Mellida*, Marston returns in *Jack Drum's Entertainment* to the satiric vein. Of the greater works, *The Dutch Courtesan*, in which the satirist yields to the dramatist, is the most attractive; *The Malcontent* best joins Marston's two literary roles and contains the essential Marstonian hero; and *Sophonisba* is "una gemma barocca, poeticamente l'opera migliore del Marston." The dramatist's overriding purpose proves to be ethical, satire serving only as a means to this end.

Among less expansive studies, Willi Egli's *John Marstons Dramen* (1956) omits not only the poems but *Eastward Ho, Jack Drum's Entertainment, Histriomastix,* and *What You Will* as not clearly attributable to the author or as mainly pertinent to the War of the Theaters. Egli does not offer an overview of the plays he does discuss because of Marston's exceptional role as "grosser Experimentator," but makes several general observations. Marston's seriousness and respect for the drama are evident in his stage directions, and his use of music is supplemented by—proportionately—more than twice the number of Shakespearean images from this area. Stoicism, not as fundamental in the plays as might at first be thought, finds its particular role in dramatic contrast. Marston's use of Machiavelli lacks discrimination, the ironic attitude toward himself which some have claimed to see is not apparent, nor does he foreshadow his subsequent ordination to the priesthood. He may be regarded as a pioneer in the new style of revenge tragedy and especially in the bitter treatment of the erotic, from *Antonio and Mellida* on. His dramas as a whole could be considered a "Phänomenologie des Lasters."

Limited but influential general comments appear elsewhere. T. S. Eliot in "John Marston," *TLS,* 26 July 1934, pp. 517–18 (rpt. in *Elizabethan Essays* [1934], pp. 177–95, and *Essays on Elizabethan Drama* [1956], pp. 162–78), sees in the playwright "an original variation of that deep discontent and rebelliousness so frequent among the Elizabethan dramatists." His verse at times has a provocatively abrupt, exasperated character, and he can give us the "sense of something behind, more real than any of his personages and their action." *Sophonisba* comes closest to expressing his irregular power. Theodore Spencer, in an early wide-ranging essay, "John Marston," *Criterion* 13 (1933–34): 581–99 (rpt. in *Selected Essays,* ed. Alan C. Purves [1966], pp. 123–38), gives only limited approval to the style, "a kind of growing pain which language was bound to suffer as it passed from the manner of Spenser to the manner of Donne." Marston's variations in diction and rhythms, while seldom successful and lacking in overtones, have a "stimulating effect" which makes him important in the foundation of the metaphysical school. Kinsayder is identified as both a pun on the author's name ("mar-stone") and a reference to the operation of kinsing, "which castrated unruly dogs and docked their tails," a suggestion of the effect that Marston, "essentially a Puritan," wished to exert on mankind through his satires. *The Dutch Courtesan* shows life as a "dark and difficult problem where reason and passion, as the two essential parts of a human being, tug violently against each other." Unlike Montaigne, Marston sees lust as "unnatural and obscene," inevitably destructive where it prevails.

Una Ellis-Fermor in *The Jacobean Drama* (1936; fourth ed. 1958) says that the dramatist carries on in his imagery the "tragic tradition of Marlowe and of Shakespeare's early work"; images provide "the essential indications of mood and underlying thought without which neither plot, character nor the true aesthetic values of the play could be rightly apprehended." During Marston's career his thought goes from unintegrated philosophic speeches to "psychological analysis, particularly self-analysis"; character likewise becomes more alive, reaching its peak in Malevole. The first four plays are greatly derivative; thereafter the playwright is his own man: i.e., divided between moralist and poet.

Marston's moral posture has been both attacked and defended. The numerous references to him in Alfred Harbage's *Shakespeare and the Rival Traditions* (I,A) generally concern his moral relevance. In using the image of the actor to suggest falsity, he may be denigrating both the artistic power and the moral tradition of the popular theaters. Marston has a "compulsion to degrade." Since he is a "coterie dramatist unadulterated," perhaps his surroundings have conditioned his thought: ". . . Marston's stylistic excesses are his own, but his conception of man is that of his milieu." The "venomous portrait" of the prostitute Franceschina in *The Dutch Courtesan* is exceptional for a private-theater play; but otherwise, whereas the popular writers simply accept the normality of woman's sexual desire, Marston glorifies it, clouding even his paragon Sophonisba and making his ingenues not "engagingly natural" but "overwhelmingly meaty."

The observation on the unreality of the actor to Marston receives some amplification in Anne Righter, *Shakespeare and the Idea of the Play* (1962). Samuel Schoenbaum, "The Precarious Balance of John Marston," *PMLA* 67 (1952): 1069-78 (rpt. in *Elizabethan Drama: Modern Essays in Criticism*, ed. Ralph J. Kaufmann [1961], pp. 123-33), describes the precarious balance between the "attraction and revulsion" toward man as a creature of soul and body, and toward courts and women. The resultant incongruity appears in the mixture of romantic melodrama and satirical comedy, especially in *Antonio's Revenge*, in imagery of physical torment and desecration and in the whole "nightmare world of lust and viciousness, intrigue and violence" of most of the plays. Since Marston's attitude participates in the "skeptical outlook," the "malaise," of his age, he was popular in the private theaters; "he stimulated the jaded tastes of his frivolous and sophisticated aristocratic audience," while adding a "gratuitous display of his own morbid tendencies."

On the other hand, Gustav Cross in "The Retrograde Genius of John Marston," *REL* 2, no. 4 (1961): 19-27, views Marston as "first and foremost a moralist." In the Elizabethan period, sexuality was widely considered "a symptom and a symbol of the disruptive power of the passions," and for Marston in particular "the over-emphasis and exaggeration . . . need not be taken as evidence of a morbid fascination with his subject: Marston writes in the tradition of the hellfire preacher who paints vice at its most vicious in the hope that his audience will look to heaven." Basically "his plays are philosophic explorations of the moral philosophy of the stoics," though he finds this ideal untenable in the face of a need for action. With a somewhat similar basic idea, Paul M. Zall in "John Marston, Moralist," *ELH* 20 (1953): 186–93, develops it differently. Marston's close attention to lust is the "key to understanding his conscious purpose as a dramatist": following conventional morality in most other respects, he has an original analysis of the "problem of the normality of concupiscence." He thus concentrates on lust as a philosophical problem; an anti-Stoic, he finds love, either idealized or natural affection, a good; and lust, either pathological hypersexuality or "acquired" desire, induced by social pressures, abnormal. Marston attempts to show "norm" characters who admit passion without letting it control them.

G. K. Hunter, in "English Folly and Italian Vice: The Moral Landscape of John Marston," in *Jacobean Theatre*, SuAS, vol. 1 (1960), pp. 84–111, finds Marston's morality empirical rather than theoretical. *Antonio and Mellida* is innovative in bringing to the stage true Machiavellian *Realpolitik*. The protagonist of *The Malcontent* "is sufficiently close to the empirical scientist to know (and demonstrate) that there is no substitute for experience, and that experience is only available to those who are, in some sense, part of the world they observe." Divided "between the desire to participate in the life of power, and the desire to condemn and withdraw," he is tortured by a world in which "the corrupt court of a Renaissance prince is in fact no less a Morality masque of skulls beneath the skin." In *The Dutch Courtesan*, Freevill is driven by sex rather than power; "Here the average self-centered man of Machiavelli and Bacon can be seen in the process of becoming the *gallant* of Caroline or Restoration Comedy, the man whose virtue (if that is the correct word) comes to him by his experience of vice and not at all by precept."

In *The Morality-Patterned Comedy of the Renaissance* (1970), Sylvia D. Feldman treats three plays of Marston. *Histriomastix* is the first of a group "omitting penance" and "the temptation to despair," but it differs from the others in having several mankind figures from different social positions, all beginning in a state of virtue. Chrisoganus is the principal "virtue figure," and his commentary shows the moral bearing of the play and the way back to virtue through pursuit of knowledge. The vices and virtues appear both as allegorical figures and as qualities implied in action and dialogue. In *Eastward Ho* Security is a vice figure, Touchstone a virtue figure, Quicksilver a mankind figure; in *The Dutch*

Courtesan the corresponding characters are Franceschina, Freevill, and Malheureux. The action concerns the danger of lust to "spiritual salvation," which seems to be accompanied by mundane happiness: Freevill saves Malheureux not only from death, but also from damnation.

A number of studies focus primarily upon the role of satire in the plays. Alvin Kernan in *The Cankered Muse: Satire of the English Renaissance* (1959) argues that the dramatist stands apart from his figures acting as satirists, who are "fully dramatic and independent characters." Thus Kernan avoids the biographical assumption of much previous Marston criticism, that the satirist of the plays "is the voice of Marston himself breaking through his character into the play and usually doing violence to both dramatic structure and characterization." In support of this interpretation the critic analyzes the speaker in *The Scourge of Villainy* and the satiric commentators in most of the plays, with special attention to *Histriomastix, Antonio and Mellida,* and *What You Will.*

John Peter, *Complaint and Satire in Early English Literature* (I,A), claims that the satires reveal Marston uneasily shuttling between Christian complaint and obscene satire influenced principally by Martial; the dramas with a satirist as character generally have something of the same difficulty. The attempt to add satire in the Latin tradition to the plays has a dubious effect upon the dramatic accomplishment. Even in *The Malcontent* "Marston has conflated and confused the Malcontent's two roles, and at the same time has given unreasonable prominence to the disguise rather than to the inner man"; as moralist Malevole is never properly motivated. Satire in *The Dutch Courtesan* is much better integrated, less merely a matter of words and more part of the situation and action; even the licentiousness is, for the first time, harmonized with the whole drama. And in *The Fawn* satire is subtly vindicated by implication, through the emphasis on its opposite, flattery. Peter pays tribute to Marston's mastery of a great range of dramatic verse, including a "colloquial freedom that was close to the suppleness and spirit of everyday speech." In an earlier article, "John Marston's Plays," *Scrutiny* 17 (1950-51): 132-53, Peter likewise censures Marston for prurience and double-entendre, but admires his variety of styles.

R. A. Foakes, "Tragedies at the Children's Theatres after 1600: A Challenge to the Adult Stage," in *The Elizabethan Theatre II,* ed. David Galloway (1970), pp. 37-59, traces Marston's development with the boy actors of a "satirical mode of tragedy" in *Antonio's Revenge* and

The Malcontent and, when this method had been exploited by the adult companies, his new departure into stylized ceremonial tragedy in *Sophonisba*. In *Shakespeare: the Dark Comedies to the Last Plays: From Satire to Celebration* (1971), Foakes repeats much of the earlier material, with additions. *Antonio and Mellida* finds a "new way of exploiting satire" by "mocking adult conventions, and then in turn mocking the mockers," though Marston could not go further in this vein and had to move on to revenge-tragedy conventions in his next play. Earlier, in "Shakespeare's Later Tragedies," *Shakespeare 1564–1964*, ed. Edward A. Bloom (1964), pp. 95–109, Foakes calls attention to the mocking parody of "the romantic tragic hero and stock villain" especially in the two parts of *Antonio and Mellida*, which he believes fostered a "new consciousness" in drama.

O. J. Campbell's *Comicall Satyre* (I,A) suggests that Marston turned to the stage because of the edict banning publication of verse satire. Adapting a satiric commentator to dramatic structure proved difficult; but Marston improved in this regard when he conceived Quadratus in *What You Will*. Campbell's *Shakespeare's Satire* (1943) reviews the Marstonian conventions of the malcontent and the deposed and disguised duke as satiric commentator. To Travis Bogard in *The Tragic Satire of John Webster* (1955), Marston is an innovator: "Chiefly because of Marston's influence, much of the serious drama after the turn of the century was informed by the spirit, the subject matter, and the techniques of Elizabethan verse satire." Even so *The Malcontent* lacks "tragic perception" because the satirist never sees the necessary final truth and order; "his concluding action is a part of the thing scourged." D. J. Palmer, "Elizabethan Tragic Heroes," in *Elizabethan Theatre*, SuAS, vol. 9, pp. 10–35, sees Marston as the "chief innovator of tragical satire," a form which outdated Kyd and Marlowe. The malcontent is the new tragic hero, the "satirical commentator who is both detached from and involved in the evil and corruption he sees around him." He is at once revolutionary and reactionary: "But while the malcontent often represented an attitude of profound skepticism which undermined the old tragic scheme of providential justice, at the same time he revived that homiletic spirit which was never far beneath the surface of Elizabethan tragedy."

Associated with satire in the plays are the sense of melancholy and the malcontent figure; the relation between the two is disputed. In *Voices of Melancholy: Studies in Literary Treatments of Melancholy in Renaissance England* (1971), Bridget Gellert Lyons analyzes Marston's attempt in the verse satires and several plays to relate satire and melancholy and "to find appropriate forms for the malcontent's voice or consciousness." As the playwright sees the satirist, the world's disorder is mirrored in his frustration and madness. After beginning crudely with *Jack Drum's Entertainment*, Marston improves his concept of the "melancholy satirist" in *What You Will*. With the *Antonio* plays, he defines a new role for the melancholy character, the "tragic victim," and in *The Malcontent* he combines satirist and victim with an inner rationale, in an environment appropriate to the attitude. Malevole, however, has only melancholy enough to support his tirades, "themselves the instruments of his revenge"; yet more than any other play except *Hamlet* this one shows the truth and heroism of the satirist. In "The Elizabethan Malcontent," *Joseph Quincy Adams Memorial Studies*, ed. James G. McManaway et al. (1948; rpt. in *Selected Essays* [above], pp. 123-38), pp. 523-35, Theodore Spencer distinguishes between melancholics like Antonio and Hamlet, changed by a grief that has altered their conception of human nature and hence devoted to solitary despair, and malcontents like Malevole, a "displaced person" in the social order, not associated with melancholy, coarse in manner and reveling in disorder, even in evil.

The Marstonian protagonist may also be seen in relation to Stoic philosophy. In "The Convention of the Stoic Hero as Handled by Marston," *MLR* 39 (1944): 338-46, Michael Higgins contends that Marston uses Stoicism partly to illustrate pessimism and the problem of evil, "in order to throw into blacker contrast the false and rotten world of human normality." His sources are Seneca's tragedies and moral treatises and Florio's Montaigne somewhat darkened in tone. The two parts of *Antonio and Mellida* furnish the best example: Andrugio "is the first attempt in English popular drama to present a philosophical sage, conducting his life according to the principles of patience and of constancy which Seneca had set forth in his moral epistles." Geoffrey D. Aggeler, "Stoicism and Revenge in Marston," *ES* 51 (1970): 507-17, analyzes the role of the Stoic protagonists modeled on Seneca's moral essays, Epictetus, and Plutarch. In *Antonio and Mellida* and *Sophonisba* they merely "endure nobly" the assaults of Machiavellian oppressors; but in two other plays in which the heroes have the obligation of revenge, "Marston is exploring the moral implications of vengeful commitment." In *Antonio's Revenge* Antonio infects the other characters and demonstrates the "total moral abandonment which inevitably follows the surrender of reason to passion." But in *The Malcontent*

Malevole renounces revenge by blood and becomes a "minister of spiritual restoration."

Marston's innovations in dramatic technique have provoked especially diverse commentary. Robert Boies Sharpe, in *The Real War of the Theaters: Shakespeare's Fellows in Rivalry with the Admiral's Men, 1594-1603* (1935), sees Marston as a dramatic trailblazer. Noting the "affinity between the growing Elizabethan mood of cynical melancholy and the Senecan dramatic accessories," he inaugurated a revival with *Antonio's Revenge* which probably led to Shakespeare's *Hamlet* among other things; and with *The Dutch Courtesan* he began the major change in Jacobean satiric drama, making cynicism "more democratic and realistic." R. W. Ingram in "Marston, Old or New Elizabethan," *HAB* 17, no. 2 (1966): 19-26, says that modern revivals of *The Dutch Courtesan* prove that "Marston made plays which work in the theatre"; in William Gaskell's phrase he has a gift like John Osborne's for the "highly rhetorical set-piece of invective." But a look at *Antonio and Mellida* shows his Elizabethan quality more clearly: struggling with the revenge tragedy tradition, he follows sympathy with ridicule, producing "something akin to a dramatic fantasia on themes suggested by revenge tragedy and the illusions of the stage." The detachment and tragedy paradoxically work together. Robert Brustein in "Slime and Snottery," a review of several English productions including one of *The Malcontent,* in *The Observer,* 22 April 1973, p. 31, speaks of Marston's "profound existential nausea" and calls him the "most innovative and experimental of all his contemporaries."

Jacobean City Comedy: A Study of Satiric Plays by Jonson, Marston, and Middleton (1968), by Brian Gibbons, finds Marston an important contributor to the type. In *Antonio and Mellida, What You Will, The Fawn,* and *The Malcontent,* parody, by the dramatist and by the characters, frustrates conventional response. Marston also offers "images of the inner anxiety and psychological confusion of the characters; they become, in a sense, emblems of their human condition." The playwright is influenced by Jonson's "comicall satyre" and by Middleton, but has his own emphasis on "expression of extremes," shown in "Italianate comic intrigue" and the "uniquely Marstonian modulation of moods." Jean Jacquot surveys several Marston plays in "Le répertoire des compagnies d'enfants à Londres (1600-1610): Essai d'interprétation socio-dramaturgique," in *Dramaturgie et société,* ed. Jacquot et al. (I,A), 2: 729-82. The satire on adult companies in *Histriomastix* may be related to the revival of the child actors and the desire of the playwrights to control the repertory of the latter. Otherwise the play utilizes the motifs of genealogy and Fortune's wheel to show the perils of an expanding society, and it foreshadows the cyclical theory of history in its economic, psychological, and moral changes. *What You Will* opposes the sociable fantasy of Quadratus to the satire of Lampatho Doria, but Marston artfully makes them at times appear contrasting aspects of the same person. He is outstandingly inventive in allying music, in precise modulation and tone, to drama. In *Antonio and Mellida* the ridiculous and the pathetic are played off against each other with the aid of music, "à donner de la condition humaine une idée misérable et dérisoire."

In another essay in the same collection, "Le théâtre de Blackfriars de 1596 à 1606," 2: 675–704, Louis Lecocq comments on Marston's dramatic technique. *What You Will* is constructed on two structural elements: disguise and "le refus d'un abandon total à l'illusion dramatique." The play achieves unity in variety: "Une harmonie existe entre tous les moyens d'expression qu'il met en oeuvre: la tonalité générale de déraison plaisante s'allie agréablement aux rappels des conventions théâtrales, grâce au rythme allègre des mouvements et des répliques, et grâce à l'utilisation pertinente des interventions musicales et des changements d'éclairage." Whereas the first version of *The Malcontent* exhibits a uniform tone reconciling oppositions, the revised version has rather "un equilibre entre deux tonalités opposées."

Michael Shapiro, "Children's Troupes: Dramatic Illusion and Acting Style," *ComD* 3 (1969): 42–53, maintains that in the *Antonio* plays, *The Fawn*, and *What You Will* Marston makes dramatic use of the audience's double awareness of characters and child actors. The bawdry stresses this disparity, as do inductions, burlesques of styles, and theatrical allusions in general. In "Toward a Reappraisal of the Children's Troupes," *Theatre Survey* 13, no. 2 (1972): 1–19, Shapiro distinguishes Marston's creation in *What You Will* of a new satiric figure: the "urbane gallant"–Quadratus in this case, the successor to Lyly's royal figure and Jonson's "scholar-poet." In earlier plays Marston flatters or insults the private-theater audience in prologues, and satirizes the "conventional satiric persona." Like Chapman, he retains in his children's plays two techniques of Jonsonian "comicall satyre": "deferential gestures toward the audience and mockery of characters resembling real persons, possibly even spectators." Arthur C. Kirsch in *Jacobean Dramatic Perspectives* (1972) follows Marston's growth, under the influence of Guarini, from self-conscious theatricalism in the *Antonio* plays to mastery in *The Malcontent* of a "play self-consciously poised between the horror and pain of reality and the absurdity and meaninglessness of a parodic make-believe." In the earlier plays derogatory references to theater reduce the value of character and action; but in *The Malcontent*, even when a character is feigning, our detachment leaves a sense of genuine emotion combined with greater understanding.

In *The Pattern of Tragicomedy in Beaumont and Fletcher* (1952), Eugene M. Waith regards Marston as an important influence on later playwrights: "For the development of the sort of characterization we have observed in *The Faithful Shepherdess* or *The Maid's Tragedy* Marston's delight in ambiguity, his reinterpretations, his assumption of contrasting roles are vitally significant." Irving Ribner in *Jacobean Tragedy: The Quest for Moral Order* (1962) finds it possible that "next to Shakespeare Marston is the most influential dramatist of his age." His use of the malcontent, the Machiavellian villain, the gory final masque, dramatic irony, and manipulation of plot by a central plotter affects Shakespeare, Tourneur, Webster, Middleton, and Ford. Yet in himself Marston, having a satiric but no tragic sense, "succeeds only in being moralistic, never in attaining the truly moral vision": he aims to remove vice, not to understand man's fate.

Also varied, though fewer, are examinations of the playwright's language, imagery, and style. Introducing "Some Notes on the Vocabulary of John Marston," *N&Q* 1 (1954): 425–27, Gustav Cross points out: "As a coiner of new words, unusual and startling images, and as a master of the telling or arresting phrase Marston is second only to Shakespeare." L. C. Stagg, *An Index to the Figurative Language of John Marston's Tragedies* (1970), provides classification under many headings of quoted passages from *Antonio's Revenge, Sophonisba*, and the tragic plot of *The Insatiate Countess*. There are cross references as well and a cross index with general categories from Caroline Spurgeon's *Shakespeare's Imagery and What It Tells Us* (1935). Mario Praz, *Studies in Seventeenth-Century Imagery*, 2nd ed. (1964), superseding his *Studi sul concettismo* (1946), lists emblematic devices, familiar or original, used in three of the plays, indicating earlier occurrences where possible.

In *The Rhetoric of Tragedy: Form in Stuart Drama* (1966), Charles Osborne McDonald examines *The Malcontent* and *Sophonisba* as examples of the way in which Marston, "an original dramatic theoretician, if no poet," used rhetoric, which he knew but found unsatisfactory. He does take pains with language, and Malevole has a "wholly verbal disguise," his rhetorical skill. In *Sophonisba* "the grammar and diction of the play seem to be Marston's attempt, often hopelessly stilted and obscure, to approximate Latinity and Senecan 'gravity' or 'majesty' in English." But in seeking to cater to a restless, overly smart audience, "the play makes the most of all these worlds, the best of none."

W. R. Gair (I,A) offers several new observations on Marston's style. From the law schools the dramatist had acquired the tradition of including "allusions étrangères au contexte immédiat de l'oeuvre." He developed this into a method of "libre association des phrases et la création de mots pour augmenter l'étendue et la valeur expressive de la langue," which is appropriate to the distributive nature of English. In language also Marston belongs to the more ornate Ciceronian school, as opposed to the Senecan school of Jonson and Bacon. His plays for the children of Paul's carry out the "gracieuse fiction" of drama as an extension of literature by and for those who "connaissaient les manières du beau monde." His main contribution is to give the audience of Paul's boys a self-aware "activité collective" in relation to the drama.

Finally, in the period under consideration, Marston's drama has furnished material for a number of studies of more restricted scope. Eudo C. Mason, "Satire on Women and Sex in Elizabethan Tragedy," *ES* 31 (1950): 1–10, singles out Marston as the "turning point in the tragico-satirical treatment of the erotic." While he violently attacks women and lechery, his very vehemence implies a "thwarted, but still not extirpated impulse to idealise love, to attribute to woman qualities one would never think of attributing to man, to look to her for some kind of healing and salvation which she cannot supply." Indeed, "that Marston deliberately constructed his plots on the framework of a dialectic of lawful and illicit love, much like a modern writer of problem plays, emerges from a note he adds to the Prologue to his *Dutch Courtesan*. . . ." Leonora Leet Brodwin, *Elizabethan Love Tragedy, 1587–1625* (1971), sees Marston in three tragedies as the "most significant figure for the study of the decadence of Courtly Love on the Elizabethan tragic stage, revealing all the possible changes that can be wrung on its theme." *Antonio's Revenge* fails to relate love to tragedy, but does inaugurate a theme of revenge against the blocking forces that influenced much Jacobean drama. In *Sophonisba* love is related to Stoic honor, a sign of weakened confidence in the ideal; facing a "totally

corrupt" society in a "conflict pattern," Sophonisba can save only herself. Marston in this play also presents the "most perceptive treatment"
of lust in the drama of the time. Finally, *The Insatiate Countess* provides a third possible variation in the "most depraved tragedy of False
Romantic Love in the Elizabethan genre."

Fredson Thayer Bowers in *Elizabethan Revenge Tragedy, 1587-
1642* (1940) is limited by his topic to *Antonio's Revenge* and *The Malcontent*. The former has at least the novelty of a setting in an Italian
Renaissance court and in Piero, a living Machiavellian villain. In the end,
however, both character and action fall victim to that "straining for
effect which was at once Marston's strength and his weakness." The
Senecan morality of letting Antonio go without the expiation exacted
from all other Elizabethan revengers also makes the play unique. *The
Malcontent* has a "tangled web of revenges" which is likewise different.

In "Shakespeare and Elizabethan Psychology: Status of the Subject,"
in *Shakespeare-Studien: Festschrift für Heinrich Mutschmann*, ed.
Walther Fischer et al. (1951), pp. 48-55, Hardin Craig notes that
Marston may have been the first dramatist in his time to utilize
abnormal psychology. Though his primary motivation is ethical, Stoic
philosophy enables him to relate ethics and psychology.

William R. Bowden's *The English Dramatic Lyric, 1603-42: A Study
in Stuart Dramatic Technique* (1951) is one of several studies concerned with Marston's "uninhibited originality" in music and song. He
"used almost every song situation that was to become important
later. . . ."; "if the development of the dramatic lyric owes a special
debt to any single man within the period covered by this study, that
man probably is Marston. . . ." Bowden furnishes an annotated list of
Marston's songs and calls attention to the number of them (an average
of seven) in the four earliest plays; to Marston's method "of plotting in
song the curve of a protagonist's career" in *Histriomastix* and (presumably) *Eastward Ho*; to an "oratorio-like scene" (I.ii) in *Sophonisba*;
and especially to the use of song in the fifth act of the three revenge
plays, for suspense, "Sophoclean irony, and the Fletcher effect of
surprise." Louis B. Wright, however, in "Extraneous Song in Elizabethan Drama after the Advent of Shakespeare," *SP* 24 (1927): 261-
74, finds songs in the drama except *The Dutch Courtesan* generally
unrelated to the action. R. W. Ingram, "The Use of Music in the Plays
of Marston," *Music & Letters* 37 (1956): 154-64, has a detailed treatment of several of the plays, especially the two parts of *Antonio and
Mellida* and *Sophonisba*: Marston "is the first consistently subtle user

of telling musical effect; the technique of weaving together words and action and sound of music is developed for the first time by him." Ingram claims that "Marston carried to its limits the use of music in drama, to that border-line where the finished work is still a play with a great deal of music and not a kind of opera with a great deal of dialogue." J. S. Manifold's *The Music in English Drama: From Shakespeare to Purcell* (1956) points out that Marston, "more than any other dramatist, sets out to link the act music with the play," and furnishes some notes on habitual use or avoidance of certain instruments in the plays. F. W. Sternfeld in *Music in Shakespearean Tragedy* (1963) similarly annotates the use of song and music in the *Antonio* plays and *Sophonisba*.

In *Act Division in Elizabethan and Jacobean Plays, 1583–1616* (1958), Wilfred T. Jewkes analyzes Marston's texts to support his conclusions: "They are generally ascribed to him, show little evidence of the playhouse, and appear to have been printed mainly from his manuscripts." In *The Malcontent* the author shows interest in the preparation of copy for the press. The distinctive number of directions for music and the division into acts are noted as characteristic of the dramatist.

Vanna Gentili in *Le figure della pazzia nel teatro elisabettiano* (1969) looks at Antonio in *Antonio's Revenge*, who resembles Hamlet in many ways and whose sanity is open to question; at Passarello and Malevole in *The Malcontent*, who are too much alike; and at Dondolo in *The Fawn*, who speaks for Marston but lacks unity of character.

Dieter Mehl in *The Elizabethan Dumb Show: The History of a Dramatic Convention* (1966; German ed. 1964) recognizes in Marston a special mastery: "The organic union between pointed pantomime and dramatic speech is Marston's particular contribution to the development of the dumb show." That is, while comparatively uninterested in the traditional dumb show, he integrates the "silent scene" with the dialogue in such a way as to reinforce the action, even the satiric effect. Mehl analyzes the *Antonio* plays, mentions several others, and includes a descriptive list of pantomime scenes in Marston.

Thelma N. Greenfield, *The Induction in Elizabethan Drama* (1969), finds that Marston's inductions, like Jonson's, "create not the world to be portrayed on the stage, but a point of view toward men and art basic to the conception of the play." In *Shakespeare's Influence on the Drama of His Age, Studied in "Hamlet"* (1938), Donald Joseph McGinn is mainly concerned with documenting allusions to Shakespeare's play in most of Marston's drama. He observes also that the style of *Antonio's Revenge,* as Jonson saw, is Marston's "old satirical" style, not a new tragic one.

C. THE WORKS AT LARGE

Several of the works already cited for analysis of the plays also make useful studies of the poetry, which is generally believed to show a close relation to the drama. Finkelpearl, *John Marston* (I,A) (which subsumes his "From Petrarch to Ovid: Metamorphoses in John Marston's *Metamorphosis of Pigmalions Image," ELH* 32 [1965] : 333–48) sees the verse satires as including in their targets young men's lechery and homosexuality. Up to the midpoint *The Metamorphosis of Pygmalion's Image* depicts satirically a Petrarchan lover (in the style of the 1590s sonneteers) madly indulging his emotions; but then he becomes an Ovidian "amatory model." In *The Scourge of Villainy* Marston, looking to a "small, select audience" of "true wits," scores sexual vice. Ironically the verse was popular with the sort of reader it is aimed against; despairing of a fit audience, Marston finally abandoned hope for verse satire.

In *John Marston, Satirist* (I,A) Anthony Caputi accepts the poet's claim that the *Metamorphosis* burlesques the amorous poem; the narrator is a simpler "spiritual kin of Jack Donne of the *Songs and Sonnets.*" The speaker of the later satires, however, is more complex: "by turns haughty and exclusive, furious to the point of hysteria, amused in the manner of Democritus, grimly hardened to the task of whipping and flaying, and then serious with the earnestness of a dedicated healer of souls." Marston uniquely integrates "fairly elaborate moral exhortation" into the calculated structure of the satires; here as in the plays his basic thought is "his personal version of Neo-Stoicism," influenced by Christianity, rejecting apathy, and accepting a rational design for nature and a perfectible rationality in man. His satires are by far the most dramatic of his time, with a host of character sketches and *exempla.*

Alvin Kernan's *The Cankered Muse* (I,B) stresses the "rough, powerful, and earnest" speaker in the satires, viewed as an invented character uttering a dramatic monologue. Kinsayder's expression is a peculiar mixture of "gutter language, stuttering style, epic constructions, and ornate bombast," and his sensitivity to human corruption is too great to permit adherence to Stoicism, which he rejects. His unmatched, almost psychotic pessimism makes him a Calvinist. In contrast, in *Complaint and Satire* (I,A), John Peter finds Marston, in the satires and *Metamorphosis*, uneasily poised between the Christian tradition of moral criticism and pagan, salacious Latin satire. "It is his subconscious awareness of that conflict and his inability to dissipate it that is at the root of Marston's querulousness and insecurity, just as it is his insecurity that accounts in turn for his truculent posturings." Finally, A. J. Axelrad, *Un malcontent élizabéthain* (I,A), views the satires as thoroughly consistent with Marston's drama: "C'est avant tout un satirique." The satires lack order and are marked by violence and invective, "qu'il manie avec une sorte de sombre jouissance." While he sees physical love as the source of most evils, he derides platonic love and lacks any "courtois" quality.

There are several other useful and substantial studies. In his edition of the *Poems* (I,A), Arnold Davenport finds the *Metamorphosis* "one of the poorest of the Ovidian, mythological, erotic poems of the late Elizabethan period," clearly influenced "in diction and detail" by *Venus and Adonis* and *Hero and Leander*. Reliance on Natalis Comes for mythology is fully documented. The original impulse was "secret disgust for readers, for amorous man and for sex itself. Such a frame of mind, while not satirical, is so closely allied to the satiric that Marston could possibly have later persuaded even himself that he wrote the poem with deliberate satiric purpose." The Scourger in the later work anticipates the moods of several characters of Shakespeare, Tourneur, and Webster; he is a "coarser-grained forerunner of Hamlet, and possibly to some extent a model on which Hamlet was fashioned"; ". . . beneath the violence and brash bluster of the satires there lurks a dark pessimistic weariness that falls little short of complete despair." In *La satire en Angleterre de 1588 à 1603* (1969), Louis Lecocq treats the poetic satire favorably. Writing for an intellectual aristocracy, Marston, alone in his generation, dared attack Ovidian poetry on literary grounds, in *The Metamorphosis of Pygmalion's Image*. "Le poème est trop mauvais pour avoir pu être écrit sans l'intention de ridiculiser une certaine forme de mauvaise poésie." There is no real neo-Stoicism in the poems. The role of Kinsayder in *The Scourge of Villainy* is ambivalent. While self-centered and at times incoherent, he also has more "raisonnements" and "discussions" than contemporary satirists; "une sorte de personnage de théâtre," he is unaware that he is guilty of the faults he attacks. At last, however, he joins intuition and reason, satire and philosophy, to form "une poésie nouvelle, annonciatrice de la poésie métaphysique."

Other recent critical work is also favorable. In "Rhetoric and Satire: New Light on John Marston's *Pigmalion* and the Satires," *JEGP* 71 (1972): 22-35, Adrian Weiss argues that *Pygmalion* is intended to be consistent with the satires, both reflecting the created figure of Kinsayder, the "most pessimistic and cynical" of Marston's dramatic characters, a victim of exaggerated self-esteem in poetry and satire. *Pygmalion* is a "parody of poetry in the vein of courtly love in general and the erotic epyllion in particular." John Scott Colley, "'Opinion' and the Reader in John Marston's *The Metamorphosis of Pigmalions Image*," *English Literary Renaissance* 3 (1973): 221-31, finds the poem a "general satire upon both literary and amatory foolishness." Marston tricks the reader into responding to mere words, poor imitations of action, as Pygmalion is drawn to an inert imitation of a woman. Both are victims of "Opinion," irrational delusion, though Pygmalion eventually comes to his senses.

Also sympathetic, Gustav Cross in "The Retrograde Genius of John Marston" (I,B) maintains that "the strength of his moral purpose shines clearly through all his writings—including the much misunderstood *Pigmalion's Image,* which turns out to be, as Marston claimed, a burlesque of the fashionable erotic epyllion of the 1590's." Indeed, "his work has the consistency of purpose one would expect from a writer who set out as a scourger of villainy and ended as a divine." In "Marston's *Metamorphosis of Pigmalions Image*: A Mock-Epyllion." *EA* 13 (1960): 331-36, Cross stresses the attitude of "enlightened naturalism" in the poem, in addition to its anti-Petrarchanism and its burlesque of "Mythological narrative poems in the Italianate Ovidian tradition."

Other general comment is of more limited extent or scope. In "Donne and His Age," in *A Garland for John Donne, 1631-1931*, ed. Theodore Spencer (1931), pp. 177-202, Spencer contends that in *The Scourge of Villainy* Marston heralds the shift from the old satire, attacks on individuals framed in "belief in the essential goodness of man," to something different and deeper. He does so by adding melancholy and "railing against mankind as a whole," with the background implication that man has forfeited the great potentialities he once displayed. By 1600 the new outlook dominates, as Donne and *Hamlet* show. Ejner J. Jensen, "Hall and Marston: The Role of the Satirist," *Satire Newsletter* 4 (1966-67): 72-83, believes that Marston tends to lose moral purpose in an obsession with his role as scourger. His didactic passages at the end of three sections of *The Scourge of Villainy* show lack of confidence in the power of his satire to make the point, and represent "perhaps Marston's most serious artistic fault." John Wilcox, "Informal Publication of Late Sixteenth Century Verse Satire," *HLQ* 13 (1949-50): 191-200, sees *The Scourge of Villainy* as epoch-making on other grounds: "the first verse that was obviously written to reach the public as serious, castigating satire, the first verse satire of the times not wholly the vehicle of youthful self-exhibition." Bernard Harris in "Dissent and Satire," *ShS* 17 (1964): 120-37, adds that Marston has the "largest claim" of contemporary satirists to attack "contemporary society."

Edward Lucie-Smith, editing the *Penguin Book of Elizabethan Verse* (1965), finds that Marston's "satire, with its feeling of impotent yet violent revulsion against the society which surrounded him, catches the spirit of Juvenal more nearly than later 'classical' English satirists." Moreover, Marston is the "most powerful" of a group of self-consciously modern poets at the end of Elizabeth's time who are aggressively and axiomatically dissatisfied with society, concentrate on subject matter rather than technique, and want "to affront the reader's susceptibilities and shatter his expectations." In *The High Design: English Renaissance Tragedy and the Natural Law* (1970), George C. Herndl asserts that Marston in *The Scourge of Villainy*, while attacking Puritanism, "is strongly Calvinistic in affirming the total corruption of human nature and the doctrine of unmerited election as the only source of righteousness, and in his obsession with loathsome and ubiquitous lust." To him free will is lacking in man. Robert Ellrodt, *L'inspiration personnelle et l'esprit du temps chez les poètes métaphysiques anglais*, 3 vols. (1960), vol. 3, finds Marston in the verse satires adorning his invectives with scholastic propositions from Duns Scotus and in his work in general combining "lucidité cynique" and "nostalgie de la pureté immaculée." Philip Hobsbaum, ed., *Ten Elizabethan Poets* (1969), places Marston in the line of Donne, Dunbar, Swift, and Joyce Cary; with Jonson and Chapman, he has a "keen knowledge of society and a violent revulsion from it." Natalis Comes's *Mythologia* is a source of "much of Marston's philosophy." Three other authorities accept Marston's statement that *The Metamorphosis of Pygmalion's Image* is intended to burlesque amorous poetry: Hallett Smith, *Elizabethan Poetry* (1952), who finds the signs of satire in the imagery and author's attitude; Louis R. Zocca, *Elizabethan Narrative Poetry* (1950); and

Douglas Bush, *Mythology and the Renaissance Tradition in English Poetry* (1932; rev. ed. 1963). All nevertheless point out a certain dwelling on sensuality in the poem.

Finally, a few more specialized analyses helpfully round out knowledge of the nondramatic (or predramatic) verse. Fidelian Burke's *Metrical Roughness in Marston's Formal Satire* (1957) defines "roughness" as "unpleasant effects in the qualities of sounds"; Marston's roughness, conventionally considered appropriate for satire, takes several forms: "frequent substitution for the basic foot of the meter; juxtapositions of strong stress and multiplication of pauses within the line; lines with more syllables or less than the decasyllabic norm; and frequent run-on lines." The study, including a number of statistical tables, is based on the first edition of *The Scourge of Villainy* in 1598, as well as the other verse; Burke raises the possibility that the two smoother editions of the same work in 1599 may be due to a reviser other than Marston. Ants Oras, *Pause Patterns in Elizabethan and Jacobean Drama: An Experiment in Prosody* (1960), studying a more limited aspect of prosody, agrees in part with Burke: Marston is "militantly antiromantic like Donne and in many ways close to Donne in his consciously roughened versification, especially in the satires of his *Scourge of Villainy.*" Nevertheless, aside from experimentation in pause patterns, he is "conspicuously conservative to the end," using the patterns of the 1590s, of Spenser and Marlowe, "when this style had been almost completely abandoned elsewhere."

Elizabeth Holmes in *Aspects of Elizabethan Imagery* (1929) finds that, for an Elizabethan, Marston has relatively little color and "few clear images." Under his images of "rigidity" and "constriction and oppression" two specific types are singled out: "a sense of narrow confinement in general, but especially of numbness and oppression, or a darkness without space like that of a cell," perhaps derived from the cave of Plato's *Republic*; and a "grasp or embrace, sometimes to suffocation, and a sense of close touch, generally with the horrible." In "The Imagery of *The Revengers Tragedie* and *The Atheists Tragedie*," *MLR* 30 (1935): 289-301, U. M. Ellis-Fermor brings in Marston's imagery by way of comparison, since to a degree Tourneur learned from Marston. Both begin with numerous body images, a young man's fault; in Marston these images, "particularly of disease, maiming and destruction," are strong in the satires and *Antonio and Mellida,* fall off in *Antonio's Revenge,* and in *The Malcontent* are down to normal.

Marston has as his two greatest defects in the use of imagery obscurity and "weakness of articulation between the image and its theme."

Arnold Stein, "The Second English Satirist," *MLR* 38 (1943): 273-78, says that Marston, more indebted to Hall than to anyone else, resented the fact and accordingly initiated a quarrel and attacked Hall more than any other figure. Marston has "few actual parallels with the Roman satirists," and it seems unlikely that he knew Juvenal and Persius well but avoided indebtedness. *Plagiarism and Imitation during the English Renaissance* (I,A) by Harold Ogden White takes a different view of the Latin connection: the satires "owe their inspiration and tone" to Juvenal, Martial, and Seneca, but "they owe their material, their ideas, to Marston's own observation and imagination." In *The Phoenix and the Turtle: Shakespeare's Poem and Chester's "Loues Martyr"* (1965), William H. Matchett says that Marston's four poems in that collection exhibit a somewhat confused but "thoroughgoing Platonism" in intention. Marston may be reacting to what he considers an attack on Platonism in Shakespeare's poem. J. B. Bamborough, *The Little World of Man* (1952), maintains that Marston in *The Scourge of Villainy,* seizing a hint in Persius, first related the "melancholy man and the satirist," and then staged such a figure in Feliche of *Antonio and Mellida,* who "mingles elements of the melancholiac, the stoic and the cynic."

Other critics are less respectful of Marston's nondramatic poetry. In *Shakespeare and Elizabethan Poetry* (1951), M. C. Bradbrook calls the "pornographic" *Metamorphosis of Pygmalion's Image* "the low-water mark of the decade." Herschel Baker, *The Wars of Truth: Studies in the Decay of Christian Humanism in the Earlier Seventeenth Century* (1952), considers *The Scourge of Villainy* "one of the most atrabiliar books in the language"; it is "a savage renunciation of humanity itself." "The accumulated moral values of two thousand years are buried in sin and crime, and the humanistic claims for human dignity are exposed as as colossal lie." Marston remains "a case for a psychiatrist."

The *Concise Bibliography* for Marston by Samuel A. Tannenbaum was published in 1940 and reprinted in *Elizabethan Bibliographies,* vol. 5 (1967). There is an updating of Tannenbaum by Charles A. Pennel and William P. Williams, *Elizabethan Bibliographies Supplements,* IV (1968). Marston is also included in Irving Ribner, *Tudor and Stuart Drama,* Goldentree Bibliographies (1966), and Clifford Chalmers Huffman, "Tudor and Stuart Drama: A Bibliography, 1966-1971," *ETJ* 24 (1972): 169-78.

II. CRITICISM OF INDIVIDUAL PLAYS AND STATE OF SCHOLARSHIP

A. INDIVIDUAL PLAYS

The Malcontent

Most interpretations suggest an artistic or moral pattern traceable through the action. M. L. Wine, in his edition for RRDS (1964), contends that the play "is a study in deception, and the mask-disguise is the central dramatic symbol; when the *masquers* step forth at the end of the play and reveal themselves, they herald the triumph of the humane world and the restoration of order." Until that moment, however, the plotting in a "topsy-turvy world of humanity preying upon itself" is shown in imagery of the hunt or chase and in the picture of a court that "betrays the ideals of the courtier and of the humanist conception of man." Marston's stagecraft uses the preliminary concert of the private theaters to distance the action, in contrast to the "vilest out-of-tune music" beginning the play, and probably also to suggest "a world of loveliness just briefly glimpsed at and struggled for in the play itself."

Reading the play more schematically, Ejner J. Jensen in "Theme and Imagery in *The Malcontent,*" *SEL* 10 (1970): 367–84, sees it as a "highly unified drama in which character, theme, language, and imagery each has a part and yet serves to contribute to the effect of the whole." Malevole successfully moves the play; his imagery projects a disorderly world of irrational bestiality, the product of a corrupt court system of "false preferment." This abuse is analogous to simony in the church, and is represented in the fable of the tortoise and the eagle, with its motifs of rise and fall. Maria and—after their reformations—Pietro, Aurelia, and Ferneze are grouped with Malevole; opposed to him in every way is Mendoza, the epitome of the ambitious, insecure, over-compensating courtier, with the hangers-on Bilioso and Maquerelle. Mendoza's images represent an ironic attempt to reassure himself by thinking in terms of strength and grasp. Jensen relates the augmentations of the third edition to the theme, and studies most of the characters.

In another reading of pattern, "Fortune in Marston's *The Malcontent,*" *PMLA* 86 (1971): 202–9, George L. Geckle regards the medieval Wheel of Fortune as a "symbol around which both the structure of the play and its most serious themes literally revolve." There were traditionally four positions on the wheel; to maintain oneself in the face of Fortune's power, Roman thought suggested prudence, fortitude, and spiritual devotion. Mendoza and his opposite in the subplot, Maquerelle, following Machiavelli, choose the first two ways; at first Malevole exhibits "Stoic prudence," and then in the latter half of the play, as he reflects, becomes more definitely Christian. Thus providence triumphs, and the drama "follows in both structure and theme an essentially moral, Christian pattern."

Three other readings also find a spiritual quality in the play. William W. E. Slights, "'Elder in a Deform'd Church': The Function of Marston's *Malcontent,*" *SEL* 13 (1973): 360-73, who sees the theme of the play as the "need for spiritual regeneration," believes that Malevole cures souls by making the sinful character aware of his own guilt. Malevole is a "distasteful parody" of his other self, from which he learns better to understand himself and the world. The process is completed when Maria's staunchness shows him the power of inner resources and, by extension, of providence. The treatment of individual rebirth in this play, *The Fawn,* and *The Dutch Courtesan* demonstrates Marston's "sexual, political, and religious orthodoxy." Brownell Salomon, "The Theological Basis of Imagery and Structure in *The Malcontent,*" *SEL* 14 (1974): 271-84, interprets the play as indicative of Marston's Calvinist tendencies, which date from his early poems. *The Malcontent* depicts fallen human nature in imagery of animality, excrement, and sterile, perverted sexual license; the world, of which Genoa is a microcosm, has been stood on its head. Yet God's providence can save man and restore moral order; and Malevole's own understanding of corrupt human nature and divine power fits in with this denouement, as do the closing events of the drama. Siegfried Korninger, "John Marston und die Bedeutung des *Malcontent,*" in *Festschrift zum 75. Geburtstag von Theodor Spira,* ed. H. Viebrock et al. (1961), pp. 152-63, discovers Christian affirmation in the play: "Die Welt der Marstonschen Dramen ist eine christliche Welt; das geht vor allem aus *The Malcontent* mit überzeugender Klarheit hervor." Altofronto is merely playing a role as Malevole; evil is shown only to contrast and emphasize the ultimate triumph of good: "Dieses Vorgehen hat mit einer negative Weltsicht nicht das Geringste zu tun." The conversion of Pietro and Aurelia, though unmotivated and not established psychologically, is in the Elizabethan tradition of spiritual transformation.

More common, however, are discussions of the play emphasizing its aesthetic or moral effect or both. In "Italian Tragicomedy on the

English Stage," *RenD* 6 (1973): 123-48, G. K. Hunter analyzes the use of Guarini's *Il pastor fido* in *The Malcontent*. Marston's adaptation, a "critical return to the roots of the genre," replaces the shepherd with the "tragi-comic urban satyr." The theme of love continues, with the pattern of an ideal pair, an imperfect pair, and a corrupt pair. "Erotic corruption provides the primary terms for the social viciousness," and throughout the action love is associated with political significance. In his edition of the play (1975), Hunter suggests that like *The Dutch Courtesan* it is built on a contrast, in this case between the tyrant and the genuine ruler. Malevole conveys both revulsion at degradation, his very language showing confusion in the world, and the control, at least in that the rhetoric outdoes the action, suitable to a head of state. Similarly he exemplifies rejection of the world, as opposed to the self-serving purposes of most of the other characters, stoicism vs. epicureanism. While citing traditional wisdom often, Marston doubts that most people can profit from it. The attempt is to ground a tragicomedy not in pastoral but in satire. As a dramatist for the boy companies, the author stresses total effect rather than inner conflict, though he does show Malevole trapped in his own concern with vice. As a playwright bending his text to performance, Marston portrays in daring controversy of reflection on church and state a "rich, highly-coloured, consciously unstable world whose contradictions are unmediated by Jonson's central rigour." Both language and mannered action punctuated by Malevole's comments display this atmosphere. Hunter's notes document indebtedness of the play to the 1602 translation of Guarini's *Pastor Fido*.

Finkelpearl, in *John Marston* (I,A)—a portion is reprinted as *"The Malcontent*: Virtuous Machiavellianism" in *Shakespeare's Contemporaries: Modern Studies in English Renaissance Drama,* ed. Max Bluestone and Norman Rabkin (2nd ed., 1970), pp. 255-69—finds the play "Marston's most successful representation of a morally debilitated world." In his time the title would have had political connotation, and one passage seems to reflect on "James's cherished doctrine of Divine Right." In "Purging the Commonwealth: Marston's Disguised Dukes and *A Knack to Know a Knave,"* *PMLA* 89 (1974): 993-1006, David J. Houser compares *The Malcontent* and *The Fawn* to the older play (1592), which is not necessarily a direct source but has more than accidental parallels. Unlike Honesty, the disguised figure in *A Knack* who seeks to know vice, Malevole tries to overcome it, to regain his rule by "benevolent Machiavellianism." In doing so he is clearly separated from his real identity as Altofronto. The play's sophisticated ending leaves some who are guilty of vice still in the court and on stage.

Less favorable views of Malevole are also common. Arthur Kirsch in *"Cymbeline* and Coterie Dramaturgy," *ELH* 34 (1967): 285-306, comments on the combined engagement and detachment in *The Malcontent:* Marston's "theatrical ambivalence is an expression of an ambivalence he sees in the real world." Before the end we cannot take "at face value" the actions or emotions of anyone, Malevole least of all. Thus the intrigue plot and "speeches representing studied exaggerations of feelings" distance us; probably the Blackfrairs version used music to the same effect. David L. Frost, *The School of Shakespeare: The Influence of Shakespeare on English Drama, 1600–42* (1968), points out some distinctive characteristics of Malevole: he is "essentially a 'plain dealer,' trading in overt insults to his enemies' faces"; Marston encourages us to look at him critically; and he hardly ever communes with himself. Nor is *The Malcontent* "properly a Revenge play at all." In *"The Malcontent* and 'Dreams, Visions, Fantasies,'" *Essays in Criticism* 24 (1974): 261-74, T. F. Wharton sees the play as a picture of role-playing in wish-fulfillment fantasies by which the characters deceive themselves. While not constructing such fancies for himself, Malevole fosters and becomes involved in those of the others; thus, unlike Pietro, the "virtuous outsider," Malevole is part of the falsity of the court. At the end he too succumbs to the temptation to play a role, the "pious and magnanimous ruler"; but the play fails to underline this final irony.

Among the more specialized approaches, J. Arthur Faber's "Rhetorical Strategy in John Marston's *The Malcontent,"* *Husson Review* 4 (1970): 18-24, sees the play as constructed in terms of the three formal modes of persuasion of Aristotle's *Rhetoric*: deliberative (Acts I and II), forensic (III and IV), and epideictic (V). The result is "not only a model of a newly emergent dramatic form, but also a monument to Marston's sense of stylistic decorum."

Christian Kiefer explores "Music and Marston's *The Malcontent,"* *SP* 51 (1954): 163-71. With more music, in performance and in allusion, than Marston's other dramas, the drama makes music symptomatic of "hypocrisy and deception"; and "the emphasis on the incongruity of musical concord and moral discord which has been evident during the play serves to make clear that the resolution is satiric." John P. Cutts, *La musique de scène de la troupe de Shakespeare, The King's Men, sous le règne de Jacques Ier* (1959; 2nd ed.,

1971), finds the use of music in *The Malcontent* well integrated into the drama. For example, the "vilest out-of-tune music" heard before the first scene and continuing to the beginning of the second "suggère l'atmosphère de discorde qui règne" in the court world, like the thunder which begins *Macbeth.*

Francesca Dunfey, "'Mighty Showes': Masque Elements in Jacobean and Caroline Drama," *Shakespeare Studies* (Shakespeare Society of Japan) 6 (1967-68): 122-46, analyzes the mask in *The Malcontent* as a "stylized presentation of the resolution." Many regular mask features appear: "The pattern is the formal one of cornets sounding, couples pairing, 'one change and rest,'" and the focus is properly upon the dance. At the same time the dancers are all "active agents in the plot, bearing significant relationships with the main character and with one another," and the mask is carefully prepared for throughout the fifth act, so that it is not merely a *deus ex machina,* but genuinely a "major concern of the characters high and low."

Brownell Salomon in "Visual and Aural Signs. in the Performed English Renaissance Play," *RenD* 5 (1972): 143-69, suggests that variations in voice intensity indicated in the text and carefully planned entrances and exits contribute to the ethical and thematic significance of *The Malcontent.*

The Dutch Courtesan

Gustav Cross, "Marston, Montaigne, and Morality: *The Dutch Courtezan* Reconsidered," *ELH* 27 (1960): 30-43, finds that "the play is clearly a morality based on the conflict between lust and love, between love for a courtezan and love for a friend, in terms of the opposition of Stoic and anti-Stoic. Montaigne's *Essaies* [III, v] gave Marston his theme, and as Montaigne's anti-Stoicism is based on a realistic view of experience, so Marston's play is given a firm foundation in reality with its City setting . . . , its gallery of prostitutes, bawds, and panders, and its frank discussion of sexuality." While producing the best "study of sexual psychology" in the drama of his time, Marston "affirms orthodox morality": lust is natural, but has no relation to love, and man enslaved by sex is ridiculous. Freevill foreshadows the naturalistic Restoration rake.

In his edition for RRDS (1965), M. L. Wine finds a comparable theme, "the recognition and control, but not the annihilation, of man's natural desires," but stresses also the comic distancing of the action. "From beginning to end . . . Marston minimizes the seriousness of the theme and invites the audience to laugh at the play with him. The numerous extra-dramatic moments destroy any possible emotional involvement." Malheureux's recognition of the failure of his way of life is a dramatic triumph; Franceschina, headlong in passion and alienated from us by confused speech, shows what he is becoming; and on the other side the unsympathetic Mulligrub is his farcical counterpart.

In his Fountainwell Drama Texts edition (1968), Peter Davison sees three varieties of love depicted, each in an appropriate style: idealized in Beatrice and Freevill, normal in Crispinella and Tysefew, and abnormal principally in Franceschina and Malheureux. As a lover, however, Freevill is no more credible than Malheureux in his early attitude, and Beatrice does not face sexuality. The comic style is basic in the play, and Cocledemoy, "a *comic* version of Freevill," is the "principal means whereby the comic aspects of venery and defecation are expressed."

Finkelpearl's book (I,A) judges the play not merely anti-Stoic or anti-Puritan; "it shows the defects of moral absolutism in any of its forms." For the first time Marston, influenced by Montaigne, shows wrongdoers capable of learning from experience. Yet he goes beyond Montaigne in idealizing love and seeing it as the crown of marriage. These attitudes are expressed in a "relatively abstract," allegorical drama; Malheureux is continually distanced from our sympathy. The comic plot helps in this respect, for Malheureux is compared to Mulligrub, just as Cocledemoy, like Freevill, acts to restore the "balance of nature." Finkelpearl also detects in the play a passage of satire on James and his Scots.

In "Language as Theme in *The Dutch Courtesan*," *RenD* 5 (1972): 75-87, Donna B. Hamilton defines the main topic of the comedy differently, as language viewed as a sign of moral integrity and intellectual acuteness. Characters showing "flexible and sensitive use of language" are Freevill, Beatrice, Crispinella (who is not in the source), Tysefew, and Cocledemoy, who has the vocabulary of Marston's satires; false language, inadvertent or calculated, is the province of Malheureux, Caqueter, and the Mulligrubs. Franceschina uses language well, but for evil ends; she must be isolated from society in prison. After trying to change Malheureux by persuasion, Freevill in Act IV subjects him to physical danger as a last resort; Cocledemoy has a parallel history with Mulligrub.

John J. O'Connor, "The Chief Source of Marston's *Dutch Courtezan*," *SP* 54 (1957): 509-15, traces the story to Nicolas de Montreux's *Le*

premier livre des bergeries de Julliette. In the play Franceschina is
original only in accent; but Freevill and Malheureux have been indi-
vidualized as very different, while their friendship is made as flawed
as the world they live in. Marston is fascinated by sin, but primarily
concerned about morality, even—though unconvincingly—about traditional morality, at the end of the comedy.

In "Dekker's *Whore* and Marston's *Courtesan,*" *ELN* 4 (1966-67):
261-66, Harry Keyishian believes that much of the play is intentional
satire upon Dekker's *1 Honest Whore.* Both plays contrast a cynical and
an earnest young man, but Marston finds the libertine justified: "The
contrast seems too pointed to be purely accidental." The fuming
Mulligrub counteracts Dekker's patient "ideal tradesman" Candido,
and the courtesans are opposites. In the tradition of the public stage
Dekker is defending conventional morality; Marston, writing for a
coterie audience, seems to find his predecessor too sentimental.

Robert K. Presson, "Marston's *Dutch Courtezan*: The Study of an
Attitude in Adaptation," *JEGP* 55 (1956): 406-13, finds the play
"a late but legitimate descendant of the *Psychomachia* literature that
numerous English plays long and popularly perpetuated." The diabolical Franceschina is contrasted to the heavenly Beatrice; Malheureux
has the position of Mankind or Humanum Genus in the moralities. It
is true that in place of the elementary debate and fall given to the central figure in a moral play, we have in Malheureux "a fearful picture of
a rational, self-critical man completely aware of his change and doom
but powerless to avert it." But his final shame and desire to be an
example to others return to the morality tradition, and the young men
of the play are like the companions of the protagonist in the older type
of drama.

Alexander Leggatt in *Citizen Comedy in the Age of Shakespeare*
(1973) also sees the work as a moral comedy, though without comparing it to the morality play. At first Freevill is flippantly teasing Malheureux, but his love for Beatrice makes him capable of informed
judgment of whoredom, a position his friend more painfully attains.
Thus the "traditional opposition of chaste maid and vicious whore"
remains. The difficulty of accepting orthodox morality is shown as
almost tragic, but the exaggerated language stresses absurdity.

In quite a different approach, Richard Horwich in "Wives, Courtesans, and the Economics of Love in the Jacobean City Comedy,"
CompD 7 (1973): 291-309, while finding *The Dutch Courtesan* a
"sort of encyclopedia of popular attitudes toward courtesans," believes

that even more it is an economic commentary, with the marital bed set against the marketplace. Franceschina is avaricious, but not witty; her schemes come from the businesswoman-bawd Mary Faugh. The parallel subplot shows the defeat of Mulligrub, an economic opposite number of Malheureux.

In "A Marston-Middleton Parallel: New Light on the Growth of City Comedy," *N&Q* 20 (1973): 459-60, Anthony Covatta begins with parallel passages in *The Dutch Courtesan* (II.ii) and Middleton's later *A Mad World, My Masters* (I.i), suggesting borrowing by Middleton, and goes on to point out a number of general resemblances between the comedies. Leo Hughes and Arthur H. Scouten in "Some Theatrical Adaptations of a Picaresque Tale," *Studies in English* (Univ. of Texas) 25 (1945-46): 98-114, trace the origins and descent of Cocledemoy's story. And James L. Jackson in "Sources of the Subplot of Marston's *The Dutch Courtezan*," *PQ* 31 (1952): 223-24, documents one additional scene as indebted more likely to Jonson than to its ultimate source, Plautus. Hanns Passmann in *Der Typus der Kurtisane im elisabethanischen Drama* (1926) considers Franceschina the central character of the play; her source is the story of the Countess of Celant presented by Bandello and recounted in Painter's *Palace of Pleasure*. Most of her characterization and motivation, however, is Marston's own; and he later used her as a preliminary study for his *Insatiate Countess*. Bonamy Dobrée in "Shakespeare and the Drama of His Time," in *A Companion to Shakespeare Studies*, ed. Harley Granville-Barker et al. (1934), pp. 243-61, notes that Crispinella "is a Restoration heroine, and many Restoration writers, Congreve himself among them, borrowed from her speeches"; Marston's world in the play resembles Wycherley's.

1 Antonio and Mellida. Antonio's Revenge

In his RRDS editions (1965), G. K. Hunter observes that in *Antonio and Mellida* Marston is interested more in contrasts than in plot: "Antonio's despair, Andrugio's nobility, Piero's *hubris*, Feliche's stoical detachment—these provide the 'figure in the carpet' which gives the play its basic interest, matching despair, or rather desperation, against the 'Babel pride' which scorns human limits; love is set against detachment . . . , and so on." Antonio's love for Mellida is outweighed by the court comedy, showing pride and folly, filling nearly half the play, and motivation is generally lacking. There is a Senecan debt, but Andrugio is more an English-model Stoic. In the second part the central

moral problem of the revenge is not solved: revenge, "which is ritualis-
tic and not ethical," contradicts the "surface language of conventional
moral concern." Yet Marston's "fable presents the religious pattern of
despair, revelation, conversion, justification, and the 'works' conse-
quent upon justification, though without the benefit of any clerical
system." The two plays were apparently not intended as one; but,
Hunter points out in *"Henry IV* and the Elizabethan Two-Part Play,"
RES 5 (1954): 236–48, there is considerable parallel structure. Still,
characterization is dim throughout, and the transition to the second
part shows no distancing change in time.

In "John Marston's Fantastical Plays: *Antonio and Mellida* and
Antonio's Revenge," PQ 41 (1962): 229–39, rpt. in *Studies in English
Drama,* ed. Charles B. Woods et al. (1962), pp. 229–39, R. A. Foakes
sees the underlying intention of both works as parody of old plays and
adult actors. He cites self-conscious speeches, and compares satire by
exaggeration in *The Metamorphosis of Pygmalion's Image.* Such a
design explains "much of the so-called clumsiness, nonsense, and bad
writing"; the target of the satire, then, is not so much folly and vice as
"conventional literary and theatrical modes and attitudes."

Finkelpearl in his book (I,A) separates the two plays. Although
"fully half" of *Antonio and Mellida* "is devoted to an assortment of
gallants very similar to those in the satires," there is a complex attitude
toward the histrionic Antonio. We are not meant to have faith in the
happy ending of this "Senecan comedy." In the *Revenge,* Antonio has
"common sense": human emotional response to suffering and recognition of the human tragedy. Yet Antonio, like Piero, with whom the
spectacle compares him, becomes a mad murderer. The terrible revenge,
causing us to give sympathy to Piero, contributes to an outlook "as
darkly pessimistic as any in Elizabethan drama."

"Theatre of Cruelty in the Middle Temple: The Plays of John
Marston," an anonymous review of Finkelpearl's book, *TLS,* 5 Feb.
1971, pp. 155–57, analyzes the *Antonio* plays to sustain the thesis that
the playwright's "double vision" has particular contemporary relevance: "The theatre of cruelty, the wild violent screams of young men
and women maddened by the established wild violence of their parents'
world of organized cruelty—*this* is the milieu of John Marston." The
plays compose a "Mannerist farcical diptych": a court farce including
satire on "affectations of stoical virtue" and a sadistic farce showing
cruelty impelled by ambition. The first play is "immensely effective
theatre," parodying both romance and theatrical convention itself.

Antonio's Revenge is a "revenge tragedy written with tongue in cheek, . . . for ever enjoying a send-up of itself"; but at the same time the author, a "prophet of nihilism," shows "genuine evil at work."

Ellen Berland in "The Function of Irony in Marston's *Antonio and Mellida,*" *SP* 66 (1969): 739-55, also believes the first *Antonio* play to be a parody intended to ridicule romantic comedy. Although Mellida is the conventional good and beautiful heroine, Antonio, Piero, and Andrugio all notably fail to take action. These characters and their accomplice, Feliche, are treated ironically; the humorous courtiers of the subplot, on the other hand, evoke satire. The connection between the two plots is the common theme of human folly, indicated in the juxtaposition of scenes.

Allen Bergson, "Dramatic Style as Parody in Marston's *Antonio and Mellida,*" *SEL* 11 (1971): 307-25, further develops some of these lines of inquiry. The two plays are united by a parodic literary orientation and by theme: "The bloody excesses of revenge tragedy are seen to grow out of the unlikely transformation of destructive feelings which characterizes the resolution of romantic comedy." The first play foreshadows the second in language and ambivalence of character. The imagery of *Antonio and Mellida* evokes a nature hostile to man and quasi-human in being divided against itself. Similarly Feliche's satire on the court's related sexual and governmental abuses is given universal resonance by Andrugio's laments on worldly fortune. While the evil men in the play are counterbalanced by Feliche, Andrugio, and the lovers Antonio and Mellida, the "vision of the world, tragic in its implications," is not qualified and ultimately outweighs the comic reconciliation. This tragic vision is related to character: the playing of two parts, which even Antonio resorts to, and especially the divided personalities of Andrugio, Antonio, and Feliche. Their avoidance of violence in *Antonio and Mellida* brings on the murders of the second play: "In a sense, the first play presents the emotional and political ethos responsible for an evil which can finally be eradicated only through violence and vengeance." In "The Ironic Tragedies of Marston and Chapman: Notes on Jacobean Tragic Form," *JEGP* 69 (1970): 613-30, Bergson finds the central irony in the *Antonio* plays to be the "dramatic revelation of the protagonist's psychological and moral disintegration." Although he seeks revenge, Antonio is forced to a political role; but his disguise betrays a wish to escape. His final "barbarism of blood-lust" is the climactic stage in his course, which could be viewed as parodying the self-understanding of the Shakespearean tragic protagonist. Similarly,

Philip J. Ayres in "Marston's *Antonio's Revenge*: The Morality of the Revenging Hero," *SEL* 12 (1972): 359-74, maintains that beginning in III.i Antonio is used to reveal by parody the lack of morality of the Kydian revenger.

The frequent recent interpretation of the *Antonio* plays as parody is challenged by T. F. Wharton in "Old Marston or New Marston: The *Antonio* Plays," *Essays in Criticism* 25 (1975): 357-69, who maintains that the careless style also indicates "incapacity to handle plot and agent in any integrated design." Marston's prologues and contemporary comment show that the aim is pathos, emotion. *Antonio's Revenge* goes even further to induce pleasure in sadistic vengeance exceeding what is shown in any contemporary work: the "electric excitement, the abruptness of actual violence" are his main accomplishment, as later imitation proves.

George L. Geckle in "*Antonio's Revenge*: 'Never more woe in lesser plot was found,'" *CompD* 6 (1972) : 323-35, regarding the play not as a parody but as a "serious tragedy," compares it with *Titus Andronicus* and Seneca's *Thyestes*. The primary Shakespearean influence is on the excessive revenge of Antonio, going beyond the eye-for-an-eye code, which is forced on him by Andrugio's ghost. Thus Antonio is intended to hold our sympathy; indeed, Marston himself may not have accepted the *lex talionis*. Pandulpho is likewise sympathetic: he realizes that Senecan doctrines are too remote from human nature. J. W. Lever, "Revenge Drama: *Antonio's Revenge, The Revenger's Tragedy*," in *The Tragedy of State* (1971), pp. 18-36, passes over *Antonio and Mellida* as a romance less spontaneous than Shakespeare's, to focus on *Antonio's Revenge*. The resemblances to *Hamlet* are probably due to the debt of both plays to the *Ur-Hamlet*. The "grim farce" does not clash with the central tragic effect; it helps smooth over possible faltering in the serious scenes by the inexperienced child actors, though parody is not intended. Marston's "classical sense of form" is shown in precise motivation and sustained control of the action without digressions.

Aldo Maugeri's *John Marston—"Antonio and Mellida": studio critico* (1951) singles out Marston's quality of conveying the passing states of his characters' minds in spontaneous dialogue, considers Antonio as a Hamlet "di tipo inferiore," and notes the significance of Antonio's role of buffoon in the *Revenge*, IV.i, as revealing alienation from society.

Robert Hunter West in *The Invisible World: A Study of Pneumatology in Elizabethan Drama* (1939) concerns himself with the ghost of

Andrugio in *Antonio's Revenge*. It is called up with a degree of necromancy, it is regarded as a real phantasm, and it is largely Senecan with a little "nondescript" Christian coloring.

G. B. Harrison in "Note sur John Marston," trans. F. W. Crosse, *Cahiers du Sud* 10 (1933): 186–88, rpt. in *Le théâtre élizabéthain,* ed. Georgette Camille and Pierre d'Exideuil [Georges Lasselin] (1940), pp. 240–43, classifies Antonio and Mellida as "le premier exemple frappant de la 'tragédie nocturne', exploitant avec succès les effets de torches qui vacillent dans les ténèbres."

In "'These Pretty Devices': A Study of Masques in Plays," *A Book of Masques: In Honour of Allardyce Nicoll* (1967), pp. 405–48, Inga-Stina Ewbank traces the dramatic effect of the mask in *Antonio's Revenge,* "the first appearance of the masque proper in tragedy" and a "fertile and vividly original device." The mask form shapes the whole scene, converting revenge into ritual and exhausting emotions so that the only conclusion left is the religious retreat.

Louis C. Stagg in "Figurative Imagery in Revenge Tragedies by Three Seventeenth-Century Contemporaries of Shakespeare," *South Central Bulletin* 26, no. 4 (1966): 43–50, analyzes the imagery in *Antonio's Revenge*. Marston's play, which receives a major share of attention, proves comparatively abundant in images relating to animals, the garden and nature, death, disease, food and drink, fire and light, and mythology and religion. Stagg shows the relevance of examples of such imagery to the drama; and in a final table he compares the three tragedies with *Hamlet* in terms of images in various categories. *Antonio's Revenge* is also unusually rich in personification.

In "The Comic Accomplice in Elizabethan Revenge Tragedy," *RenD* 9 (1966): 125–39, Douglas Cole recognizes a burlesque element in both *Antonio* plays, but finds a serious purpose in *Antonio's Revenge*: "the interaction of the philosophical Stoic and the passionate revenger," supplemented by the Kydian theme of madness. Of the comic accomplices, Balurdo and Gaspar Strotzo, the first may be carried over simply because he was popular in the first part, and both reflect the "disjointed quality" of the play itself. But their ridiculousness may help to keep the pathos sounding serious.

Paul N. Siegel in *Shakespearean Tragedy and the Elizabethan Compromise* (1957) believes the prologue to *Antonio's Revenge* as important as that to *Tamburlaine* or *Every Man in His Humour,* for voicing a "conception of tragedy as the exposure of universal, affrighting evil." The pessimistic view of man held by Marston and Donne countered the Christian humanist view and "furnished the emotional material for later Elizabethan and Jacobean tragedy." And Rolf Soellner in "Baroque Passion in Shakespeare and His Contemporaries," *ShakS* 1 (1965): 294-302, examines the extreme violence of Antonio's passion, set off by parallels and contrasts, as an example of the baroque hero in an "art which strives to go beyond probability."

The Wonder of Women, or The Tragedy of Sophonisba

Peter Ure's "John Marston's *Sophonisba*: A Reconsideration," *DUJ* 10, no. 3 (1949): 81-90, rpt. in *Elizabethan and Jacobean Drama: Critical Essays by Peter Ure*, ed. J. C. Maxwell (1974), pp. 75-92, sees three main components of this "austere and melancholy Roman tragedy": Stoicism, the failure of "policy," and "lust in action." As in *Gorboduc*, the characters receive a morality-play grouping, with the good constituted by Massinissa and Sophonisba, representing the Stoic position, and Gelosso, the anti-Machiavellian; opposed are the Machiavellian councillors of Carthage and Syphax, worked upon by Erictho as Lust herself. The treatment is generally classical, with some similarity in content and tone to Daniel and Greville. Sophonisba receives a "Senecan apotheosis" in the end, and Stoicism is justified by a demonstrated dichotomy in the world.

Finkelpearl (book, I,A) points out that the author calls *Sophonisba*, alone among his dramas, a "poeme"; it is his "most serious, carefully contrived work." In Sophonisba, Marston "tried to express an ideal of human perfection about which he had a nearly obsessional preoccupation." The play's form "is nearer to some kind of quasi-religious spectacle than to conventional tragedy." The result is uneven: the language "tends to be elliptical, condensed, and sententious"; the play, "thoughtful, earnest, high-minded, tedious."

Gerhard Saupe, *Die Sophonisbatragödien der englischen Literatur des 17. und 18. Jahrhunderts* (1929), finds the play oriented to sensational appeals: it seeks to dramatize as many events as possible and particularly to show the extreme of passion. Sophonisba is less a nationalist than a woman in love, and more a rhetorician than either. Her suicide is viewed as heroic, but Massinissa is also a memorable character.

In *Le thème de Sophonisbe dans les principales tragédies de la littérature occidentale* (1956), A. José Axelrad notes that in addition to Appian, Marston made some use of a French play, the *Sophonisbe* of Nicolas de Montreux (1601). The egregious use of Erictho remains controversial, and Sophonisba's devotion to her virtue does not grip us. "Marston se montre panégyriste maladroit de la vertu féminine; c'est que cette vertu l'étonne, et qu'il n'est pas bien convaincu de sa réalité." John Orrell in "The Sources of Marston's *The Wonder of Women or The Tragedie of Sophonisba,*" *N&Q* 10 (1963): 102-3, supplementing the notes in the Wood edition, points out details suggesting Livy as a minor source for the play. He also quotes moralistic marginal annotations in the 1578 translation of Appian which may have suggested to Marston his favorable view of Sophonisba.

Eldred Jones, *Othello's Countrymen: The African in English Renaissance Drama* (1965), believes that the play is concerned with the "sacrifice of the individual to state and policy" and the renunciation of morality for the sake of his own will by Syphax. In the latter connection Erictho, whose rites are presented with "sensitive use of darkness and blackness," represents the degeneration of Syphax; and the two Africans seem to be deliberately worked into the unity of the play: the treacherous Zanthia and Vangue, "the visible black symbol, the agent of Syphax' heart." Robert Rentoul Reed, Jr., in *The Occult on the Tudor and Stuart Stage* (1965), calls Erictho the "most horrifying enchantress on the English stage."

Parasitaster, or The Fawn

Finkelpearl's "The Use of the Middle Temple's Christmas Revels in Marston's *The Fawne,*" *SP* 64 (1967): 199-209, is included in his book (I,A). Several features of the "Prince d'Amour" celebration seem to be echoed in the fifth act of the play: the laws of love, the prognostication, a defense of women's inconstancy, paradoxes, and a defense of drunkenness. In addition, the play has jokes about law and lawyers; and the plot, manifesting the superiority of youth over age, "registers the spirit of the Christmas revels, which abounded in the same sort of jokes as *The Fawne's* directed against slow-witted, impotent, aging, tight-fisted, pedantic fathers and teachers." The comparison also suggests that Marston's choice of material is considerably indebted to tradition and that there is more comedy in this and his other plays than is always realized. Finkelpearl agrees with Albert W. Upton, "Allusions to James I and His Court in Marston's *Fawn* and Beaumont's *Woman Hater,*" *PMLA* 44 (1929): 1048-65, that Gonzago satirizes James. B. N. De Luna, reviewing Finkelpearl's book in *ELN* 8 (1970-71): 149-53, points out other possible allusions to James: pregnancy, a favorite subject of the king, is frequently mentioned; and the proceedings of the two "parliaments" called by James in January and March 1604 might be more comparable to Cupid's parliament in the play than the "Prince d'Amour" revels are.

Joel Kaplan, "John Marston's *Fawn*: A Saturnalian Satire," *SEL* 9 (1969): 335–50, regards the play as the triumph of Marston's satiric comedy. Marston saw the Hercules of myth as a type of the satirist, in cleaning the Augean stables, but also liked the creative implication of the supposed thirteenth labor, making pregnant in one night the fifty daughters of King Thespius. In *The Fawn* Duke Hercules is both "satiric and saturnalian," carrying out both Herculean tasks in festive spirit, fostering the marriage of his son to continue his line and flattering the courtiers (with the dominant figure of swelling) until their delusions burst and drain away. In the final masque satire and saturnalia, the Ship of Fools and the Court of Love, combine as Hercules becomes Bacchic and the inflated figure of Drunkenness looms forth.

In his RRDS edition of the play (1965), Gerald A. Smith looks at the characters and their analogues. Gonzago is a "close imitation" of Polonius; the Fawn is a flatterer and a "classical giver of oracles and a Renaissance forest figure, the satyr." By giving them an exaggerated dose of their own medicine, he joyously plays upon the "flatterers who prevent princes from knowing themselves."

David J. Houser in "Purging the Commonwealth: Marston's Disguised Dukes and *A Knack to Know a Knave*" (above, *"The Malcontent"*) finds that most of the vice figures in *The Fawn* are not flatterers, but "corrupters of love." The Tiberio-Dulcimel plot treats flattery and especially "abused love," and shows a relation to the Honesty theme in *A Knack*. But the satiric subplot is detachable, there is no education of the ruling Cupid, and the whole is rather carelessly joined.

Histriomastix

Alvin Kernan, "John Marston's Play *Histriomastix*," *MLQ* 19 (1958): 134–40, also in condensed form in his book (I,B), views the play as roughly unified, a study in English social breakdown. There is no evidence that it is not entirely Marston's original work. The heterogeneous texture can be attributed to "the tastes of its specialized audience and the peculiar abilities of the boy choristers who played it." Each act shows one stage of decline on four social levels: "nobility, tradesmen and lawyers, the artisans turned players, and the scholar Chrisoganus"— who, although he should guide others to knowledge, is at the beginning a proud, pedantic scholastic. By the end he has become a "snarling, malcontent satirist." The repetition of sins from the preceding poetry suggests that the play is "Marston's first attempt to order for the stage the sensational and highly popular material of his formal verse satires."

In "John Marston's *Histrio-Mastix* as an Inns of Court Play: A Hypothesis," *HLQ* 29 (1965-66): 223-34, Finkelpearl agrees on the closeness to the satires, but goes further: "The language, the attitudes, the processional structure . . . of *Histrio-Mastix* are very close to those expressed in the satires and unlike what we find in his subsequent work." Pointing out academic relevance and references to lawyers, he contends that the play was probably written for the Middle Temple Christmas revels of 1598-99; the cast of a hundred and twenty would give "every Inner Barrister in residence" a role. Chrisoganus is favorably treated: ". . . he is the one who has maintained standards, the one who shows the path to reformation through law at the end." In his book (I,A) Finkelpearl further classifies the play as "made-to-order professional entertainment," and as "a quasi-pageant for the edification and glorification of his Society and of his Queen." A second ending, apparently for court presentation, is traceable in the text.

George L. Geckle, "John Marston's *Histriomastix* and the Golden Age," *CompD* 6 (1972): 205-22, agrees with Kernan on the theme of social breakdown, but would emphasize the role of Chrisoganus as chorus-commentator and the cyclical turn from a "vision of the Golden Age" through gradual decline to the Iron Age and return to the Golden in a tribute to Elizabeth. Important sources are Spenser and Juvenal, and the Wheel of Fortune becomes a structural principle. The play shows many typical qualities of Marston, who proves a conservative wishing to preserve the Christian values, like Shakespeare and Jonson. Chrisoganus, who Geckle (unlike Kernan) believes does not deteriorate during the action, is the first of a line of Marston's "educated social critics and political leaders." In this play as in his others, "female chastity is an absolute good, levity in dress or manner is questioned and usually satirized, and true 'law . . . Love and Peace' reside in an ideal union of chaste women and wisely educated men."

The apparent attack on Anthony Munday as Posthaste in *Histrio-mastix*, noted by Chambers, which seems separate from the Poetomachia, is supported by the readings of Eduard Eckhardt in *Das englische Drama im Zeitalter der Reformation und der Hochrenaissance: Vorstufen, Shakespeare und seine Zeit* (1928) and *Das englische Drama der Spätrenaissance* (1929) and J. B. Leishman in his edition of *The Three Parnassus Plays* (I,A). On the other hand, David Bevington in

Tudor Drama and Politics: A Critical Approach to Topical Meaning (1968) considers the identification of Posthaste as Munday or Shakespeare "unnecessary and inconclusive": the character is a social abstraction.

What You Will

According to Finkelpearl's book (I,A), *What You Will* again presents the world of the verse satires, but with a significant difference: the author has freed himself of "an intrusive representation of his own point of view." There are resemblances to Shakespeare's plays, especially *The Comedy of Errors* and *Twelfth Night;* but the "festive atmosphere" lacks the purging quality of that in the latter play. Marston's world is his metaphor for reality—libertine, inhuman, heedless of tradition, and demanding conformity.

In *Italian Renaissance Drama in England before 1625: The Influence of "Erudita" Tragedy, Comedy, and Pastoral on Elizabethan and Jacobean Drama* (1970), David Orr examines the extensive changes made by Marston in adapting his source, Sforza d'Oddi's *I Morti Vivi* (1576), for *What You Will*: ". . . it is nevertheless a completely different play, and wholly English in nature." Marston has discarded at least half of d'Oddi's material and largely substituted the stuff of satire, though this includes the stock pedant of Italian comedy.

Michael Shapiro, "Audience vs. Dramatist in Jonson's *Epicoene* and Other Plays of the Children's Troupes," *English Literary Renaissance* 3 (1973): 400–417, points out two ways in which Marston in *What You Will* flatters the audience so as to prevent unruly interruption. In the Induction Doricus seems to speak for the audience and deny that its members would be guilty of disturbance. And Quadratus offers the audience a favorable self-image, while at the same time suggesting conventional targets for its mockery, including Lampatho Doria, the "professional satirist." In short, "Quadratus' graceful superiority to the other characters in the play and his effortless enactment of his own chosen role were nicely calculated to produce sympathetic vibrations among the aristocratic spectators at Paul's, and thereby to prevent disruptive counterperformances."

Richard L. DeMolen, "Richard Mulcaster and the Elizabethan Theatre," *Theatre Survey* 13, no. 1 (1972): 28–41, raises the possibility that Pedante in *What You Will* may be cautiously drawn from Mulcaster and influenced by Shakespeare's similarly-based portrait in

Love's Labour's Lost; if so, the fact that Marston had no more plays acted by Saint Paul's Boys is understandable.

The Herford and Simpson edition of Jonson notes that the Induction to *What You Will,* like the prologue to *The Dutch Courtesan,* opposes the Horatian concept of delightful teaching, which Sidney and Jonson had accepted, and thus foreshadows Dryden's view.

Jack Drum's Entertainment

In *John Marston* (I,A), Finkelpearl sees the plot as seemingly conventional and romantic for the most part, but actually satiric in purpose; the target is "young gallants blinded by fashions and pursuing false gods," especially "linguistic mannerisms," and their superior, condescending exploiter, Brabant Senior. Marston may have been influenced by John Hoskins's *Directions for Speech and Style.* Through most of the play Planet is the familiar "satiric persona"; but at the end, in an attack on "uninvolved, condescending, satiric commentators," he seems to express the "recantation of an attitude Marston now found odious."

Michael C. Andrews, *"Jack Drum's Entertainment* as Burlesque," *RenQ* 24 (1971): 226-31, maintains that Marston's play not only borrows, as is generally known, from Sidney's *Arcadia,* but burlesques the more serious use of the same material in the anonymous public theater drama *The Trial of Chivalry,* which must have come first. Since the Marston work also mocks the "romantic crudities of the public theatres in general," it is relevant to the War of the Theaters, whether or not Brabant Senior (not part of the burlesqued material) also involves the Poetomachia. Whereas Marston seems to know both prior treatments of the Pasquill-Katherine-Mamon story, he makes his version "as farcical as possible"; with child actors it must have been "unmistakably comic throughout."

Fred L. Jones, "Echoes of Shakespeare in Later Elizabethan Drama," *PMLA* 45 (1930): 791-803, sees Mamon as only partly imitated from Shylock, in losses and speech mannerisms; Marston's character does not evoke the pathos and hatred that Shylock receives, but "only scorn." In the swift punishment he gets from fate and the rejoicing of his victims, Mamon may be indebted to the Prior of Munday's *Downfall of Robert Earl of Huntington.* Gilbert R. Davis in "The Characterization of Mamon in *Jack Drum's Entertainment,"* *ELN* 3 (1965-66): 22-24, points out that Mamon is called, not a Jew, but a "Jebusite—i.e., in the 17th century a Catholic, especially a Jesuit." He is a conventional

Elizabethan non-Jewish usurer, one of the "holdovers from the moralities."

The Insatiate Countess

According to Finkelpearl's book (I,A), the Countess contrasts to Sophonisba as in *The Dutch Courtesan* Franceschina does to Beatrice. "Marston was apparently trying to contrast three ways of loving: the Countess' psychopathic lust, the comic husbands' psychopathic hate, jealousy, and shame, and the altruistic and civilized devotion of the Count Mendoza and the Lady Lentulus." But while Marston's touch is traceable throughout (as is Barksted's), the lack of relation of two of the plots and the failure to resolve the third suggest that Marston did not finish his work. His style is especially visible in the love letter of the subplot and the scenes with Count Gniaca, "a kind of Malheureux."

Jean Prévost in *"L'insatiable comtesse," Cahiers du Sud* 10 (1933): 189-91, rpt. in *Le théâtre élizabéthain* (above, *"Antonio and Mellida"*), pp. 244-47, believes that the play dramatizes Marston's own inner conflicts: "pas seulement le drame de la vie sexuelle sans frein, mais le drame du scandale, et non pas seulement social: scandale intérieur dans les âmes mêmes qui s'en trouvent frappées." The playwright lacks humor; he is a somber Juvenal or Boccaccio. A biblical sense of sin also afflicts him, and the English belief "que la vie sociale et la cérémonie sont les choses les plus saintes, les plus sacrées qu'il y ait au monde." Ferdinando Neri in "La Contessa di Challant," in *Storia e Poesia* (1944), pp. 83-129, sees the countess as "alquanto gelida, ermetica ne' suoi apparenti furori," rather dominated than animated by her drives. Hanns Passmann in *Der Typus der Kurtisane im elisabethanischen Drama* (above) finds the countess developed from Franceschina in *The Dutch Courtesan* (also based on the Countess of Challant), and modern in her pathological nature.

Eastward Ho

In their edition of Jonson, vol. 1, Herford and Simpson judge the play "one of the best made of Elizabethan comedies. Its clear-cut strength and simplicity of structure was rarely, if ever, approached by any one of its three authors elsewhere." Touchstone is not ridiculed, but justifies "all the thrifty virtues of the honest tradesman." Quicksilver is inconsistent, especially in his conversion; but Gertrude is drawn with spirit, and her mother, "piteous as well as laughable," is neatly hit off. Mildred's characterization is neglected; and Golding, not a congenial role or essentially Elizabethan, if treated rather gingerly, is more likable than one would expect.

In his edition (1973), C. G. Petter sees the play as criticizing not only city comedy, but the city itself for prodigality, greed, and bourgeois smugness, which make for disorder. *Eastward Ho* parodies morality play endings, and even treats the prodigal son parable ironically. Yet Slitgut is like a chorus celebrating the downfall of those who would prey on the city, and Golding's gentlemanly compromise restores a harmony which the play seeks. Probably Marston, a shareholder in the Queen's Revels, got Chapman and Jonson to join with him in a challenge to other successful citizen comedies. Julia H. Harris's edition (1926) stresses that the play "is related to the principal members of the prodigal-son group, and to the *Glass of Government* in particular; that the authors have used the comedy of London life to emphasize, by its very reality, the stereotyped situations of the prodigal-son drama, and to fuse incidents from Italian drama with the main plot." *Eastward Ho* contains less Protestantism than "citizen morality, honesty-is-the-best-policy morality." In Quicksilver and others Marston achieves a certain modulation of style to character.

In *George Chapman* (I,A), Jean Jacquot considers that the play, while seeking a return to traditional morality, views Touchstone with "une bienveillance amusée" and plays with the old naive moral ending; thus *Eastward Ho* is halfway between *The Shoemaker's Holiday* and *The Knight of the Burning Pestle*. John Doebler, "Beaumont's *The Knight of the Burning Pestle* and the Prodigal Son Plays," *SEL* 5 (1965): 333–44, compares *Eastward Ho* with the contemporary *London Prodigal* and with Beaumont's play, which uses the Marston-Chapman-Jonson comedy as a source and also parodies it.

Clifford Leech, "The Dramatists' Independence," *RORD* 10 (1967): 17–23, sees the play as introducing "a new sub-genre, the journey-comedy where the journey is minimal and abortive, and, in the case of *Eastward Ho*, is presented with a subtle irony." The planned journey to Virginia becomes a short trip to the east, Gertrude tries vainly to find Sir Petronel's fictional castle, and Golding figuratively moves up in the citizen world. "The first two journeys end in comic disaster, which carries over to Golding's successful journey and thus colors that with irony: all citizens' journeys, it is implied, are trifling matters." In "Three Times *Ho* and a Brace of Widows: Some Plays for the Private

Theatre," in *The Elizabethan Theatre III,* ed. David Galloway (1973), pp. 14–32, Leech is interested in the audience and tone. Although the play does not attack the Dekker-Webster *Westward Ho,* it does seem to envisage an audience which could appreciate inside jokes on plays of the public or other private theaters. *Eastward Ho* shows the prosperity of "city virtue," but laughs at it, and shows the pitfalls of prodigality, but makes its prodigals attractive. The goldsmith's occupation may not have seemed very moral to the audience, and the play has a good deal of bawdry.

In *"Eastward Ho,* 1605, by Chapman, Jonson, and Marston, Bibliography and Circumstances of Production," *Library* 9 (1928-29): 287–302, R. E. Brettle considers whether the trouble over the play was caused by the production or the printing. He believes that "a three-author play usually and perhaps always meant that a manager wanted it quickly," and cites "the great probability that any trouble over an Elizabethan or Jacobean play . . . would arise at its production and before its printing." W. W. Greg, however, in *"Eastward Ho,* 1605," a note appended to Brettle's article, pp. 303-4, finds that on balance the printed version of the play more likely aroused the royal anger: Chapman refers to two offending clauses, and two sentences were excised from the printed play. Petter's edition (above) suggests that after setting but before printing some fourteen lines of text may have been revised. On the other hand, Joseph Quincy Adams in *"Eastward Hoe* and Its Satire against the Scots," *SP* 28 (1931): 689-701, like Brettle thinks that the production gave offense. Jonson claims that his responsibility and Chapman's for the difficulty are due only to *"Rumour,"* which does not seem to be the right expression for a text; and the fact that the production was in trouble might account for the speedy printing of the play.

B. OVER-ALL STATE OF CRITICISM

Criticism may often have unduly stressed certain superficial or ill-defined lines of inquiry: Ejner J. Jensen in "Theme and Imagery in *The Malcontent"* (II,A) speaks of "those objections to the excesses of his language and that concentration on the man which have been the dominant strains of Marston criticism in the past." At any rate, in comparatively few areas have students of Marston built upon each other's work: attention to such stage effects as music, a new reading of *The Dutch Courtesan,* awareness of originality of wording, a suggestion of parody especially in the *Antonio* plays, an increased sense of significance in the satire. Although Louis Lecocq in "Travaux récents sur John Marston," *EA* 16 (1963): 351-63, believes it to be generally admitted now that Marston stands detached from his heroes, there is a point of appreciation beyond which some critics could not go. Yet some change of evaluation has occurred. Much of the earlier criticism sought to judge the works as a whole and the author's complete artistic and moral personality as well. Intensive studies of the individual plays have indicated that these previous judgments may have been too sweeping; the latest larger studies have, without whitewashing, done more justice to the magnitude and variety of the playwright's experiments and given him more credit for knowledge and originality. Much that has been touched on, however, remains to be explored further: Marston's language and rhetoric, the stageworthiness of his dialogue, his acceptance of neo-Stoicism and his criticism of it, his knowledge of classical and Italian literature, his conception of dramatic satire, his attitude toward courts, the rationale of his peculiar treatment and subordination of female characters. The motive behind his sensational effects, if it is not simply to gain an audience, should be discoverable. The question of his intention to parody other plays will probably continue to arouse vigorous reaction on both sides.

III. CANON

A. PLAYS IN CHRONOLOGICAL ORDER

The order, date limits (in italics before semicolon), first publication date, and classification by type are those of Alfred Harbage, *Annals of English Drama, 975-1700,* rev. Samuel Schoenbaum (1964). E. K. Chambers treats canon and dating in *The Elizabethan Stage* (I,A), vols. 3 and 4; and see Gerald Eades Bentley, *The Jacobean and Caroline Stage,* 7 vols., 1941-68. The first quartos are described in W. W. Greg, *A Bibliography of the English Printed Drama to the Restoration,* 4 vols. (1939-59).

Histriomastix, or The Player Whipped (revised by
Marston? and others?), comedy (*1598-1599*; 1610)

Robert Boies Sharpe in *The Real War of the Theaters* (I,B) believes the play dated by an unmistakable reference to the alarm in London on 7 August, 1599, aroused by the rumor that a Spanish invasion had begun. Anthony Caputi in *John Marston, Satirist* (I,A) judges from the style that Marston revised an old play, and dates the production in the late summer or early autumn of 1599, because of the time of reopening of Paul's Boys and Jonson's apparent allusion in *Every Man Out*. In *The Three Parnassus Plays* (I,A), J. B. Leishman argues for 1598, principally on the ground that Jonson's declaration of 1601 that his enemies had provoked him on the stage for three years accurately designated the time. Philip J. Finkelpearl in "John Marston's *Histro-Mastix* as an Inns of Court Play: A Hypothesis" (II,B) and in his book (I,A) would put production at the Middle Temple Christmas revels of 1598/99 on the basis of structure, local relevance, Marston's stylistic development, two reputed topical allusions, and evidence of a performance for the court not available to Paul's Boys at the time.

Harbage and Schoenbaum suggest that Marston may have revised an old play, possibly by Chapman. R. E. Brettle, "John Marston," *University of Oxford . . . Abstracts of Dissertations for the Degree of Doctor of Philosophy* 1 (1928): 20–31, allows Marston a fourth of the play. On the basis of the text, Jean Jacquot in *George Chapman* (I,A) concludes that Chapman wrote the original drama in the style of his early works, probably between 1592 and 1596. Perhaps Chapman and Marston later revised it together. Arthur Acheson, *Shakespeare, Chapman, and "Sir Thomas More"* (1931), while seeing Chapman as the primary author, thinks that Nashe contributed a little also.

1 Antonio and Mellida, tragicomedy (*1599-1600*; 1602)

Caputi (book, I,A) finds on stylistic grounds that the play must follow *Jack Drum's Entertainment*, and considers the second half of 1600 the only open date. Finkelpearl's book (I,A) interprets a reference in the Induction as pointing to late 1600 and notes four possible allusions to *Hamlet* also supporting a later date. In "A New Date for *Antonio's Revenge*," D. J. McGinn (I,A), rejecting the "painter's scene" as an autobiographical clue, places the play in 1600 on internal evidence. But Gustav Cross in "The Date of Marston's *Antonio and Mellida*," *MLN* 72 (1957): 328–32, accepting the same scene as a reference by Marston to himself, puts the writing and probably the performance between September 1599 and the end of March 1600. In *The School of Shakespeare* David Frost (II,A) agrees with Cross: Marston frequently puts personal data into a play. The Armed Epilogue, reflecting on Jonson's *Cynthia's Revels*, may be a later addition.

Antonio's Revenge (*2 Antonio and Mellida*), tragedy (*1599-1601*: 1602)

Caputi (book, I,A) dates the play in the winter of 1600/1, from references to winter in the prologue and to the current problem of monopoly. Frost (II,A) agrees, pointing out that this date accounts for Jonson's being able to ridicule the piece in *Poetaster* and (since *Jack Drum's Entertainment* would then come before) allows for changes from *Antonio and Mellida*. Believing that both the *Antonio* plays follow *Hamlet*, Finkelpearl (book, I,A) prefers a time between late 1600 and the Stationers' Register entry of 24 October 1601. E. A. J. Honigmann in "The Date of *Hamlet*," *ShS* 9 (1956), 24-34, is willing to accept that *Hamlet* may in a small way imitate Marston's play, which may then date from the autumn or early winter of 1599. McGinn's article (I,A) suggests the late winter or early spring of 1601 because of the influence of *Hamlet*, which turned Marston's attention, not previously thus inclined, to revenge tragedy.

Jack Drum's Entertainment, domestic comedy (*1600*; 1601)

Brettle, in his review of the first volume of Wood's edition of the plays, *RES* 11 (1935): 221-28, considers the play to be wholly Marston's and mentions "almost contemporary manuscript evidence of his authorship." Sharpe in *The Real War of the Theaters* (I,B) dates the play May 1600, partly on the basis of an allusion to Kemp's morris dance to Norwich. Caputi (book, I,A) identifies the manuscript evidence mentioned by Brettle and cites several references, of which that to Kemp is chief, indicating a production in late spring or early summer of 1600.

What You Will, comedy (*1601*; 1607)

Largely on structural and stylistic grounds, Caputi (book, I,A) puts the play probably in 1601 or 1602; he rejects the thesis that it necessarily comes between Jonson's *Cynthia's Revels* and *Poetaster*.

The Dutch Courtesan, comedy (*1603-1604*; 1605)

Caputi (book, I,A) would date the play "concurrently, or very nearly concurrently" with *Eastward Ho*—that is, early 1605—because he believes that Marston learned something about structure from the collaborative play.

The Malcontent, tragicomedy (*1600-1604*; 1604)

Although Harbage and Schoenbaum mention "additions by Webster," there seems to be no study in the period challenging Marston's authorship of the text of the play proper, including the additions, as opposed to the Induction. On the other hand, the date has been argued. In "The Dates of *Hamlet* and Marston's *The Malcontent*," *RES* 9 (1933): 397-409, Harold R. Walley places both productions of the play in 1604, the first coming in the spring. He believes the playwright complimented in the epilogue to be Chapman, the chief Blackfriars dramatist of the time, who was completing *Monsieur D'Olive*. In "The Date of *The Malcontent*: A Rejoinder," *RES* 11 (1935): 42-50, Elmer Edgar Stoll maintains his view—originally stated in *John Webster* (1905)—that the first production of *The Malcontent* as a Blackfriars play came in 1600. He thinks that Marston would not have abandoned Senecan revenge tragedy after the *Antonio* plays, only to return three years and more later; and the King's Men would have wished to take over a play new enough to be interesting, but old enough to have been forgotten by audiences and to have fallen from the Blackfriars repertory. Gustav Cross also argues for the earlier date, "not later than 1600," in "The Date of *The Malcontent* Once More," *PQ* 39 (1960): 104-13. There are many similarities to the *Antonio* plays, and Malevole is the fuller version of Feliche promised in *Antonio and Mellida*. The quotations in *The Malcontent* from Thomas Bastard's *Chrestoleros* (1598) and other works would lack topical relevance as late as 1604. Like the *Antonio* plays, *The Malcontent* is Stoical, whereas after the appearance of Florio's translation of Montaigne in 1603 Marston became "fired with enthusiasm for Montaigne's anti-Stoicism," as the plays clearly of the later time, *The Dutch Courtesan* and *The Fawn*, attest. There is a reference in *The Fawn* (II.i) to Duke Pietro's discovery of his duchess's unfaithfulness four years before. If, as Cross believes, *The Fawn* was written in 1604, the playwright himself may be indicating a date of 1600 for *The Malcontent*. A table of the percentages of neologisms in Marston's plays puts *The Malcontent* in the earlier group, before Jonson's inhibiting satire in the *Poetaster* of 1601. Finkelpearl (book, I,A), however, says that since Bernard Harris (edition; I,A) has demonstrated dependence upon a 1602 translation of *Il PastorFido*, Marston's play must be later. Caputi (book, I,A) thinks it unlikely that both versions of the play, as well as three editions, appeared in the same year; in addition, a remark in the Induction suggests that the shorter version was not new. Hence he would put the Blackfriars production before May 1603, when the theaters were closed for the year.

In his edition (II,A), G. K. Hunter agrees on the year: 1603 is as close as we can come, though some time before March may have been appropriate for a play designed to bolster the slipping children's company. The translation of Guarini came in 1602, and other references make the play at least that late; but Florio's Montaigne of 1603, quoted in Marston's next two plays, is not used. As stylistic evidence shows, Marston wrote at least six of the eleven passages added to the third quarto; he or Webster or some other may have written the remainder.

Parasitaster, or The Fawn, comedy (*1604-1606*; 1606)

Caputi (book, I,A) would put the play after *The Malcontent*, to which it has resemblances, because of the use in *The Fawn* of Florio's Montaigne; Marston's presumptive occupation with other plays after 1604 and the productions by two different companies noted on the title page of the second edition make 1604 the most likely date.

Eastward Ho, with Chapman and Jonson, comedy (*1605*; 1605)

By general agreement Marston is given the first act and various parts thereafter. Percy Simpson in "The Problem of Authorship of *Eastward Ho*," *PMLA* 59 (1944): 715-25, presents an analysis also supported by C. H. Herford and included in their edition of Jonson (I,A), vols. 1 and 9: "Marston originated the idea of the play," and created at least in draft such characters as Touchstone, Sindefy, Quicksilver, Golding, Mildred, and Gertrude. Julia H. Harris (II,A) would give the "general scheme of the play" to Jonson; Marston's style is identifiable by reason of its "balanced structure." After the first act her attributions differ somewhat from those of Herford and Simpson; and she specifies Marston's working with Chapman (to whom she assigns the largest share) in the three middle acts. Petter's edition (II,A) sets up its own series of Marstonian language tests and on this basis divides the authorship, with results close to but not identical with Simpson's. In *George Chapman* (I,A), Jean Jacquot finds Chapman's contribution beginning at II.ii, with signs of Marston's collaboration; after IV.i the play is more difficult to break down in authorship.

The Wonder of Women, or The Tragedy of Sophonisba, tragedy (*1605-1606*; 1606)

From the title page, which indicates performances after the queen's patronage had been withdrawn from the Revels Children, and from the fact that *Sophonisba* is announced in the second edition of *The Fawn*, Caputi (book, I,A) dates production in late spring, 1606, with publication in the summer.

City Pageant, royal entertainment (*31 July 1606*; MS)

R. E. Brettle, "Notes on John Marston" (I,A), attributes most of the manuscript to Marston.

The Entertainment at Ashby, mask and speeches (*Aug. 1607*; MSS)

Brettle, "Notes on John Marston" (I,A), finds Marston's handwriting at several points in the manuscript.

The Insatiate Countess, with William Barkstead; tragedy (*ca. 1610-1613*; 1613)

Caputi (book, I,A) does not find Marston's hand in the "general conception"—either ideas or terms—of the play; there is even a "philosophical disparity." He probably planned and wrote the lesser action, the comic—in view of what is known of his working schedule and later imprisonment, between August 1607 and June 1608. Production may have come at any time between 1608 and 1613. Finkelpearl (book, I,A) sees touches of Marston, as of Barkstead, throughout. H. Harvey Wood, *The Plays of John Marston*, 3 vols. (1934-39), vol. 3, finds Marston's style in the play "more frequent and more obvious" than Barkstead's: "indeed, the play as a whole could, in my opinion, be attributed to no other hand, on stylistic evidence, than Marston's."

B. UNCERTAIN ASCRIPTIONS; APOCRYPHA

Robert II King of Scots, with Chettle, Dekker, and Jonson; history (*3-27 Sept. 1599*; lost)

The only evidence for attribution to Marston is an apparent reference to him in Henslowe's *Diary*, cited in Chambers (I,A), vol. 3.

A Larum for London, or The Siege of Antwerp, history (*ca. 1598–1600*; 1602)

See under *The Puritan* below.

Charlemagne, or The Distracted Emperor, tragedy (*1584–ca. 1605*; MS)

See under *The Puritan* below.

The Spanish Moor's Tragedy, with Day, Dekker, and Haughton; tragedy (*13 Feb. 1600*; 1657?)

This is probably the same play as the following.

Lust's Dominion, or The Lascivious Queen, with Day, Dekker (and Haughton?); tragedy (*13 Feb. 1600*; 1657)

In "The Authorship of *Lust's Dominion*," *SP* 55 (1958): 39–61, Gustav Cross suggests that this is the play called by Henslowe *The Spanish Moor's Tragedy*, originally written some time before 1600. Marston was the first to revise or rewrite it, during his brief period as a Henslowe hack; and it was later rehandled by Day, Haughton, and Dekker. Cross believes that Marston sharpened both the action and the characters of Eleazar and the Queen Mother, "was responsible for the 'finer scenes,'" and in general contributed what Bullen calls the play's "tragic lurid-ness" and "iron gloom." Marston's hand appears at intervals throughout the play, especially in I.ii and iii; II.vi; IV.iii; "and a good deal of the last act, especially Eleazar's long speeches in V.vi." Possibly Kirkman, printing the play in 1657, misread Marston's name on a manuscript copy as Marlowe. Evidence for this attribution includes Marston's initi-ation of the revival of revenge tragedy with the *Antonio* plays; the use "of music as an illustration of character" in the opening scenes of *Lust's Dominion* and *The Malcontent*; a parallel passage, numerous "tricks of expression," and similarities in thought; and a comparison of *Lust's Dominion* and Marston's early plays in terms of coinages and new uses of words. Nearly a third of such examples in *Lust's Dominion* "either correspond to or are closely linked with similar coinages in Marston's acknowledged works." In "The Vocabulary of *Lust's Domin-ion*," *NM* 59 (1958): 41–48, Cross lists these coinages and new uses. Caputi (book, I,A) judges Cross's argument on this attribution imper-fect but "impressive."

J. L. Simmons in *"Lust's Dominion*: A Showpiece for the Globe?" *TSE* 20 (1972): 11-22, also argues for Marston's authorship. Like *Antonio's Revenge*, the play is a sophisticated parody "in the spirit of coterie drama" of Kyd, Marlowe in *The Jew of Malta,* and Shakespeare in *Titus Andronicus.* The conclusions equally depart from popular drama in letting the wrongdoer go unpunished. In *Lust's Dominion* we may find the transitional phase between the "careless plotting of *Antonio's Revenge* and the masterly control of *The Malcontent.*" The play may also establish an earlier connection with the Lord Chamberlain's Men. Specific parallels with *The Malcontent* are the use of music and the names Mendoza and Maria for villain and emblem of chastity. But there is always the possibility that in *Lust's Dominion* someone else is imitating Marston and his antecedents.

Satiromastix, or The Untrussing of the Humorous Poet, with Dekker; comedy (*1601*; 1602)

That Marston helped Dekker write *Satiromastix* has been denied by M. T. Jones-Davies, *Un peintre de la vie londonienne: Thomas Dekker* (I,A). Ants Oras in *Pause Patterns in Elizabethan and Jacobean Drama* (I,C), however, finds a similarity of pause patterns between this play and Marston's known work: "There is more split-line thrust and parry of repartee and clash of series of abrupt short speeches in this play of Dekker's than anywhere else in his early work, recalling Marston's experimentation with the same devices in the second part of his first tragedy and in *Sophonisba,* and lending some support to those critics, including Chambers, who see Marston's hand in it." Ernest A. Gerrard, *Elizabethan Drama and Dramatists, 1583-1603* (1928), sees Marston's touch in the comic situations of Horace.

The London Prodigal, Shakespeare? Dekker? Drayton?; comedy (*1603-1605*; 1605)

See under *The Puritan* below.

The Puritan, or The Widow of Watling Street, Shakespeare? Middleton?; comedy (*1606*; 1607)

The attributions of *A Larum for London, Charlemagne, The London Prodigal,* and this play are listed in Chambers (I,A), vol. 4. Brettle (diss. abstract, above) rejects the hypothesis that Marston wrote *The Puritan* and *The London Prodigal*—suggested by C. F. Tucker Brooke in his edition of *Shakespeare Apocrypha* (1908)—or *Charlemagne*; the attribution of *A Larum for London* is "very doubtful." Baldwin Maxwell, "Conjectures on *The London Prodigal,*" in *Studies in Honor of T. W. Baldwin*, ed. Don Cameron Allen (1958), pp. 171-84, finds Marston's authorship "hardly conceivable." In *Studies in the Shakespeare Apocrypha* (1956), Maxwell considers Middleton the most likely author of *The Puritan*.

The Silver Mine, perhaps also known as *The Conspiracy of Charles Duke of Byron*, comedy (*Feb.–March 1608*; lost)

The *Annals* accepts Chambers's assigned title, cites the play as of anonymous authorship, and questions Chapman or Marston as author.

The First Anti-Mask of Mountebanks, Christmas entertainment (*2 and 19 Feb. 1618*; MSS)

Brettle (diss. abstract, above) believes that Marston wrote this mask before 1617, perhaps before 1606. Caputi (book, I,A) doubts that Marston wrote it. Harbage and Schoenbaum suggest Thomas Campion as a possible author.

C. CRITIQUE OF THE STANDARD EDITION

The only collected edition of Marston's plays in this century, that of H. Harvey Wood, 3 vols. (1934-39), includes all the dramas in which the playwright is known to have a hand. The old spelling is largely preserved; but *Jack Drum's Entertainment*, *Histriomastix*, and *Eastward Ho* are not annotated. The quality of this edition is not high. Introductions and notes, while at times useful, are open to objection; and the editing is uneven, as reviews of the first volume point out. R. E. Brettle's analysis (III,A) finds that "it is neither full enough nor accurate enough—in Introduction, text, textual apparatus and explanatory notes—for the scholar and the specialist, and it is too expensive and 'finicking' for the ordinary student and the general reader." W. W. Greg in *MLR* 30 (1935): 90-94 is even more blunt: "Altogether a slovenly piece of work, unredeemed by either judgment or taste." Both reviews contain substantial lists of mistakes.

While many Marston studies cite Wood's edition, others still use *The Works of John Marston,* edited by A. H. Bullen, 3 vols. (1887), with modernized spelling, and with line numbers, which the Wood edition lacks.

D. TEXTUAL STUDIES

In his edition of *Antonio and Mellida* and *Antonio's Revenge* (1921), W. W. Greg suggests, on the basis of the ornaments, that the quartos were printed by Richard Bradock—an ascription repeated in his *Bibliography of the English Printed Drama to the Restoration* (III,A). The earlier work lists variant, dubious, and irregular readings and discusses unusual punctuation in the texts.

In his edition of *The Dutch Courtesan* (II,A), Peter Davison believes the 1605 quarto "to have been set from a final draft of the play, not prepared fully for the theatre, but lightly prepared by Marston for the printer." Apparently one press is involved, and there was considerable, though somewhat clumsy, proofreading.

W. W. Greg, "Notes on Old Books," *Library* 2 (1921-22): 49-57, traces the three 1604 printings of *The Malcontent*. The first "was very carelessly printed from a rather confused manuscript"; the second is an "emended impression" using part at least of the same type, incorporating numerous quite rough corrections, "most likely by the author." From this altered impression came the augmented edition, which was also carelessly printed and which, while making corrections in later impressions, never received an authoritative proofreading. W. Craig Ferguson, *Valentine Simmes, Printer to Drayton, Shakespeare . . . Marston, Heywood, and Other Elizabethans* (1968), a fresh and full examination, corroborates Greg's order for the three 1604 quartos, and adds notes on relations of the manuscript to Q1 and Q2 and of Q2 to Q3. Brettle in "Bibliographical Notes on Some Marston Quartos and Early Collected Editions" (I,A), notes addition of an omitted line in the second state of the first edition and omission of a satirical reference to the church in the third state. M. L. Wine in his edition (II,A) records discovery of a unique copy of the second edition with an entire sheet recast. E. E. Stoll's article on *The Malcontent* (III,A) argues that passages added to the text in the augmented edition are not due to later revision, but represent restoration of the original, in line with Elizabethan and Marstonian dramaturgy. D. C. Gunby, however, in "The Third Quarto of *The Malcontent*: Marston's Additions and Their Effects," *AUMLA* 31 (1969): 20-27, believes the additions "unfortunate" in reducing both coherence of theme and dramatic effect. Aside from the Induction and minor changes, the new text may be classified as satire, mostly amplified dialogue for Malevole, Bilioso, and Passarello, and serious attempts to explain more clearly Malevole and his relation to the theme. But the first group of changes affects the balance of the play by expanding the satire without further relating it to the whole, and the second gives a misleading idea of the central character. Thus Marston often augments in a "cavalier manner," adding "red herrings"; in I.iv he may be trying to step up dramatic interest at the expense of the play as a whole, but in all he was perhaps simply in too much of a hurry.

G. K. Hunter, editing the play (II,A), studies the three quartos anew. Agreeing with Greg on their order, he adds that the first quarto was printed from a manuscript of literary rather than theatrical provenance, and underwent correction while in press. The second quarto includes not only corrections but some changes, seemingly by Marston. The third and best quarto reflects close reading of the text of the second, with much correction.

In his bibliographical article Brettle observes that the corrections in the second edition of *The Fawn*, although attributed by both the publisher and Marston himself to the author, are "not many nor very important." W. L. Halstead, "An Explanation for the Two Editions of Marston's *Fawne*," *SP* 40 (1943): 25-32, finds that the first edition must have been set with the playwright's approval from a personal, not a professional, copy; in the second edition there are some "changes to improve the understanding by the reader and to give the exact intentions of the author, " made by Marston, who shows unusual interest in this publication.

Julia H. Harris, editing *Eastward Ho* (II,B) believes the printer of the 1605 editions, on the basis of ornaments used, to be G. Eld; Herford and Simpson in their edition of Jonson (I,A), vol. 4, and Greg, *Bibliography of the English Printed Drama to the Restoration* (above), vol. 1, adopt the suggestion. Harris also believes the third edition to have been printed from the earlier editions, not the manuscript. Brettle in his article on the play (II,A) discusses the omission of about seven lines from the first issue of the first edition, the substitution of a shorter passage, and the revision of one phrase; he indicates the relation of the three editions of 1605. Perhaps in other places a "passage or passages were suppressed in proof." Herford and Simpson (I,A) suggest that in the primary example of omission and substitution cited by Brettle presumably one or more of the authors were consulted, and raise the possibility that, before the second of the two pages in question was reset, a further cut, shown by unusual spacing, occurred. They agree that the text was also cut, seemingly by the printer, at three of the four possible places suggested by Brettle, and note two other possible excisions. The first of the three divisions of the play affected they assign to Marston, the others to Chapman. In "*Eastward Ho* and Its Satire against the Scots" (II,A), J. Q. Adams reviews all the omissions suggested by Brettle and the apparent additional cut before the printing of two pages, to show that the acting text is not reproduced even in the first issue, the publisher seemingly having made the changes after setting type. In "Bibliographical Notes on Some Marston Quartos and Early Collected Editions" (I,A), Brettle looks at the printing history of *The Insatiate Countess* and the *Plays* of 1633. There may have been a second issue of the first edition of *The Insatiate Countess* in 1613; if so, either Marston refused to have his name appear as partial author or it had no right to be there, the first hypothesis being the more likely. William Sheares, publisher of the collected *Plays* in 1633, may have had doubts about Marston's authorship of *The Malcontent* and *The Insatiate Countess*, since he did not include these.

Sydney Race, "Collier and the Mountebank's Masque," *N&Q* 197 (1952): 281–83, while denying Marston's authorship of the work, contends that John Payne Collier, contrary to his statement introducing his edition, did not find a manuscript of the mask in the Duke of Devonshire's library; instead he essentially copied the version already printed by John Nichols in his *Progresses of Queen Elizabeth*, with an unacknowledged use of the British Museum manuscript. Race lists Collier's corrections of the Nichols version, and compares a manuscript of the mask from the Gray's Inn Library which may be the one transcribed, without complete accuracy, by Nichols.

E. SINGLE-WORK EDITIONS

The Malcontent has been edited by M. L. Wine, RRDS (1964), by Bernard Harris (1967), and by George K. Hunter (1975). All three are modernized texts based upon extensive collation, with listing of substantive variants, full explanatory notes, and critical introductions. G. B. Harrison also edited the play for the Temple Dramatists (1933). There has been a reprint of the third 1604 quarto (1970). A translation by Giorgio Melchiori appears in *Teatro elisabettiano*, ed. Mario Praz (1948).

The Dutch Courtesan has also been edited by M. L. Wine, RRDS (1965), with a comprehensive introduction. Peter Davison has edited an old-spelling text (1968). *The Cheater Cheated*, a droll made from the play, is in *The Wits: Or, Sport upon Sport*, ed. John James Elson (1932).

Antonio and Mellida and *Antonio's Revenge* have separate editions by G. K. Hunter for the RRDS (1965). Each play has been edited by W. W. Greg for the Malone Society (1921).

The Fawn has been edited by Gerald A. Smith for the RRDS (1965).

Eastward Ho was edited by Julia H. Harris (1926) and by C. H. Herford and Percy Simpson in *Ben Jonson* (I,A), vol. 4; both editions have substantial introductions and notes. Herford and Simpson do not regard the Harris text as satisfactory. The latest editor is C. G. Petter (1973).

F. NONDRAMATIC WORKS

The standard edition of *The Poems of John Marston* by Arnold Davenport (1961) has a collated text with list of variants and full introduction and notes. A small illustrated edition of *The Metamorphosis of Pygmalion's Image* with slight editing was published in 1926. G. B. Harrison has edited *The Scourge of Villainy* in the second (1599) edition (1925). Marston's contribution to *The Phoenix and the Turtle* may be found in the edition of that work by Bernard H. Newdigate (1937).

IV. SEE ALSO

A. GENERAL

Biographical

Acheson, Arthur. *Shakespeare's Sonnet Story, 1592-1598, Restoring the Sonnets Written to the Earl of Southampton to Their Original Books* .... 1922.

Atkins, Sidney H. "Marston and Everard Guilpin." *TLS*, 9 June 1932, p. 427.

Beckwith, E. A. "On the Hall-Marston Controversy." *JEGP* 25 (1926): 84-89.

Cross, Gustav. "Manningham's Libel on Marston." *N&Q* 3 (1956): 377-78.

Cunningham, John E. *Elizabethan and Early Stuart Drama*. 1965.

Davenport, Arnold. "An Elizabethan Controversy: Harvey and Nashe." *N&Q* 182 (1942): 116-19.

———, ed. *The Whipper Pamphlets (1601)*. 2 vols. 1951.

Enck, John J. "The Peace of the Poetomachia." *PMLA* 77 (1962): 386-96.

Flood, W. H. Grattan. "A John Marston Letter." *RES* 4 (1928): 86-87.

George, J. "John Marston in the Trumbull Correspondence." *N&Q* 4 (1957): 226.

Greg, W. W., et al., eds. *English Literary Autographs, 1550-1650*, 1932.

Harrison, G. B. *Elizabethan Plays and Players*. 1940.

Huntley, Frank L. "Ben Jonson and Anthony Munday, or, *The Case Is Altered Altered Again*." *PQ* 41 (1962): 205-14.

Jenkins, Gladys. "Manningham, Marston, and Alderman More's Wife's Daughter." *N&Q* 4 (1957): 243-44.

Jones, P. E. "Manningham and Marston." *N&Q* 4 (1957): 180.

King, Arthur H. *The Language of Satirized Characters in "Poëtaster": A Socio-Stylistic Analysis 1597-1602*. 1941.

Knoll, Robert E. *Ben Jonson's Plays: An Introduction*. 1964.

Linklater, Eric. *Ben Jonson and King James: Biography and Portrait*. 1931.

Nicoll, Allardyce. *British Drama: An Historical Survey from the Beginnings to the Present Time*. 1925; 5th ed. 1963.

Palmer, John. *Ben Jonson*. 1934.

Pokorný, Jaroslav. *Shakespeares Zeit und das Theater*. 1959.

Race, Sydney. "Manningham's Diary: The Case for Re-examination." *N&Q* 1 (1954): 380-83.

———. "Manningham and Marston." *N&Q* 4 (1957): 147, 244.

Wagner, Bernard M. "Elizabethan Dramatists." *TLS*, 28 Sept. 1933, p. 651.

General

Adams, Joseph Quincy. *A Life of William Shakespeare*. 1923.

Albright, Evelyn May. *Dramatic Publication in England, 1580-1640: A Study of Conditions Affecting Content and Form in Drama*. 1927.

Alexander, Nigel, comp. *Elizabethan Narrative Verse*. 1968.

Allen, Don Cameron. *The Star-Crossed Renaissance: The Quarrel about Astrology and Its Influence in England*. 1941.

Amico, Silvio d'. *Storia del teatro drammatico*. 2 vols. 1939; rev. ed. 1950.

Anderson, Donald K., Jr. "The Banquet of Love in English Drama (1595-1642)." *JEGP* 63 (1964): 422-32.

Anikst, Alexandr. *Teatr epokhi Shekspira* [The theater of the age of Shakespeare] 1965. [Not seen]

Anniah Gowda, H. H. *Dramatic Poetry from Mediaeval to Modern Times: A Philosophic Inquiry into the Nature of Poetic Drama in England, Ireland, and the United States of America*. 1972.

Aronstein, Philipp. *Das englische Renaissancedrama*. 1929.

Babb, Lawrence. "The Background of 'Il Penseroso.'" *SP* 37 (1940): 257-73.

———. "Melancholy and the Elizabethan Man of Letters." *HLQ* 4 (1940-41): 247-61.

———. "Love Melancholy in the Elizabethan and Early Stuart Drama." *Bulletin of the History of Medicine* 13 (1943): 117-32.

———. *The Elizabethan Malady: A Study of Melancholia in English Literature from 1580 to 1642*. 1951.

Barish, Jonas A. *Ben Jonson and the Language of Prose Comedy*. 1960.

Baskervill, Charles Read. *The Elizabethan Jig and Related Song Drama*. 1929.

Bastiaenen, Johannes Adam. *The Moral Tone of Jacobean and Caroline Drama*. 1930.

Beckingham, C. F. "Seneca's Fatalism and Elizabethan Tragedy." *MLR* 32 (1937): 434-38.

Bentley, Gerald Eades. "John Cotgrave's *English Treasury of Wit and Language* and the Elizabethan Drama." *SP* 40 (1943): 186-203.

———. *The Profession of Dramatist in Shakespeare's Time, 1590-1642.* 1971.

Blayney, Glenn H. "Enforcement of Marriage in English Drama (1600-1650)." *PQ* 38 (1959): 459-72.

Bluestone, Max. *From Story to Stage: The Dramatic Adaptation of Prose Fiction in the Period of Shakespeare and His Contemporaries.* 1974.

Boas, Frederick S. *An Introduction to Stuart Drama.* 1946.

———. *Queen Elizabeth in Drama and Related Studies.* 1950.

Bradbrook, M. C. *Themes and Conventions of Elizabethan Tragedy.* 1935; 2nd ed. 1952.

———. *The Growth and Structure of Elizabethan Comedy.* 1956.

Bradley, Jesse Franklin, and Joseph Quincy Adams, eds. *The Jonson Allusion-Book: A Collection of Allusions to Ben Jonson from 1597 to 1700.* 1922.

Bridges-Adams, W. *The Irresistible Theatre.* 1957.

Brooks, Alden. *Will Shakspere and the Dyer's Hand.* 1943.

Campbell, Oscar James. *Shakespeare's Satire.* 1943.

———, and Edward G. Quinn, eds. *The Reader's Encyclopedia of Shakespeare.* 1966.

Cawley, Robert Ralston. *The Voyagers and Elizabethan Drama.* 1938.

———. *Unpathed Waters: Studies in the Influence of the Voyagers on Elizabethan Literature.* 1940.

Cazamian, Louis F. *The Development of English Humor.* 1952.

Charney, Maurice. "The Children's Plays in Performance." *RORD* 18 (1975): 19-23.

Chew, Samuel C. *The Crescent and the Rose: Islam and England during the Renaissance.* 1937.

Clark, Arthur Melville. *Thomas Heywood: Playwright and Miscellanist.* 1958.

Clark, Eleanor Grace. *Elizabethan Fustian: A Study in the Social and Political Backgrounds of the Drama, with Particular Reference to Christopher Marlowe.* 1937.

Clarkson, Paul S., and Clyde T. Warren. *The Law of Property in Shakespeare and the Elizabethan Drama.* 1942.

Clough, Wilson O. "The Broken English of Foreign Characters of the Elizabethan Stage." *PQ* 12 (1933): 255-68.

Cookman, A. V. "Shakespeare's Contemporaries on the Modern English Stage." *SJ* 94 (1958): 29-41.

Coon, Arthur M. "Southey and Marston." *TLS*, 31 Jan. 1942, p. 55.

Craig, Hardin. *The Enchanted Glass: The Elizabethan Mind in Literature.* 1936.

———. "Revised Elizabethan Quartos: An Attempt to Form a Class." In *Studies in the English Renaissance Drama in Memory of Karl Julius Holzknecht*, ed. Josephine W. Bennett et al. (1959), pp. 43-57.

Cross, Gustav. "Some Notes on the Vocabulary of John Marston." *N&Q* 1 (1954): 425-27; 2 (1955): 20-21, 57-58, 186-87, 335-36, 427-28, 480-82; 3 (1956):

330-32, 470-71; 4 (1957): 65-66, 221-23, 283-85, 524-26; 5 (1958): 5-6, 103-4; 6 (1959): 101-2, 137-39, 254-55, 355-56; 7 (1960): 135-36; 8 (1961): 123-26, 298-300, 388-91; 10 (1963): 308-12.

————. "An Unrecognized Poem by John Marston?" *MLQ* 19 (1958): 325-30.

Crundell, H. W. "Marston's 'Drusus.'" *TLS*, 30 Oct. 1937, p. 803.

Curry, John V. *Deception in Elizabethan Comedy.* 1955.

Damon, S. Foster. "Milton and Marston." *PMLA* 42 (1927): 873-74.

Davenport, Arnold. "Some Notes on References to Joseph Hall in Marston's Satires." *RES* 9 (1933): 192-96.

David, Richard. *The Janus of Poets: Being an Essay on the Dramatic Value of Shakspere's Poetry Both Good and Bad.* 1935.

Davis, Joe Lee. *The Sons of Ben: Jonsonian Comedy in Caroline England.* 1967.

Dawson, Giles E. "An Early List of Elizabethan Plays." *Library* 15 (1934-35): 445-56.

Doran, Madeleine. *Endeavors of Art: A Study of Form in Elizabethan Drama.* 1954.

Downer, Alan S. *The British Drama: A Handbook and Brief Chronicle.* 1950.

Duckles, Vincent. "The Music for the Lyrics in Early Seventeenth-Century English Drama: A Bibliography of the Primary Sources." In *Music in English Renaissance Drama*, ed. John H. Long (1968), pp. 117-60.

"Elizabethan Pamphlets." *New Statesman*, 26 Sept. 1925, pp. 666, 668.

Elliott, Robert C. *The Power of Satire: Magic, Ritual, Art.* 1960.

Farnham, Willard. *The Medieval Heritage of Elizabethan Tragedy.* 1936.

Fenton, Doris. *The Extra-Dramatic Moment in Elizabethan Plays before 1616.* 1930.

Fink, Z. S. "Jaques and the Malcontent Traveler." *PQ* 14 (1935): 237-52.

Foakes, R. A., ed. *The Revenger's Tragedy*, by Cyril Tourneur. 1966.

Frantz, David O. "'Leud Priapians' and Renaissance Pornography," *SEL* 12 (1972): 157-72.

Gassner, John. *Masters of the Drama.* 1940; 3rd ed. 1954.

Gibbons, Brian, ed. *The Revenger's Tragedy*, by Cyril Tourneur. 1967.

Gilbert, Allan H. "Logic in the Elizabethan Drama." *SP* 32 (1935): 527-45.

Goldsmith, Robert Hillis. *Wise Fools in Shakespeare.* 1955.

Gransden, K. W., ed. *Tudor Verse Satire.* 1970.

Grivelet, Michel. *Thomas Heywood et le drame domestique élizabéthain.* 1957.

Harbage, Alfred. "Elizabethan Acting." *PMLA* 54 (1939): 685-708.

Harrison, G. B. *Shakespeare under Elizabeth.* 1933.

Haydn, Hiram. *The Counter-Renaissance.* 1950.

Heltzel, Virgil B. "The Dedication of Tudor and Stuart Plays." In *Studies in English Language and Literature, Presented to Professor Dr. Karl Brunner on the Occasion of His Seventieth Birthday*, ed. Siegfried Korninger (1957), pp. 74-86.

Henderson, Sam H. "Neo-Stoic Influence on Elizabethan Formal Verse Satire." In *Studies in English Renaissance Literature*, ed. Waldo F. McNeir (1962), pp. 56-86, 217-21.

Herrick, Marvin T. *Tragicomedy: Its Origin and Development in Italy, France, and England.* 1955.

Hibbard, G. R. "Review of Philip J. Finkelpearl, *John Marston of the Middle Temple*." *N&Q* 19 (1972): 39-40.

Highet, Gilbert. *Juvenal the Satirist, a Study*. 1954.

Hillebrand, Harold Newcomb. *The Child Actors: A Chapter in Elizabethan Stage History*. 2 vols. 1926.

Hirst, Désirée. "The Enigmatic Mr. Marston." *Antigonish Review* 1, no. 2 (1970): 97-99.

Hobsbaum, Philip. "Elizabethan Poetry." *Poetry Review* 56 (1965): 80-97.

Höhna, Heinrich. *Der Physiologus in der elisabethanischen Literatur*. 1930.

Holden, William P. *Anti-Puritan Satire, 1572-1642*. 1954.

Holzknecht, Karl J. *Outlines of Tudor and Stuart Plays, 1497-1642*. 1947. [*Dutch Courtesan; Malcontent*]

Hotson, Leslie. *Shakespeare's Sonnets Dated, and Other Essays*. 1949.

Howarth, R. G. "John Marston." *N&Q* 197 (1952): 518.

―――. "John Marston." *N&Q* 1 (1954): 179.

Hunter, G. K. "Review of Philip J. Finkelpearl, *John Marston of the Middle Temple*." *MLQ* 31 (1970): 375-77.

―――. "Further Borrowings in Webster and Marston." *N&Q* 19 (1972): 452-53.

Jacquot, Jean. "Les tragédies de Sénèque et le théâtre élizabéthain." *EA* 14 (1961): 343-44.

Jenkins, Gladys. "Marston the Poet." *N&Q* 4 (1957): 243-44.

Jensen, Ejner J. "Kyd's *Spanish Tragedy*: The Play Explains Itself." *JEGP* 64 (1965): 7-16.

―――. "The Changing Faces of Love in English Renaissance Comedy." *CompD* 6 (1972): 294-309.

Jones, Robert C. "Italian Settings and the 'World' of Elizabethan Tragedy." *SEL* 10 (1970): 251-68.

Joseph, B. L. *Elizabethan Acting*. 1951.

Keyishian, Harry. "A Checklist of Medieval and Renaissance Plays (excluding Shakespeare) on Film, Tape, and Recording." *RORD* 17 (1974): 45-58.

Kimbrough, Robert. *Shakespeare's "Troilus & Cressida" and Its Setting*. 1964.

Klein, David. *The Elizabethan Dramatists as Critics*. 1963.

Knight, G. Wilson. *The Mutual Flame: On Shakespeare's "Sonnets" and "The Phoenix and the Turtle."* 1955.

―――. *The Golden Labyrinth: A Study of British Drama*. 1962.

Koch, J. "Thomas Nabbes, ein zu wenig beachteter Dichter." *Anglia* 47 (1923): 32-82.

Krzyzanowski, J. "Some Conjectural Remarks on Elizabethan Dramatists." *N&Q* 193 (1948): 233-34.

Lawrence, William J. *Pre-Restoration Stage Studies*. 1927.

Lea, Kathleen M. "An Emendation for Satire X of *The Scourge of Villanie*." *RES* 7 (1931): 334-36.

―――. *Italian Popular Comedy: A Study in the Commedia dell'arte, 1560-1620, with Special Reference to the English Stage*. 2 vols. 1934.

Leech, Clifford. *Shakespeare's Tragedies, and Other Studies in Seventeenth-Century Drama*. 1950.

————. "Review of Anthony Caputi, *John Marston, Satirist.*" *RES* 14 (1963): 292–94.

Legouis, Emile. *The Middle Ages and the Renascence (650–1660)*, trans. Helen Douglas Irvine. Vol. 1 in *A History of English Literature*, with Louis Cazamian. 2 vols. 1926.

Lewis, C. S. *English Literature in the Sixteenth Century, Excluding Drama.* 1954.

Lievsay, John Leon. "Some Research Opportunities in Anglo-Italian Renaissance Drama." *RenD* 7, Supplement (1964): 10–12.

Lindabury, Richard Vliet. *A Study of Patriotism in the Elizabethan Drama.* 1931.

Linthicum, M. Channing. *Costume in the Drama of Shakespeare and His Contemporaries.* 1936.

Loane, George G. "Notes on Marston." *N&Q* 184 (1943): 71–74.

Lucas, Richard Macdonald. *Shakespeare's Vital Secret (Known to His Queen).* 1937.

McNeir, Waldo F. "Marston versus Davies and Terpsichore." *PQ* 29 (1950): 430–34.

Main, William W. "Dramaturgical Norms in the Elizabethan Repertory." *SP* 54 (1957): 128–48.

Maxwell, J. C. "Review of *The Poems of John Marston*, ed. Arnold Davenport." *N&Q* 9 (1963): 478–79.

Mincoff, Marco. "Verbal Repetition in Elizabethan Tragedy." *Annuaire de l'Université de Sofia, Faculté Historico-Philologique* 41 (1944–45): 1–128.

Moore, John Robert. "The Songs of the Public Theaters in the Time of Shakespeare." *JEGP* 28 (1929): 166–202.

Munce, T. Edward, Jr. "Southey and Marston." *TLS*, 25 Oct. 1941, p. 536.

Murray, Peter B. *A Study of Cyril Tourneur.* 1965.

Myers, Aaron Michael. *Representation and Misrepresentation of the Puritan in Elizabethan Drama.* 1931.

Nicoll, Allardyce. *Stuart Masques and the Renaissance Stage.* 1938.

————, ed. *The Works of Cyril Tourneur.* 1930.

Nozaki, Mutsumi. "John Marston the Dramatist." *Studies in English Literature* (English Literary Society of Japan) (English no.) (1973): 187–88. [Abstract of article in Japanese no.; not seen]

Obertello, Alfredo, ed. *Teatro elisabettiano: raccolta di drammi.* 2 vols. 1951.

Ornstein, Robert, *The Moral Vision of Jacobean Tragedy.* 1960.

————. "Review of Anthony Caputi, *John Marston, Satirist.*" *MP* 60 (1962–63): 218–20.

Orsini, Napoleone. "'Policy' or the Language of Elizabethan Machiavellianism." *JWCI* 9 (1946): 122–34.

Palmer, Ralph Graham. *Seneca's "De Remediis Fortuitorum" and the Elizabethans: An Essay on the Influence of Seneca's Ethical Thought in the Sixteenth Century* . . . . 1953.

Parkes, H. B. "Nature's Diverse Laws: The Double Vision of the Elizabethans." *SR* 58 (1950): 402–18.

Parrott, Thomas Marc, and Robert Hamilton Ball. *A Short View of Elizabethan Drama.* 1943.

Patterson, Annabel M. *Hermogenes and the Renaissance: Seven Ideas of Style.* 1970.

Pearn, B. R. "Dumb-Show in Elizabethan Drama." *RES* 11 (1935): 385-405.

Pellegrini, G. "Symbols and Significances." *ShS* 17 (1964): 180-87.

"The Plays of John Marston: Tragedy and Social Satire." *TLS*, 26 March 1938, p. 209.

Poggi, Valentina. *L'uomo e le corti nel teatro elisabettiano.* 1968.

Praz, Mario. "Reviews of H. Harvey Wood, ed., *The Plays of John Marston.*" *ES* 17 (1935): 149-54; 21 (1939): 24-26; 23 (1941): 55-58.

―――. *Machiavelli in Inghilterra, ed altri saggi.* 2nd. ed. 1943.

―――. *The Flaming Heart: Essays on Crashaw, Machiavelli, and Other Studies in the Relations between Italian and English Literature from Chaucer to T. S. Eliot.* 1958.

Prosser, Eleanor. *Hamlet and Revenge.* 1967; 2nd ed. 1971.

Putt, S. Gorley. "The Relevance of Jacobean Drama." *E&S* 23 (1970): 18-33.

Rabkin, Norman. "The Double Plot: Notes on the History of a Convention." *RenD* 7 (1964): 55-69.

Randolph, Mary Claire. "The Medical Concept in English Renaissance Satiric Theory: Its Possible Relationships and Implications." *SP* 38 (1941): 129-57.

Rébora, Piero. *L'Italia nel dramma inglese (1558-1642).* 1925.

―――. *Civiltà italiana e civiltà inglese.* 1936.

Reed, Robert Rentoul. *Bedlam on the Jacobean Stage.* 1952.

Reese, Max Meredith, ed. *Elizabethan Verse Romances.* 1968.

Reibetanz, John. "Theatrical Emblems in *King Lear.*" In *Some Facets of King Lear: Essays in Prismatic Criticism*, ed. Rosalie L. Colie and F. T. Flahiff (1974), pp. 39-57.

Reul, Paul de. *Présentation du théâtre jacobéen de Marston à Beaumont and Fletcher (1660-1625).* N. D.

Ribner, Irving. "Criticism of Elizabethan and Jacobean Drama." *RORD* 6 (1963): 7-13.

Ricci, Seymour de, and W. J. Wilson. *Census of Medieval and Renaissance Manuscripts in the United States and Canada.* 3 vols. 1935-40.

Riesner, Dieter. "Shakespeares Zeitgenossen in deutschen Übersetzungen." *Archiv* 202 (1965-66): 361-69.

Robertson, J. M. *Marlowe: A Conspectus.* 1931.

Rossiter, A. P. *English Drama from Early Times to the Elizabethans: Its Background, Origins, and Developments.* 1950.

Rostenberg, Leona. *Literary, Political, Scientific, Religious & Legal Publishing, Printing & Bookselling in England, 1551-1700: Twelve Studies.* 2 vols. 1965.

Sackton, Alexander. "The Paradoxical Encomium in Elizabethan Drama." *Studies in English* (Univ. of Texas) 28 (1949): 83-104.

Salingar, L. G. "The Elizabethan Literary Renaissance." In *The Age of Shakespeare* (1955; vol. 2 of The Pelican *Guide to English Literature*, ed. Boris Ford), pp. 51-116.

―――. "Tourneur and the Tragedy of Revenge." In *The Age of Shakespeare* (ibid.), pp. 334-54.

―――. Gerald Harrison, and Bruce Cochrane. "Les comédiens et leur public en angleterre de 1520 à 1640." In *Dramaturgie et société: rapports entre l'oeuvre théâtrale, son interprétation, et son public aux 16. et 17. siècles*, ed. Jean Jacquot et al. 2 vols. (1968); 2: 525–76.

Schäfer, Jürgen. *Wort und Begriff 'Humour' in der elisabethanischen Komödie.* 1966.

Schelling, Felix E. *Foreign Influences in Elizabethan Plays.* 1923.

————. *Elizabethan Playwrights: A Short History of the English Drama from Mediaeval Times to the Closing of the Theatres in 1642.* 1925.

Scherer, Bernhard. *Vers und Prosa bei den . . . Zeitgenossen Shakespeares.* 1932.

Schoenbaum, Samuel. "John Day and Elizabethan Drama." *Boston Public Library Quarterly* 5 (1953): 140–52.

————. "Marston, Middleton, and Massinger." In *English Drama (excluding Shakespeare): Select Bibliographical Studies*, ed. Stanley Wells (1975), pp. 69–99.

Schrickx, W. *Shakespeare's Early Contemporaries: The Background of the Harvey-Nashe Polemic and "Love's Labour's Lost."* 1956.

Schücking, Levin L. *Shakespeare und der Tragödienstil seiner Zeit.* 1947.

"The Scourge of Villanie." *TLS*, 27 Aug. 1925, p. 555.

Sehrt, Ernst Th. *Der dramatische Auftakt in der elisabethanischen Tragödie.* 1960.

Seznec, Jean. *The Survival of the Pagan Gods: The Mythological Tradition and Its Place in Renaissance Humanism and Art.* 1953.

Shapiro, Michael. "Three Notes on the Theatre at Paul's c. 1569–c. 1607." *Theatre Notebook* 24 (1969–70): 147–54.

————. "Theatrical Perspectives of Children's Companies." *RORD* 18 (1975): 13–18.

Simpson, Claude M. *The British Broadside Ballad and Its Music.* 1966.

Sjögren, Gunnar. *Shakespeares samtida och deras dramatik.* 1969. [Not seen.]

Smet, Robert de [Romain Sanvic]. *Le théâtre élisabéthain.* 1955.

Smith, John Hazel, ed. *The Gentleman Usher*, by George Chapman. 1970.

Sorelius, Gunnar. *"The Giant Race before the Flood": Pre-Restoration Drama on the Stage and in the Criticism of the Restoration.* 1966.

Spencer, Theodore. *Death and Elizabethan Tragedy: A Study of Convention and Opinion in the Elizabethan Drama.* 1936.

————. "Hamlet and the Nature of Reality." *ELH* 5 (1938): 253–77. Rpt. in *Selected Essays*, ed. Alan C. Purves (1966), pp. 196–219.

Spivack, Bernard. *Shakespeare and the Allegory of Evil: The History of a Metaphor in Relation to His Major Villains.* 1958.

Stein, Arnold. "Donne's Harshness and the Elizabethan Tradition." *SP* 41 (1944): 390–409.

————. "Donne's Obscurity and the Elizabethan Tradition." *ELH* 13 (1946): 98–118.

Stewart, Bain Tate. "Characterization through Dreams in the Drama of Shakespeare's Day." In *Studies in Honor of John C. Hodges and Alwin Thaler*, ed. Richard Beale Davis and John Leon Lievsay, *TSL* Special Number (1961), pp. 27–34.

Stodder, Joseph H. *Satire in Jacobean Tragedy.* 1974.

Stoll, Elmer Edgar. *Shakespeare and Other Masters.* 1940.

Stratman, Carl J. *Bibliography of English Printed Tragedy, 1565–1900.* 1966.

Stroup, Thomas B. *Microcosmos: The Shape of the Elizabethan Play.* 1965.

Sugden, Edward H. *A Topographical Dictionary to the Works of Shakespeare and His Fellow Dramatists.* 1925.

Talbert, Ernest William. "The Purpose and Technique of Jonson's *Poetaster.*" *SP* 42 (1945): 225-52.

Taylor, Archer. "Proverbs and Proverbial Phrases in the Plays of John Marston." *SFQ* 24 (1960): 193-216.

Thorndike, Ashley H. *English Comedy.* 1929.

Thorp, Willard. *The Triumph of Realism in Elizabethan Drama, 1558-1612.* 1928.

Tiegs, Alexander. *Zur Zusammenarbeit englischer Berufsdramatiker unmittelbar vor, neben und nach Shakespeare.* 1933.

Tomlinson, T. B. *A Study of Elizabethan and Jacobean Tragedy.* 1964.

Traversi, Derek A. *An Approach to Shakespeare.* 1939; 2nd ed. 1956.

Ure, Peter. "A Note on 'Opinion' in Daniel, Greville, and Chapman." *MLR* 46 (1951): 331-38. Rpt. in *Elizabethan and Jacobean Drama: Critical Essays by Peter Ure,* ed. J. C. Maxwell (1974), pp. 209-20.

Vandiver, E. P., Jr. "The Elizabethan Dramatic Parasite." *SP* 32 (1935): 411-27.

Venezky, Alice S. *Pageantry on the Shakespearean Stage.* 1951.

Viswanathan, S. "Is Touchstone Marston?" *AN&Q* 10 (1971-72): 99-102.

Waith, Eugene M. "Characterization in John Fletcher's Tragicomedies." *RES* 19 (1943): 141-64.

Walker, Hugh. *English Satire and Satirists.* 1925.

Weiner, Albert B. "Elizabethan Interior and Aloft Scenes: A Speculative Essay." *Theatre Survey* 2 (1961): 15-34.

Wells, Henry W. *Elizabethan and Jacobean Playwrights.* 1939.

––––––. *A Chronological List of Extant Plays Produced in or about London, 1581-1642.* 1940.

––––––. "Senecan Influence on Elizabethan Tragedy: A Re-estimation." *ShAB* 19 (1944): 71-84.

Wilson, Edward M. "Family Honour in the Plays of Shakespeare's Predecessors and Contemporaries." *E&S* 6 (1953): 19-40.

Wolfe, Humber. *Notes on English Verse Satire.* 1929.

Wren, Robert M. "The Five-Entry Stage at Blackfriars." *Theatre Research* 8 (1966-67): 130-38.

––––––. "Salisbury and the Blackfriars Theatre." *Theatre Notebook* 23 (1968-69): 103-9.

Wright, Louis B. "Extraneous Song in Elizabethan Drama after the Advent of Shakespeare." *SP* 24 (1927): 261-74.

––––––. "Vaudeville Dancing and Acrobatics in Elizabethan Plays." *Englische Studien* 63 (1928-29): 59-76.

––––––. "The Reading of Plays during the Puritan Revolution." *Huntington Library Bulletin* 6 (1934): 73-108.

B. INDIVIDUAL PLAYS

The Malcontent

Babb, Lawrence. "Melancholic Villainy in the Elizabethan Drama." *Papers of the Michigan Academy of Science, Arts, & Letters* 29 (1943): 527-35.

————. "Scientific Theories of Grief in Some Elizabethan Plays." *SP* 40 (1943): 502-19.

Boyce, Benjamin. *The Theophrastan Character in England to 1642.* 1947.

Brustein, Robert. "The Monstrous Regiment of Women: Sources for the Satiric View of the Court Lady in English Drama." In *Renaissance and Modern Essays: Presented to Vivian de Sola Pinto in Celebration of His Seventieth Birthday*, ed. G. R. Hibbard et al. (1966), pp. 35-50.

Cross, Gustav. "Webster and Marston: A Note on *The White Devil*, V.iii.106." *N&Q* 7 (1960): 337.

Dunn, Esther Cloudman. *The Literature of Shakespeare's England.* 1936.

Hawkins, Harriett. *Likenesses of Truth in Elizabethan and Restoration Drama.* 1972.

Heuser, Georg. *Die aktlose Dramaturgie William Shakespeares: Eine Untersuchung über das Problem der Akteinteilung und angeblichen Aktstruktur der Shakespeareschen Dramen.* 1956.

Howard, R. G. "Dipsas in Lyly and Marston." *N&Q* 175 (1938): 24-25.

Hunter, G. K. "A Census of Renaissance Drama Productions." *RORD* 17 (1974): 59-66.

Isaacs, J. *Production and Stage-Management at the Blackfriars Theatre.* 1933.

Joseph, Bertram L. "Scenes Invented Merely to be Spoken." *DramS* 1 (1961-62): 18-33.

Lambert, J. W. "The Tonic Comedy of Disillusion." *Sunday Times* (London), 17 June 1973, p. 35.

Levin, Harry. *The Question of Hamlet.* 1959.

Long, John H. *Shakespeare's Use of Music.* 3 vols. 1955-71.

Madelaine, R. E. R. "'When Griffon Saw the Reconciled Quean': Marston, Ariosto, and Haydocke." *N&Q* 19 (1972): 453-54.

Nightingale, Benedict. "Fair Swap." *New Statesman*, 20 April 1973, pp. 592-93.

Salingar, L. G. "*The Revenger's Tragedy*: Some Possible Sources." *MLR* 60 (1965): 3-12.

Shaw, Sharon K. "Medea on Pegasus: Some Speculations on the Parallel Rise of Women and Melodrama on the Jacobean Stage." *Ball State University Forum* 14, no. 4 (1973): 13-21.

Sider, John Wm. "Shakespeare's Cornetts." *SQ* 22 (1971): 401-4.

Slights, William W. E. "Political Morality and the Ending of *The Malcontent*." *MP* 69 (1971-72): 138-39.

Stoll, Elmer Edgar. "Jaques, and the Antiquaries." *MLN* 54 (1939): 79-85.

Stroup, Thomas B. "The Testing Pattern in Elizabethan Tragedy." *SEL* 3 (1963): 175-90.

Tilley, M. P. "Charles Lamb, John Marston, and Du Bartas." *MLN* 53 (1938): 494-98.

Viglione, Francesco. *Genova nella storia della letteratura inglese.* 1937.

Wallis, Lawrence B. *Fletcher, Beaumont & Company: Entertainers to the Jacobean Gentry.* 1947.

Withington, Robert. "Notes on Dramatic Nomenclature." *N&Q* 149 (1925): 399-401.

The Dutch Courtesan

Adlard, John. "Marston and Jorrocks." *TLS*, 16 April 1971, p. 449.

Boyd, Morrison Comegys. *Elizabethan Music and Musical Criticism.* 1940.

Chambers, E. K. *William Shakespeare: A Study of Facts and Problems.* 2 vols. 1930.

Cope, Jackson I. *The Theater and the Dream: From Metaphor to Form in Renaissance Drama.* 1973.

Covatta, Anthony. *Thomas Middleton's City Comedies.* 1973.

Cox, Frank. "Marston, Beaumont, Fletcher, Dekker, Marlowe: Dwarfed by Shakespeare." *Plays and Players*, July 1964, p. 10.

Cross, Gustav. "The Way of All Flesh." *N&Q* 5 (1958): 257.

Finkelpearl, Philip J. "Beaumont, Fletcher, and 'Beaumont & Fletcher': Some Distinctions." *English Literary Renaissance* 1 (1971): 144-64.

Hoy, Cyrus. *The Hyacinth Room: An Investigation into the Nature of Comedy, Tragedy, & Tragicomedy.* 1964.

Hughes, Leo, and A. H. Scouten, eds. *Ten English Farces.* 1948.

Hyde, Mary Crapo. *Playwriting for Elizabethans, 1600-1605.* 1949.

Jensen, Ejner J. "The Boy Actors: Plays and Playing." *RORD* 18 (1975): 5-11.

M., H. G. "Review of Performance of *The Dutch Courtesan.*" *Theatre World*, Aug. 1964, p. 31.

Olson, Wm. Bruce. "Marston and Jorrocks." *TLS*, 28 May 1971, p. 621.

Piggott, Stuart. "Marston and Jorrocks." *TLS*, 30 April 1971, p. 505.

Powell, Anthony. "Marston and Jorrocks." *TLS*, 2 April 1971, p. 396.

Roberts, Peter. "After the Fanfare . . . ." *Plays and Players*, Sept. 1964, pp. 26-28.

Sabol, Andrew J. "Two Unpublished Stage Songs for the 'Aery of Children.'" *RN* 13 (1960): 222-32.

Styan, J. L. "Dwarfed by Shakespeare? In Search of an Elizabethan Heritage." *Plays and Players*, July 1964, pp. 8-9.

Antonio and Mellida and *Antonio's Revenge*

Anderson, Ruth L. "Kingship in Renaissance Drama." *SP* 41 (1944): 136-55.

Armstrong, William Arthur. "The Influence of Seneca and Machiavelli on the Elizabethan Tyrant." *RES* 24 (1948): 19-35.

―――. *The Elizabethan Private Theatres: Facts and Problems.* 1958.

Black, A. Bruce, and Robert Metcalf Smith. *Shakespeare Allusions and Parallels.* 1931.

Boas, Frederick S. "Review of H. Harvey Wood, ed., *The Plays of John Marston*, vol. 1." *Observer* (London), 9 Sept. 1934, p. 7.

Borish, M. E. "John Day's *Humour out of Breath.*" *Harvard Studies and Notes in Philology and Literature* 16 (1934): 1-11.

Bradbrook, M. C. *Shakespeare, the Craftsman.* 1969.

Coghill, Nevill. *Shakespeare's Professional Skills.* 1964.

Cross, Gustav. "Ovid Metamorphosed: Marston, Webster, and Nathaniel Lee." *N&Q* 3 (1956): 244-45, 508-9.

―――. "Tilley's *Dictionary of Proverbs in England*, H348, and Marston's *Antonio and Mellida.*" *N&Q* 8 (1961): 143-44.

Eidson, John Olin. "Senecan Elements in Marston's *Antonio and Mellida.*" *MLN* 52 (1937): 196-97.

————. "A Marston Note." *MLN* 52 (1937): 198.

Eisinger, Fritz. *Das Problem des Selbstmordes in der Literatur der englischen Renaissance.* 1926.

Exideuil, Pierre d'. "Vengeance." *Cahiers du Sud* 10 (1933): 67-74. Rpt. in *Le théâtre élizabéthain*, ed. Georgette Camille and Pierre d'Exideuil (1940), pp. 92-100.

Foakes, R. A. "Mr. Levin and 'Good Bad Drama.'" *Essays in Criticism* 22 (1972): 327-29.

Forker, Charles R. "Tennyson's 'Tithonus' and Marston's *Antonio's Revenge.*" *N&Q* 6 (1959): 445.

Fuzier, Jean. "La tragédie de vengeance Élisabéthaine et le théâtre dans le théâtre." *Revue des science humaines* 145 (1972): 17-33.

Galinsky, G. Karl. *The Herakles Theme: The Adaptations of the Hero in Literature from Homer to the Twentieth Century.* 1972.

Gilbert, Allan H. "Italian Names in *Everyman out of His Humour.*" *SP* 44 (1947): 195-208.

Grossmann, Rudolf. *Spanien und das elisabethanische Drama.* 1920.

Halio, Jay L. "*Perfection* and Elizabethan Ideas of Conception." *ELN* 1 (1963-64): 179-82.

Harbage, Alfred. "Intrigue in Elizabethan Tragedy." In *Essays on Shakespeare and Elizabethan Drama in Honor of Hardin Craig*, ed. Richard Hosley (1962), pp. 37-44.

Heilman, Robert Bechtold. *Tragedy and Melodrama: Versions of Experience.* 1968.

Hunter, G. K. "The Spoken Dirge in Kyd, Marston, and Shakespeare: A Background to *Cymbeline.*" *N&Q* 11 (1964): 146-47.

————. "Seneca and the Elizabethans: A Case-Study in 'Influence.'" *ShS* 20 (1967): 17-26.

Ingram, R. W. "Operatic Tendencies in Stuart Drama." *Musical Quarterly* 44 (1958): 489-502.

Jacquot, Jean. "Sénèque, la Renaissance et nous." In *Les tragédies de Sénèque et le théâtre de la Renaissance*, ed. Jean Jacquot et al. (1964), pp. 271-307.

Jensen, Ejner J. "The Style of the Boy Actors." *CompD* 2 (1968): 100-114.

————. "A New Allusion to the Sign of the Globe Theater." *SQ* 21 (1970): 95-97.

Korninger, Siegfried. "Die Geisterszene im elisabethanischen Drama." *SJH* (1966): 124-45.

Lawrence, W. J. "The Date of *Hamlet.*" *TLS*, 8 April 1926, p. 263.

Levin, Harry. "An Echo from *The Spanish Tragedy.*" *MLN* 64 (1949): 297-302.

Levin, Richard. "The New *New Inn* and the Proliferation of Good Bad Drama." *Essays in Criticism* 22 (1972): 41-47.

————. "The Proof of the Parody." *Essays in Criticism* 24 (1974): 312-17.

Lucas, F. L. *Seneca and Elizabethan Tragedy.* 1922.

Mahl, Mary R. "Our Earlier Drama." *Personalist* 48 (1967): 420-27.

Margeson, J. M. R. "Dramatic Form: The Huntington Plays." *SEL* 14 (1974): 223-38.

Mehl, Dieter. "Zur Entwicklung des 'Play within a Play' im elisabethanischen Drama." *SJ* 97 (1961): 134–52.

———. "Emblems in English Renaissance Drama." *RenD* 2 (1969): 39–57.

Nakata, Yasushi. *"Antonio and Mellida and Hamlet."* [In Japanese.] *Hokkaido Eigo Eibangaku* 10 (1965): 13–22. [Not seen.]

Nicoll, Allardyce. "'Tragical-Comical-Historical-Pastoral': Elizabethan Dramatic Nomenclature." *BJRL* 43 (1960–61): 70–87.

Nungezer, Edwin. *A Dictionary of Actors and of Other Persons Associated with the Public Representation of Plays in England before 1642.* 1929.

O'Donnell, Norbert F. "Shakespeare, Marston, and the University: The Sources of Thomas Goffe's *Orestes*." *SP* 50 (1953): 476–84.

Orsini, Napoleone. "Caratteri estetici del dramma elisabettiano." *Anglica* 2, no. 2 (1948): 1–19.

———. "T. S. Eliot e la teoria delle convenzioni drammatiche." *Letterature Moderne* 4 (1953): 621–35.

Peter, John. "Marston's Use of Seneca." *N&Q* 1 (1954): 145–49.

Reibetanz, John. "Hieronimo in Decimosexto: A Private-Theater Burlesque." *RenD* 5 (1972): 89–121.

Reiman, Donald H. "Marston, Jonson, and the *Spanish Tragedy* Additions." *N&Q* 7 (1960): 336–37.

Schücking, Levin L. *The Meaning of "Hamlet."* Trans. Graham Rawson. 1937.

———. "The Baroque Character of the Elizabethan Tragic Hero." *PBA* 24 (1938): 85–111.

Sibly, John. "The Duty of Revenge in Tudor and Stuart Drama." *REL* 8, no. 3 (1967): 46–54.

Simpson, Percy. "The Theme of Revenge in Elizabethan Tragedy." *PBA* 21 (1935): 101–36. Rpt. in his *Studies in Elizabethan Drama* (1955), pp. 138–78.

Smith, Gerald. "A Note on the Death of Lear." *MLN* 70 (1955): 403–4.

Smith, John Harrington, Lois D. Pizer, and Edward K. Kaufman. *"Hamlet, Antonio's Revenge,* and the *Ur-Hamlet*." *SQ* 9 (1958): 493–98.

Soellner, Rolf. "The Madness of Hercules and the Elizabethans." *CL* 10 (1958): 309–24.

Spencer, Theodore. *Shakespeare and the Nature of Man.* 1942; 2nd ed. 1949.

Stoll, Elmer Edgar. *Shakespeare Studies.* 1927.

Walley, Harold R. "Shakespeare's Conception of *Hamlet*." *PMLA* 48 (1933): 777–98.

Weidhorn, Manfred. *Dreams in Seventeenth-Century English Literature.* 1970.

Sophonisba

Axelrad, A. José. "Sur une source possible de la *Sophonisbe* de John Marston (1606)." *RLC* 27 (1935): 182–85.

Bland, D. S. *"Macbeth* and *Sophonisba*." *TLS*, 16 Oct. 1948, p. 583.

Briggs, K. M. *Pale Hecate's Team: An Examination of the Beliefs on Witchcraft and Magic among Shakespeare's Contemporaries and His Immediate Successors.* 1962.

Chang, Joseph S. M. J. "'Of Mighty Opposites': Stoicism and Machiavellianism." *RenD* 9 (1966): 37–57.

Maxwell, J. C. "The Relation of *Macbeth* to *Sophonisba*." *N&Q* 2 (1955): 373–74.

Muir, Kenneth. "Macbeth and Sophonisba." *TLS*, 9 Oct. 1948, p. 569.

———. "*Macbeth* and *Sophonisba*." *TLS*, 23 Oct. 1948, p. 597.

———, ed. *Macbeth*. 1957.

Peery, William. "A Latin Quotation in *Wonder of Women* and *Woman Is a Weathercock*." *N&Q* 191 (1946): 33–34.

Tetzeli von Rosador, Kurt. *Magie im elisabethanischen Drama*. 1970.

Waith, Eugene M. *Ideas of Greatness: Heroic Drama in England*. 1971.

Wright, Louis B. "Juggling Tricks and Conjury on the English Stage before 1642." *MP* 24 (1926–27): 269–84.

———. "Stage Duelling in the Elizabethan Theatre." *MLR* 22 (1927): 265–75.

Parasitaster, or The Fawn

Eccles, Mark. "Recent Studies in Elizabethan and Jacobean Drama." *SEL* 13 (1973): 374–406.

Levin, Richard. "A Marston-Wilkins Borrowing." *N&Q* 19 (1972): 453.

Maxwell, J. C. "A Reading in Marston." *N&Q* 8 (1961): 195.

———. "An Echo of Tacitus in Marston." *N&Q* 18 (1971): 13–14.

Morris, Brian. "Elizabethan and Jacobean Drama." In *English Drama to 1710*, ed. Christopher Ricks (1971; vol. 3 of *History of Literature in the English Language*), pp. 65–117.

Price, Lawrence M. *English Literature in Germany*. 1953.

Schäfer, Jürgen. "Huarte: A Marston Source." *N&Q* 18 (1971): 16–17.

Smith, Gerald. "A Reading in Marston." *N&Q* 8 (1961): 397.

Wilson, F. P. *Elizabethan and Jacobean*. 1945.

Histriomastix

Armstrong, William A. "Actors and Theatres." *ShS* 17 (1964): 191–204.

Schoell, Franck L. "Shakespeare, Chapman and *Sir Thomas More*." *RAA* 3 (1925–26): 428–34.

Turner, Robert Y. "The Causal Induction in Some Elizabethan Plays." *SP* 60 (1963): 183–90.

Williams, Sheila, and Jean Jacquot. "Ommegangs anversois du temps de Bruegel et de Van Heemskerk." In *Les fêtes de la Renaissance*, ed. Jean Jacquot, 2 vols. (1956, 1960), 2: 359–88.

Wright, Louis B. "Animal Actors on the English Stage before 1642." *PMLA* 42 (1927): 656–69.

What You Will

Gray, Henry David. "Schoolmaster Shakespeare." *TLS*, 5 Feb. 1931, p. 99.

Jack Drum's Entertainment

Crundell, H. W. "Dekker's Theatrical Allusiveness." *TLS* 13 Feb. 1937, p. 111.

Kilby, James A. "'Drinking Danes' in Shakespeare and Marston." *N&Q* 10 (1963): 347.

Sabol, Andrew J. "Two Songs with Accompaniment for an Elizabethan Choirboy Play." *SRen* 5 (1958): 145-59.

The Insatiate Countess

Dent, R. W. "Ovid, Marlowe, and *The Insatiate Countess*." *N&Q* 10 (1963): 334-35.

Gunby, D. C. "Further Borrowings by Webster? " *N&Q* 13 (1966): 296-97.

Kramer, Mary D. "The Roman Catholic Cleric on the Jacobean Stage." *Costerus* 2 (1972): 109-17.

Turner, Robert K., Jr. "Dekker's 'Back-door'd Italian': *I Honest Whore*, II.i.355." *N&Q* 7 (1960): 25-26.

Eastward Ho

Camp, Charles W. *The Artisan in Elizabethan Literature*. 1924.

Cope, Jackson I. "*Volpone* and the Authorship of *Eastward Hoe*." *MLN* 72 (1957): 253-56.

Farmer, A. J. "Une source d'*Eastward Hoe*: Rabelais." *EA* 1 (1937): 325.

Greg, W. W. "Review of *Eastward Ho*, ed. Julia Harris." *MLR* 23 (1928): 76.

Harbage, Alfred. "The Mystery of *Perkin Warbeck*." In *Studies in the English Renaissance Drama in Memory of Karl Julius Holzknecht*, ed. Josephine W. Bennett et al. (1959), pp. 125-41.

Horwich, Richard. "*Hamlet* and *Eastward Ho*." *SEL* 11 (1971): 223-33.

Levin, Richard. "The Elizabethan 'Three-Level' Play." *RenD* 2 (1969): 23-37.

Peery, William. "*Eastward Ho!* and *A Woman Is a Weathercock*." *MLN* 62 (1947): 131-32.

"Plays of Ben Jonson." *TLS*, 21 July 1927, p. 500.

Schoenbaum, Samuel. "Internal Evidence and the Attribution of Elizabethan Plays." *BNYPL* 65 (1961): 102-24.

———. *Internal Evidence and Elizabethan Dramatic Authorship: An Essay in Literary History and Method*. 1966.

City Pageant

Bergeron, David M. *English Civic Pageantry, 1558-1642*. 1971.

D. TEXTUAL STUDIES

Bowers, Fredson. "Notes on Standing Type in Elizabethan Printing." *PBSA* 40 (1946): 205-24.

Brettle, R. E. "More Bibliographical Notes on Marston." *Library* 12 (1931-32): 235-42.

———. "Marston Bibliography: A Correction." *Library* 15 (1934-35): 241-42.

Crundell, H. W. "John Marston." *N&Q* 184 (1943): 175.

Haselden, Reginald B. *Scientific Aids for the Study of Manuscripts*. 1935.

McKerrow, Ronald B. *An Introduction to Bibliography for Literary Students*. 1927.

Turner, Robert K., Jr. "The Composition of *The Insatiate Countess*, Q2." *SB* 12 (1959): 198-203.

Yamada, Akihiro. *Shakespeare Jidai no Gikyoku to Shoshigakuteki Kenkyu-Josetsu* [*Bibliographical studies in Elizabethan dramatic texts: An introduction*], 1969. [Not seen.]

E. UNCERTAIN ASCRIPTIONS: APOCRYPHA

Bevington, David. "Shakespeare vs. Jonson on Satire." In *Shakespeare 1971: Proceedings of the World Shakespeare Congress, Vancouver, August 1971*, ed. Clifford Leech and J. M. R. Margeson (1972), pp. 107-22.

Cross, Gustav. "More's *Historie of Kyng Rycharde the Thirde* and *Lust's Dominion*." *N&Q* 4 (1957): 198-99.

Cutts, John P. "Jacobean Masque and Stage Music." *Music & Letters* 35 (1954): 185-200.

Green, Adwin Wigfall. *The Inns of Court and Early English Drama*. 1931.

Guha, P. K. "The Plot Structure of *Troilus and Cressida*." In *Essays on Shakespeare*, ed. Bhabatosh Chatterjee (1965), pp. 1-20.

Lucas, F. L., ed. *The Complete Works of John Webster*. 4 vols. 1937. [Induction to *The Malcontent*]

Muir, Kenneth. "Collier Fabrications." *N&Q* 197 (1952): 150.

Race, Sydney. "John Payne Collier and His Fabrications." *N&Q* 197 (1952): 54-56.

Sibley, Gertrude Marian. *The Lost Plays and Masques, 1500-1642*. 1933.

Spens, Janet. *Elizabethan Drama*. 1922.

Steele, Mary Susan. *Plays & Masques at Court during the Reigns of Elizabeth, James, and Charles*. 1926.

Welsford, Enid. *The Court Masque: A Study in the Relationship between Poetry and the Revels*. 1927.

F. EDITIONS

Ingram, R. W. "Editions of English Renaissance in Progress and Planned: A Rough Checklist." *RenD* 7, Supplement (1964): 13-28.

Anthologies

Baskervill, Charles Read, et al., eds. *Elizabethan and Stuart Plays*. 1934; rev. ed. 1971. [*Malcontent*]

Brooke, C. F. Tucker, et al., eds. *English Drama 1580-1642*. 1933. [*Eastward Ho, Malcontent*]

Chapman, Robin, et al., eds. *The City and the Court: Five Seventeenth-Century Comedies of London Life*. 1968. [*Eastward Ho*]

Donno, Elisabeth Story, ed. *Elizabethan Minor Epics*. 1963. [*Metamorphosis of Pygmalion's Image*]

Fraser, Russell A., et al., eds. *Drama of the English Renaissance II: The Stuart Period*. 1976. [*Dutch Courtesan*]

Gomme, A. H., ed. *Jacobean Tragedies*. 1969. [*Malcontent*]

Harrier, Richard C., ed. *The Anchor Anthology of Jacobean Drama.* Vol. 1, 1963. [*Malcontent*]

Lawrence, Robert Gifford, comp. *Early Seventeenth-Century Drama.* 1963. [*Malcontent*]

Oliphant, E. H. C., ed. *Shakespeare and His Fellow Dramatists: A Selection of Plays Illustrating the Glories of the Golden Age of English Drama.* 2 vols. 1929. [*Eastward Ho*]

————. *Elizabethan Dramatists Other than Shakespeare: A Selection of Plays Illustrating the Glories of the Golden Age of English Drama.* 1931. [Same as above except for omission of Shakespeare][*Eastward Ho*]

Rubinstein, H. F., ed. *Great English Plays: Twenty-Three Masterpieces.* 1928. [*Eastward Ho*]

Salgādo, Gāmini, ed. *Four Jacobean City Comedies.* 1975. [*Dutch Courtesan*]

Schelling, Felix E., ed. *Typical Elizabethan Plays.* 1926; 3rd ed. (with Matthew Black) 1949. [*Eastward Ho*]

Spencer, Hazelton, ed. *Elizabethan Plays.* 1933. [*Dutch Courtesan; Malcontent*]

Walley, Harold Reinohl, et al., eds. *Early Seventeenth-Century Plays.* 1930. [*Dutch Courtesan; Eastward Ho*]

CYRIL TOURNEUR

Charles R. Forker

The standard edition is Allardyce Nicoll's one-volume *The Works of Cyril Tourneur* (n.d. [1929]; reissued in 1963). Separate editions of *The Revenger's Tragedy,* ed. R. A. Foakes (1966), and *The Atheist's Tragedy,* ed. Irving Ribner (1964), in The Revels Plays have superseded Nicoll. For the sake of convenience, I include *The Revenger's Tragedy* among Tourneur's works; the problems of ascription are discussed in Section III (Canon).

I. GENERAL

A. BIOGRAPHICAL

Tourneur, one of the more shadowy figures of Renaissance drama, has been the subject of much biographical conjecture. The few facts known about his life are fully given in Nicoll's introduction to the *Works*. One significant addition to Nicoll's factual account, a reference to Tourneur in a letter from James Bathurst to William Trumbull, was discovered by James R. Sutherland: "Cyril Tourneur," *TLS,* 16 April 1931, p. 307. Peter B. Murray's *A Study of Cyril Tourneur* (1964), Ribner's edition of *The Atheist's Tragedy,* Brian Gibbons's New Mermaid edition of *The Revenger's Tragedy* (1967), Henri Fluchère's bilingual edition of *La tragédie du vengeur* (1958), and Arthur H. Nethercot's edition of *The Revenger's Tragedy* in *Stuart Plays,* ed. Arthur H. Nethercot, Charles R. Baskervill, and Virgil B. Heltzel (1971), provide convenient biographical summaries. Tourneur's activity as a dramatist was brief; he seems to have written for the theater only when not employed in military and diplomatic affairs. He was apparently born between 1570 and 1580; he had close connections with the Low Countries and with

248

the prominent Vere and Cecil families. Tourneur died at Kinsale, Ireland, on 28 February 1625/26.

B. GENERAL STUDIES OF THE PLAYS

The only general book-length treatment to date is Peter B. Murray's *A Study of Cyril Tourneur* (1964), a revision of a University of Pennsylvania doctoral thesis (1962). It contains critical analyses of *The Transformed Metamorphosis, The Atheist's Tragedy,* and *The Revenger's Tragedy,* as well as an important bibliographical chapter, which is the most elaborate attempt yet made to prove, on the basis of internal evidence, that *The Revenger's Tragedy* is by Middleton. Murray's volume illustrates an unfortunate but characteristic irony of Tourneur scholarship; half of it is devoted to discussing a play the author believes to be the work of another dramatist. (See III, A, below, for specific comments on Murray's bibliographical contribution.) This study nevertheless provides a useful introduction to Tourneur, since Murray absorbs and synthesizes the important commentary and scholarship of his predecessors. He also introduces significant judgments of his own.

Noting the critical drift away from the late Victorian and early twentieth-century emphasis on Tourneur's supposed horror and loathing of life, Murray builds his interpretation upon the thesis that Tourneur shows himself an orthodox Christian moralist in both *The Transformed Metamorphosis* and *The Atheist's Tragedy,* a poet who occupies "the Anglican center against attack from all extremes." He offers a complicated interpretation of *The Transformed Metamorphosis,* seeing in the dark allegory of this baffling poem mythic, religious, apocalyptic, historical, and biographical meanings. And he goes on to read both *The Atheist's Tragedy* and *The Revenger's Tragedy* in terms that often seem more theological than dramatic: the damnation of D'Amville and the salvation of Charlemont in *The Atheist's Tragedy* become complementary aspects of the "quest for fulfillment," the major forces of a conflict in which "events, characters and language are arranged into symbolic patterns" and "given significance by their relation to Christian ritual and legend." Vindici's "quest for justice" in the corrupt, inverted, "transformed" world of *The Revenger's Tragedy* is traced in successive stages as a terrible "journey to damnation." Despite significant limitations, Murray's book is the most comprehensive assessment available of the work traditionally attributed to Tourneur.

Three older and briefer discussions of Tourneur appear in *Elizabethan and Jacobean Playwrights* (1939) by Henry W. Wells, *A Short View of Elizabethan Drama* (1943) by Thomas Marc Parrott and Robert Hamilton Ball, and *An Introduction to Stuart Drama* (1946) by Frederick S. Boas. Refusing to commit himself on the authorship of *The Revenger's Tragedy*, Wells notes the self-conscious theatricality of the play, its deliberately artificial and intellectual appeal, and judges it but slightly inferior to "the masterpieces of Webster and Jonson because it lacks their ampler humanity." Wells comments on the atmosphere "of bustling tragicomedy" that informs *The Atheist's Tragedy* and "the unusual interest" of "some of the minor roles." Parrott and Ball are sensible on the authorship controversy (they lean toward the traditionalists) and suggestive on influences, but their account is weakened by an attempt to postulate a religious "conversion" on Tourneur's part to explain the shift in moral outlook from *The Revenger's Tragedy* to *The Atheist's Tragedy*. Boas shuns biographical heresies, is equally good on influences, and leaves the attribution of *The Revenger's Tragedy* "an open question." He offers a balanced, though necessarily general, appreciation of Tourneur's dramatic and poetic powers.

M. C. Bradbrook's pages on Tourneur in *Themes and Conventions of Elizabethan Tragedy* (1935) remain influential for their elucidation of the playwright's dramatic style. Bradbrook is especially illuminating on Tourneur's irony, whether verbal, thematic, or structural, and makes important observations on the imagery of both *The Revenger's Tragedy* and *The Atheist's Tragedy*. L. G. Salingar, "Tourneur and the Tragedy of Revenge," in *The Age of Shakespeare* (1955; vol. 2 of the Pelican *Guide to English Literature,* ed. Boris Ford), pp. 355–68, treats intellectual, historical, social, religious, and literary contexts, and analyzes Tourneur's rhythm. Salingar also considers the symbolic and psychological sides of Tourneur and suggests, for instance, that *The Revenger's Tragedy* "involves tense equilibrium between seeing human actions as personal, individual, and seeing them allegorically, as incidents of an eternal design."

John Peter's *Complaint and Satire in Early English Literature* (1956) examines Tourneur's didactic intentions and his "closeness to the established traditions of Complaint and the Morality." Tourneur is no "embittered nullifidian"; rather his "characters have a predetermined significance" as in medieval allegory; "they behave consistently in terms of that significance"; and his dramatic method, unlike Shakespeare's, is rigidly to define and limit the scope of his plays according to the moral orthodoxies they illustrate. Irving Ribner's chapter on Tourneur in *Jacobean Tragedy: The Quest for Moral Order* (1962) is equally certain about Tourneur's moralistic and religious purpose. Attributing to Tourneur "a crusading missionary tone," Ribner detects no trace of skepticism in the plays, stresses their links with medieval rather than Calvinistic theology, and thinks they "teach doctrines corollary to a belief in heaven: divine justice, retribution for sinners, the futility of earthly vengeance, and above all the fallacy of any system of human reason which may lead a man to place his faith in physical nature rather than in God." Robert Ornstein in *The Moral Vision of Jacobean Tragedy* (1960) also emphasizes Tourneur's "moralistic passion," though less categorically than Ribner. He notes the constant association of the sexual with the macabre and finds in *The Revenger's Tragedy* "an ethical design as sophisticated and intellectual as that of Jonson's greatest comedies." Vindici plays the villain for purposes of revenge only to become what he feigns. Noel Annan underscores Tourneur's sense of sin and his obsession with damnation in "Books in General," *New Statesman and Nation,* 24 June 1944, p. 423.

A very different view of Tourneur is advanced by Una Ellis-Fermor in *The Jacobean Drama: An Interpretation* (1936; 5th ed., 1965). Tourneur's universe is "inherently evil," "denuded of spiritual significance," and dominated by one emotion—horror; nevertheless Tourneur is "a poet-philosopher" whose "lucid and admirably thought-out psychological theories break through" and who attains an "underlying harmony of image and character, image and setting, or image and situation." *The High Design: English Renaissance Tragedy and the Natural Law* (1970) by George C. Herndl also emphasizes the "gloom and revulsion" of Tourneur's moral outlook, his Calvinistic insistence on a world in which depravity is "total and universal": the "teleological order of nature" which operates in Shakespeare's tragedies "is nowhere visible or tangible and certainly does not shape events." Herndl argues that in lieu of "the retributive working of the natural law" Tourneur gives us "a merciless avenger and a demonstration that whoever indulges himself at the expense of others will meet his match among his intended victims (as in *The Revenger's Tragedy*) or be blasted by divine lightning (as in *The Atheist's Tragedy*)."

Several writers have discussed Tourneur's place in the evolution and development of the revenge play. Percy Simpson in "The Theme of Revenge in Elizabethan Tragedy," *PBA* 21 (1935): 101-36, rpt. in his

Studies in Elizabethan Drama (1955), pp. 138-78, treats both Tourneur's tragedies as decadent variations on earlier conventions, though he admires the "powerfully sustained" characterization of Vindici. Fredson Thayer Bowers takes a similar line in *Elizabethan Revenge Tragedy, 1587-1642* (1940): *The Revenger's Tragedy,* which verges on incoherence and "moral chaos," is transitional between earlier plays, such as Kyd's *Spanish Tragedy,* in which revenge is the main interest, and later dramas, in which "horror and tortuous intrigue" are exploited by means of revenge conventions for their own sake. *The Atheist's Tragedy,* on the other hand, is an uncertain experiment—an unsuccessful attempt to reconcile old dramatic conventions and Christian ethics. François André Camoin, *The Revenge Convention in Tourneur, Webster, and Middleton* (1972), discusses Vindici's balance between involvement and detachment in a world where "free will is not a major factor" and "in which the ultimate attempt to assert identity (the death of others) paradoxically results in a gradual relinquishing of that identity, even unto death . . . ." Camoin sees *The Atheist's Tragedy,* in which Tourneur's outlook is more optimistic and revenge less central, as weaker than its companion play. Henry Hitch Adams traces a progression of ideas from *The Revenger's Tragedy* to *The Atheist's Tragedy* which argues "a common approach to the problem of revenge" and therefore "common authorship" in "Cyril Tourneur on Revenge," *JEGP* 48 (1949): 72-87.

Madeleine Doran, *Endeavors of Art: A Study of Form in Elizabethan Drama* (1954), speaks of the "unexamined ethical formula" that prevents *The Atheist's Tragedy* from realizing its potential and of Tourneur's "failure to assimilate different attitudes" in *The Revenger's Tragedy* so that our response to Vindici remains puzzled: Tourneur "is not really interested in how a man may be drawn into doing wrong to right wrong . . . but simply in the mordant depiction of a vicious and ugly world . . . ." Harold Jenkins's "Cyril Tourneur," *RES* 17 (1941): 21-36, accounts for stylistic differences between *The Revenger's Tragedy* and *The Atheist's Tragedy* in terms of "the supplanting of a fiery instinct by a reasoning purpose." J. M. R. Margeson analyzes the ironic structure of Tourneur's two dramas in *The Origins of English Tragedy* (1967). The title character of *The Revenger's Tragedy* is not only a manipulator but a satiric commentator who gradually loses his objectivity and is drawn increasingly into the evil upon which he comments; Vindici's growing cynicism betrays him into fallible judgments. *The Atheist's Tragedy,* in which the villains are attacking the virtuous as well as the evil elements of society, presents a less subtle pattern; the play's providential emphasis tends to undercut the irony of evil destroying itself.

Modern revival of interest in Tourneur owes much to four nineteenth-century critics who are still quoted with respect. Charles Lamb's *Specimens of English Dramatic Poets Who Lived About the Time of Shakespeare* (1808) reprints excerpts from both Tourneur's plays with richly appreciative commentary. His instinct for the most opulent passages and electric scenes is unerring, and his observations, though brief, are worth consulting. Algernon Charles Swinburne's effusions on Tourneur are impressionistic and unspecific; his ranking of Tourneur with Aeschylus and Shakespeare and his characterization of *The Revenger's Tragedy* as "a thunderstorm of a play" with its "fiery jet" of "molten verse" are frequently cited. For Swinburne's reactions see "Cyril Tourneur," *Nineteenth Century* 21 (1887): 415-27, rpt. in his *The Age of Shakespeare* (1908), pp. 259-86; his *Contemporaries of Shakespeare*, ed. E. Gosse and T. J. Wise (1919); and "Cyril Tourneur," a sonnet, and "Prologue to *The Revenger's Tragedy*" in *The Complete Works of Algernon Charles Swinburne,* ed. E. Gosse and T. J. Wise, 20 vols. (1925-27), vols. 3 and 6. John Addington Symonds in his Mermaid edition of *Webster and Tourneur* (1893) and Edmund Gosse in *The Jacobean Poets* (1894) offer general but sensitive appreciations of Tourneur in conjunction with Webster.

T. S. Eliot's essay "Cyril Tourneur," prompted by the publication of Nicoll's edition (*TLS*, 13 Nov. 1930, pp. 925-26; rpt. in both his *Selected Essays* [1932] and *Elizabethan Essays* [1934]), is one of the *loci classici* of criticism. Eliot regards the plays chiefly as a commentary on their author's personality, detecting in *The Revenger's Tragedy* an adolescent cynicism and disgust for life, an immature expression of "the death motive" which, though excessive, was nevertheless realized in verse of superb concentration, originality, and power. The influence of Marston is stressed. Eliot's biographical approach, though outdated, is nevertheless suggestive and remains influential. Padraic Fallon in "The Unique Genius," *Dublin Magazine* 12 (1937): 62-69, amplifies some of Eliot's ideas, inferring a kind of literary biography from the works. In *Death and Elizabethan Tragedy: A Study of Convention and Opinion in the Elizabethan Drama* (1936), Theodore Spencer shows that Tourneur's fascination with mortality is partly traditional, though the Jacobean, unlike his medieval predecessors, tends to think of death as an end, a climax, rather than as a spiritual beginning.

William Archer's *The Old Drama and the New* (1923) deserves mention for its extremism. Archer, reading by the light of Ibsen, sees the author of *The Revenger's Tragedy* as "a sanguinary maniac who cannot even write tolerable verse" and the play as "a product either of sheer barbarism, or of some pitiable psychopathic perversion." C. V. Boyer also bases largely negative judgments on unfounded assumptions about psychological realism in Tourneur. His *The Villain as Hero in Elizabethan Tragedy* (1914) discusses both Vindici and D'Amville together with other villainous protagonists of the period. In a more sophisticated vein, Robert B. Heilman's *Tragedy and Melodrama* (1968) treats both Tourneur's plays as different but self-conscious alterations of a melodramatic stereotype: *The Atheist's Tragedy* is "tragedy *manqué*" while in *The Revenger's Tragedy* the dramatist's "considerable achievement . . . is to analyze the stereotype revenger, who is also the voluble defender of outraged virtue, and discover an enthusiast for wily stratagems, third-degree tortures, and unsubtle vigilantism." Among the denigrations of Tourneur's work, Christopher Ricks's "The Tragedies of Webster, Tourneur, and Middleton: Symbols, Imagery, and Conventions" in *English Drama to 1710,* ed. Ricks (1971), pp. 306-51, is perhaps the most discriminating. Concurring in part with Archer's view of the unnaturalness and improbability of much Jacobean tragedy, Ricks distinguishes between dramatists (such as Shakespeare and Middleton) who use theatrical conventions responsibly without violating our sense of natural life, and those (like Webster and Tourneur) who employ them as mere devices or conveniences, as solutions for technical embarrassments. More routinely, Donald Joseph McGinn, *Shakespeare's Influence on the Drama of His Age Studied in "Hamlet,"* (1938), investigates Tourneur's imitations of and reactions to Shakespeare's masterpiece. Richard Proudfoot, "Shakespeare and the New Dramatists of the King's Men, 1606-1613," in *Later Shakespeare,* SuAS, vol. 8 (1966), pp. 235-61, also illuminates Shakespeare's influence upon his immediate contemporaries and successors including Tourneur: *The Revenger's Tragedy* imitates both *Hamlet* and *Lear* for themes and characterization, while *The Atheist's Tragedy* "draws more heavily and less creatively on Shakespeare." For an earlier discussion, see Levin L. Schücking, "Eine Anleihe Shakespeares bei Tourneur," *Englische Studien* 50 (1916-17): 80-105.

Michael Kelly, "The Dramaturgy of Tourneur's Trial Scene," *Cithara* 8 (1968): 26-38, argues that the trial scenes of *The Revenger's Tragedy* and *The Atheist's Tragedy* illustrate "significant differences" of technique and conception between the two plays: whereas *The Atheist's Tragedy* "is the epitome of overt thesis drama" in which "theme does not emerge from action and situation" but "is superimposed" upon them, *The Revenger's Tragedy* succeeds in embodying its moral ideas convincingly in character and plot. In *Microcosmos: The Shape of the Elizabethan Play* (1965), Thomas B. Stroup treats a different aspect of Tourneur's dramaturgy—his encompassing of the sphere of human action by a supernatural sphere and his use of the testing motif.

Ever since Frederic I. Carpenter in *Metaphor and Simile in the Minor Elizabethan Drama* (1895) called attention to Tourneur's "imaginative brevity," his tendency, particularly in *The Revenger's Tragedy,* to make effective use of "ellipsis and condensation," the poet's imagery has provoked commentary. Una Ellis-Fermor's "The Imagery of *The Revengers Tragedie* and *The Atheists Tragedie,*" *MLR* 30 (1935), 289-301, and Marco K. Mincoff's "The Authorship of *The Revenger's Tragedy,*" *Studia Historico-Philologica Serdicensia* 2 (1939): 1-87, both compare the imagery of the two plays with a view to resolving the authorship problem of the earlier one. Ellis-Fermor's categories are arbitrary, and she draws unwarranted biographical inferences from them; she concludes that Tourneur wrote both plays. Mincoff, using similar methods, independently decides that *The Revenger's Tragedy* is Middleton's. Both scholars contribute to our appreciation of Tourneur's language; neither settles attribution. Inga-Stina Ekeblad, "An Approach to Tourneur's Imagery," *MLR* 54 (1959): 489-98, argues that Tourneur wrote *The Revenger's Tragedy* and, without minimizing stylistic differences between the plays, that both tragedies evince "important similarities . . . in the function of imagery as part of dramatic structure and technique." Dieter Mehl, "Emblems in English Renaissance Drama," *RenD* 2 (1969): 39-57, includes both Tourneur's plays among his illustrations. Louis Charles Stagg lists images in *An Index to the Figurative Language of Cyril Tourneur's Tragedies* (1970).

Pre-Restoration Stage Studies (1927) by William J. Lawrence comments on several aspects of the staging of both *The Revenger's Tragedy* and *The Atheist's Tragedy.* Elmer Edgar Stoll takes up the chronology and dating of Tourneur's plays in an appendix to *John Webster: The Periods of His Work as Determined by His Relations to the Drama of His Day* (1905). The matter of chronology is, of course, intertwined with the controversy about attribution. E. H. C. Oliphant, responding to T. S. Eliot's review-essay (above), reopens the question of the priority of *The Revenger's Tragedy* over *The Atheist's Tragedy* in

"Tourneur and *The Revenger's Tragedy,*" *TLS,* 18 Dec. 1930, p. 1087. Eliot answers Oliphant's letter in *TLS,* 1 Jan. 1931, p. 12; Oliphant replies once more in *TLS,* 5 Feb. 1931, p. 99, and again at greater length in "Tourneur and Mr. T. S. Eliot," *SP* 32 (1935): 546-52.

C. THE WORKS AT LARGE

Apart from the two tragedies, Tourneur's work has received scant attention. Bernard M. Wagner adds two occasional poems to the canon (omitted from Nicoll's edition of the *Works*) in "Elizabethan Dramatists," *TLS,* 28 Sept. 1933, p. 651 (see III,B, below). Murray's book (I,B) deals at length with only one of the nondramatic works, *The Transformed Metamorphosis* (1600). Allardyce Nicoll in his introduction to the *Works* discusses this poem along with the prose pamphlet *Laugh and Lie Down* (1605; signed "C.T." and doubtfully ascribed to Tourneur), the funeral elegy on Sir Francis Vere (1609), *The Character of Robert, Earl of Salisbury* (1612), and *A Grief on the Death of Prince Henry* (1612), all in necessarily general terms, as had John Churton Collins in his edition of *The Plays and Poems of Cyril Tourneur,* 2 vols. (1878), vol. 1. Ruth Wallerstein in *Studies in Seventeenth-Century Poetic* (1950) offers a discerning critique of *A Grief on the Death of Prince Henry,* comparing it favorably with companion pieces composed for the same occasion by contemporaries and with Tourneur's earlier poem on the death of Vere.

Discussion of *The Transformed Metamorphosis* has centered on the identity of Mavortio, the poem's allegorical hero: J. C. Collins thought he was the Earl of Essex (*The Plays and Poems of Cyril Tourneur,* vol. 2); Dorothy Pym favored Spenser in "A Theory on the Identification of Cyril Tourneur's 'Mavortio,'" *N&Q* 174 (1938): 201-4; Kenneth N. Cameron's candidate in "Cyril Tourneur and *The Transformed Metamorphosis,*" *RES* 16 (1940): 18-24, was Sir Christopher Heydon, to whom the poem is dedicated; and J. D. Peter advanced a claim for Henry VIII in "The Identity of Mavortio in Tourneur's *Transformed Metamorphosis,*" *N&Q* 193 (1948): 408-12. A. C. Hamilton made the most persuasive argument by reopening the case for Spenser on broader grounds than Pym's in "Spenser and Tourneur's *Transformed Metamorphosis,*" *RES* 8 (1957): 127-36. Finally Murray, in his chapter on the poem, attempts to reconcile these positions by regarding Mavortio as a type, a composite mythic figure. C. S. Lewis in *English Literature in the Sixteenth Century* (1954) writes on the aesthetic effect of the poem, which he variously characterizes as "a freak" and "a surrealist mixture of horror and nonsense."

The following works supply bibliographical information: E. K. Chambers, *The Elizabethan Stage,* 4 vols. (1923); Samuel A. and Dorothy R. Tannenbaum, *Cyril Tourneur: A Concise Bibliography* (1946), rpt. in *Elizabethan Bibliographies,* vol. 10 (1967); Dennis Donovan, *Elizabethan Bibliographies Supplements II, Cyril Tourneur: 1945-1965* (1967); Irving Ribner, *Tudor and Stuart Drama,* Goldentree Bibliographies (1966).

II. CRITICISM OF INDIVIDUAL PLAYS AND STATE OF SCHOLARSHIP

A. INDIVIDUAL PLAYS

The Revenger's Tragedy

Praise of this play has been multifarious but far from universal. Felix E. Schelling objected to "the ingenuity of its horror, its straining of all the legitimate devices of tragedy, its pruriency in an attitude of assumed righteousness, and its bitterly cynical outlook on life" (*Elizabethan Drama: 1558-1642* [1908]). Alfred Harbage provides a more recent condemnation in "Intrigue in Elizabethan Tragedy" in *Essays on Shakespeare and Elizabethan Drama in Honor of Hardin Craig,* ed. Richard Hosley (1962), pp. 37-44: *The Revenger's Tragedy* is "a bad play" despite "its widely acclaimed poetry, which proves upon examination to appear only in the first and a few later bravura speeches" and "less because of its intrigue, thickened to the point of coagulation, but because it has so little else to offer." Harbage also believes that Vindici not only "ends thoroughly corrupted" but "seems also to have begun corrupted." Most writers, however, have been more sympathetic.

Lacy Lockert's "The Greatest of Elizabethan Melodramas" in *Essays in Dramatic Literature: The Parrott Presentation Volume,* ed. Hardin Craig (1935), pp. 103-26, reviews commentary on the play and offers appreciation of its poetry, atmosphere, plotting, and characterization. L. G. Salingar, *"The Revenger's Tragedy* and the Morality Tradition," *Scrutiny* 6 (1938): 402-24, rpt. in *Elizabethan Drama: Modern Essays in Criticism,* ed. R. J. Kaufmann (1961), pp. 208-24, corrects more romantically inclined critics and shows that the play is "a logical

development from the mediaeval drama." Salingar suggests that
Tourneur inevitably failed when he left off "dealing with types" and
"tried to examine individual motives" or "argue out the reasons for his
judgments." In a later and broader essay on Tourneur (see I,B), Salingar
modified this opinion. Peter Lisca's *"The Revenger's Tragedy:* A Study
in Irony," *PQ* 38 (1959): 242-51, rpt. in *Shakespeare's Contemporaries: Modern Studies in English Renaissance Drama,* ed. Max Bluestone and
Norman Rabkin (1961), pp. 239-49, 2nd ed. (1970), pp. 307-17,
analyzes the dramatic structure and demonstrates how Tourneur objectifies his moral attitude at the levels of action and language to achieve a
macabre but complex unity.

Samuel Schoenbaum illuminates the relationship of the play to late
medieval visual art in *"The Revenger's Tragedy:* Jacobean Dance of
Death," *MLQ* 15 (1954): 201-7, arguing that the play fuses elements of
tragedy, melodrama, and farce. In *Middleton's Tragedies: A Critical
Study* (1955), Schoenbaum expands this discussion, synthesizing earlier
commentary, reexamining the imagery, and concluding that Middleton,
to whom he here attributes the tragedy (but see III,A, below), " is telling a timeless parable of man's wickedness and God's punishment for
sin." Robert Ornstein in "The Ethical Design of *The Revenger's
Tragedy," ELH* 21 (1954): 81-93, revised in *The Moral Vision of
Jacobean Tragedy* (1960), also finds a sermon in the play: despite its
lurid eccentricities and dark tone, it "expresses the intense, but only
temporary, disillusion of a very orthodox and very conservative mind."
John Peter's *"The Revenger's Tragedy* Reconsidered," *Essays in
Criticism* 6 (1956): 131-43, examines the emphasis on lechery, acquisitiveness, and death in early parts of the play as a basis for arguing that
the later parts "consolidate and advance the ethical positives" already
implied at the beginning. T. W. Craik, replying in the same journal (6
[1956] : 482-85) thinks Peter "underestimates the moral difficulties";
and Peter defends himself (pp. 485-86). Peter's discussion reappears in
altered form in his *Complaint and Satire in Early English Literature*
(1956).

Philip J. Ayres approaches morality and structure differently in
"Parallel Action and Reductive Techniques in *The Revenger's
Tragedy," ELN* 8 (1970): 103-7, arguing that the subsidiary revenge
actions serve to deglamorize the main action and thus "provide comment" on Vindici by undermining his dignity and his moral justification. In "Morality and Inevitability in *The Revenger's Tragedy," JEGP*
71 (1972): 36-46, Arthur L. Kistner contends that the tragedy presents

"a mutually interdependent structure of inevitability and morality, but not the simple reward-for-the-good and punishment-for-the-bad morality that has generally been imposed on the play": Vindici degenerates morally, to be replaced by Antonio as spokesman for decency and order, but Antonio's values represent only an imperfect "silver age" and disclose the ethical limits of so corrupt a society.

B. J. Layman, "Tourneur's Artificial Noon: The Design of *The Revenger's Tragedy,*" *MLQ* 34 (1973): 20–35, also disagrees with those who interpret the play as a demonstration of "doctrinal orthodoxy": Vindici's role calls upon him to combine "the righteous fury of a Savonarola, the virtuosic cruelty of a Cesare Borgia, and the self-regarding, defamatory satire of an Aretino"; his use of and obsession with the skull of Gloriana become Tourneur's conceit for the "horrible oneness" of life and death, night and noon. Layman believes that Tourneur "channeled the power of his intelligence and imagination into a reiterated definition of that convulsive moment when the time-ridden destroy themselves" and so dramatized a response to life that, "while sporadically moving and brilliant, is ultimately self-entangling and self-nullifying." J. W. Lever in *The Tragedy of State* (1971) voices a similar view of the play's moral nihilism: "There is no norm of a virtuous polity against which the Duke's regime can be offset; no supposition that a good ruler has been overthrown or murdered before the action began; no appearance of an uncorrupted heir to take over the injured state." Lever notes the absence of supernatural powers in the play, a feature which sets it apart from earlier products of "the Senecan tradition," and concludes that it is "a revenge drama without political perspectives, a morality without positive standards."

Alvin Kernan's *The Cankered Muse: Satire of the English Renaissance* (1959) treats Vindici as an unmasker of pretense, a stripper-away of illusion; the play is a "tragical satire" in which the tension between apparently contradictory attitudes is resolved by the hero's self-exposure, self-recognition, and death. Max Bluestone and Norman Rabkin reprint Kernan's discussion in *Shakespeare's Contemporaries* (2nd ed., 1970), pp. 317–27. In *The Language of Tragedy* (1947), Moody E. Prior compares the procedure of *The Revenger's Tragedy* to a chess exhibition in which the author "demonstrates the solution in such a way as to encompass the maximum number of variant situations latent in the problem"; Prior locates "both the distinction and the limitations of Tourneur's performance" in his "great fertility of invention" and in his capacity for "relating the diction to the perverse and false values of a life of sin."

Several commentators have been struck by the relationship of the play to comedy. J. C. Oates, "The Comedy of Metamorphosis in *The Revenger's Tragedy*," *Bucknell Review* 11 (1962): 38–52, speaks of "the essential savagery of its comic vision," seeing in Vindici "the force of the unconscious controlling the conscious self and ultimately destroying it." Cyrus Hoy's *The Hyacinth Room: An Investigation into the Nature of Comedy, Tragedy, and Tragicomedy* (1964) views the play as a systematic exposure "of the incongruous nature of man," a "representation of human folly . . . in all its guises." In *Jacobean City Comedy* (1968) Brian Gibbons points out links between *The Revenger's Tragedy* and the citizen comedy of the period, particularly Middleton's. Douglas Cole comments briefly on an aspect of the play's characterization in "The Comic Accomplice in Elizabethan Revenge Tragedy," *RenD* 9 (1966): 125–39.

A Study of Elizabethan and Jacobean Tragedy (1964) by T. B. Tomlinson discusses *The Revenger's Tragedy* at length. Tomlinson thinks Tourneur triumphs "only precariously over incipient decadence" and that the play's strength lies not in its attitude of "moral superiority over lust and corruption," but in its "ability to realize and place its own attraction to them." The "key to a true reading" is "in the movement of attention we are constantly forced to make between the almost naïvely simple clarity of Revenge morality . . . and the richer, more complex wit of metaphysical or near-metaphysical verse." Tomlinson's attraction to the anti-sentimental qualities of the play is of the school of F. R. Leavis; his treatment suffers from an anti-historical bias, over-subtlety, and a dogmatism which would elevate Tourneur's achievement by sinking Webster's. (An earlier version appeared as "The Morality of Revenge: Tourneur's Critics" in *Essays in Criticism* 10 [1960]: 134–47.)

Charles Osborne McDonald's chapter on *The Revenger's Tragedy* in *The Rhetoric of Tragedy: Form in Stuart Drama* (1966) endorses the high estimate of Tourneur's poetic intensity. McDonald provides a usefully detailed analysis of the play's imagery and thematic juxtapositions but vitiates his discussion of the verbal and structural patterns by insisting that they infallibly obey the laws of "sophistic rhetoric," practiced by Euripides and other Greek writers of the fifth century B.C. and transmitted to the English Renaissance through Seneca.

R. A. Foakes, as part of the introduction to his Revels edition (see III,E), tries to reconcile the strong points of critics who tend to identify Tourneur's attitudes with Vindici's and those who read the play more objectively. The many proverbs, maxims, and sententiae in the play have the dramatic function of ironic distancing: "The generalizing force" of many characters' speeches "suggests a concern for morality and truth which is quite unrelated to their behaviour, and is never tested against principles. It is a mechanical sententiousness, comically horrible." Foakes also argues against Murray's notion of a Vindici who is gradually corrupted, regarding his moral superiority over the other characters as, at best, very limited. In *Shakespeare: The Dark Comedies to the Last Plays; From Satire to Celebration* (1971), Foakes enlarges upon these ideas: the combination of tragic and satiric elements in Tourneur's play takes us "as it were, to the edge of a precipice" and shows us "in the gulf beyond, a limiting possibility of a society where social, legal and moral restraints have crumbled away." Like Foakes, Anders Dallby concerns himself with the distancing effect of the dramatist's "detached comments, so general and so nearly anonymous that they might have been spoken by a presenter," which make Tourneur's dramatic writing more stylized and direct, and less ambiguous, than Webster's (*The Anatomy of Evil: A Study of John Webster's "The White Devil"* [1974]).

Wylie Sypher's *Four Stages of Renaissance Style: Transformations in Art and Literature, 1400-1700* (1955), relates *The Revenger's Tragedy* briefly to the "mannerist" tradition: "Tourneur's scale of moral values is always being adjusted to the needs of the immediate dramatic crisis. This means that the motives and the actions need not be consistent with any one scheme of morality, but effective only for the instant."

Although Alan Brissenden's "Impediments to Love: A Theme in John Ford," *RenD* 7 (1964): 95-102, is primarily concerned with the motif of incest in the later dramatist, *The Revenger's Tragedy* is discussed for purposes of comparison. Jeffrey L. Johnson in "The Spoils of Love and Vengeance: A Study of the Jacobean Revenge Tragedy Motivated by Lust," *Xavier University Studies* 7.3 (1968): 31-43, is also interested in the sexual emphasis of the drama, regarding it as transitional between the Kydian revenge plays where the death of a relative is paramount and those plays which depict the consequences of lust rather than the fulfillment of a family obligation. George L. Geckle studies Tourneur's idea of justice in "Justice in *The Revenger's*

Tragedy," *RenP 1973* (1974), pp. 75-82, relating it to Renaissance iconography and specifically to Spenser's *Faerie Queene*. Geckle finds the play's morality "implicitly orthodox" and discerns "a complex interrelationship between Justice, Queen Elizabeth, Vindice's dead financée, Gloriana, and Vindice's sister, Castiza."

The most extended and comprehensive analysis of style in the tragedy is Daniel Jonathan Jacobson's monograph, *The Language of "The Revenger's Tragedy,"* (1974), which treats such features as condensation, irony, antithesis, paradox, metonymy, word play, and the blending of literal and figurative meanings. In "Synecdoche and Cyril Tourneur: Language in *The Revenger's Tragedy,"* *Massachusetts Studies in English* 2 (1970): 103-6, Eugene P. Walz comments on the vividness in diction achieved by substituting a part for the whole. Characteristically the synecdochial figures apply to the body, especially the head and tongue, by which means the playwright dissects human nature and stresses "the grossness and mortality of the world of the flesh." F. R. Leavis in "Imagery and Movement: Notes in the Analysis of Poetry," *Scrutiny* 13 (1945): 119-34, devotes a section to a close reading of Vindici's famous "silkworm" speech (III.v.69-106). Robert C. Jones, "Italian Settings and the 'World' of Elizabethan Tragedy," *SEL* 10 (1970): 251-68, surveys the treatment of location in *The Revenger's Tragedy* and other contemporary plays, pointing out that direct allusions to Italy are sparse and that through patterns of imagery Tourneur shows us "a way of life, not a place." Maurice Charney remarks the combination of bloody violence and artifice in *The Revenger's Tragedy,* the "curious mixture of crude formulas and sophisticated poetry" ("The Persuasiveness of Violence in Elizabethan Plays," *RenD* 2 [1969]: 59-70).

A determinative primary source for *The Revenger's Tragedy* has yet to be discovered. Samuel Schoenbaum in *"The Revenger's Tragedy*: A Neglected Source," *N&Q* 195 (1950): 338, calls attention to statements by Vernon Lee and J. A. Symonds which point to Varchi's *Storia Fiorentina* or possibly some other version of events in the life of Alessandro de' Medici. N. W. Bawcutt follows up in *"The Revenger's Tragedy* and the Medici Family," *N&Q* 4 (1957): 192-93, and concludes that Tourneur is most likely to have come by his knowledge of the Medici in the twelfth novel of the Queen of Navarre's *Heptaméron* englished by William Painter in *The Palace of Pleasure*. Pierre Legouis independently reaches the same conclusion in "Réflexions sur la recherche des sources à propos de *La Tragédie du Vengeur,"* *EA* 12

(1959): 47-55. Lever's *Tragedy of State* (above) also discusses the play's rendering of Medician history. G. K. Hunter suggests that an episode in II.ii derives from Heliodorus's *Aethiopica,* probably through the English translation of Thomas Underdowne, in "A Source for *The Revenger's Tragedy,*" *RES* 10 (1959): 181-82. L. G. Salingar discusses similarities of plot in the play to a story in Cinthio's *Hecatommithi* (translated by Barnabe Riche in his *Farewell to the Military Profession)* and to a *novelle* by Bandello in *"The Revenger's Tragedy:* Some Possible Sources," *MLR* 60 (1965): 3-12. Foakes also treats sources in his Revels edition; he points out, as have others, that John Florio's dictionary, *A Worlde of Wordes* (1598), serves as a gloss for most of the characters' names.

The impact of Shakespeare's *Hamlet* upon the play has been discussed by Ashley H. Thorndike in "The Relations of *Hamlet* to Contemporary Revenge Plays," *PMLA* 17 (1902): 125-220; by Levin L. Schücking in "Eine Anleihe Shakespeares bei Tourneur" (I,B); and by Donald Joseph McGinn in *Shakespeare's Influence on the Drama of His Age Studied in "Hamlet"* (I,B). David L. Frost, *The School of Shakespeare: The Influence of Shakespeare on English Drama, 1600–42* (1968), not only classifies *The Revenger's Tragedy* as a lineal descendant of Shakespeare's tragedy but contends that it is a play Hamlet "might well have . . . written." See also Richard Proudfoot, "Shakespeare and the New Dramatists of the King's Men, 1606-1613" (I,B). R. A. Foakes in "The Art of Cruelty: Hamlet and Vindici," *ShS* 26 (1973): 21-31, distinguishes between Hamlet's tendency to displace actual cruelty by venting it in artistic or merely verbal terms and Vindici's attraction to the means of vengeance as an end in itself; whereas "Hamlet is concerned with the nature of revenge and the horror of the act of cruelty," Vindici falls in love with his own art and commits himself wholly to it. Peter B. Murray comments briefly on the influence of *The Spanish Tragedy* on *The Revenger's Tragedy* in *Thomas Kyd* (1969).

The Atheist's Tragedy, or the Honest Man's Revenge

Michael H. Higgins in "The Influence of Calvinistic Thought in Tourneur's *Atheist's Tragedy,*" *RES* 19 (1943): 255-62, makes a case for theological significance in the play: its language, thought, and moral conception portray "the gloomy, sadistic, and logical universe" of Calvin's *Christian Institutions,* and its central theme is "the secret providence of God." The structure of the tragedy is based on the contrast between D'Amville (who represents, by his atheism, the sinful, doomed majority) and Charlemont (who exemplifies, by his pious faith, the blessed condition of the elect). Robert Ornstein in *"The Atheist's Tragedy* and Renaissance Naturalism," *SP* 51 (1954): 194-207, is also concerned with the play's philosophical content: D'Amville, a farcical character who makes an absurd anti-religion out of his beliefs, is a "curious compound of atheist, materialist, sensualist, nature worshipper, and politician," but nevertheless a character recognizable to Elizabethan audiences as "the archetypal Renaissance atheist synthesized from contemporary opinion about, and refutations of, atheism." Ornstein holds that "D'Amville's view of nature is never actually refuted" in the play and that therefore Tourneur tacitly accepts a premise of Baconian rationalism—the split between nature and providence. The conclusions of this argument are assimilated into Ornstein's *The Moral Vision of Jacobean Tragedy* (I,B).

Clifford Leech, *"The Atheist's Tragedy* as a Dramatic Comment on Chapman's *Bussy* Plays," *JEGP* 52 (1953): 525-30, notes the similarity of the names Charlemont and Clermont, D'Amville and D'Ambois, and refines a point made by Henry Hitch Adams in "Cyril Tourneur on Revenge" (I,B) on the relation of Tourneur's play to Chapman's *Revenge of Bussy D'Ambois.* Leech argues that *The Atheist's Tragedy* "presents a christianization of themes which Tourneur found" in both of Chapman's *Bussy* plays; that Bussy, "the supreme individualist," and Clermont, "the man suspicious of action," undergo a transmutation into D'Amville and Charlemont; and that speeches of Bussy's and Montferrers's ghosts illustrate the difference in moral attitude between Chapman and Tourneur.

William Empson in *Some Versions of Pastoral* (1935) outlines the contrast between Levidulcia and Castabella and discusses its thematic implications for the structure of *The Atheist's Tragedy.* In "The Subplot of *The Atheist's Tragedy,"* *HLQ* 29 (1965): 17-33, Richard Levin greatly elaborates Empson's point. Levin views the affair of Levidulcia and Sebastian "as part of a carefully planned schematism which integrates the separate actions . . . on a much more elaborate and comprehensive scale than is found in many other double-plot plays of the period." He arranges the central figures of both plots in a kind of moral-philosophical hierarchy extending from true wisdom to mere physical appetite, and he relates the Snuff-Soquette episode to both the main and subplots in such a manner as to suggest that Tourneur placed all three actions not only in a "scale of descending importance" but in a "sequence of causation," thereby establishing "three distinct levels of tone and value" which "tend to reinforce each other." Levin also treats the plotting briefly in "The Elizabethan 'Three-Level' Play," *RenD* 2 (1969): 23-37. In revised form this material is incorporated into Levin's *The Multiple Plot in English Renaissance Drama* (1971). Glen A. Love analyzes the dramatic structure in "Morality and Style in *The Atheist's Tragedy,*" *HAB* 15 (1964): 38-45. Like Levin, Love sees antithesis as an organizational principle of the play, but he emphasizes its function not merely at the levels of character and plot but also as a rhetorical characteristic which pervades "the smaller elements of language, such as imagery, diction, and syntax": Tourneur's antithetical habit of mind reveals a "two-valued orientation" and serves the dramatist's "moral—and tragic—perception of a world divided into irreconcilable opposites."

"Tourneur and the Stars" by J. M. S. Tompkins, *RES* 22 (1946): 315-19, draws attention to the importance of astrology as a theme in *The Atheist's Tragedy.* D'Amville denies the stars' influence as instruments of divine purpose at two significant turning points in the action: "first, when he has accomplished the murder of his brother, and secondly, just before the strokes of God's vengeance begin to rain on him." Una Ellis-Fermor in *The Frontiers of Drama* (1945) and Joseph T. McCullen, Jr., in "Madness and the Isolation of Characters in Elizabethan and Early Stuart Drama," *SP* 48 (1951): 206-18, provide brief discussions of two facets of Tourneur's characterization in *The Atheist's Tragedy*: Ellis-Fermor notes how the character and mental preoccupation of figures such as D'Amville, Sebastian, and Levidulcia are precisely differentiated through imagery; and McCullen how D'Amville's tragic isolation, like that of many other such characters, is dramatized through madness.

Irving Ribner, in his introduction to the Revels edition of *The Atheist's Tragedy* (III,E), accepts the notion that Tourneur felt impelled to respond to Chapman's *Bussy* plays and confirms influence on the play from *Doctor Faustus, Hamlet, Macbeth,* and *Lear.* Ribner analyzes the dramatic structure in terms of "two parallel movements, the one devoted to a systematic refutation of D'Amville's creed . . . , the other to a demonstration of Charlemont's way as the only one which can assure man's happiness" so that the play becomes a sort of "medieval *débat*" in which the two antagonists symbolize the conflict between animalism, mechanism, and determinism on the one side and Christian transcendence on the other. The tragedy is "a new kind of revenge play in that the revenger is victorious through refusal to revenge, rather than destroyed, like Vindice, for the vehemence of his vengeance." Despite its heavy didacticism, *The Atheist's Tragedy* "offers as comprehensive and realistic a view of Jacobean daily life as any play of the period."

R. J. Kaufmann's "Theodicy, Tragedy, and the Psalmist: Tourneur's *Atheist's Tragedy*," *CompD* 3 (1969-70): 241-62, groups Tourneur's piece, along with others by Marlowe, Shakespeare, Jonson, and Marston, as an example of a special sub-genre of Renaissance tragedy in which "the protagonist is both enlarged and belittled by the framing theoretical assumptions. These assumptions are clearly too narrow to contain his spirit, but, equally, he is not invested with enough *axiologically independent* initiative to shatter the frame." Thus, halting between theological orthodoxy and subversiveness, Tourneur drives a wedge between our sympathy for D'Amville and our moral disapproval, evoking an oxymoric response to him as a "tiny monster," "dangerous trifler," "vigilant blind man" or "life-hoarding suicide." *The Atheist's Tragedy* emerges as "an explicit . . . projection of the themes of the 127th Psalm, '*Nisi Dominus*, nothing can be done without God's grace,' and a Calvinist reading at that."

Four essays may be mentioned which relate Tourneur's tragedy to Shakespeare: J. J. Lawlor in "The Tragic Conflict in *Hamlet*," *RES* 1 (1950): 97-113, suggests that both *The Atheist's Tragedy* and *The Revenge of Bussy D'Ambois* reflect Shakespeare's handling of the problem of delay, but that, whereas Tourneur and Chapman make the conflict between the duty of revenge and justice explicit, Shakespeare makes his hero "call in question all things under the sun *except* the duty that is enjoined upon him." S. L. Bethell compares D'Amville and Iago as characters who reject divine providence and who are diabolically inspired in "Shakespeare's Imagery: The Diabolic Images in *Othello*," *ShS* 5 (1952): 62-80. Carolyn S. French sees a connection between *King Lear* and *The Atheist's Tragedy* in the treatment of the paradox of wisdom in foolishness ("Shakespeare's 'Folly': *King Lear*," *SQ* 10 [1959]: 523-29). In "Time, Providence, and Tragedy in *The Atheist's Tragedy* and *King Lear*," *EM* 23 (1972), 55-74, G. F. Waller illustrates Tourneur's conformity with Protestant solutions to the problem of reconciling evil with divine justice and contrasts this with Shakespeare's more profound handling of the issue. See also Levin L. Schücking, "Eine Anleihe Shakespeares bei Tourneur" (I,B).

No major source for *The Atheist's Tragedy* is known. Ribner's Revels edition (III,E) provides the best discussion of the problem. Jackson I. Cope and Robert Ornstein suggest sources for different incidents. Cope in "Tourneur's *Atheist's Tragedy* and the Jig of 'Singing Simpkin,'" *MLN* 70 (1955): 571-73, rejects Boccaccio and puts forward a contemporary jig as being closer to the scene (II.v) in which Levidulcia manages the escape of Sebastian and Fresco from her bedchamber (see Ribner's edition for objections). Ornstein in *"The Atheist's Tragedy," N&Q* 2 (1955): 284-85, thinks Tourneur may have been influenced by the account of Marlowe's death in Thomas Beard's *The Theatre of God's Judgement* for the incredible scene in which D'Amville knocks out his own brains.

B. OVER-ALL STATE OF CRITICISM

Appreciation of Tourneur's plays has grown markedly in recent years. Generally speaking, the quality of criticism has increased with quantity. Too many critics have used perceptions about *The Revenger's Tragedy*, often valid in themselves, as weapons in the argument over authorship. Modern critical perspective has lessened the emphasis on Tourneur's moral pessimism and psychological horror and seen the plays less as expressions of the author's immaturity or neurosis than as non-naturalistic, symbolic structures, didactic and religious in purpose and traditional in thought and feeling. Very recently readings of Tourneur as a dramatist of the absurd or irrational strains in human experience have been gaining ground. There has been detailed analysis of Tourneur's poetry, irony, dramatic structure, and moral outlook; with a heightened awareness of such influences as the medieval morality plays, the attitude *de contemptu mundi*, Calvinistic theology, and the traditions of Renaissance satire, we have learned to judge Tourneur's significance more historically and objectively. The volume of critical activity and the scholarly editions of both plays suggest that Tourneur has been better served than almost any other dramatist of the period save Shakespeare.

III. CANON

A. PLAYS IN CHRONOLOGICAL ORDER

The chronology and type of play are from Alfred Harbage, *Annals of English Drama, 975-1700*, rev. Samuel Schoenbaum (1964); the acting date appears in italics, followed by the date of the earliest authoritative edition. W. W. Greg describes the quartos in *A Bibliography of the English Printed Drama to the Restoration,* 4 vols. (1939-59). E. K. Chambers treats the canon in *The Elizabethan Stage,* 4 vols. (1923).

The Revenger's Tragedy, tragedy *(1606-7;* 1607 [or 1608])

The tragedy was entered in the Stationers' Register by the printer George Eld on 7 October 1607 in conjunction with *A Trick to Catch the Old One.* Both plays were immediately printed without designation of author. Some copies of *The Revenger's Tragedy* bear a title page dated 1607, but this was corrected while the play was still in press to 1608. All the copies of *A Trick* are dated 1608, but the sheets of Middleton's comedy were reissued the same year with a new title page ascribing it to "T.M." and referring to performances at Paul's, Blackfriars, and court. The title page of *The Revenger's Tragedy* advertises that play as having *"beene sundry times Acted, by the Kings Maiesties Seruants."* Proponents of the theory that Middleton wrote both plays have often cited the publicationary link and even suggested, despite the evidence of the title pages, that the same company acted both. Borrowings, echoes, and influences in *The Revenger's Tragedy* from very recent plays (by Middleton, Marston, Shakespeare, and others) make 1605-1606 the likeliest date of composition (see Foakes's Revels edition).

The dispute over the authorship of this play is notorious. Since neither the Stationers' Register nor the 1607-08 title page mentions an author, the tragedy remained anonymous until it was attributed to "Tournour" by Edward Archer in a list of plays appended to *The Old Law* (1656) and to "Cyrill Tourneur" by Francis Kirkman in similar lists printed with *Tom Tyler and His Wife* (1661) and *Nicomede* (1671). Though unreliable, these lists were accepted uncritically for two centuries as establishing Tourneur's claim. Then Frederick Gard Fleay in *A Biographical Chronicle of the English Drama, 1559-1642,* 2 vols. (1891), suggested that *The Revenger's Tragedy* was "far superior to anything Turner (judging from his known writings) could have produced" and pronounced its meter "purely Websterian." In *Cyril Tourneurs Stellung in der Geschichte des englischen Dramas* (1918), Paul Wenzel hesitantly detected the voice of Marston in the tragedy, but E. H. C. Oliphant raised the question of authorship to new urgency by proposing Middleton—at first uncertainly in "Problems of Author-ship in Elizabethan Dramatic Literature," *SP* 8 (1911): 411-59, and then with greater conviction in "The Authorship of *The Revenger's Tragedy,*" *SP* 23 (1926): 157-68. Since Oliphant's second essay, scholarly opinion has settled down to a steady tussle between Tour-neurians and Middletonians.

Samuel Schoenbaum, a former convert to the Middletonians, accu-rately sums up our present state of knowledge: "the external evidence does not sweep all before it, and the situation, as it stands, is that neither Middleton's nor Tourneur's advocates have been able to bring forward the kind of proof to which one party or the other must submit. Hence the seemingly endless exchanges of replies and counter-replies in our journals" ("Internal Evidence and the Attribution of Elizabethan Plays," *BNYPL* 65 [1961]: 102-24). Marshalling the evidence for Middleton, Schoenbaum summarized the previous scholarship in *Middleton's Tragedies* (II,B) and, after revising his opinion in the article quoted above, again surveyed the scholarship as a cautionary tale in *Internal Evidence and Elizabethan Dramatic Authorship: An Essay in Literary History and Method* (1966). Concise accounts of the authorship debate appear in the editions of *The Revenger's Tragedy* by Foakes and Ross (III,E).

The most "scientific" attempt to press the claim for Middleton is Peter B. Murray's "The Authorship of *The Revenger's Tragedy,*" *PBSA* 56 (1962): 195-218, rpt. in *A Study of Cyril Tourneur* (I,B). Murray's argument rests chiefly upon an extensive application of the test of colloquial contractions and uses statistical tables to present average and actual incidences of various linguistic forms in plays by Middleton and Tourneur and in other plays issued by the respective printers of *The Revenger's Tragedy* and *The Atheist's Tragedy*. The weaknesses of Murray's method are pointed out in important reviews by W. T. Jewkes, "The Nightmare of Internal Evidence in Jacobean Drama," *Seventeenth-Century News* 24 (1966): 4, 6-8, and by G. R. Proudfoot, *N&Q* 14 (1967): 233-37; his case remains unproved.

For additional studies of the attribution problem and attempted resolution (in chronological order), see the following:

For Middleton: H. N. Hillebrand, "Thomas Middleton's *The Viper's Brood,*" *MLN* 42 (1927): 35-38; E. H. C. Oliphant, "Tourneur and *The Revenger's Tragedy,*" *TLS,* 18 Dec. 1930, p. 1087, and 5 Feb. 1931, p. 99; Wilbur D. Dunkel, "The Authorship of *The Revenger's Tragedy,*" *PMLA* 46 (1931): 781-85; Bernard M. Wagner, "Cyril

Tourneur," *TLS,* 23 April 1931, p. 327; Fred L. Jones, "Cyril Tourneur," *TLS,* 18 June 1931, p. 487; E. H. C. Oliphant, "Tourneur and Mr. T. S. Eliot," *SP* 32 (1935): 546-52; Marco K. Mincoff, "The Authorship of *The Revenger's Tragedy," Studia Historico-Philologica Serdicensia* 2 (1939): 1-87; Richard H. Barker, "The Authorship of *The Second Maiden's Tragedy* and *The Revenger's Tragedy," ShAB* 20 (1945): 51-62, 121-33; Samuel Schoenbaum, "*The Revenger's Tragedy* and Middleton's Moral Outlook," *N&Q* 196 (1951): 8-10; Alfred Harbage, *Shakespeare and the Rival Traditions* (1952); C. L. Barber, "A Rare Use of the Word *Honour* as a Criterion of Middleton's Authorship," *ES* 38 (1957): 161-68; Richard H. Barker, *Thomas Middleton* (1958); William Power, "Middleton's Way with Names," *N&Q* 7 (1960): 26-29, 56-60, 95-98, 136-40, 175-79; George R. Price, "The Authorship and the Bibliography of *The Revenger's Tragedy," Library* 15 (1960): 262-77; MacD. P. Jackson, "Affirmative Particles in *Henry VIII," N&Q* 9 (1962): 374; David L. Frost, *The School of Shakespeare* (1968); Sanford Sternlicht, "Tourneur's Imagery and *The Revenger's Tragedy," Papers on Language and Literature* 6 (1970): 192-97; D. J. Lake, "*The Revenger's Tragedy*: Internal Evidence for Tourneur's Authorship Negated," *N&Q* 18 (1971): 455-56.

For Tourneur: H. Dugdale Sykes, "Cyril Tourneur: *The Revenger's Tragedy; The Second Maiden's Tragedy," N&Q* 5 (1919): 225-29; T. S. Eliot, "Cyril Tourneur," *TLS,* 13 Nov. 1930, pp. 925-26, and "Tourneur and *The Revenger's Tragedy," TLS,* 1 Jan. 1931, p. 12; Una Ellis-Fermor, "The Imagery of *The Revengers Tragedie* and *The Atheists Tragedie," MLR* 30 (1935): 289-301; Harold Jenkins, "Cyril Tourneur," *RES* 17 (1941): 21-36; Thomas Marc Parrott and Robert Hamilton Ball, *A Short View of Elizabethan Drama* (1943); Henry Hitch Adams, "Cyril Tourneur on Revenge," *JEGP* 48 (1949): 72-87; R. A. Foakes, "On the Authorship of *The Revenger's Tragedy," MLR* 48 (1953): 129-38; Frank W. Wadsworth, "*The Revenger's Tragedy,*" *MLR* 50 (1955): 307; Inga-Stina Ekeblad, "A Note on *The Revenger's Tragedy," N&Q* 2 (1955), 98-99; Henri Fluchère, ed., *La tragédie du vengeur* (1958); Inga-Stina Ekeblad, "An Approach to Tourneur's Imagery," *MLR* 54 (1959): 489-98, and "On the Authorship of *The Revenger's Tragedy," ES* 41 (1960): 225-40; Irving Ribner, *Jacobean Tragedy* (1962).

Also of interest are: G. E. Bentley, "Authenticity and Attribution in the Jacobean and Caroline Drama," *English Institute Annual, 1942* (1943), pp. 101-18; W. W. Greg, "Authorship Attribution in the Early

Play-Lists, 1656-1671," *Edinburgh Bibliographical Society Transactions* 2 (1938-45): 305-29; Francis Berry, "Pronouns in *The Revenger's Tragedy"* in his *Poets' Grammar: Person, Time, and Mood in Poetry* (1958), pp. 80-86; Allardyce Nicoll, *"The Revenger's Tragedy* and the Virtue of Anonymity," in *Essays on Shakespeare and the Elizabethan Drama in Honor of Hardin Craig,* ed. Richard Hosley (1962), pp. 309-16.

The issue of the canonicity of *The Revenger's Tragedy* cries out for fresh external evidence. Until it can be produced, solution of the difficulties is not likely.

The Atheist's Tragedy, or The Honest Man's Revenge, tragedy (*1607-11*; 1611 [or 1612])

Early historians and editors tended to date this play well before 7 October 1607, when Eld entered *The Revenger's Tragedy* in the Stationers' Register. Their arguments rested on an allusion in the play (II.i.40-94) to the siege of Ostend (1601-4), the possibility of a reference to Sir Francis Vere's illness in August 1602 (I.ii.108-15), and the belief that Tourneur's lesser artistic achievement must have preceded his greater. More recent scholarship, stressing Tourneur's probable indebtedness to Shakespeare's *King Lear* (1606-7) and to Chapman's *Revenge of Bussy D'Ambois* (ca. 1610), has tended to favor a later date, 1610 or 1611 (see Ribner's edition).

The entry in the Stationers' Register is dated 14 September 1611. The tragedy immediately appeared in quarto with a title page claiming that *"in diuers places it hath often beene Acted."* Some copies of the first edition carry 1611 on their title pages, but the date was altered during the printing to 1612.

B. UNCERTAIN ASCRIPTIONS; APOCRYPHA; INFLUENCE

The Life of Timon of Athens, tragedy (*ca. 1606-8*; 1607 and 1623 [folio])

F. G. Fleay attributed the secondary authorship of Shakespeare's play to Tourneur on the "evidence of general style" in *Shakespeare Manual* (1876). H. Dugdale Sykes denied the part-authorship (*Sidelights on Elizabethan Drama* [1924]), and since then the claim has been universally repudiated.

The Second Maiden's Tragedy, tragedy (*1611*; MS)

This anonymous play (written for the King's Men and licensed 31 October 1611) survives in a unique manuscript at the British Museum. It has been attributed to Chapman, Tourneur, Middleton, and Massinger, invariably (and inconclusively) on the basis of evidence that is almost totally internal. Tourneur's claim rests wholly on certain similarities of plot, style, and theme which the play shares with *The Revenger's Tragedy,* and since the authorship of the latter play is also in doubt, the ascription must remain conjectural. H. Dugdale Sykes argued for Tourneur in "Cyril Tourneur: *The Revenger's Tragedy; The Second Maiden's Tragedy,*" *N&Q* 5 (1919): 225-29, but Sykes himself had second thoughts about this essay and excluded it from his *Sidelights on Elizabethan Drama* (1924). Allardyce Nicoll was not sufficiently impressed to include the play in his edition of Tourneur's *Works* (1929). Richard H. Barker in "The Authorship of *The Second Maiden's Tragedy* and *The Revenger's Tragedy,*" and again in *Thomas Middleton* (III,A), argued that both plays are by Middleton; he was supported by Samuel Schoenbaum in *Middleton's Tragedies* (1955), but Schoenbaum later admitted in *Internal Evidence and Elizabethan Dramatic Authorship* (1966) that he had "attached insufficient weight" to the significance of scribal corrections and revisions in the manuscript. Summaries of previous scholarship are supplied by Schoenbaum (see both *Middleton's Tragedies* and *Internal Evidence*) and by Leonora Leet Brodwin in "Authorship of *The Second Maiden's Tragedy*: A Reconsideration of the Manuscript Attribution to Chapman," *SP* 63 (1966): 51-77. The best edition is by W. W. Greg (1909) for the Malone Society. See also Harold L. Stenger, Jr., ed., "*The Second Maiden's Tragedy*: A Modernized Edition with an Introduction," Ph. D. dissertation, Univ. of Pennsylvania, 1954.

The Nobleman, tragicomedy (*1612*; lost)

This "tragicomedy," written by "Cyrill Tourneur," and entered in the Stationers' Register on 15 February 1611/12 and again on 9 September 1653 (where it is subtitled *The Great Man*), may have perished at the hands of Warburton's cook (see W. W. Greg, "The Bakings of Betsy," *Library* 2 [1911]: 225-59). The play was acted by the King's players at court on 23 February 1612, and later at the Christmas season of 1612-13. Nicoll prints some incidental music probably used for performances in 1612 (*Works*).

The Arraignment of London, comedy? (*1613*; lost)

A letter dated 5 June 1613 from Robert Daborne to Philip Henslowe records that Daborne gave "Cyrill Tourneur an act of yᵉ Arreignment of London to write" (see W. W. Greg, ed., *The Henslowe Papers* [1907]). The play, in the repertory of the Princess Elizabeth's Company, is probably to be identified with *The Bellman of London,* another lost play mentioned in Henslowe's papers and perhaps founded on Thomas Dekker's tract, *The Bellman of London,* or its sequel, *Lanthorn and Candlelight, or the Bellman's Second Night'swalk* (both 1608). See Nicoll's edition of the *Works.*

The Honest Man's Fortune, tragicomedy (*1613*; 1647 and MS)

This tragicomedy, which presents one of the most complex authorial problems of the entire Beaumont and Fletcher canon, exists in two versions: in a manuscript at the Victoria and Albert Museum, London, and in the folio of 1647. It has been variously divided up among several dramatists including, at times, Tourneur. Adducing resemblances to *The Atheist's Tragedy,* E. H. C. Oliphant, *The Plays of Beaumont and Fletcher* (1927), gives Tourneur Acts I and II.i and iii; the remainder he divides among Field, Fletcher, and Massinger. Bernard M. Wagner supports the part-attribution to Tourneur on the evidence of characteristic spellings ("Cyril Tourneur," *TLS,* 23 April 1931, p. 327). J. Gerritsen in his critical edition of the play (1952) concludes on the basis of metrical and grammatical tests that Tourneur wrote Act I (he assigns the residue to Fletcher and Field). Cyrus Hoy, on the evidence of linguistic forms, rejects Tourneur's claim, probably correctly, in "The Shares of Fletcher and His Collaborators in the Beaumont and Fletcher Canon (IV)," *SB* 12 (1959): 91-116.

Poems

Two occasional poems probably by Tourneur were omitted from Nicoll's edition of the *Works* and added to the canon by Bernard M. Wagner, "Elizabethan Dramatists," *TLS,* 28 Sept. 1933, p. 651. The first, a six-line elegy "On the Death of a Child But One Year Old" has been printed by Alexander B. Grosart in "Literary Finds in Trinity College, Dublin, and Elsewhere," *Englische Studien* 26 (1899): 1-19. The signature is "Cecill Turner," which, as Wagner notes, may be a scribal error but, in any case, is an "appropriate transformation of Tourneur's Christian name to that of the house which he served and eulogized." The second poem, which Wagner assigns to Tourneur's "doubtful works," is a piece of eight seven-line stanzas entitled, "Of My Lady Anne Cecill, the Lord Burleigh's Daughter" signed "C.T." It is printed in "A Collection of Several Ingenious Poems and Songs" appended to *Le Prince D'Amour* (1660). Wagner points out that Tourneur's known association with other members of Lady Anne's family make the ascription very likely; he dates the poem before 1600.

Influence

A. R. Skemp, in his edition of *Nathanael Richards' Tragedy of Messalina* (1910), records several of Richards's imitations of *The Revenger's Tragedy*. In "A Note on *The White Devil*," *N&Q* 3 (1956): 99–100, Gustav Cross argues that Webster may have taken the title of his play from a line in *The Revenger's Tragedy* (III.v.153). David George, "The Problem of Middleton's *The Witch* and Its Sources," *N&Q* 14 (1967): 209–11, contends that Tourneur's *Atheist's Tragedy* furnished Middleton with part of the subplot.

C. CRITIQUE OF THE STANDARD EDITION

The single-volume edition of the *Works* by Allardyce Nicoll (1929) is not only the most complete but the only one to preserve the spelling of the original quartos. Though regrettably it omits the two occasional poems to which Bernard M. Wagner called attention (see III,B), it offers a generally reliable text, an introduction treating Tourneur's life and canon as a whole, and an appendix of textual footnotes (with variant readings) and literary-historical commentary. Although produced in the days before collation of multiple copies of the same edition had become standard practice, the text is conservatively and carefully treated. Emendation is kept to a minimum, though Nicoll has altered the original punctuation with some freedom. The annotations are slender. The only other "complete" edition, much inferior to Nicoll's, is *The Plays and Poems of Cyril Tourneur* (1878) in two volumes by John Churton Collins.

D. TEXTUAL STUDIES

The most important textual scholarship on both *The Revenger's Tragedy* and *The Atheist's Tragedy* is consolidated in the two Revels editions by Foakes and Ribner (III,E). Understandably, textual study of *The Revenger's Tragedy* has often been wedded to considerations of the disputed authorship (see III,A, above, especially Murray's *Study of Cyril Tourneur*). George R. Price examines the 1607 quarto bibliographically, treating spelling, punctuation, stage directions, act headings, and the like with "a prior conviction of Middleton's authorship" in "The Authorship and the Bibliography of *The Revenger's Tragedy*," *Library* 15 (1960): 262-77. A. T. Brissenden describes a British Museum copy of Q1 which contains annotations and textual alterations in the hand of Robert Dodsley, the editor of *A Select Collection of Old Plays* (1744) in "Dodsley's Copy-Text for *The Revenger's Tragedy* in his *Select Collection*," *Library* 19 (1964): 254-58. C. S. Napier in *"The Revenger's Tragedy,"* *TLS*, 13 March 1937, p. 188, and Clifford Leech in "A Speech-Heading in *The Revengers Tragædie*," *RES* 17 (1941): 335-36, both suggest that Q's Spurio is an error for Supervacuo at V.iii.53. Eugene M. Waith proposes a more radical solution to the difficulties in "The Ascription of Speeches in *The Revenger's Tragedy*," *MLN* 57 (1942): 119-21.

In "Cyril Tourneur: *Atheist's Tragedy*, Act IV, sc. i," *MLR* 16 (1921): 324, R. C. Bald corrects J. A. Symonds's interpretation of the musical term "laerg" (IV.i.52); J. C. Maxwell points out that two eighteenth-century reprints of *The Atheist's Tragedy*, unconsulted by Ribner and other modern editors, right some obvious errors in the 1611 quarto ("*The Atheist's Tragedy*, 1792 and 1794," *N&Q* 17 [1970]: 214-15).

Bernard M. Wagner, "Cyril Tourneur," *TLS*, 23 April 1931, p. 327, describes a Bodleian Library manuscript of Tourneur's "Character of Robert; late Earle of salisburie" (the only one which is signed "Cyrill Tourneur"), contrasts spelling habits in the manuscript of *The Honest Man's Fortune* with those in *The Revenger's Tragedy*, and draws attention to a ballad ("to the tune of O the wind, the winde and the Raine") to which Tourneur may allude in *Laugh and Lie Down* (1605). Samuel Tannenbaum, reexamining the signatures in various manuscripts of the *Character of Salisbury*, presents paleographical and other evidence to weaken the attribution to Tourneur in "A Tourneur Mystification," *MLN* 47 (1932): 141-43.

E. SINGLE-WORK EDITIONS OF THE PLAYS

The Revels edition of *The Revenger's Tragedy* by R. A. Foakes (1966), although it modernizes the spelling, is the first to deal seriously with the haphazard lineation and stage directions of the quarto. It offers a valuable introduction, a reliably conservative text, and an apparatus considerably fuller than Nicoll's (including reprints of the source material). At least for the present, it is the most authoritative. Two other useful editions are those by Lawrence J. Ross in the Regents Renaissance Drama Series (1966) and by Brian Gibbons in The New Mermaids (1967)—the first for its concise introduction and good text, the second for its revealing illustrations from the emblems and iconography of the period. A "popular" reprint of limited use has been prepared by James L. Rosenberg for the Chandler drama series (1962), and the play is freshly edited in three recent anthologies: Richard C. Harrier includes an old-spelling edition with important textual footnotes in *An Anthology of Jacobean Drama*, 2 vols. (1963), vol. 2; Gāmini Salgādo prints a modernized version with introductory material in his Penguin edition of *Three Jacobean Tragedies* (1965); and Arthur H. Nethercot surveys the critical and authorial controversies surrounding the play in his annotated and modernized text (*Stuart Plays*, ed. Arthur H. Nethercot, Charles R. Baskervill, and Virgil B. Heltzel [1971]).

Henri Fluchère has produced a bilingual edition, *La tragédie du vengeur* (1958); it contains a long introduction, a verse translation, and extensive notes. The play had twice earlier been translated into French— by Camille Cé and Henri Servajean in *Cyril Tourneur: "La tragédie de la vengeance" suivie de "La tragédie de l'athée"* (n.d., [1925]), and by Pierre Messiaen in *Théâtre anglais, moyen-age et XVIᵉ siècle* (1948). Pier Luigi Valente offers an Italian version, *La tragedia de vendicatore*, in *Teatro elisabettiano: raccolta di drammi a cura di Alfredo Obertello*, 2 vols. (1951), vol. 2. Weöres Sándor has translated the play into Hungarian as *A bosszúálló tragédiája* in *Angol reneszánsz drámák*, ed. Szenczi Miklós, 3 vols. (1961), vol. 2.

The Revels edition of *The Atheist's Tragedy* by Irving Ribner (1964) is more authoritative than Nicoll's despite its modernized orthography and punctuation. The text is based upon a collation of many copies of the quarto, a full introduction is provided, source material is reprinted in an appendix, and annotations are more ample and up to date than Nicoll's. The Scolar Press has issued a photographic facsimile of a copy of the 1611 quarto in the Bodleian Library (1969). There have been translations into Russian, French, and Italian: see I. A. Aksenov, *Tragedia ateista* in *Elisabetintsi* (1916); Camille Cé and Henri Servajean, *Cyril Tourneur: "La tragédie de la vengeance" suivie de "La tragédie de l'athée"* (n.d. [1925]); Ottiero Ottieri, *La tragedia dell' ateo* in *Teatro elisabettiano* (1948), ed. Mario Praz.

F. EDITIONS OF NONDRAMATIC WORKS

There is no separate edition of Tourneur's nondramatic works. Nicoll's edition includes them all except the two minor poems (see III,B, "Poems"). Ruth Wallerstein reprints Tourneur's *A Grief on the Death of Prince Henry* (in old spelling) in her *Studies in Seventeenth-Century Poetic* (1950).

IV. SEE ALSO

A. GENERAL

Aronstein, Philipp. *Das englische Renaissancedrama.* 1929.

Axelrad, A. José. *Un malcontent élizabéthain: John Marston.* 1955.

Baker, Herschel. *The Wars of Truth: Studies in the Decay of Christian Humanism in the Earlier Seventeenth Century.* 1952.

Bastiaenen, Johannes Adam. *The Moral Tone of Jacobean and Caroline Drama.* 1930.

Bridges-Adams, W. *The Irresistible Theatre.* 1957.

Brodwin, Leonora Leet. *Elizabethan Love Tragedy, 1587-1625.* 1971.

Brustein, Robert. "The Monstrous Regiment of Women: Sources for the Satiric View of the Court Lady in English Drama." In *Renaissance and Modern Essays Presented to Vivian de Sola Pinto in Celebration of His Seventieth Birthday,* ed. G. R. Hibbard (1966), pp. 35-50.

Cazamian, Louis. *The Development of English Humour.* 1952.

Clarkson, Paul S., and Clyde T. Warren. *The Law of Property in Shakespeare and the Elizabethan Drama.* 1942.

Courthope, W. J. *A History of English Poetry.* 1903.

Davril, Robert. *Le drame de John Ford.* 1954.

Dent, Robert W. "'Quality of Insight' in Elizabethan and Jacobean Tragedy," *MP* 63 (1966): 252-56.

D'Exideuil, Pierre. "Vengeance." *CS* 10 (1933): 67-74; rpt. in *Le théâtre élizabéthain* (1940), pp. 92-100.

Downer, Alan S. *The British Drama: A Handbook and Brief Chronicle.* 1950.

Evans, B. Ifor. *A Short History of English Drama.* 1948; rev. ed., 1965.

Forker, Charles R. "Love, Death, and Fame: The Grotesque Tragedy of John Webster." *Anglia* 91 (1973): 194-218.

Gassner, John. *Masters of the Drama.* 1940.

Holmes, Elizabeth. *Aspects of Elizabethan Imagery.* 1929.

Holzknecht, Karl J. *Outlines of Tudor and Stuart Plays, 1497-1642.* 1947. [*Revenger's Tragedy, Atheist's Tragedy*]

Hunter, G. K. "English Folly and Italian Vice." In *Jacobean Theatre*, SuAS, vol. 1 (1960), pp. 85-110.

Imai, Sachiko. "The Two Revenge Tragedies: Dramatic Failure in the Revengers." *Ochanomizu Univ. Studies in Arts and Culture* 25, part ii (1972): 49-64. [In Japanese; summary in English.]

Knight, G. Wilson. *The Golden Labyrinth: A Study of British Drama.* 1962.

Kurtz, Leonard P. *The Dance of Death and the Macabre Spirit in European Literature.* 1934.

Lagarde, Fernand. *John Webster.* 2 vols. 1968.

Leech, Clifford. *Shakespeare's Tragedies and Other Studies in Seventeenth-Century Drama.* 1950.

————. *The John Fletcher Plays.* 1962.

Lucas, F. L. *Seneca and Elizabethan Tragedy.* 1922.

Mackenzie, Agnes Mure. *The Playgoer's Handbook to the English Renaissance Drama.* 1927.

Manifold, J. S. *The Music in English Drama from Shakespeare to Purcell.* 1956.

Mincoff, Marco K. *Verbal Repetition in Elizabethan Tragedy.* 1944.

Nicoll, Allardyce. *British Drama: An Historical Survey from the Beginnings to the Present Time.* 1925; rev. ed. 1963.

————. "Passing over the Stage." *ShS* 12 (1959): 47-55.

————. *English Drama: A Modern Viewpoint.* 1968.

Nosworthy, J. M. "Music and its Function in the Romances of Shakespeare." *ShS* 11 (1958): 60-69. [Robert Johnson, composer for the King's Men from 1607 to 1616.]

Oras, Ants. *Pause Patterns in Elizabethan and Jacobean Drama: An Experiment in Prosody.* 1960.

Ottieri, Ottiero. "I personaggi negativi di Tourneur." *Inventario* 3 (Summer, 1950): 110-20.

Praz, Mario. *The Flaming Heart: Essays on Crashaw, Machiavelli, and Other Studies in the Relations between Italian and English Literature from Chaucer to T. S. Eliot.* 1958.

Putt, S. Gorley. "The Relevance of Jacobean Drama." *E&S* 23 (1970): 18-33.

Quéneau, Raymond. "Cyril Tourneur, dramaturge noir." *CS* 10 (1933): 207-9; rpt. in *Le théâtre élizabethain* (1940), pp. 268-71.

Quennell, Peter. *The Singular Preference: Portraits and Essays.* 1953.

Sanna, A. *Considerazioni sulla tragedia di C. Tourneur.* 1949.

Schelling, Felix E. *Elizabethan Playwrights: A Short History of the English Drama from Medieval Times to the Closing of the Theaters in 1642.* 1925.

Schwob, Marcel. "Cyril Tourneur, Tragic Poet." In his *Imaginary Lives*, trans. Lorimer Hammond (1924), pp. 191-200.

Sharpe, Robert Boies. *Irony in the Drama: An Essay on Impersonation, Shock, and Catharsis.* 1959.

Sinclair, Francis D. "The Jacobean Anguish." In his *Three Papers on Tragedy* (1960), pp. 5-12.

Smet, Robert de [Romain Sanvic]. *Le théâtre élisabéthain.* 1955.

Speaight, Robert. *Christian Theatre.* 1960.

Spencer, Theodore. "The Elizabethan Malcontent." In *Joseph Quincy Adams Memorial Studies,* ed. James G. McManaway et al. (1948), pp. 523–35.
Stavig, Mark. *John Ford and the Traditional Moral Order.* 1968.
Thomas, Sidney. *The Antic Hamlet and Richard III.* 1943.
Wilson, F. P. *Elizabethan and Jacobean.* 1945.

B. INDIVIDUAL PLAYS

The Revenger's Tragedy

Babb, Lawrence. *The Elizabethan Malady: A Study of Melancholia in English Literature from 1580 to 1642.* 1951.
Bradbrook, M. C. *The Growth and Structure of Elizabethan Comedy.* 1961.
Champion, Larry S. "Tourneur's *The Revenger's Tragedy* and the Jacobean Tragic Perspective." *SP* 72 (1975): 299–321.
Cookman, A. V. "Shakespeare's Contemporaries on the Modern English Stage." *SJ* 94 (1958): 29–41. [Production of *The Revenger's Tragedy* by The Marlowe Society.]
Fuzier, Jean. "La tragédie de vengeance élisabéthaine et le théâtre dans le théâtre." *Revue des sciences humaines* 145 (1972): 17–33.
Guha, P. K. *Tragic Relief.* 1932.
Howarth, R. G. "Who's Who in *The Revenger's Tragedy.*" In his *A Pot of Gillyflowers: Studies and Notes* (1964), pp. 70–71.
Kalem, T. E. [Review of *The Revenger's Tragedy* as performed by the Yale Repertory Theatre.] *Time,* 14 Dec. 1970, p. 63.
Mehl, Dieter. *The Elizabethan Dumb Show: The History of a Dramatic Convention.* 1966; German ed. 1964.
Muller, Herbert. *The Spirit of Tragedy.* 1956.
[Review of *The Revenger's Tragedy* as performed by The Royal Shakespeare Company.] *Times* (London), 6 Oct. 1966, p. 18.
Rylands, George. [Review of *The Revenger's Tragedy* as performed by The Marlowe Society.] *Spectator,* 12 March 1937, p. 471.
Stagg, Louis Charles. "Figurative Imagery in Revenge Tragedies by Three Seventeenth-Century Contemporaries of Shakespeare." *South Central Bulletin* 26, no. 4, (1966; pub. 1967): 43–50.

The Atheist's Tragedy

Beckingham, C. F. "Seneca's Fatalism and Elizabethan Tragedy." *MLR* 32 (1937): 434–38.
Higgins, Michael H. "The Convention of the Stoic Hero as Handled by Marston." *MLR* 39 (1944): 338–46.
———. "The Development of the 'Senecal' Man." *RES* 23 (1947): 24–33.
Reed, Robert Rentoul, Jr. *Bedlam on the Jacobean Stage.* 1952.
Smith, Grover. "Tourneur and *Little Gidding;* Corbière and *East Coker.*" *MLN* 65 (1950): 418–21.
Spens, Janet. *Elizabethan Drama.* 1922.

C. CANON AND TEXT

Feldman, Abraham. "Cyril Tourneur." *TLS*, 5 Aug. 1949, p. 505.
———. "Cyril Tourneur." *TLS*, 18 Aug. 1950, p. 517.
Maxwell, J. C. "Two Notes on *The Revenger's Tragedy*." *MLR* 44 (1949): 545.

D. EDITIONS

The Revenger's Tragedy

Gomme, A. H., ed. *Jacobean Tragedies*. 1969.
Harrison, G. B., ed. *The Revenger's Tragedy*. The Temple Dramatists. 1934.
Huston, Dennis J., and Alvin B. Kernan, eds. *Classics of the Renaissance Theater: Seven English Plays*. 1969.
Oliphant, E. H. C., ed. *Elizabethan Dramatists Other than Shakespeare*. 1931.
Rylands, George, ed. *Elizabethan Tragedy: Six Representative Plays (Excluding Shakespeare) Selected with an Introduction*. 1933.

The Atheist's Tragedy

Gomme, A. H., ed. *Jacobean Tragedies*. 1969.

ADDENDA

The following items which appeared too late for inclusion in the essay above deserve mention: a new annotated edition of *The Revenger's Tragedy* in *Drama of the English Renaissance*, ed. Russell A. Fraser and Norman Rabkin, 2 vols. (1976), vol. 2; yet another ascription of *The Revenger's Tragedy* to Middleton on the basis of a fresh and highly detailed examination of the play's linguistic forms in David J. Lake, *The Canon of Thomas Middleton's Plays: Internal Evidence for the Major Problems of Authorship* (1975); Leslie Sanders, "*The Revenger's Tragedy*: A Play on the Revenge Play," *Renaissance and Reformation* 10 (1974): 25–36; discussion of the amorous theme in plays by Tourneur and contemporaries in Charles R. Forker's "The Love-Death Nexus in English Renaissance Tragedy," *Shakespeare Studies* 8 (1975): 211–30.

SAMUEL DANIEL

William L. Godshalk

The Complete Works in Verse and Prose of Samuel Daniel, ed. Alexander Grosart, 5 vols. (1885-96; rpt. 1963), remains the standard edition.

I. GENERAL

A. BIOGRAPHICAL

Joan Rees's *Samuel Daniel: A Critical and Biographical Study* (1964) is a complete survey of Daniel's life and works. He was born in 1562 or 1563 and matriculated at Magdalen Hall, Oxford, in 1581. In 1592, he was in Lincolnshire at the home of Sir Edward Dymoke, with whom he had traveled on the Continent. Later in that year Daniel entered the service of the Pembrokes at Wilton, where he wrote *Delia* and *Rosamond,* which were dedicated to the Countess of Pembroke. After writing *Cleopatra* (1593-94), he left Wilton, and under the patronage of Fulke Greville and Charles Blount composed *Musophilus.* From 1604 to 1607 he was at court where he composed *Panegyrike Congratulatorie* and *The Vision of the Twelve Goddesses,* as well as *Philotas* and *The Queen's Arcadia.* After Blount's death in 1606, Daniel "seems to have entered into the Earl of Hertford's service at about the time of the production of *The Queenes Arcadia* in 1605." Retiring to a farm of the earl's, Daniel tried to finish the *Civil Wars* (1605-8). During his last years, he worked on the mask *Tethys' Festival,* the pastoral play *Hymen's Triumph,* and the prose *History of England.* His last poem, on the sickness of James Montague, Bishop of Winchester, was written in 1618. Daniel himself died in October 1619, and was buried on the 14th.

Rees offers a unified picture of Daniel as an artist. His tone is quiet, and "what he has to say does not immediately grip the imagination."

She underlines his ambivalence, "the duality of his apprehensions," which "goes without false simplification into his work, the faith in poetry and the doubt, the love of England and the historian's scepticism, the love of beauty and the distrust for the outside of things." She offers a select bibliography.

In his five biographical chapters, Pierre Spriet, *Samuel Daniel (1563-1619): sa vie, son oeuvre* (1969), reveals that Daniel was with Sir Edward Dymoke in Lincolnshire as early as 1588, and he contends that Daniel was in the service of the Pembrokes at Wilton from 1584 to 1588. Spriet deals comprehensively with Daniel's life, treating his family background, his youth and his years at Oxford and Paris, the influence of Florio and Bruno, and the years as a patronized poet.

A briefer sketch of Daniel's life and works is in Raymond Himelick's edition *Samuel Daniel's "Musophilus: Containing a General Defense of All Learning"* (1965). Mark Eccles, "Samuel Daniel in France and Italy," *SP* 34 (1937): 148-67, and Leslie Hotson, "Marigold of the Poets," *EDH* 17 (1938): 47-68, explore a rather obscure period in Daniel's life and his connection with Sir Edward Dymoke. Eccles notes that Daniel "went to France about December, 1585," and "in the spring of 1586 he took the first step towards a career in the foreign service by securing employment with the English ambassador at Paris, Sir Edward Stafford." Sometime after 1586 and before 1592, Daniel was probably in Italy with Dymoke. Eccles points out the Italian influence, especially Guarini, on Daniel's work. Hotson discusses a 1592 lawsuit in which Daniel's name is linked with Dymoke's.

Cecil Seronsy, "Daniel's *Panegyrike* and the Earl of Hertford," *PQ* 32 (1953): 342-44, presents some bibliographical evidence to suggest that Daniel met the earl and sought his patronage in 1603. Joan Rees, "Samuel Daniel and the Earl of Hertford," *N&Q* 5 (1958): 408, believes that, though Daniel may have sought the earl's patronage in 1603, it did not begin until 1605. She uses evidence from *The Queen's Arcadia* (ll. 2406-15) to support her claim. Patricia Thomson, "The Literature of Patronage, 1580-1630," *Essays in Criticism* 2 (1952): 267-84, senses that Daniel "retained his individuality" as a patronized poet; "the 'poetry of patronage' written by Daniel has a quiet steadiness lacking in Donne." J. W. Saunders, "Donne and Daniel," *Essays in Criticism* 3 (1953): 109-14, questions putting Donne and Daniel in the same category. Cecil Seronsy's "The Case for Daniel's Letter to Egerton Reopened," *HLQ* 29 (1965-66): 79-82, offers "some grounds for accepting its authenticity." The letter is printed by Grosart (vol. 1). If authentic, it "is of considerable value as a document of Daniel's relationships and activities and offers a testimony of his artistic intentions around 1602." Virgil B. Heltzel, "Sir Thomas Egerton as Patron," *HLQ* 11 (1948): 105-27, also touches on this question and on Egerton's patronage of Daniel. Cecil Seronsy's *Samuel Daniel* (1967) discusses the possible influence of John Florio, Tailboys Dymoke, Mary Sidney, and Hugh Sanford on the young poet. John Buxton, *Sir Philip Sidney and the English Renaissance* (1954; 2nd ed. 1964), contains a brief discussion.

B. GENERAL STUDIES OF THE PLAYS

Cecil Seronsy's *Samuel Daniel* (I,A) is a general study of Daniel's work, containing separate chapters on the plays, touching on every aspect of Daniel's literary career, and summing up the major contributions of scholarship. Daniel's career falls into two parts. "In the first age of poetry he had sung of love and 'passionate mischance,' and now he had successfully written of war, of 'tumultuous Broyles' [i.e., *The Civil Wars*], the theme of the mature poet. He was about to enter the second half of his career [in 1595], taking the lead among English poets in a variety of new forms." Seronsy believes that Daniel "had in a sense led the way in three aspects of English drama: French Senecan closet tragedy, the masque, and Italian pastoral. Although not spectacular, his achievement was distinctive and sometimes of high quality." The study concludes with a chapter on Daniel as "poet and thinker." Joan Rees, *Samuel Daniel* (I,A), deals with each of Daniel's plays and masks, but does not concentrate on them as separate elements in Daniel's literary career. Her study is closely tied to the vicissitudes of Daniel's biography. Pierre Spriet, *Samuel Daniel* (I,A), carefully scrutinizes the sources and the style of the plays and masks, commenting on such issues as originality and underlying intentions.

C. THE WORKS AT LARGE

May McKisack, "Samuel Daniel as Historian," *RES* 23 (1947): 226-43, describes Daniel's critical temper and historical imagination. Qualities of mind rather than depth of reading are Daniel's strong points as historian. Because of his "natural scepticism" he distrusts legends, although he is "one of the few Elizabethans to write of the Middle Ages with a sense of loss." His work also reveals his historical interest in law and justice. William Blissett, "Samuel Daniel's Sense of the Past," *ES*

38 (1957): 49-63, emphasizes that Daniel's imagination was stimulated by history's "pattern and moral significance"; Daniel "had a 'sense of the past'—of its opportunities and pitfalls, its lessons for the present, its place in the continuity of history." In the *Civil Wars*, "Daniel is less a chronicler than a commentator." What he loses in immediacy, he gains in perspective and historical irony.

Cecil Seronsy, "The Doctrine of Cyclical Recurrence and Some Related Ideas in the Works of Samuel Daniel," *SP* 54 (1957): 387-407, feels that Daniel is preeminently a meditative poet, and he sets out "(1) to sketch the background and possible origins of Daniel's particular brand of cyclical theory, (2) to present the precise nature of his ideas on recurrence and the way in which he artistically utilizes these ideas, and (3) to show the extent to which the cyclical theory supports his attitudes towards tragedy, fame, and literary history—all given great prominence in his work." Arthur B. Ferguson, "The Historical Thought of Samuel Daniel: A Study in Renaissance Ambivalence," *JHI* 32 (1971): 185-202, carefully traces Daniel's philosophy of history and his various theories through the *Civil Wars, Defence of Ryme,* and *History of England.* Rudolf B. Gottfried, "Samuel Daniel's Method of Writing History," *SRen* 3 (1956): 157-74, investigates Daniel's use of *L'Histoire et cronique de Normandie* (1581). "Daniel frequently uses more than one of his sources in a single episode, and he not only sews them together, as he says, but he condenses, amalgamates, and interprets his material into a narrative which is characteristically his own."

In "The Authorship of *A Breviary of the History of England*," *SP* 53 (1956): 172-90, Gottfried argues that the *Breviary* should be dated before 20 April 1612 and that the piece was not written by Raleigh; it is Daniel's brief sketch of the historical material which was later incorporated into the *History of England.* W. L. Godshalk, "Daniel's *History*," *JEGP* 63 (1964): 45-57, adds to Gottfried's argument and continues with a survey of Daniel's growth as a writer of history, touching on the structure of Daniel's prose history, his use of sources, and his sharp sense of historical perspective. The study ends with a consideration of Daniel's use of John Speed's *History of Great Britain* as a structural source for his history of Edward III. Daniel may have gone to other historians for the basis of his structure, but the reflections upon historic events are his own.

Joan Rees, *Samuel Daniel* (I,A), in her account of *The Civil Wars,* emphasizes Daniel's growing skepticism. "The whole movement of Daniel's thought about *The Civil Wars* over the years" is "towards a blurring of the distinctions between a 'right' side and a 'wrong' which at the outset had seemed clear-cut." Inhibited as a poet by the preconceived pattern of history imposed by Tudor propaganda, Daniel had to give up the project. In the prose *History,* things are different; the poet is subdued to the historian; "there are none of the uneasy tensions that occurred in *The Civil Wars* and Daniel is clearly much happier with this work than he was with the latter books of his poem." Spriet, *Samuel Daniel* (I,A), has a long section on Daniel as historian in which he deals with the poet's political thought, his relationship to earlier historians, and his deviations from historical fact in *The Civil Wars.* Joseph S. M. J. Chang, "Machiavellianism in Daniel's *The Civil Wars,*" *TSE* 14 (1965): 5-16, demonstrates how the Duke of York, Edward III, Henry V and others display the traits of a Machiavellian villain. Daniel, however, "refuses to make moral judgments not because he does not wish to cast the first stone, but because hs is aware of the political implication which follows from the decision to make a given figure consciously responsible for historical events." In "Daniel's *Civil Wars* and Lucan's *Pharsalia,*" *SEL* 11 (1971): 53-68, George M. Logan attempts a precise demonstration of just how much Daniel modeled his work on that of Lucan. Bolingbroke is identified with Lucan's Caesar, Richard II with Pompey. Other overt similarities are pointed out, as well as scattered reminiscences.

Laurence Michel and Cecil Seronsy, "Shakespeare's History Plays and Daniel: An Assessment," *SP* 52 (1955): 549-77, consider Daniel as a source for Shakespeare and evaluate "evidence of mutual influence." Daniel was a shaping force in the development of Shakespeare's craftsmanship and conception of history. However, Shakespeare's influence on Daniel seems apparent in the 1609 edition of *The Civil Wars* in which he alters certain historical ideas following Shakespeare's lead. This material is incorporated into *The Civil Wars,* ed. Laurence Michel (1958). Joan Rees, "Shakespeare's Use of Daniel," *MLR* 55 (1960): 79-82, brings further evidence to show "how Shakespeare's craftsmanship may be illuminated by recognition of his source in Daniel." She compares *Civil Wars,* II.xv, with *Julius Caesar,* II.i.21-27, and *Civil Wars* I.xciv, with *Julius Caesar,* II.i.15-17; "these points of contact between *The Civil Wars* and *Julius Caesar* serve to illuminate some of the trains of thought in Shakespeare's mind at the time of writing and to illustrate the way in which his study of English history influenced his treatment of Roman history." In this context, see Matthew W. Black, "The Sources of Shakespeare's *Richard II,*" in

Joseph Quincy Adams Memorial Studies, ed. James G. McManaway et al. (1948), pp. 199-216, and Peter Ure, ed., *Richard II* (1956). C. A. Greer, "Did Shakespeare Use Daniel's *Civile Warres*?" *N&Q* 196 (1951): 53-54, argues against the indebtedness of Shakespeare's *Richard II* to Daniel. Charles Knight, *Works of Shakespere* (1838-45), "was first to suggest that Shakespeare used Daniel's *Civile Warres* of 1595 as a source . . . and his suggestion has been almost universally accepted." There are no verbal reminiscences of Daniel in Shakespeare, and certain allusions in Shakespeare are not found in Daniel. Their treatments of history are "completely different."

For the complicated textual background of *The Civil Wars,* see James G. McManaway, "Some Bibliographical Notes on Samuel Daniel's *Civil Wars,*" *SB* 4 (1951-52): 31-39, who discusses the printing and publishing of the first five books; Laurence Michel's "Introduction" to his edition (above); W. L. Godshalk, "Samuel Daniel and Sir Peter Leigh," *N&Q* 11 (1964): 333-34; Cecil Seronsy, "Daniel's Manuscript *Civil Wars* with Some Previously Unpublished Stanzas," *JEGP* 52 (1953): 153-60 and his correction of that article, *JEGP* 52 (1953): 594; and Cecil Seronsy and Robert Krueger, "A Manuscript of Daniel's *Civil Wars,* Book III," *SP* 63 (1966): 157-62.

The imagery of *The Civil Wars* is touched on by Laurence Michel, "'Sommers Heate' Again," *N&Q* 195 (1950): 292-93, who questions the meaning of Daniel's Book VI, stanza 10 and especially "*Mountioyes* solitarie rest,/ Be'ing checkt with Sommers heate." There may be a pun involved which hints at trouble between Edward Somerset and Mountjoy. Several items concern Daniel as historical poet: George Burke Johnston, "Camden, Shakespeare, and Young Henry Percy," *PMLA* 76 (1961): 298, with a reply by Laurence Michel and a rejoinder by Johnston, "Camden, Daniel, and Shakespeare," *PMLA* 77 (1962): 510-12; Homer Nearing, Jr., *English Historical Poetry, 1599-1641* (1945); Louis R. Zocca, *Elizabethan Narrative Poetry* (1950); E. M. W. Tillyard, *The English Epic and Its Background* (1954) and *Shakespeare's History Plays* (1959).

Daniel's poetry in general is discussed by Rees, *Samuel Daniel* (I,A). Cecil Seronsy, "Well-Languaged Daniel: A Reconsideration," *MLR* 52 (1957): 481-97, examines "the specific ingredients of Daniel's style as a poet." There are introductions in Peter Ure's "Two Elizabethan Poets: Samuel Daniel and Sir Walter Ralegh," in *The Age of Shakespeare* (1955; vol. 2 of the Pelican *Guide to English Literature,* ed. Boris Ford), pp. 131-46, C. S. Lewis's *English Literature in the Sixteenth*

Century (1954), and Douglas Bush's *English Literature in the Earlier Seventeenth Century* (1945; 2nd ed. 1962).

J. W. Lever, *The Elizabethan Love Sonnet* (1956; 2nd ed. 1966), discusses Daniel's use of Ronsard and Tasso. Lever feels that Daniel "should be credited with two major contributions to the formal development of the late Elizabethan sequence." Daniel uses metaphoric imagery as a structuring device to bind together groups of sonnets within the series, and he realizes the latent potential in Surrey's verse form. Lloyd Goldman, "Samuel Daniel's *Delia* and the Emblem Tradition," *JEGP* 67 (1968): 49-63, illustrates, through a critical analysis, how Daniel blended the form and content of his sonnets. "The principles of the English sonnet as Daniel exploited them also verbally contained the five specific properties of an impresa." Daniel's "Petrarchan sonnets are verbalized emblems," and the emblem tradition was the "inspiration that controlled the conceits" in Daniel's sequence. Distinguishing between emblem and impresa, Joseph Kau, "Daniel's *Delia* and the *Imprese* of Bishop Paolo Giovio: Some Iconological Influences," *JWCI* 33 (1970): 325-28, argues that "what can be definitely shown in the sonnets is Daniel's debt to *imprese* which stress wit and simple thoughts like love rather than *emblemi* which emphasize plain statement and sententiae." Kau finds Giovio's influence in several of Daniel's sonnets. Assessing Daniel's sonnets eternizing Delia, Kau, *"Delia's* Gentle Lover and the Eternizing Conceit in Elizabethan Sonnets," *Anglia* 92 (1974): 334-48, "reveals the way in which Daniel refines the Petrarchan sonnet tradition."

F. T. Prince, "The Sonnet from Wyatt to Shakespeare," in *Elizabethan Poetry*, SuAS, vol. 2 (1960), pp. 11-29, believes that Sonnets 30 to 36 are "unmistakably Shakespeare's inspiration for many of the earlier sonnets in his own book," and investigates Daniel's techniques. In the same volume, see R. G. Rees's "Italian and Italianate Poetry," pp. 52-69. Claes Schaar, *An Elizabethan Sonnet Problem: Shakespeare's Sonnets, Daniel's "Delia," and Their Literary Background* (1960), examines the sonnet sequences against their continental literary background, questions Daniel's influence on Shakespeare, and indicates the possibility of the direct opposite of Prince's theory. J. B. Leishman, *Themes and Variations in Shakespeare's Sonnets* (1961), also discusses Daniel's sonnets in relation to Shakespeare's.

C. F. Williamson, "The Design of Daniel's *Delia*," *RES* 19 (1968): 251-60, gives a word analysis to demonstrate that the sequence falls into two parts. In the first, Daniel projects, through his use of language, "the poet's despair" and Delia's "domination"; in the second, Delia's beauty is "transient" and Time becomes the "tyrant." In the last two sonnets, Daniel returns to despair and humility. Diethild Bludau, "Sonettstruktur bei Samuel Daniel," *SJ* 94 (1958): 63–89, finds the greatness of Daniel's sonnets in "die Verbindung von Form und Bewegung, Sinn und Zeit zur Sinnbewegung." Patricia Thomson's "Sonnet 15 of Samuel Daniel's *Delia*: A Petrarchan Imitation," *CL* 17 (1965): 151–57, points out that *Delia* "presents a difficult case of mixed Italian and French influences modified by an English genius." Theodore C. Hoepfner, "Daniel's *Delia,* Sonnet XL," *Expl* 6 (1952): item 38, gives an explanatory paraphrase, while Claes Schaar, "A Textual Puzzle in Daniel's *Delia,*" *ES* 40 (1959): 382–85, argues that Berardino Rota may have influenced Daniel's imagery. Edwin Haviland Miller, "Samuel Daniel's Revisions in *Delia,*" *JEGP* 53 (1954):58–68, points out that *Delia* was printed four times and revised thrice; the results are "a diminution of youthful romantic fervor and a pallid conventionalization of his lines."

Virgil B. Heltzel, *Fair Rosamond: A Study of the Development of a Literary Theme* (1947), notes that Daniel contributes "at least three new features in one form or another." His comments are extended by Cecil Seronsy, "Daniel's *Complaint of Rosamond:* Origins and Influence of an Elizabethan Poem," *Lock Haven Bulletin,* ser. 1, no. 2 (1960), pp. 39–57, who suggests that "before the end of the century *Rosamond* had spent its force as an influence over narrative poetry." Ira Clark, "Samuel Daniel's *Complaint of Rosamond,*" *Renaissance Quarterly* 23 (1970): 152–62, discusses the mythological embellishments of the work and describes several of Daniel's innovations. Ronald Primeau, "Daniel and the *Mirror* Tradition: Dramatic Irony in *The Complaint of Rosamond,*" *SEL* 15 (1975): 21–36, believes that there evolved in the "Mirror" tradition "an increase in consciously ironic treatment of psychology. These developments began as early as Sackville's contributions of 1563 . . . and reached maturity in Samuel Daniel's 1592 edition . . . of *The Complaint of Rosamond.*"

Joseph Kau, "Samuel Daniel and the Renaissance *Impresa*-makers: Sources for the First English Collection of *Imprese,*" *Harvard Library Bulletin* 18 (1970): 183–204, argues that the chapter containing twenty-six specific *imprese* appended to Daniel's translation, *The Worthy Tract of Paulus Iovius,* is not an original collection; the sources are Domenichi and Simeoni. In "Daniel's Influence on an Image in *Pericles* and Sonnet 73: An *Impresa* of Destruction," *SQ* 26 (1975):

51-53, Kau argues that the image of the down-turned torch in *Pericles* (II.ii. 32-35) and in Sonnet 73 is indebted to Daniel's impresa. Katherine Duncan-Jones, "Two Elizabethan Versions of Giovio's Treatise on Imprese," *ES* 52 (1971): 118-23, contends that Abraham Fraunce and Daniel were not original. Daniel's heading to his prefatory essay misleads one to believe that it is his own work; it is translated from Ruscelli's *Discorso*. She also notes that Daniel's supplementary chapter is indebted to Domenichi. Werner von Koppenfels, "Two Notes on *Imprese* in Elizabethan Literature: Daniel's Additions to *The Worthy Tract of Paulus Iovius*; Sidney's *Arcadia* and the Tournament Scene in *The Unfortunate Traveller*," *Renaissance Quarterly* (1971): 13-25, claims that Daniel used a French text, not the Italian original, in his translation of Giovio.

J. I. M. Stewart, "Montaigne's *Essays* and *A Defence of Ryme*," *RES* 9 (1933): 311-12, traces parallels and suggests that Daniel had read Montaigne thoroughly. Raymond Himelick, "Samuel Daniel, Montaigne and Seneca," *N&Q* 3 (1956): 61-64, feels that "doctrinally . . . Daniel stays closer to the Roman; and one suspects that Montaigne's growing naturalism provided some things to puzzle and disturb the poet's orthodoxy." In "Montaigne and Daniel's *To Sir Thomas Egerton*," *PQ* 36 (1957): 500-504, Himelick points out that "in 1603 Samuel Daniel prefaced the first edition of Florio's translation of Montaigne with lines indicative of warm admiration." Daniel uses the essayist "for material which allows him to combine earnest advice with adroit compliment."

Seneca also influenced some of the verse epistles. Ann Louise Hentz, "A Senecan Source for Samuel Daniel's Verse Epistle to Southampton," *N&Q* 9 (1962): 208-9, traces parallels with Seneca's *On Providence*. Martha Hale Shackford, "Samuel Daniel's Poetical *Epistles,* Especially That to the Countess of Cumberland," *SP* 45 (1948): 180-95, contains critical observations on Daniel's use of the epistolary form, along with comments on his style and on the biographical and literary backgrounds. Arthur Freeman, "An Epistle for Two," *Library* 25 (1970): 226-36, comments on Daniel's *Epistle to the Lady Margaret, Countess of Cumberland*. Freeman possesses the Hatton Manuscript of the poem which is copied in a "scribal secretary hand," but which has "marginal and interlined corrections and revisions almost certainly in Daniel's distinctive autograph." He argues that Daniel dedicated the poem a second time, this time to Elizabeth, widow of Sir William Hatton. Daniel's epistles are briefly touched on by Rees, *Samuel Daniel* (I,A).

For *Musophilus,* Rees, *Samuel Daniel* (I,A), gives a personal background. "The courtier-scholar of the Renaissance, the Humanist ideal, typified in Daniel's day by such men as Sidney and Essex and Mountjoy, lends warmth and colour to *Musophilus* but the sense of human sinfulness which was so strong in Greville has its place also in the poem." Raymond Himelick, "*A Fig for Momus* and Daniel's *Musophilus,*" *MLQ* 18 (1957): 247-50, notes that Hoby's translation of *The Courtier* has often been seen as a source for the poem. Greville's "redoubtable opposition to Daniel's optimistic humanism could have served as catalyst to this concretion of defense." See Geoffrey Bullough, ed., *Poems and Dramas of Fulke Greville, First Lord Brooke* (1939), vol. l. But most probably Lodge's inadequate presentation in the *Fig for Momus* influenced Daniel to write his fuller discussion. Himelick's edition, *Samuel Daniel's "Musophilus"* (I,A), has a thorough introduction. Irving Blum, "The Paradox of Money Imagery in English Renaissance Poetry," *SRen* 8 (1961): 144-54, notes that *Musophilus* and *The Complaint of Rosamond* make use of monetary and wealth imagery while at the same time disdaining "fruitlesse riches." After considering *Musophilus* as a critical piece, J. W. H. Atkins, *English Literary Criticism: The Renascence* (1947), concludes: "Of Daniel's place among the major Elizabethan critics there can . . . be no question."

Daniel's influence on English literature has been investigated. Anthony LaBranche, "Poetry, History, and Oratory: The Renaissance Historical Poem," *SEL* 9 (1969): 1-19, observes the influence of Daniel's *Rosamond* on Drayton's *Barons Warres.* "Samuel Daniel and Milton," *N&Q* 197 (1952): 135-36, by Cecil Seronsy, points to parallels between the *Civil Wars* and *Paradise Lost.* In "The Historical Sources of Patrick Hannay's *Sheretine and Mariana,*" *JEGP* 43 (1944): 242-47, N. T. Ting suggests Daniel as a source of Hannay's poem. Seronsy, "Wordsworth's Annotations in Daniel's *Poetical Works,*" *MLN* 68 (1953): 403-6, presents the manuscript notes and markings made by Wordsworth in the 1718 edition of Daniel's *Works*; in "Daniel and Wordsworth," *SP* 56 (1959): 187-213, Seronsy reveals that there are similarities of style and phraseology indicating direct influence. Joan Rees, "Wordsworth and Samuel Daniel," *N&Q* 6 (1959): 26-27, notes that Wordsworth quoted Daniel in *The Excursion* and compares Wordsworth's retrospective account of Godwinism in *The Prelude* (XI) with *Civil Wars,* VI, stanzas 35-36. Seronsy, "Coleridge Marginalia in Lamb's Copy of Daniel's *Poetical Works,*" *Harvard Library Bulletin* 7 (1953): 105-12, transcribes the notes made by Coleridge. Seronsy's "An

Autograph Letter by Swinburne on Daniel and Drummond of Hawthornden," *N&Q* 12 (1965): 303-4, indicates Swinburne's interest in Daniel. Raymond Himelick, "Thoreau and Samuel Daniel," *American Literature* 24 (1952-53): 177-85, notes that a critical appraisal of Daniel appears in Thoreau's commonplace book, and that, in *A Week on the Concord and Merrimack Rivers*, Thoreau quotes from *Philotas, Musophilus,* and *To the Lady Margaret, Countess of Cumberland.*

Samuel A. Tannenbaum's *Samuel Daniel: A Concise Bibliography* (1942) is reprinted in *Elizabethan Bibliographies*, vol. 2 (1967). George Robert Guffey's chronological listing for 1942-65 is included in *Elizabethan Bibliographies Supplements,* vol. 7 (1967), ed. Charles A. Pennel. Harry Sellers gives a primary bibliography in "A Bibliography of the Works of Samuel Daniel, 1585-1623: With an Appendix of Daniel's Letters," *Oxford Bibliographical Society Proceedings and Papers* 2 (1927-30): 29-54, with "Supplementary Note," pp. 341-42.

II. CRITICISM OF INDIVIDUAL PLAYS AND STATE OF SCHOLARSHIP

A. INDIVIDUAL PLAYS

Cleopatra

The relations between Daniel's *Cleopatra* and Shakespeare's *Antony and Cleopatra* result in *Cleopatra* receiving at least passing attention in most studies of the sources and influences of Shakespeare's play.

Joan Rees, *Samuel Daniel* (I,A), fills in the background of Daniel's first tragedy: i.e., Sidney's *Apology for Poetry, Gorboduc,* Garnier's *Marc-Antoine,* Jodelle's *Cléopâtre Captive,* and the classical atmosphere at Wilton. Daniel uses his sources with independence, emphasizing the conflict between "Cleopatra's instincts as a Queen and her instincts as a mother." After discussing the maternal conflict in the play, Rees concludes that Daniel has evolved "a closely integrated action," and has produced "a study of character remarkable for its sympathy and insight." The characteristics of the mature poet are already emerging, and "*Cleopatra* deserves much better than to be dismissed merely as an aberration from the path of true drama; in its relation to Daniel's career, it is a very important document."

Daniel rewrote his *Cleopatra* in 1607, and it has been thought that he worked under the influence of Shakespeare's *Antony and Cleopatra.*

Rees feels that the reasons for revision were to give the play greater "vitality and movement" than it had and "to show how the bounds of neo-classical drama could be enlarged beyond the narrow limits of the earlier Pembroke examples and yet remain uncontaminated by sensationalism and technical 'licence.'" Seronsy, *Samuel Daniel* (I,A), believes that it is "the best of the English Senecan group," and that Daniel did not use Shakespeare's play for the revision of *Cleopatra*: "(1) That portion of new material added to the 1607 revision of Daniel's play, material that might have been suggested by either Plutarch or Shakespeare, or both, is narrated rather than cast into dramatic form. (2) With the exception of the final scene . . . , those portions of the early version of Daniel's play that are converted into direct dramatic presentation are almost entirely elements of the story to which Shakespeare gave no attention."

Willard Farnham, *Shakespeare's Tragic Frontier: The World of His Final Tragedies* (1950), feels that Shakespeare was influenced by the earliest version of Daniel's play. Holger Nørgaard, "The Bleeding Captain Scene in *Macbeth* and Daniel's *Cleopatra*," *RES* 6 (1955): 395-96, suggests that the "spent swimmers" image in *Macbeth,* I,ii, was influenced by the similar image in *Cleopatra,* scene i. This parallel is further discussed by Joan Rees, "Shakespeare's Use of Daniel," *MLR* 55 (1960): 79-82. J. C. Maxwell, "'Rebel Powers': Shakespeare and Daniel," *N&Q* 14 (1967): 139, feels that the expression in the second line of Shakespeare's Sonnet 146 may have been taken from Daniel's *Cleopatra.*

The problem of mutual influence is also discussed by Arthur M. Z. Norman, "*The Tragedie of Cleopatra* and the Date of *Antony and Cleopatra*," *MLR* 54 (1959): 1-9, who summarizes the sceptical arguments of Johannes Schütze, "Daniels *Cleopatra* und Shakespeare," *Englische Studien* 71 (1936): 58-72. Norman notes that Schütze "damages the theory that Daniel's recasting and revitalization of scenes suggests the influence of Shakespeare," and he concludes: "*Antony and Cleopatra* was written some time in 1606 or 1607; Shakespeare's source was North's Plutarch, but he consulted and echoed one of the 1594-1605 editions of Daniel's *Cleopatra*. Daniel, who had already emerged from under the shadow of Senecan drama, witnessed a performance of Shakespeare's play and found in it the spur he needed to reconsider his early tragedy; thus the influence became reciprocal." In "Daniel's *The Tragedie of Cleopatra* and *Antony and Cleopatra*," *SQ* 9 (1958): 11-18, Norman contends that *Cleopatra* "provides an explanation of

Shakespeare's daring use of two climaxes and of his conception of Cleopatra as the embodiment of a love transcending worldly obligations." The case for Shakespeare having read Daniel rests upon a "number of verbal echoes," which in turn "raise the question of Daniel's influence upon Shakespeare in the greater parallels of character, content, and theme." "Shakespeare's Cleopatra, though she is the amoral, willful person described by Plutarch, is equally close to Daniel's heroine as the embodiment of an enduring passion."

Joan Rees, "An Elizabethan Eyewitness of *Antony and Cleopatra?*" *ShS* 6 (1953): 91-93, quotes Daniel's play (I.ii.238-64) and suggests that "the dramatic pauses and the picture of the suspended body [in "taffaty"] which give vividness and reality to Dircetus's story might be a reminiscence of the way the *Antony and Cleopatra* scene was actually managed by an imaginative company." Later, Rees (*Samuel Daniel,* I,A) changed her mind: "I now think that this explanation is less likely than" that Daniel was trying to revitalize the play by adding action descriptions. Ernest Schanzer, "Daniel's Revision of His *Cleopatra,*" *RES* 8 (1957): 375-81, extends the arguments of Schütze (above), contending that "most of the additions supposed to be inspired by Shakespeare's play are far more closely paralleled in *Antonius* [by Mary Sidney], and . . . there can be no doubt that it was this play rather than Shakespeare's that furnished Daniel with suggestions and much of the material for his revision." In an untitled letter to the editor, Joan Rees (*RES* 9 [1958]: 294-95) notes that not all Schanzer's assertions are correct, and feels that the Countess of Pembroke's account of Cleopatra's pulling Antony into the tomb did not influence Daniel. Both are vivid accounts, but "they are quite different from each other." Brents Stirling, "Cleopatra's Scene with Seleucus: Plutarch, Daniel, and Shakespeare," *SQ* 15, no. 2 (1964): 299-311 (also in *Shakespeare 400: Essays by American Scholars on the Anniversary of the Poet's Birth,* ed. James G. McManaway [1964], pp. 299-311), uses Daniel to discuss Shakespeare: "Daniel did follow Plutarch quite literally and Shakespeare knew Daniel's play. Hence any major difference between the two is likely to be significant. As an example of what Shakespeare strives not to do with Cleopatra, Seleucus, and Caesar, nothing serves better than Daniel's *Tragedie.*"

Joan Rees, "Samuel Daniel's *Cleopatra* and Two French Plays," *MLR* 47 (1952): 1-10, takes as her "standpoint for a re-examination of the *Cleopatra* a detailed study of Daniel's use of the two French treatments of his theme," and emphasizes "the life and humanity which inform" the play "and the artistic skill in handling material." Daniel uses Garnier's *Marc-Antoine* and Jodelle's *Cléopâtra Captive.* Rees suggests that Daniel's 1607 revision of the play was a "great mistake." Daniel's genius was for the "mature contemplation of event and character."

Philotas

Daniel's second tragedy was acted before the king by the Children of the Queen's Revels early in January 1605. Daniel was called before the privy council because of the play's possible reflection of the Essex affair, although it is possible to read the play without drawing parallels. Rees (*Samuel Daniel,* I,A) emphasizes the complexity of the characters, and concludes that "Daniel is describing the effects of fear and ambition in high places. . . . 'The frailty of greatnesse, and the usuall workings of ambition' are in a very full sense the themes of the play and the characterisation." *Philotas* is not "closet drama."

A general introduction to the play is found in Laurence Michel's edition (1949) which deals with the possible relationship of *Philotas* to the Essex revolt, the play's literary sources, its bibliographical history, and Daniel's revisions in the editions of 1607 and 1611. Michel believes that Daniel fully realized the parallels with Essex's ill-fated rebellion. Brents Stirling, "Daniel's *Philotas* and the Essex Case," *MLQ* 3 (1942): 583–94, reconstructs the case for the charges the privy council brought against Daniel.

Defending Daniel's innocence against Michel and Stirling, G. A. Wilkes, "Daniel's *Philotas* and the Essex Case: A Reconsideration," *MLQ* 23 (1962): 233–42, points out that Daniel was exonerated by the privy council. Wilkes feels that, "on the evidence available, the connection of *Philotas* with the Essex case cannot be proved with any more finality than it can be disproved." Daniel may imbue his play with ambivalence, but he does not consciously allegorize the Essex affair. Ernest William Talbert, *The Problem of Order: Elizabethan Political Commonplaces and an Example of Shakespeare's Art* (1962), admits that "Daniel manipulates the sources in at least three major incidents to place Philotas in a relatively favorable light." But *Philotas* is a "debate-like play" which deals with "conflicting aspects of certain ideas, with the conflicting relevance of political commonplaces, and with the conflicting interpretation of events." With Wilkes, Talbert finds that the play can be appreciated without direct reference to Essex. Although Seronsy (*Samuel Daniel,* I,A) believes that the "Essex affair does seem to have affected the structure of Daniel's play," he points out that it has general themes: "the limits of government and . . . the abuse of tyranny." J. C. Maxwell, "'Enjealous': An Antedating," *N&Q* 18 (1971): 286, reports that Michel's edition restores the verb "in-jealous" in line 23 of *Philotas* (1607).

The Queen's Arcadia

Joan Rees, *Samuel Daniel* (I,A), notes the Italian sources: the play is "Italianate pastoral drama" which Daniel contrived "perhaps as a deliberate counterstroke to the Jonsonian masque." The theme of the play is "the contrast between the demoralizing effects of sophistication and the wholesome goodness of simpler, less pretentious ways." It implies that "knowledge . . . unless allied to faith and to humanity, is a curse and not a blessing." Certain portions of the play may represent "a bout in a running battle with Jonson." Madeleine Doran, *Endeavors of Art: A Study of Form in Elizabethan Drama* (1954), feels that the play puts the pastoral convention to "the service of social criticism, not, perhaps, to be taken too seriously."

Kenneth Muir, *Shakespeare's Sources*, vol. 1 (1957), suggests this play may have influenced the language and imagery of *Macbeth*; *The Queen's Arcadia* was performed at Oxford in 1605 during a visit by King James and was possibly seen by Shakespeare at the time. Cecil Seronsy, "Shakespeare and Daniel: More Echoes," *N&Q* 7 (1960): 328–29, also believes this play influenced *Macbeth* and suggests that *Hamlet* may have provided Daniel with some images. Seronsy, *Samuel Daniel* (I,A), emphasizes the play's "harsh, satirical overtones." W. W. Greg's *Pastoral Poetry and Pastoral Drama: A Literary Inquiry, with Special Reference to the Pre-Restoration Stage in England* (1906), contains an analysis.

Hymen's Triumph

Daniel's second pastoral play has been highly praised. It was produced for the marriage of Robert Ker, Lord Roxborough, to Jean Drummond, a relative of William Drummond, who owned a manuscript copy of the play (see W. W. Greg, *"Hymen's Triumph* and the Drummond MS," *Modern Language Quarterly* [London] 6 [1903] : 59-64). Joan Rees, *Samuel Daniel* (I,A), feels that the play may have some relation to Jonson's *Sad Shepherd*. Noting that Daniel was especially adept at creating female characters, she suggests that "his delicacy and respect and intuitive sympathy contribute a great deal to the general atmosphere of *Hymens Triumph,* not only in Thirsis's formal defence but in the sweetness of the whole." Following Greg's evaluation in *Pastoral Poetry and Pastoral Drama* (above), Cecil Seronsy, *Samuel Daniel* (I,A), feels that the play is greatly superior to *The Queen's Arcadia* and bears "a good many traces of some of the earlier romantic comedies of Shakespeare," a point which he also makes in "Shakespeare and Daniel: More Echoes," *N&Q* 7 (1960): 328-29. Madeleine Doran, *Endeavors of Art* (above), feels that the play is "outside the main line of English drama." John P. Cutts, "Original Music to Browne's Inner Temple Masque, and Other Jacobean Masque Music," *N&Q* 1 (1954): 194-95, treats the original music for Daniel's play.

Tethys' Festival

This work has not been well liked. Joan Rees, *Samuel Daniel* (I,A), believes that, beyond its one good lyric ("Are they shadowes that we see?"), "only marginal interests can engage the modern reader." Cecil Seronsy, *Samuel Daniel* (I,A), passes rapidly over this mask. Thomas Gardner, "'A Parodie! A Parodie!': Conjectures on the Jonson-Daniel Feud," in *Lebende Antike: Symposion für Rudolf Sühnel,* ed. Horst Meller and Hans-Joachim Zimmermann (1967), pp. 197-206, reconstructs the court background of the mask and suggests that it is aimed at criticizing Ben Jonson.

The Vision of the Twelve Goddesses

Geoffrey Creigh, "Samuel Daniel's Masque *The Vision of the Twelve Goddesses,*" *E&S* 24 (1971): 322-35, touches on Daniel's use of the mask in general, recounts his feud with Jonson, but concentrates on *The Vision.* He feels that this mask "warrants greater respect than it has been paid."

B. OVER-ALL STATE OF CRITICISM

Daniel is not generally thought of as a dramatist. Although his lyric poetry and histories have been regarded with critical interest, the masks have been almost entirely neglected except in derogatory comparison to Jonson's, and the pastoral plays are usually passed over in silence. His tragedies have received most of the critical attention devoted to his drama. Work on Daniel is impeded by the lack of a reliable standard edition.

III. CANON

A. PLAYS IN CHRONOLOGICAL ORDER

This list follows Alfred Harbage, *Annals of English Drama, 975–1700*, rev. S. Schoenbaum (1964). There has been little controversy over the Daniel canon or its dating. See E. K. Chambers, *Elizabethan Stage* (1923), vols. 2 and 3, and W. W. Greg, *A Bibliography of the English Printed Drama to the Restoration*, 4 vols. (1939–59). The form of the following entries is name of the play, type, date of performance in italics, and the date of first publication.

Cleopatra, tragedy (*1593* [revised *1599* and *1607*] ; 1594)

Philotas, tragedy (*1604* [three acts written in *1600*] ; 1605)

The Vision of the Twelve Goddesses (The Masque at Hampton Court), mask (*8 Jan. 1604;* 1604)

The Queen's Arcadia (Arcadia Reformed); pastoral (30 Aug. 1605; 1606)

Tethys' Festival, or The Queen's Wake, mask (*5 June 1610*; 1610)

Hymen's Triumph, pastoral (*2 Feb. 1614;* 1615 and MS)

B. CRITIQUE OF THE STANDARD EDITION

The Complete Works in Verse and Prose of Samuel Daniel, ed. Alexander B. Grosart (1885–96; rpt. 1963), is textually weak, careless in incidental readings, and not fully reliable in substantial readings. Grosart's notes may be misleading: see Hibernicus, "Daniel: Stray Notes on the Text," *N&Q* 186 (1944): 6-8. This edition should be replaced.

C. SINGLE-WORK EDITIONS OF THE PLAYS

The Tragedy of Philotas (1949), ed. Laurence Michel, contains textual apparatus, annotations, and appendices. Helen L. Sampson, "A Critical Edition of Samuel Daniel's *The Tragedie of Cleopatra*," *DA* 27 (1967): 3017A, edits the play, with introduction and explanatory notes. A complete text of *Cleopatra* is in Geoffrey Bullough's *Narrative and Dramatic Sources of Shakespeare,* vol. 5 (1964). *The Tragedie of Cleopatra nach dem Drucke von 1611,* ed. M. Lederer (1911), is still valuable. Lyle H. Butrick, "*The Queenes Arcadia* by Samuel Daniel, Edited, with Introduction and Notes," *DA* 29 (1968): 1863A, suggests that the play is a court satire. *The Vision of the Twelve Goddesses* is edited by Joan Rees for *A Book of Masques in Honour of Allardyce Nicoll* (1967), pp. 17-42.

D. EDITIONS OF NONDRAMATIC WORKS

Daniel's *Civil Wars,* ed. Laurence Michel (I,C), has a full introduction and notes. Geoffrey Bullough, *Narrative and Dramatic Sources of Shakespeare,* vol. 4 (1962), prints excerpts from the poem. Raymond Himelick, ed., *Samuel Daniel's "Musophilus"* (I,A), offers a full introduction, discussing sources, analogues, revisions, and style. Both Himelick and Michel have made some textual errors, for which see G. Blakemore Evans, *JEGP* 57 (1958): 808-10, and Joan Rees, *RN* 19 (1966): 153-54. James Harry Smith and Edd Winfield Parks, ed., include the *Defence of Ryme* in *Great Critics: An Anthology of Literary Criticism* (1932; 3rd ed., rev., 1951). Selections from the *Defence* are printed by O. B. Hardison, ed., *English Literary Criticism: The Renaissance* (1963). Arthur Colby Sprague's *Poems and A Defence of Ryme* (1930), contains *To the Reader* (1607), *Delia, The Complaint of Rosamond, Musophilus, Epistles, A Defence of Ryme,* and *Ulisses and the Syren.* Ruth Hughey, ed., *The Arundel Harington Manuscript of Tudor Poetry,* 2 vols. (1960), prints an early version of *A Letter from Octavia.*

IV. SEE ALSO

Adelman, Janet. *The Common Liar: An Essay on "Antony and Cleopatra."* 1973.

Bald, R. C. "Shakespeare and Daniel." *TLS,* 20 Nov. 1924, p. 776.

Berthelot, Joseph A. *Michael Drayton.* 1967.

Bowden, William R. *The English Dramatic Lyric, 1603-42: A Study in Stuart Dramatic Technique.* 1951.

Brady, George Keyports. *Samuel Daniel: A Critical Study.* 1926.

Brettle, R. E. "Samuel Daniel and the Children of the Queen's Revels, 1604-5." *RES* 3 (1927): 162-68.

Broadbent, J. B. *Poetic Love.* 1964.

Bullen, A. H. *Elizabethans.* 1924.

Bullough, Geoffrey. "The Grand Style in English Poetry." In *Cairo Studies in English,* ed. Magdi Wahba (1959), pp. 9-25.

————, ed. *Narrative and Dramatic Sources of Shakespeare.* Vol. 3. 1960.

Bush, Douglas. *Mythology and the Renaissance Tradition in English Poetry.* 1932; rev. ed. 1963.

Buxton, John. *Elizabethan Taste.* 1963.

Caldwell, Harry B., and David L. Middleton, comp. *English Tragedy, 1370-1600: Fifty Years of Criticism.* 1971.

Cawley, Robert Ralston. *The Voyagers and Elizabethan Drama.* 1938.

Clifford, Anne. *The Diary of Lady Anne Clifford,* ed. V. Sackville-West. 1924.

Daniel, M. S. "An Elizabethan Wordsworth," *Dublin Review* 176 (Jan. 1925): 108-17.

Daniel, Samuel. *A Defence of Ryme against a Pamphlet entituled: Observations in the Art of English Poesie.* Ed. G. B. Harrison. 1925.

————. "Love Is a Sickness Full of Woes." *Golden Book* 21 (Jan. 1935): 71.

————. *Delia: with, The Complaint of Rosamond (1592).* 1969.

————. *A Panegyrike with A Defence of Ryme (1603).* 1969.

————. "Song by Samuel Daniel, 1590." *Prairie Schooner* 48 (1974-75): 55.

————, trans. *The Worthy Tract of Paulus Iovius (1585),* ed. Norman K. Farmer, Jr. 1976.

Dickey, Franklin M. *Not Wisely but Too Well: Shakespeare's Love Tragedies.* 1957.

Dobrée, Bonamy. "Cleopatra and 'That Criticall Warr.'" *TLS,* 11 Oct. 1928, pp. 717-18. Rpt. in *Twentieth-Century Interpretations of "All for Love,"* ed. Bruce King (1968), pp. 19-31.

Donow, Herbert S., ed. *A Concordance to the Sonnet Sequences of Daniel, Drayton, Sidney, and Spenser.* 1969.

Evans, Maurice. *English Poetry in the Sixteenth Century.* 1955.

Farnham, Willard. *The Medieval Heritage of Elizabethan Tragedy.* 1936.

Farrand, Margaret L. "Samuel Daniel and His 'Worthy Lord.'" *MLN* 45 (1930): 23-24.

Flood, W. H. Grattan. "Was Samuel Daniel in France in 1584-1586?" *RES* 2 (1926): 98-99.

Francis, F. C. "The Shakespeare Collection in the British Museum." *ShS* 3 (1950): 43-57.

Greg, W. W. *English Literary Autographs.* 4 vols. 1925-32.

Grierson, H. J. C., and J. C. Smith. *Critical History of English Poetry.* 1946.

Grove, Robin. "Ralegh's Courteous Art." *Melbourne Critical Review* 7 (1964): 104-13.

Grundy, Joan, ed. *The Poems of Henry Constable.* 1960.

Haines, C. R. "Shakespeare Allusions." *TLS,* 5 June 1924, p. 356.

Hanson, L. W. "The Shakespeare Collection in the Bodleian Library, Oxford." *ShS* 4 (1951): 78-96.

Hardin, Richard F. *Michael Drayton and the Passing of Elizabethan England.* 1973.

Harrison, G. B. "Books and Readers, 1591-4." *Library* 8 (1927): 273-302.

Hebel, J. William. "Drayton's Sirena." *PMLA* 39 (1924): 814-36.

Herbert, C. A. "Belinda and Rosamond." *CEA Critic* 30, no. 2 (1967): 10.

Herrick, Marvin T. *Tragicomedy: Its Origin and Development in Italy, France, and England.* 1955.

Hutcheson, W. J. Fraser. *Shakespeare's Other Anne.* 1950. [Anne Whateley, a nun, is Daniel's Delia.]

Jeffery, V. M. "Italian and English Pastoral Drama of the Renaissance: III. Sources of Daniel's *Queen's Arcadia* and Randolph's *Amyntas.*" *MLR* 19 (1924): 435–44.

Jones, J. *"Musophilus* Revisited." *School and Society* 65 (1947): 97–100.

Jorgensen, Paul A. *Shakespeare's Military World.* 1956.

Koskenniemi, Inna. *Studies in the Vocabulary of English Drama, 1550–1600, Excluding Shakespeare and Ben Jonson.* 1962.

LaBranche, A. "Samuel Daniel: A Voice of Thoughtfulness." In *The Rhetoric of Renaissance Poetry,* ed. Thomas Sloan and R. B. Waddington (1974), pp. 123–39.

Law, Robert Adger. "Daniel's *Rosamond* and Shakespeare." *Studies in English* (Univ. of Texas), 26 (1947): 42–48.

Leavenworth, Russell Edwin. "Daniel's *Cleopatra*: A Critical Study." *University of Colorado Studies* (General Series) 29, no. 3 (1954): 26–27.

Leishman, J. B. "Variations on a Theme in Shakespeare's Sonnets." In *Elizabethan and Jacobean Studies Presented to Frank Percy Wilson in Honour of his Seventieth Birthday,* ed. Herbert Davis and Helen Gardner (1959), pp. 112–49.

Levine, Jay Arnold. "The Status of the Verse Epistle Before Pope." *SP* 59 (1962): 658–84.

[Maxwell, J. C.] "Samuel Daniel and Milton." *N&Q* 197 (1952): 239.

Miles, Josephine. *Renaissance, Eighteenth-Century, and Modern Language in English Poetry: A Tabular View.* 1960.

Miller, Edwin Haviland. *The Professional Writer in Elizabethan England: A Study of Nondramatic Literature.* 1959.

Morris, Helen. *Elizabethan Literature.* 1957.

Nearing, Homer, Jr. "'Yorke in Choller' and Other Unrecorded Allusions to *Richard II,*" *N&Q* 191 (1946): 46–47.

Nicoll, Alardyce. *Stuart Masques and the Renaissance Stage.* 1937.

Nørgaard, Holger. "Shakespeare and Daniel's *Letter from Octavia.*" *N&Q* 2 (1955): 56–57.

Nungezer, Edwin. "Samuel Daniel." *TLS,* 27 March 1937, p. 240.

———. "Inedited Poems of Daniel." *N&Q* 175 (1938): 421.

Paradise, Nathaniel B. *Thomas Lodge: The History of an Elizabethan.* 1931.

Pearson, Lu Emily. *Elizabethan Love Conventions.* 1933.

Pellegrini, Angelo. "Giordano Bruno on Translations." *ELH* 10 (1943): 193–207.

Pevsner, N. *The Buildings of England: Somerset.* 1951.

Rae, Wesley D. *Thomas Lodge.* 1967.

Rice, Julian C. "The Allegorical Dolabella." *CLAJ* 13 (1970): 402–7.

Roberts, John Hawley. "A Note on Samuel Daniel's *Civile Wars.*" *MLN* 41 (1926): 48–50.

Rollins, Hyder E. *A New Variorum Edition of Shakespeare.* Vols. 24, 25. 1944.

Schaar, Claes. *Elizabethan Sonnet Themes and the Dating of Shakespeare's "Sonnets."* 1962.

Schelling, F. E. *Foreign Influences in Elizabethan Plays.* 1923.

Scott, Janet G. "The Names of the Heroines of Elizabethan Sonnet-Sequences." *RES* 2 (1926): 159–62. [Delia]

————. [Janet Girvan Espiner]. *Les sonnets élisabéthains: les sources et l'apport personnel.* 1929.

Sellers, H. "Two New Letters of Samuel Daniel." *TLS,* 24 March 1927, p. 215.

Sells, A. Lytton. *The Italian Influence on English Poetry from Chaucer to Southwell.* 1955.

Short, R. W. "Jonson's Sanguine Rival." *RES* 15 (1939): 315–17.

Steele, Mary Susan. *Plays and Masques at Court during the Reigns of Elizabeth, James, and Charles.* 1926.

Thaler, Alwin. "Shakespere, Daniel, and *Everyman.*" *PQ* 15 (1936): 217–18.

Tobin, James E. "A 1609 Concept of Comparative Literature." *Comparative Literature News-Letter* 1 (1943): 3–4.

Ure, Peter. "A Note on 'Opinion' in Daniel, Greville and Chapman." *MLR* 46 (1951): 331–38.

————. *Elizabethan and Jacobean Drama,* ed. J. C. Maxwell. 1974.

Welsford, Enid. *The Court Masque: A Study of the Relationship between Poetry and Revels.* 1927.

Wickham, Glynne. *Early English Stages, 1300–1660.* Vol. 2. 1963.

Witherspoon, Alexander M. *The Influence of Robert Garnier on Elizabethan Drama.* 1924.

Yates, Frances A. *John Florio: The Life of an Italian in Shakespeare's England.* 1934.

————. "The Emblematic Conceit in Giordano Bruno's *De Gli Eroici Furori* and in the Elizabethan Sonnet Sequences." *JWCI* 6 (1943): 101–21.

ANONYMOUS PLAYS

Anne Lancashire   Jill Levenson

Books and articles consulted date from the publication of E. K. Chambers, The Elizabethan Stage, *4 vols. (1923), to the end of 1967; works published 1920-23 and not cited in Chambers are included, as are some post-1967 works. For additional information, see: G. E. Bentley,* The Jacobean and Caroline Stage, *7 vols. (1941-68); W. W. Greg,* A Bibliography of the English Printed Drama to the Restoration, *4 vols. (1939-59); Alfred Harbage,* Annals of English Drama, 975-1700, *rev. Samuel Schoenbaum (1964), and the* Supplement *by Schoenbaum (1966). A list of works dealing generally with a large number of anonymous plays appears at the end of this section. The dates following play titles indicate the preferred date of first performance (in italics) and the date of the first edition from the* Annals *and the* Supplement; *type classifications are from the* Annals. *Full bibliographical citation is given only for the first reference to a work in each essay; short titles are used for subsequent references. In longer essays, a shortened title of the section in which the work is first cited ("Edition," "Text," etc.) is usually given in parentheses following the short title.*

The Wisdom of Doctor Dodypoll, comedy (*1599*; 1600)

Editions

The play has been edited by Marshall Nyvall Matson in a 1967 Ph. D. dissertation for Northwestern University, "A Critical Edition of *The Wisdom of Doctor Dodypoll* (1600) with a Study of *Dodypoll*'s Place in the Repertory of Paul's Boys" (*DA* 28 [1967] : 2213A-14A), and in the Malone Society series (1965, for 1964). The dissertation introduction deals with date (ca. 1600), authorship (left as anonymous), the place of the play in the Paul's repertory, and the play's connections with other dramatic works and literature of the time, and gives an analysis of plot, character, and language, and a discussion of the text (which was printed, Matson finds, with a single skeleton-forme and apparently from an authorial draft). In the Malone Society edition Matson summarizes previous scholarship on authorship, date, and sources, himself accepting a date of ca. 1600 and finding no author, direct source, or evidence of revision. Textual matters, including printing method and copy text, are briefly discussed.

The Wisdom of Doctor Dodypoll is also available in microprint in Henry W. Wells, ed., *Three Centuries of Drama* (Readex Microprint Corp., 1955-56).

Authorship and Date

J. M. Robertson, *An Introduction to the Study of the Shakespeare Canon* (1924), thinks that the play may have had several authors and was probably written ca. 1590; he cannot accept Fleay's Peele attribution. Ernest A. Gerrard, *Elizabethan Drama and Dramatists, 1583–1603* (1928), implausibly suggests that *Dodypoll* is an old Lyly play, written ca. 1592 and revised by Dekker and others (probably one or more of Chettle, Day, and Haughton) in 1599. Robert Boies Sharpe, *The Real War of the Theaters* (1935), leans towards a form of the old Peele attribution: the play is possibly an old romantic drama by Peele "with a new satirical title and a fairly thorough rewriting [ca. 1599] to bring it up to date. The folk-lore elements are interestingly characteristic of Peele; and Doctor Dodipoll himself . . . may be a modernization of the doctor of the mumming plays." The plot, Sharpe declares, resembles that of *A Midsummer Night's Dream* and that of Henry Porter's *Two Angry Women of Abingdon,* but, most of all, that of *The Old Wives Tale*; and there are also resemblances to *Shoemakers' Holiday* (1599) and *Julius Caesar* (1599). "In general, *Doctor Dodipoll* shows a clever furbishing up of old romantic material to please the fashionable taste." Robert Rentoul Reed, Jr., *The Occult on the Tudor and Stuart Stage* (1965), finds the author to be craftsmanlike but not brilliant, inferior to Peele in *The Old Wives Tale,* whom he imitates. Leonard R. N. Ashley, *Authorship and Evidence* (1968), attacks attributions based on parallels and specifically rejects the assignment of *Dodypoll* to Peele.

John P. Cutts, "Peele's *Hunting of Cupid,*" *SRen* 5 (1958): 121–32, calls for a "complete reinvestigation . . . of the anonymous play *The Wisdom of Doctor Dodypoll* which was first attributed to Peele on then unacceptable evidence and was subsequently denied to Peele on evidence that now seems equally unacceptable." Cutts deals with the song, "What thing is love," found in both Peele's *Hunting of Cupid* and *Dodypoll,* giving, from a 1606 collection by John Bartlet, the musical version probably sung in *Dodypoll;* he believes that the song does suggest Peele's authorship of *Dodypoll,* and that the "echo" of *Julius Caesar* or of Jonson's *Every Man Out of His Humour* in the play, which would place the composition of *Dodypoll* after Peele's death, is not necessarily an echo at all.

Harold Newcomb Hillebrand, *The Child Actors* (1926), has "no quarrel with the accepted theory that *Doddipole* was revived by Paul's at the beginning of their activities in 1599-1600 from their older repertory of before 1590."

Other Studies

Critical comments on the play are brief and miscellaneous. Willard Thorp, *The Triumph of Realism in Elizabethan Drama, 1558-1612* (1928), deals with *Dodypoll* in his section on plays on the theme of the abused wife, dates it 1596-1600, and calls it "a curious gallimaufry of romantic leftovers." In *The Anatomy of Puck* (1959), K. M. Briggs points out that the drama contains a large amount of folklore, and that throughout the play runs the idea that enchantments have no final power over love; she links *Dodypoll* with Milton's *Comus.* The style, she declares, is crude, but with occasional flashes of poetry. The fairies, maintains Robert Reed, *The Occult,* are basically unnecessary to the play and therefore must have been in vogue when it was written.

Dodypoll is linked with Shakespeare's *King Lear* by Arthur M. Sampley, "Two Analogues to Shakespeare's Treatment of the Wooing of Cordelia," *SQ* 12 (1961): 468-69, who finds an analogue to Cordelia's wooing by Burgundy (who rejects her) and France (who accepts her) in the *Dodypoll* wooing of Cornelia by Albertus, Dodypoll, and finally Earl Cassimer, and suggests the existence of "some vogue for this effective turn of plot on the stage shortly before Shakespeare wrote *King Lear.*"

Two scholars find historical models for characters in *Dodypoll.* Abraham Feldman, "Hans Ewouts, Artist of the Tudor Court Theatre," *N&Q* 195 (1950): 257-58, suggests that the character of Hans is a tribute to Hans Ewouts; Dutchmen in Elizabethan drama usually are buffoons and drunkards, but the function of *Dodypoll*'s Hans is "mainly in arrangement of melodious amusement for royalty," and the character speaks excellent English and is witty. "Doctor Dodypoll is patterned," maintains Hersch L. Zitt ("The Jew in the Elizabethan World-Picture," *Historia Judaica* 14 [1952] : 53-60), "after Dr. Roderigo Lopez, the Queen's physician, who was a Jew," and who was tried and executed for treason and attempted murder in 1594.

Louis B. Wright, "Extraneous Song in Elizabethan Drama after the Advent of Shakespeare," *SP* 24 (1927): 261-74, believes that the sole function of much of the music and song in *Dodypoll* was to give the actors, the children of Paul's, an opportunity to furnish musical entertainment. Several songs, he maintains, have no relation whatever to the play.

Wilfred T. Jewkes, *Act Division in Elizabethan and Jacobean Plays, 1583-1616* (1958), states that the quarto text seems to have been printed from authorial manuscript (or a copy close to it); it contains no trace of playhouse preparation.

See Also

Albright, Evelyn May. *Dramatic Publication in England, 1580-1640.* 1927.
Clough, Wilson O. "The Broken English of Foreign Characters of the Elizabethan Stage." *PQ* 12 (1933): 255-68.

A. L.

The Maid's Metamorphosis, comedy (*1600*; 1600)

Introduction

Although *The Maid's Metamorphosis* has not been neglected by modern scholars, there has been no recent edition of the play. The 1600 edition is available in microprint in Henry W. Wells, ed., *Three Centuries of Drama* (Readex Corp., 1955-56).

Attribution

The question of attribution is unresolved. Several scholars consider the possibility that Lyly contributed to the anonymous comedy. In *The Child Actors: A Chapter in Elizabethan Stage History* (1926), Harold Newcomb Hillebrand accepts the consensus of earlier critics who assign part of *Maid's Metamorphosis* to Lyly but thinks that the author of the rest of the play is still to be discovered. Benvenuto Cellini, ed., *Drammi pre-Shakespeariani,* Collana di Letterature Moderne, no. 4 (1958), suggests that the play is a collaborate work by Lyly and either Daniel or Day. Two scholars seriously question the Lyly ascription: W. W. Greg, ed., *English Literary Autographs, 1550-1650,* pt. 1 (1925), and "Authorship Attributions in the Early Play-Lists, 1656-1671," *Edinburgh Bibliographical Society Transactions* 2 (1938-45): 303-29; and M. P. Tilley, *"The Maid's Metamorphosis* and Ovid's *Metamorphoses," MLN* 46 (1931): 139-43. William J. Lawrence, "Thomas Ravenscroft's Theatrical Associations," *MLR* 19 (1924): 418-23, believes the Lyly ascription to be a mistake; he feels that the comedy may be Day's. After a summary of previous attribution scholarship, S. R. Golding, "The Authorship of *The Maid's Metamorphosis,"* *RES* 2 (1926): 270-79, disagrees with those who ascribe the play to Day, Lyly, or Daniel; finding correspondences with Peele's work, he theorizes that Peele or, more probably, an imitator of Peele, composed the comedy. M. C. Bradbrook, *The Growth and Structure of Elizabethan Comedy* (1955), does not accept the Day ascription; the style, in her opinion, resembles Lyly's.

Date and Source

William J. Lawrence, "A Plummet for Bottom's Dream," *Fortnightly Review* 111 (1922): 833-44, and "Thomas Ravenscroft's Theatrical Associations" ("Attribution"), proposes that *Maid's Metamorphosis* was a new play or a revival when it was entered on the Stationers' Register on 24 July 1600 and performed at the wedding of Henry, Lord Herbert and Anne Russell on 16 June 1600. Golding ("Attribution") finds internal evidence which suggests a composition date in the first half of 1600. He comments also that Spenserian imitations in *Maid's Metamorphosis* indicate that the play could not have been written before 1596. More emphatically than Golding, Hillebrand ("Attribution") puts forth internal evidence which he feels establishes a date of 1600 for *Maid's Metamorphosis.* Like Lawrence, Hillebrand thinks that the play was performed at the Herbert-Russell wedding. Hector Genouy, *L'élément pastoral dans la poésie narrative et le drame en Angleterre, de 1579 à 1640* (1928), says that the comedy could not have been written before 1590-91, because it imitates the work of both Lyly and Sidney. In *The Real War of the Theaters: Shakespeare's Fellows in Rivalry with the Admiral's Men, 1594-1603* (1935), Robert Boies Sharpe speculates that *Maid's Metamorphosis* may have been performed at court during Christmas 1600 as an old play revised or a new play. Peter Saccio, *The Court Comedies of John Lyly: A Study in Allegorical Dramaturgy* (1969), remarks that *Maid's Metamorphosis* was performed in 1600, possibly at a noble wedding.

Tilley ("Attribution") shows how the author of *Maid's Metamorphosis* borrowed incidents, characters, speeches, words, phrases, and rhymes from Golding's translation of Ovid's *Metamorphoses* (1565-67). Sharpe (above) mentions the anonymous play's indebtedness to Ovid.

Literary Connections and Genre

A number of scholars have noticed in *Maid's Metamorphosis* correspondences not only with plays by Lyly, Peele, and Shakespeare, but also with Sidney's *Arcadia* and Spenser's *Fairie Queene:* see, for example, Lawrence's two articles ("Attribution" and "Date and Source"); Golding ("Attribution"); Genouy, Sharpe, and Saccio (all in "Date and Source"); C. F. Tucker Brooke, in *A Literary History of England,* ed. Albert C. Baugh (1948). Traudl Eichhorn, "Prosa und Vers im vorshakespeareschen Drama," *SJ* 84-86 (1948-50): 140-98; Katharine M. Briggs, *The Anatomy of Puck* (1959); and David Bevington, *Tudor Drama and Politics* (1968); Violet M. Jeffery, "Italian and English Pastoral Drama of the Renaissance: III," *MLR* 19 (1924): 435-44, and *John Lyly and the Italian Renaissance* (1928), points out resemblances between *Maid's Metamorphosis* and the dramas of Luigi Groto, whose influence she finds in the anonymous play. Sharpe ("Date and Source") remarks that Chapman's *May-Day* (1602) may contain a burlesque of *Maid's Metamorphosis.*

Several writers discuss the genre of *Maid's Metamorphosis* and its affinities with the pastoral mode: see, for instance, Jeffery's article and book (above); Genouy and Sharpe (both in "Date and Source"); Murray Krieger, "*Measure for Measure* and Elizabethan Comedy," *PMLA* 66 (1951): 775-84; Marvin T. Herrick, *Tragicomedy* (1955); Jerry H. Bryant, "*The Winter's Tale* and the Pastoral Tradition," *SQ* 14 (1963): 387-98; and Bevington (above). Saccio ("Date and Source") offers the most extensive discussion of genre as he explains why and how *Maid's Metamorphosis* signals the end of what he calls "situational drama."

Miscellaneous

The music in the play receives attention from Lawrence in both of his articles ("Attribution" and "Date and Source"); Edward Bliss Reed, ed., *Songs from the British Drama* (1925); Germaine Bontoux, *La chanson en Angleterre au temps d'Élisabeth* (1936); John P. Cutts, "The Second Coventry Carol and a Note on *The Maydes Metamorphosis,*" *RN* 10 (1957): 3-8, and "A Note on *The Maydes Metamorphosis,*"

N&Q 4 (1957): 292-93; Andrew J. Sabol, "Two Songs with Accompaniment for an Elizabethan Choirboy Play," *SRen* 5 (1958): 145-59, and "Ravenscroft's *Melismata* and the Children of Paul's," *RN* 12 (1959): 3-9; Vincent Duckles, "The Music for the Lyrics in Early Seventeenth-Century English Drama: A Bibliography of the Primary Sources," in *Music in English Renaissance Drama,* ed. John H. Long (1968), pp. 117-60.

Wilfred T. Jewkes, *Act Division in Elizabethan and Jacobean Plays, 1583-1616* (1958), concludes that copy for the play "was either an author's manuscript which had never been prepared for the stage, or a non-theatrical transcript of it." Briggs ("Literary Connections and Genre") and Robert Rentoul Reed, Jr., *The Occult on the Tudor and Stuart Stage* (1965), discuss the role of the fairies in *Maid's Metamorphosis*. In *Playwriting for Elizabethans, 1600-1605* (1949), Mary Crapo Hyde describes the love-chase in the play as well as the function of Echo in IV.i. Bain Tate Stewart, "The Misunderstood Dreams in the Plays of Shakespeare and His Contemporaries," in *Essays in Honor of Walter Clyde Curry,* VUSH, vol. 2 (1954), pp. 197-206, remarks the use of dream in *Maid's Metamorphosis,* and Glenn H. Blayney, "Enforcement of Marriage in English Drama (1600-1650)," *PQ* 38 (1959): 459-72, explains how the play treats the theme of enforced marriage.

See Also

Chambers, E. K. *William Shakespeare.* 1930. Vol. 1.

Kimbrough, Robert. *Shakespeare's "Troilus and Cressida" and Its Setting.* 1964.

Linton, Marion. "The Bute Collection of English Plays." *TLS,* 21 Dec. 1956, p. 772.

———. "National Library of Scotland and Edinburgh University Library Copies of Plays in Greg's *Bibliography of the English Printed Drama.*" *SB* 15 (1962): 91-104.

Long, John H. *Shakespeare's Use of Music: The Final Comedies.* 1961.

Schoenbaum, S. *Internal Evidence and Elizabethan Dramatic Authorship.* 1966.

Stříbrný, Zdeněk. "John Lyly a Dvorské Drama" [John Lyly and the court drama]. *PP* 6 (1963): 100-112.

Willcox, Alice. "Medical References in the Dramas of John Lyly." *Annals of Medical History* 10 (1938): 117-26.

Winslow, Ola Elizabeth. *Low Comedy as a Structural Element in English Drama from the Beginnings to 1642.* 1926.

J. L.

The Contention between Liberality and Prodigality, moral interlude
(*1601*; 1602)

Introduction and Attribution

The Contention between Liberality and Prodigality (L&P) has not
been edited since the Malone Society edition by W. W. Greg in 1913.
The 1602 text is available in microprint in Henry W. Wells, ed., *Three
Centuries of Drama* (Readex Corp., 1955-56).

The most important candidate for authorship is Sebastian Westcote.
In "Sebastian Westcote, Dramatist and Master of the Children of
Paul's," *JEGP* 14 (1915): 568-84, Harold Newcomb Hillebrand argues
that *L&P* was a new version of the play *Prodigality* (1567), that both
dramas belonged to the repertory of Paul's boys, and that Westcote
probably created the original play. Hillebrand summarizes these arguments in *The Child Actors: A Chapter in Elizabethan Stage History*
(1926), where he attempts to distinguish Westcote's part of *L&P* from
those portions of the old play which have been rewritten. Considering
Hillebrand's theory, Charles W. Roberts, "The Authorship of *Gammer
Gurton's Needle,*" *PQ* 19 (1940): 97-113, compares *L&P* with *Gammer
Gurton's Needle*, points out stylistic features in the two plays which
suggest that Westcote contributed to them, and puts forth additional
dubious evidence to show that Westcote and John Heywood may have
collaborated on *L&P*. T. W. Baldwin, *Shakspere's Five-Act Structure*
(1947), suggests, with some qualification, additional evidence to support Hillebrand's attribution. One scholar seriously questions Hillebrand's argument and conclusion: Arthur Brown, "A Note on Sebastian
Westcott and the Plays Presented by the Children of Paul's," *MLQ* 12
(1951): 134-36.

Date and Sources

Most scholars agree that *L&P* was probably performed in 1601 as
either a newly written play or a revised version of *Prodigality* (1567):
see, for example, Hillebrand's article and book ("Introduction and
Attribution"); Louis B. Wright, "Social Aspects of Some Belated
Moralities," *Anglia* 54 (1930): 107-48; Robert Boies Sharpe, *The
Real War of the Theaters: Shakespeare's Fellows in Rivalry with the
Admiral's Men, 1594-1603* (1935); Harold Jenkins, "Peele's *Old
Wives' Tale,*" *MLR* 34 (1939): 177-85 (rpt. in *Shakespeare's Contem-
poraries*, ed. Max Bluestone and Norman Rabkin [1961], pp. 22-30);

Baldwin ("Introduction and Attribution"); G. K. Hunter, *John Lyly: The Humanist as Courtier* (1962); Allardyce Nicoll, *British Drama* (1925; 5th ed., 1962); and John Doebler, "Beaumont's *The Knight of the Burning Pestle* and the Prodigal Son Plays," *SEL* 5 (1965): 333–44.

A few writers find the question of date problematical. In *Pre-Restoration Stage Studies* (1927), William J. Lawrence discovers an imitation of Marlowe's *Tamburlaine* in *L&P* which causes him to take issue with E. K. Chambers's dating of the anonymous play in *The Elizabethan Stage* (1923), vol. 4. Like Lawrence, Samuel C. Chew, "Time and Fortune," *ELH* 6 (1939): 83–113, and *The Pilgrimage of Life* (1962), discerns in *L&P* resemblances to *Tamburlaine*. According to his view, the anonymous play may have been new or revised in the early seventeenth century, "or at any rate it was refurbished at a date later than *Tamburlaine* (1587)." T. W. Craik, *The Tudor Interlude: Stage, Costume, and Acting* (1958), is not convinced that *Tamburlaine* influenced *L&P* and takes issue with Lawrence's argument about date.

The only scholar who mentions sources is Baldwin ("Introduction and Attribution"), who remarks that part of the third act of *L&P* uses as a model the early play *Acolastus* (trans. 1540).

Literary Connections and Genre

At least two scholars think that Marlowe's *Tamburlaine* influenced *L&P* (see "Date and Sources"), and Robert E. Knoll, *Ben Jonson's Plays: An Introduction* (1964), agrees with Arthur Bivins Stonex, "The Sources of Jonson's *The Staple of News,*" *PMLA* 30 (1915): 821–30, that the anonymous drama may have been a source for *The Staple of News* (1626).

The genre of *L&P*, which is a belated morality play, has been often discussed: see, for example, Willard Thorp, *The Triumph of Realism in Elizabethan Drama, 1558–1612* (1928); Wright ("Date and Sources"); Chew's article and book ("Date and Sources"); Baldwin ("Introduction and Attribution"); A. P. Rossiter, *English Drama from Early Times to the Elizabethans* (1950); Madeleine Doran, *Endeavors of Art: A Study of Form in Elizabethan Drama* (1954); Craik, Hunter, Nicoll, and Doebler (all in "Date and Sources"). Both Wright and Sharpe ("Date and Sources") point out that this late morality play had contemporary relevance; it attempted to advise Queen Elizabeth to improve certain political and economic policies. Chew's article and book ("Date and Sources") interpret some of the emblematic features in *L&P*.

Miscellaneous

Baldwin ("Introduction and Attribution") describes the five-act structure and staging of *L&P*. Craik ("Date and Sources"), in his attempt to illustrate how Tudor interludes were performed, discusses the setting, costumes, properties, and action. Hunter ("Date and Sources") speculates about the use of a platform.

J. E. Bernard, Jr., *The Prosody of the Tudor Interlude* (1939), offers a detailed analysis of the play's prosody; and Daniel C. Boughner, *The Braggart in Renaissance Comedy* (1954), and "Vice, Braggart, and Falstaff," *Anglia* 72 (1954): 35-61, briefly explains the role of Prodigality.

See Also

Bradbrook, M. C. "'Silk? Satin? Kersey? Rags?'—The Choristers' Theater under Elizabeth and James." *SEL* 1 (1961): 53-64.

Brawner, James Paul. "Early Classical Narrative Plays by Sebastian Westcott and Richard Mulcaster." *MLQ* 4 (1943): 455-64.

Calmann, Gerta. "The Picture of Nobody: An Iconographical Study." *JWCI* 23 (1960): 60-104.

Fredén, Gustaf. *Friedrich Menius und das Repertoire der englischen Komödianten in Deutschland.* 1939.

Hapgood, Robert. "Falstaff's Vocation." *SQ* 16 (1965): 91-98.

Harbage, Alfred. *Shakespeare and the Rival Traditions.* 1952.

Koskenniemi, Inna. "On the Use of 'Figurative Negation' in English Renaissance Drama." *NM* 67 (1966): 385-401.

Lawrence, William J. *Those Nut-Cracking Elizabethans.* 1935.

Morris, Helen. *Elizabethan Literature.* 1958.

Partridge, Edward B. *The Broken Compass: A Study of the Major Comedies of Ben Jonson.* 1958.

Reed, Edward Bliss, ed. *Songs from the British Drama.* 1925.

Spivack, Bernard. *Shakespeare and the Allegory of Evil.* 1958.

Steele, Mary Susan. *Plays & Masques at Court during the Reigns of Elizabeth, James, and Charles.* 1926.

Wright, Celeste Turner. "The Usurer's Sin in Elizabethan Literature." *SP* 35 (1938): 178-94.

Wright, Louis B. "Animal Actors on the English Stage before 1642." *PMLA* 42 (1927): 656-69.

J. L.

Wily Beguiled, comedy (*1602;* 1606)

Editions

Wily Beguiled is available in microprint in Henry W. Wells, ed., *Three Centuries of Drama* (Readex Microprint Corp., 1955-56).

Date and Authorship

There has been no agreement on a date or an author for *Wily Beguiled.* The extant text has been identified both as an original work of ca. 1600 and as a revision of an older drama, and Dekker, Greene, Marston, Peele, Henry Porter, and Samuel Rowley have all been considered as authorship candidates.

The revision theory is presented by Baldwin Maxwell, *"Wily Beguiled,"* *SP* 19 (1922): 206-37, at considerable length, and by Robert Boies Sharpe, *The Real War of the Theaters* (1935). Maxwell identifies *Wily Beguiled* with the "lost" *Wylie Beguylie* performed at Merton College, Oxford, at Christmas 1566-67. The extant text he finds to be a thorough revision of the original, which was in doggerel or prose and doggerel; the revision is to be dated late 1601 to early 1602, because of the connections of the present text with the poetomachia between Jonson and his fellow dramatists and (as noted in previous criticism) with *The Merchant of Venice, Romeo and Juliet, Hamlet,* and *The Spanish Tragedy.* He argues against Peele and Jonson as possible authors, and also considers and rejects Marston as author or reviser. Sharpe calls *Wily Beguiled* "an evidently old [romantic] play which seems to have been revived by Paul's boys about 1602" and "fitted up with new comic material." It contains, he states, numerous similarities and allusions to productions of other companies, but these productions cover so long a period that no exact date for *Wily Beguiled* can be ascertained from them. W. W. Greg, *Two Elizabethan Stage Abridgements* (1923; Malone Society), discusses an older attribution by H. Dugdale Sykes of the prose scenes to Samuel Rowley, and, dating *Wily Beguiled* at least as early as 1596, calls it "obviously of composite origin," considering the possibility of revision.

Other scholars consider date and authorship without positing or commenting on an earlier version of the play. H. Dugdale Sykes, in *Sidelights on Elizabethan Drama* (1924), reprints his earlier attribution of the prose scenes to Rowley and of the verse parts of the play to the unknown author of the verse portions of *The Taming of a Shrew.* This author, he states, borrows from Kyd's *Spanish Tragedy* and *Soliman and Perseda.* Against Sykes's methods, see M. St. C. Byrne, "Bibliographical Clues in Collaborate Plays," *Library* 13 (1932-33): 21-48. Sykes's attribution work is dismissed by Baldwin Maxwell, *"The Two Angry Women of Abington* and *Wily Beguiled,"* *PQ* 20 (1941): 334-39, and the Rowley assignment is also rejected, though on weak grounds, by Matthew P. McDiarmid, "The Stage Quarrel in *Wily Beguiled," N&Q* 3 (1956): 380–83. McDiarmid dates the play ca. 1602, through allusions he finds in it to the poetomachia between Jonson and Marston and Dekker, especially to Jonson and *Poetaster* (1601) and to Dekker and *Satiromastix* (1601), and through echoes in *Wily Beguiled* of *Sir Giles Goosecap* (1601–2) and *Antonio and Mellida* (1599), as well as echoes (noted by previous scholars) of *Merchant of Venice, Twelfth Night,* and possibly *Hamlet.* The character Churms "at odd moments . . . represents Marston." M. T. Jones-Davies, *Un peintre de la vie londonienne, Thomas Dekker* (1958), vol. 2, states that there is no proof that our *Wily Beguiled* text is a revision of the 1567 Oxford play, and declines to give the play to Dekker; the similarities between it and Dekker's known works are to be found in many Elizabethan plays. The drama is assigned to Dekker, however, by William Amos Abrams, ed., *The Merry Devil of Edmonton, 1608* (1942).

J. M. Robertson, *An Introduction to the Study of the Shakespeare Canon* (1924), without dating the play or considering revisions, discusses previous attribution work, finds the Prologue to echo *Hamlet* and "the Marston-Jonson wrangle," and, doubting that Greene or Peele is the author, gives the work to "young play-haunters penning it for a University audience." The Prologue, he says, might be Marston's or Jonson's. Frederick S. Boas, *Shakespeare and the Universities* (1923), declares *Wily Beguiled* to be "almost certainly a Cambridge play" and to make use of *Romeo and Juliet* and *Merchant of Venice.* William J. Lawrence, *Pre-Restoration Stage Studies* (1927), enters the play in his index under Peele.

In *"Two Angry Women"* Baldwin Maxwell points out similarities between the extant *Wily Beguiled* text and Henry Porter's *Two Angry Women of Abingdon,* but hesitates, because of the superiority of *Two Angry Women,* to suggest common authorship of the two dramas, and states only that these similarities, together with others pointed out by previous scholars between *Wily* and Kyd's works, *The Taming of a Shrew,* etc., are of value in showing that the *Wily Beguiled* author was widely acquainted with the drama of his time.

Other scholars noting echoes in *Wily Beguiled,* relevant to the question of date, of other plays of the period, are: Sharpe, *Real War* [*Merchant of Venice*]; K. M. Lea, *Italian Popular Comedy* (1934), vol. 2 [*Merchant of Venice*]; Ashley H. Thorndike, *English Comedy* (1929) [*Midsummer Night's Dream*].

Leonard R. N. Ashley, *Authorship and Evidence* (1968), sums up previous scholarship on the date, authorship, and origin of the text, and, rejecting the Peele attribution, concludes only that the style is "certainly" late Elizabethan, typical of a date before 1606.

Other Studies

Glenn H. Blayney, "Enforcement of Marriage in English Drama (1600-1650)," *PQ* 38 (1959): 459-72, views the play as focused for comic and satiric purposes on the theme of enforced marriage. It "satirizes the crass stupidity of a man whose single aim in his daughter's marriage is the wealth of the prospective mate." K. M. Briggs, *The Anatomy of Puck* (1959), calls *Wily Beguiled* a "rationalized fairy-tale," and points out that Mother Midnight, Will Cricket, Robin Goodfellow, and Fortunatus are all fairy-tale names but here belong to mortals. She examines especially Robin Goodfellow.

Two scholars comment on Will Cricket's courtship of Peg as a burlesque of the serious, traditional, main-plot wooing: Ola Elizabeth Winslow, *Low Comedy as a Structural Element in English Drama from the Beginnings to 1642* (1926), and J. W. Ashton, "Conventional Material in Munday's *John a Kent and John a Cumber*," *PMLA* 49 (1934): 752-61. John B. Moore, *The Comic and the Realistic in English Drama* (1925), in a footnote calls Gripe a type comic figure who "imitates the serious complication," and Bernard Spivack, *Shakespeare and the Allegory of Evil* (1958), finds Robin Goodfellow to be "a figure derived from the morality Vice."

In *The Elizabethan Jig and Related Song Drama* (1929), Charles R. Baskervill points out that the dialogue of the Broughton Play [a mummers' wooing play] includes a large part of the Induction of *Wily Beguiled;* and *Wily Beguiled* as a source for *The Knight of the Burning Pestle* is argued by Baldwin Maxwell, "*The Knight of the Burning Pestle* and *Wily Beguiled*," *MLN* 35 (1920): 503-4, who repeats this view in his *Studies in Beaumont, Fletcher, and Massinger* (1939). Louis B. Wright, "Extraneous Song in Elizabethan Drama after the Advent of Shakespeare," *SP* 24 (1927): 261-74, calls a song in *Wily Beguiled* purely extraneous.

Wilfred T. Jewkes, *Act Division in Elizabethan and Jacobean Plays, 1583-1616* (1958), states that "*Wily Beguiled* is associated with a private company only on grounds of its quasi-academic note" [cf. E. K. Chambers, *Elizabethan Stage* (1923), vol. 4], and that the printer's copy was "probably a set of author's papers, or a non-theatrical transcript from them."

The best overall view of the play is Maxwell's in *"Wily Beguiled."*

See Also

Blayney, Glenn H. "Wardship in English Drama (1600–1650)." *SP* 53 (1956): 470–84.

Cellini, Benvenuto, ed. *Drammi pre-Shakespeariani.* Collana di Letterature Moderne, no. 4 (1958).

Chambers, E. K. *The English Folk-Play.* 1933.

Curry, John V. *Deception in Elizabethan Comedy.* 1955.

Feldman, A. Bronson. "The Flemings in Shakespeare's Theatre." *N&Q* 197 (1952): 265–69.

Mares, Francis Hugh. "The Origin of the Figure Called 'the Vice' in Tudor Drama." *HLQ* 22 (1958–59): 11–29.

Ogburn, Dorothy and Charlton. *This Star of England.* 1952.

A. L.

Philotus, comedy (*1603*; 1603)

Editions

The only recent edition is by A. J. Mill for the Scottish Text Society in its *Miscellany Volume* (1933). Mill briefly sums up and evaluates previous scholarship on authorship, date, and sources; she places the play simply during the reign of James VI, finds no author (rejecting the Robert Semple attribution), and states that the source is possibly the eighth tale in Barnaby Rich's *Farewell to Military Profession* (1581) or (directly or indirectly) the Italian comedy *Gli Ingannati*. The two black letter quartos (1603 and 1612) are described, and a list of modern editions is given.

Philotus is also available in microprint in Henry W. Wells, ed., *Three Centuries of Drama* (Readex Microprint Corp., 1955–56).

Other Studies

In *An Historical Survey of Scottish Literature to 1714* (1933), Agnes Mure Mackenzie deals with *Philotus* at some length. She places the drama, from internal evidence, "little later than the *Thrie Estaitis"* (ca. 1540) of Sir David Lindsay, and earlier than 1542. Rich's *Farewell,* she states, may have borrowed from *Philotus,* or both Rich and the *Philotus* author may have used a now-lost source. "[The play's] form is as unlike the English work of the late [sixteenth] century as its content is unlike that of anything English before Greene." *Philotus* contains "a hint of both Terence and the novelle, and touches of what was to grow into Molière," and is a "genuine romantic comedy." The characters, however, she declares, are mere outlines, and the text may be incomplete.

Philotus is not much examined again until ca. 1950, but from then to the present receives attention from a number of scholars. The question of source and date is the focus of concern, and it has now been generally agreed that the play draws on the eighth tale in Rich's *Farewell* and therefore was written not before 1581. See: James Craigie, "Rich's *Farewell to Military Profession*," *TLS*, 1 Nov. 1934, p. 755, and "More About *Philotus*: Sources and Problem of Authorship," *The Scotsman*, 18 Dec. 1948; Thomas M. Cranfill and Dorothy Hart Bruce, *Barnaby Rich: A Short Biography* (1953); Thomas Mabry Cranfill, ed., *Rich's Farewell to Military Profession, 1581* (1959); M. P. McDiarmid, "*Philotus*: A Play of the Scottish Renaissance," *Forum for Modern Language Studies* (Univ. of St. Andrews, Scotland) 3 (1967): 223-35; Helena Mennie Shire, *Song, Dance and Poetry of the Court of Scotland under King James VI* (1969). Cranfill in his edition maintains that not only the eighth story but also definitely the first, sixth, and seventh and probably the second, third, and fifth tales as well are used in *Philotus*; McDiarmid accepts Cranfill's main points, although believing that Cranfill exaggerates the debt of *Philotus* to Rich. McDiarmid also finds the dialogue-poem "Pamphilus and Galatea" to be a source and influence, and comments as well on the possible influence of *The Bugbears*.

Craigie (above, two articles) calls attention to the apparent existence of a 1594 edition of the *Farewell* [now extant and known], and places *Philotus* at the end of the sixteenth century; Mill, in her edition, cites Sir William Craigie's opinion that, on the evidence of vocabulary, *Philotus* "cannot be much earlier than 1600." See also Lewis Spence, "*Philotus*: Scotland's One Jacobean Comedy," *The Scotsman*, 11 Dec. 1948, p. 7. McDiarmid and Shire, however, both date the play ca. 1583-86.

Authorship is also a disputed matter. Spence, "*Philotus*," rejects previous arguments for the authorship of Robert Semple, as does Craigie, "More About *Philotus*," who is also disinclined to accept the possible candidacy of Alexander Montgomerie and argues for King James himself as the author of the work. Cranfill, *Rich's Farewell*, is drawn, however, towards Robert Semple, and McDiarmid and Shire support Montgomerie. McDiarmid argues for Montgomerie at length, finding *Philotus* to be in his spirit, style, language, and phrasing, and rejects both James VI and Semple on stylistic grounds.

"The Court was the home of *Philotus*," states Kurt Wittig, *The Scottish Tradition in Literature* (1958), and the court origin of the play is also mentioned by Craigie, "More About *Philotus*," McDiarmid, and Shire, McDiarmid arguing at some length that the play was definitely written for (court) performance and that its acting procedure comes in part from the morality tradition.

Spence, *"Philotus,"* calls the play "an Italian *vignette de théâtre* in a Scots frame"; Craigie, "More About *Philotus*," finds the drama to be "amateurish" and to combine the characteristics of the Italian comedy of intrigue and of the earlier sixteenth-century interlude.

See Also

Bowden, William R. *The English Dramatic Lyric, 1603–42.* 1951.

Cranfill, Thomas Mabry. "Barnaby Rich's *Farewell* and the Drama." Ph. D. dissertation, Harvard Univ., 1944.

Mill, Anna Jean. *Mediaeval Plays in Scotland.* 1927.

Whiting, B. J. "Proverbs and Proverbial Sayings from Scottish Writings Before 1600." *Mediaeval Studies* 11 (1949): 123–205, and 13 (1951): 87–164.

A. L.

Claudius Tiberius Nero, tragedy (*1607*; 1607)

Edition and Introduction

The only recent edition of *Claudius Tiberius Nero* is John Francis Abbick's 1967 University of North Carolina (Chapel Hill) dissertation (*DA* 28 [1968] : 3134-A). In his introduction, Abbick discusses attribution, sources, the dramatic structure of the play, genre, and the 1607 edition. The 1607 text is available in microprint in Henry W. Wells, ed., *Three Centuries of Drama* (Readex Corp., 1955–56).

Except for Abbick's edition, scholarship on *Claudius* consists of short notices. Only two of these deal with attribution: both William J. Lawrence, *The Physical Conditions of the Elizabethan Public Playhouse* (1927), and C. F. Tucker Brooke, in *A Literary History of England,* ed. Albert C. Baugh (1948), believe that the play was written by a university scholar.

Questions of date and sources have received no attention in the short notices.

Literary Connections and Miscellaneous

Brooke links the play with Shakespeare's *Julius Caesar* (1599) and Jonson's *Sejanus His Fall* (1603), plays based on Roman subjects by dramatists not connected with the Senecan school. In *Elizabethan Revenge Tragedy, 1587–1642* (1940), Fredson Bowers describes *Claudius* as a combination of conventions from Elizabethan and Jacobean revenge tragedies. He mentions also that *Revenge for Honour* (1640) borrows from *Claudius*. Brief references to stage directions in *Claudius* and the play's use of the stage appear in: Lawrence; John Cranford Adams, *The Globe Playhouse: Its Design and Equipment* (1942; 2nd ed. 1961); Richard Hosley, "Was there a Music-Room in Shakespeare's Globe?" *ShS* 13 (1960): 113–23; Leslie Hotson, *Shakespeare's Wooden O* (1959). Fredson Bowers, "Kyd's Pedringano: Sources and Parallels," *Harvard Studies and Notes in Philology and Literature* 13 (1931): 241–49, notes some attempts at irony in *Claudius*; Dieter Mehl, *The Elizabethan Dumb Show* (1966; German ed. 1964), comments that the tragedy includes formal processions and entrances but no genuine dumb shows; and Waldo F. McNeir, "Trial by Combat in Elizabethan Literature," *NS* 65 (1966): 101–12, remarks the use of the trial-by-combat theme. The precedent for and implications of the dedication are mentioned by William J. Lawrence in both "The Dedication of Early English Plays," *Life and Letters* 3 (1929): 30–44, and *Speeding up Shakespeare* (1937); and by Virgil B. Heltzel, "The Dedication of Tudor and Stuart Plays," in *Studies in English Language and Literature Presented to Professor Dr. Karl Brunner on the Occasion of his Seventieth Birthday*, ed. Siegfried Korninger (1957), pp. 74–86.

See Also

Bentley, G. E. *The Jacobean and Caroline Stage.* Vol. 5. 1956.

Bowden, William R. *The English Dramatic Lyric, 1603–42: A Study in Stuart Dramatic Technique.* 1951.

Cawley, Robert Ralston. *Unpathed Waters: Studies in the Influence of the Voyagers on Elizabethan Literature.* 1940.

Chew, Samuel C. *The Crescent and the Rose.* 1937.

Linton, Marion. "National Library of Scotland and Edinburgh University Library Copies of Plays in Greg's *Bibliography of the English Printed Drama.*" *SB* 15 (1962): 91–104.

J. L.

Every Woman in Her Humour, comedy (*1607*; 1609)

Introduction

The single recent edition of *Every Woman in Her Humour (EWH)* is Archie M. Tyson's 1952 University of Pennsylvania dissertation (*Doctoral Dissertations* 19 [1951-52] : 230). The 1609 text is available in microprint in Henry W. Wells, ed., *Three Centuries of Drama* (Readex Corp., 1955-56).

Scholarship on this anonymous play is sparse. Since the study of *EWH* by Joseph Quincy Adams, Jr., in *"Every Woman in Her Humor and The Dumb Knight,"* *MP* 10 (1913): 413-32, the comedy has received attention in only one brief article and a number of short notices. Two of the notices mention sources: Jesse Franklin Bradley and Joseph Quincy Adams, *The Jonson Allusion-Book* (1922), and Louis B. Wright, "Animal Actors on the English Stage before 1642," *PMLA* 42 (1927): 656-69, remark the indebtedness of *EWH* to Jonson's *Every Man in His Humour* (1598). None of the notices comment on attribution or date.

Literary Connections and Miscellaneous

R. P. Cowl, *Some "Echoes" in Elizabethan Drama of Shakespeare's "King Henry the Fourth," Parts I and II, Considered in Relation to the Text of Those Plays* (1926), notices an allusion to *1 Henry IV* in *EWH*. J. L. Cardozo, *The Contemporary Jew in the Elizabethan Drama* (1925), considers the anonymous play a Roman rather than a London comedy, and Thomas P. Harrison, Jr., "The Literary Background of Renaissance Poisons," *Studies in English* (Univ. of Texas) 27 (1948): 35-67, groups *EWH* with ten other English Renaissance dramas where a sleeping potion is taken purposely. The burlesque masque which concludes *EWH* receives attention from Louis B. Wright, "Vaudeville Dancing and Acrobatics in Elizabethan Plays," *Englische Studien* 63 (1928): 59-76, and the prologue is commented on by Autrey Nell Wiley, "Female Prologues and Epilogues in English Plays," *PMLA* 48 (1933): 1060-79. Wilfred T. Jewkes, *Act Division in Elizabethan and Jacobean Plays, 1583-1616* (1958), thinks that the text must have been printed from author's copy.

The music in *EWH* has inspired more discussion than any of the play's other features. In *Songs from the British Drama* (1925), Edward Bliss Reed, ed., quotes and identifies three songs in *EWH*, and mentions several others. William R. Bowden, *The English Dramatic Lyric, 1603-42: A Study in Stuart Dramatic Technique* (1951), lists the songs and disagrees with some of Reed's conclusions about them. Reviewing the use of vocal music in *EWH*, John P. Cutts, *"Everie Woman in Her Humor," RN* 18 (1965): 209-13, also discovers a contemporary musical setting for one of the songs. He suggests that knowledge of the kind of music the play employs makes it possible to speculate about the type of company for which *EWH* was written. Vincent Duckles, "The Music for the Lyrics in Early Seventeenth-Century English Drama: A Bibliography of the Primary Sources," in *Music in English Renaissance Drama,* ed. John H. Long (1968), pp. 117-60, lists the sources of the tunes of five popular airs in *EWH*.

See Also

Dawson, Giles E. "An Early List of Elizabethan Plays." *Library* 15 (1935): 445-56.

Gray, H. David, and Percy Simpson. "Shakespeare or Heminge? A Rejoinder and a Surrejoinder." *MLR* 45 (1950): 148-52.

Greg, W. W. "Authorship Attributions in the Early Play-Lists, 1656-1671." *Edinburgh Bibliographical Society Transactions* 2 (1938-45): 303-29.

Lawrence, William J. *Pre-Restoration Stage Studies.* 1927.

Modder, Montagu Frank. *The Jew in the Literature of England to the End of the Nineteenth Century.* 1939.

Myers, Aaron Michael. *Representation and Misrepresentation of the Puritan in Elizabethan Drama.* 1931.

Wright, Celeste Turner. "Something More about Eve." *SP* 41 (1944): 156-68.

J. L.

A SELECTED LIST OF USEFUL STUDIES

The books and articles in this list deal with or apply to a large number of anonymous plays, including those in other volumes of this series. Works which center on a specific play are cited in the essay on the play.

Adams, John Cranford. *The Globe Playhouse.* 1942; rev. ed. 1961.

Aronstein, Philipp. *Das englische Renaissancedrama.* 1929.

Ashley, Leonard R. N. *Authorship and Evidence.* 1968.

Babb, Lawrence. *The Elizabethan Malady.* 1951.

Bentley, Gerald Eades. "Authenticity and Attribution in the Jacobean and Caroline Drama." *English Institute Annual* (1942): 101-18.

Bowden, William R. *The English Dramatic Lyric, 1603-42.* 1951.

Chambers, E. K. *William Shakespeare.* 2 vols. 1930.

Craig, Hardin. *A New Look at Shakespeare's Quartos.* 1961.

Dawson, Giles E. "An Early List of Elizabethan Plays." *Library* 15 (1934-35): 445-56.

Eckhardt, Eduard. *Das englische Drama im Zeitalter der Reformation und der Hochrenaissance.* 1928.

————. *Das englische Drama der Spätrenaissance.* 1929.

Eichhorn, Traudl. "Prosa und Vers im vorshakespeareschen Drama." *SJ* 84/86 (1948-50): 140-98.

Greg, W. W. *Dramatic Documents from the Elizabethan Playhouses.* 2 vols. 1931.

————. "Authorship Attributions in the Early Play-Lists, 1656-1671." *Edinburgh Bibliographical Society Transactions* 2 (1938-45): 303-29.

Grossmann, Rudolf. *Spanien und das elisabethanische Drama.* 1920.

Harbage, Alfred. *Shakespeare and the Rival Traditions.* 1952.

Hewett-Thayer, Harvey W. "Tieck and the Elizabethan Drama: His Marginalia." *JEGP* 34 (1935): 377-407.

Hoffmann, Friedrich. "Die typischen Situationen im elisabethanischen Drama und ihr Pattern." *SJ* 94 (1958): 107-20.

Jewkes, Wilfred T. *Act Division in Elizabethan and Jacobean Plays, 1583-1616.* 1958.

Koskenniemi, Inna. *Studies in the Vocabulary of English Drama, 1550-1600, excluding Shakespeare and Ben Jonson.* 1962.

Lawrence, William J. *Pre-Restoration Stage Studies.* 1927.

Linthicum, M. Channing. *Costume in the Drama of Shakespeare and His Contemporaries.* 1936.

Linton, Marion. "National Library of Scotland and Edinburgh University Library Copies of Plays in Greg's *Bibliography of the English Printed Drama.*" *SB* 15 (1962): 91-104.

Lüdeke, H. *Ludwig Tieck und das alte englische Theater.* Deutsche Forschungen, vol. 6 (1922).

Main, William W. "Dramaturgical Norms in the Elizabethan Repertory." *SP* 54 (1957): 128-48.

Maxwell, Baldwin. "The Shakespeare Apocrypha." *ShN* 14 (1964): 45.

Nicoll, Allardyce. "'Tragical-Comical-Historical-Pastoral': Elizabethan Dramatic Nomenclature." *BJRL* 43 (1960-61): 70-87.

Oras, Ants. *Pause Patterns in Elizabethan and Jacobean Drama: An Experiment in Prosody.* 1960.

Parks, Edd Winfield. "Simms's Edition of the Shakespeare Apocrypha." In *Studies in Shakespeare,* ed. Arthur D. Matthews and Clark M. Emery (1953), pp. 30-39.

Prior, Moody E. "Imagery as a Test of Authorship." *SQ* 6 (1955): 381-86.

Schelling, Felix E. *Elizabethan Playwrights.* 1925.

Schoenbaum, S. *Internal Evidence and Elizabethan Dramatic Authorship.* 1966.

Sehrt, Ernst T. *Der dramatische Auftakt in der elisabethanischen Tragödie.* 1960.

Stroup, Thomas B. *Microcosmos: The Shape of the Elizabethan Play.* 1965.

Talbert, E. W. *Elizabethan Drama and Shakespeare's Early Plays.* 1963.

Tillyard, E. M. W. *Shakespeare's History Plays.* 1944.

Trainer, James. "Some Unpublished Shakespeare Notes of Ludwig Tieck." *MLR* 54 (1959): 368–77.

Studies of Shakespeare often comment on the anonymous plays, especially the apocrypha and plays closely connected to the Shakespeare canon.

Microfilms of the early quarto editions of the following plays are included in Henry W. Wells, ed., *Three Centuries of Drama* (Readex Microprint Corp., 1955–56): *Arden of Feversham, Edward III, Fair Em, The Famous Victories of Henry V, King Leir, A Knack to Know a Knave, The Life and Death of Jack Straw, Locrine, Mucedorus, The Rare Triumphs of Love and Fortune, Selimus, Soliman and Perseda, The Taming of a Shrew, I & II The Troublesome Reign of King John, The True Tragedy of Richard III, The Wars of Cyrus.*

A. L. & J. L.

OTHER DRAMATISTS

Terence P. Logan   Denzell S. Smith

The figures included here were active at the same time as the major playwrights treated in this volume; all or a majority of their plays were initially performed under auspices other than those of companies primarily active in the London open-air public theaters. They are included because their plays have been the subject of some recent scholarship. Articles and books dealing exclusively or primarily with their nondramatic works are not included. For additional information see: G. E. Bentley, The Jacobean and Caroline Stage, *7 vols. (1941–68), E. K. Chambers,* The Elizabethan Stage, *4 vols. (1923), W. W. Greg,* A Bibliography of the English Printed Drama to the Restoration, *4 vols. (1939–59), Alfred Harbage,* Annals of English Drama, 975–1700, *rev. Samuel Schoenbaum (1964), and the* Supplements *by Schoenbaum (1966, 1970). The essays on anonymous plays and on appropriate major authors in this volume, as well as those in* The Predecessors of Shakespeare *and* The Popular School, *ed. Terence P. Logan and Denzell S. Smith (1973, 1975), include more extensive treatments of the plays of uncertain authorship and the collaborative plays that are dealt with here. Playwrights are discussed in alphabetical order. Entries are listed in chronological order for each playwright and include items listed in the available source bibliographies from the publication of* The Elizabethan Stage *(1923) to the end of 1974; the title of each work is followed by a brief summary of its contents.*

WILLIAM ALEXANDER

Kastner, L. E., and H. B. Charlton, ed. *The Poetical Works of Sir William Alexander, Earl of Stirling.* 2 vols. 1921–29. (Publ. also as Scottish Text Society Pubs., n. s., no. 11 [1921], no. 24 [1929].) Volume one contains four plays, *Croesus, The Tragedy of Darius, The*

Alexandraean Tragedy, and *Julius Caesar,* each with explanatory notes and variants, and a two-hundred-page essay on the Senecan tradition in Europe (rpt. separately as *The Senecan Tradition in Renaissance Tragedy,* 1946). The essay discusses Seneca's tragedies, Latin and Greek tragedy in the Renaissance, and the Senecan tradition in Italy, France, and England. The section on the Senecan tradition in England treats in detail the growth of Senecan influence and its relationship to French and Italian models. Alexander's plays, with Greville's, represent the "final crystallisation of all the tendencies of Seneca and of the French school." Alexander's life-long revisions (of vocabulary, syntax, and pronunciation) point to a conscious standardization of the language. Volume two contains the poems and a bibliographical description of early editions of the works.

McGrail, Thomas H. *Sir William Alexander, First Earl of Stirling: A Biographical Study.* 1940. This full-length biography includes a chapter titled "Literary Life and Reputation." That Alexander's literary work was well known and praised by his contemporaries is established from the written records of his relations with William Drummond (a thirty-year friendship), Michael Drayton (mutual regard), Samuel Daniel (who praised Alexander in verse as early as 1605), William Habington, and many other English and Scots men of letters. After his death his reputation declined quickly.

Dent, Robert W. "John Webster's Debt to William Alexander." *MLN* 65 (1950): 73–83. Seventeen verbal parallels in *The Duchess of Malfi* and *The White Devil,* and one in *The Devil's Law Case,* support the contention that Webster borrowed from Alexander. No common source for the parallels is likely; Alexander, like Webster, reveals no direct verbal imitation of earlier writers.

Gordon, T. Crouther. *Four Notable Scots.* 1960. Alexander's literary work receives brief evaluative notice in this forty-page biographical survey of his life as striving, successful, and finally bankrupt courtier to James and Charles.

Ure, Peter. "*The Duchess of Malfi*: Another Debt to Sir William Alexander." *N&Q* 13 (1966): 296. Webster's source for "We are merely the stars' tennis balls" probably is *The Alexandraean Tragedy,* V.i.

ROBERT ANTON

Lloyd, Bertram. "The Authorship of *The Valiant Welshman.*" *N&Q* 197 (1952): 425-27. Lloyd ascribes the play to Anton on the basis of parallels with works of proven authorship. The claim for Robert Armin is rejected. See the discussion of attribution under the play title in the Anonymous Plays section of *The Popular School.*

ROBERT ARMIN

For Armin's connections with The Valiant Welshman, *see the discussion of that play in* The Popular School.

Baldwin, T. W. "Shakespeare's Jester: The Dates of *Much Ado* and *As You Like It.*" *MLN* 39 (1924): 447-55. Using facts from theater history, Baldwin dates the performance of *Two Maids of More-Clacke* in the autumn and winter of 1597 or 1598. [The *Annals* cites the dating limits as 1607-8.]

Denkinger, Emma Marshall. "Actors' Names in the Registers of St. Bodolph Aldgate." *PMLA* 41 (1926): 91-109. A summary of the known facts about Armin is followed by new information found in the Registers (Armin married, had three children, and died on 30 Nov. 1615) and records of the Goldsmiths' Company (the entry for Armin's apprenticeship).

Gray, Austin K. "Robert Armine, the Foole." *PMLA* 42 (1927): 673-85. Gray re-states the facts of Armin's life, lists his works, and speculates on his character. Armin hid his kindness, wisdom, and charity "behind a veil of mirth." The characters of the fools acted by Armin in *As You Like It, Twelfth Night,* and *King Lear* are discussed briefly.

Murry, John Middleton. "A 'Fellow' of Shakespeare: Robert Armin." *New Adelphi* 1 (1928): 251-53. Armin's works, including *The Two Maids of More-Clacke,* contain many reminiscences of Shakespeare's lines, and none of other writers. *Two Maids* parodies the situation in *Hamlet.*

Herring, Robert. "The Whale Has a Wide Mouth, or Harlequin Faustus." *Life and Letters Today* 36 (1943): 44-65. In this survey of minor plays, Herring accepts *The Valiant Welshman* as Armin's, quoting

frequently to show that his language had "individuality and force. . . .
He knew what he wanted to say and had the words for it."

Dudley, O. H. T. "John in the Hospital." *TLS*, 17 June 1949, p. 397.
The woodcut on the title page of the 1609 quarto of *Two Maids of
More-Clacke* unmistakably depicts the uniform worn by schoolboys of
Christ's Hospital, and suggests that John, the natural fool in the play,
was modeled on a living contemporary who, because he was a fool,
"enjoyed the protection of the uniform as long as he lived."

Williams, Philip. "The Compositor of the 'Pied Bull' *Lear.*" *SB* 1
(1949): 61–68. The two compositors of the quarto text of *Two Maids
of More-Clacke,* printed by Nicholas Okes in 1609, also set *The White
Devil*; one of them, compositor B, set the "Pied Bull" *Lear* quarto
(1608).

Lloyd, Bertram. "The Authorship of *The Valiant Welshman.*" *N&Q*
197 (1952): 425–27. Robert Anton, not Armin, is the author because
of similarities to Anton's known work in style and in astronomical and
classical allusions.

Long, John H. *Shakespeare's Use of Music: A Study of the Music and
Its Performance in the Original Production of Seven Comedies.* 1955.
Contains a brief summary of Armin's career and scattered references to
him as a singer.

Felver, Charles S. "Robert Armin, Shakespeare's Source for Touchstone." *SQ* 7 (1956): 135–37. The evidence indicates that Armin's *Two
Maids* "was written and acted in by him before his engagement by the
Shakespearian company." Thus Shakespeare compliments Armin "by
naming his first important role with the Chamberlain's Men, Touchstone in *As You Like It,* after the part (Tutch) Armin created in his
own play."

————. "Robert Armin's Fragment of a Bawdy Ballad of 'Mary
Ambree.'" *N&Q* 7 (1960): 14–16. Allusions to Mary Ambree in Elizabethan drama imply moral laxity not found in the preserved ballads,
but a song in *Two Maids of More-Clacke* explicitly states it. Felver
suggests that Armin wrote as well as sang a bawdy ballad about Mary
Ambree.

————. *Robert Armin, Shakespeare's Fool: A Biographical Essay.* 1961. While emphasizing Armin's life, this eighty-two page essay places him in the clowning tradition of the English theater, examines the clown in his play *The Two Maids of More-Clacke,* traces the development of the Feste-Touchstone type of fool in his works, and analyzes his roles as fool in Shakespeare.

Sternfeld, F. W. "Twentieth-Century Studies in Shakespeare's Songs, Sonnets, and Poems. 1. Songs and Music." *ShS* 15 (1962): 1-10. Several of the studies mentioned in this survey refer to the songs in Armin's plays, the relationship of Armin to the songs in Shakespeare's plays, and Armin as a singer.

Bradbrook, M. C. *Shakespeare the Craftsman: The Clark Lectures, 1968.* 1969. Details from contemporary records support an overview of Armin's dramatic career, style as a clown, influence on *Twelfth Night,* and later career. Similarities in scenes between plays Armin acted in and *The Valiant Welshman* (as well as other arguments) suggest that he was the author of *VW.*

Feather, John. "A Check-List of the Works of Robert Armin." *Library* 26 (1971): 165-72. The check-list contains simplified title-page transcriptions with collations, traces copies, and cites *STC* references and other matter for pre-1641 editions. It supplies short titles and dates and places of publication for post-1641 editions.

WILLIAM BARKSTEAD

Turner, Robert K., Jr. "The Compositors of *The Insatiate Countess,* Q2." *SB* 12 (1958): 198-203. Two, possibly three, compositors set the 1614 edition using the 1613 edition as copy-text. See the discussion in the Marston essay (II,A, and III,A) in this volume.

Gunby, D. C. "Further Borrowings by Webster?" *N&Q* 13 (1966): 296-97. Supplements R. W. Dent's *John Webster's Borrowing* (1960) with additional items from *The Insatiate Countess.*

LORDING BARRY

Ewen, C. L'Estrange. "Lording Barry, Dramatist." *N&Q* 174 (1938): 111-12. The author of *Ram Alley* is Lording Barry, not the elder son of David, Lord Barry. Biographical details of Barry's life as pirate and adventurer are cited (he made peace with the Lord Admiral in 1615 by presenting him with gifts: silver cloth, silver lace, a Negro wench, and a Flemish ship laden with cod).

―――. *Lording Barry, Poet and Pirate.* 1938. Contemporary records establish Barry's given name, genealogy, authorship, financial involvement as shareholder in the Whitefrairs theater, and later life as a pirate and adventurer. [16 p. pamphlet.]

Jones, Claude E., ed. *Ram-Alley or Merrie-Trickes: A Comedy by Lording Barry.* 1952. The introduction summarizes the facts of Barry's life, describes the characters and action of the play, and establishes the fact of three quartos, two dated 1611, the third 1636. The text is a reprint of the first edition; textual variants and useful explanatory notes are supplied.

Leggatt, Alexander. *Citizen Comedy in the Age of Shakespeare.* 1973. Although *Ram Alley* creates a "pungent satiric picture of society" which goes beyond its model, Middleton's *A Trick to Catch the Old One,* "the response it evokes . . . is entirely amoral." There are "few plays of the period in which moral considerations are so successfully excluded."

WILLIAM BROWNE

Cutts, John P. "Original Music to Browne's Inner Temple Masque, and Other Jacobean Masque Music." *N&Q* 1 (1954): 194-95. Some of the original music, perhaps set by Robert Johnson, is preserved in a manuscript found in Wells.

Jones, Gwyn, ed. *Circe and Ulysses.* 1954. A deluxe edition which includes woodcuts by Mark Severin and a prefatory essay by Jones on Browne and the masque tradition.

Hill, R. F., ed. *The Masque of the Inner Temple (Ulysses and Circe).* In *A Book of Masques: In Honour of Allardyce Nicoll,* ed. T. J. B. Spencer and Stanley W. Wells (1967), pp. 179-206. Includes full glossarial notes and an analysis of the text. The mask was probably written for Christmas, 1641.

ROBERT DABORNE

Flood, W. H. Grattan. "Fennor and Daborne at Youghal in 1618." *MLR* 20 (1925): 321-22. The article supplies details about Daborne's career in the church (ordained in 1616, he was fellow of Youghal College 1616-19), preferment by Baron Boyle, owner of Youghal, and involvement in Boyle's forging of deeds for the sequestration of endowments for the College.

Bacon, Wallace A. "The Source of Robert Daborne's *The Poor-Mans Comfort*," *MLN* 57 (1942): 345-48. William Warner's *Pan His Syrinx* (1584; 2d ed. 1597, titled *Syrinx*) provided story and moral for the main plot and details for the subplot.

————, ed. *William Warner's Syrinx, or a Sevenfold History*. 1950. The introduction summarizes the editor's article in *MLN*, above.

Palmer, Kenneth, ed. *The Poor Man's Comfort*. 1955, for 1954. This Malone Society edition is meant to "provide a basis for further investigation" of the relationship between the quarto and the manuscript. [BM Egerton 1994 is treated at length in Frederick S. Boas, *Shakespeare and the Universities and Other Studies in Elizabethan Drama*, 1923.] The editor describes the physical characteristics of the manuscript, which is "not a playhouse copy," and discusses its provenance. Substantive differences between the 1655 quarto and the manuscript are listed; the quarto was printed from a prompt-book. Certain details in the play are explained by its known source, Warner's *Pan His Syrinx*. The date of composition is ca. 1615-17. [The *Annals* cites limits as 1610-17.]

Maxwell, Baldwin. "Notes on Robert Daborne's Extant Plays." *PQ* 50 (1971): 85-98. Daborne's habit of working on more than one play at a time, alone and in collaboration, and of forwarding finished portions to Henslowe, precluded his writing plays of real merit. *A Christian Turned Turk* was composed "not before late 1610, and perhaps more likely in 1611"; the 1612 quarto probably was printed from an authorial manuscript. The supposed allusion to the Porters' Hall Theatre in *The Poor Man's Comfort* is insufficient to date the play 1615-17; repetition in it of passages in *A Christian Turned Turk,* and Daborne's habit of working on more than one play, suggest an earlier date, perhaps 1610. Hints in the preface to *A Christian Turned Turk* lead Maxwell to believe that Edmund Verney may have secured the play's suppression, since a London audience would have recognized his half brother, Sir Francis, in the character Francisco.

PHINEAS FLETCHER

Langdale, Abram Barnett. *Phineas Fletcher: Man of Letters, Science, and Divinity.* 1937. This full-length study treats Fletcher's biography, scientific interest, poetic sources and tradition, and, briefly, the occasion, publication, and sources of *Siceledes*.

————. "Phineas Fletcher's Marriage: A Parallel to the Shakespeare Marriage Records," *N&Q* 177 (1939): 327-28. Carelessness about spelling and inaccurate recording of details by parish clerks account for discrepancies in the marriage records.

Berry, Lloyd E. "Phineas Fletcher: Additions and Corrections." *N&Q* 7 (1960): 54. Three biographical details supplement Langdale, above.

Baldwin, R. G. "Phineas Fletcher: His Modern Readers and His Renaissance Ideas." *PQ* 40 (1961): 462-75. In support of his claim that recent Fletcher scholarship typically is "piecemeal and superficial," Baldwin cites errors in Langdale (above), M. H. Nicolson (*The Breaking of the Circle,* 1950), and others. Fletcher is a "valuable source of Renaissance ideas in their clearest, most settled, simplest form"; the "fantastic, eccentric, and obscure Fletcher of the literary historians never existed."

Grundy, Joan. *The Spenserian Poets: A Study in Elizabethan and Jacobean Poetry.* 1969. *Sicelides* is a "tedious, complicated entertainment" indebted to Italian pastoral drama.

FULKE GREVILLE

Kuhl, E. P. "Contemporary Politics in Elizabethan Drama: Fulke Greville," *PQ* 7 (1928): 299-302. Greville believed plays should use thinly disguised allusions to contemporary political situations as a means of correcting abuses.

Rice, Warner G. "The Sources of Fulke Greville's *Alaham.*" *JEGP* 30 (1931): 179-87. "Greville obviously drew upon the narrative of

Ludovico di Varthema, an Italian traveller whose *Itinerary* was first published in Rome in 1510." Seneca, perhaps in Jasper Heywood's translation, was also an influence.

Bullough, Geoffrey. "Fulke Greville, First Lord Brooke." *MLR* 28 (1933): 1–20. Greville's life is reconstructed from contemporary records.

Shaver, Chester L. "The Date of *Revenge for Honour.*" *MLN* 53 (1938): 96–98. Shaver rejects Fredson Bowers's hypothesis, in an article with the same title (*MLN* 52 [1937]: 192–96), that the French Ambassador saw a performance of *Alaham*; he also disputes the early date Bowers advances for *Revenge for Honour.*

Bullough, Geoffrey, ed. *Poems and Dramas of Fulke Greville, First Lord Brooke.* 2 vols. 1939. The second volume includes texts of the plays with a full apparatus. The critical introduction concludes: "The history of Greville's dramatic career is one of failure, but of failure qualified by noble experiment."

Edwards, A. C. "Fulke Greville on Tragedy." *TLS,* 8 June 1940, p. 279. Greville held that an important function of tragedy was to show ambitious governors how they hasten to ruination.

Orsini, Napoleone. *Fulke Greville tra il mondo e Dio.* 1941. Greville's enigmatic sadness is part of his special fascination. His thought reflects the unresolved conflicts between his Italian artistic ideals, his Calvinism, and his strong nationalistic feelings.

Morgan, Marjorie McC. "Fulke Greville's Birth." *TLS,* 4 Nov. 1944, p. 535. Letters in the University of Aberdeen Library give Greville's birth hour as 7:00 A.M., 3 Oct. 1554.

Utz, Hans Werner. *Die Anschauungen über Wissenschaft und Religion im Werke Fulke Grevilles.* 1948. A biographical sketch is followed by two chapters establishing the basic conflict in Greville's views on science (a follower of Bacon's empiricism) and religion (a believer in traditional Christianity). The final chapter traces the duality and tension in Greville's political thought to his—and his age's—underlying conflict between science and religion.

Newman, Franklin B. "Sir Fulke Greville and Giordano Bruno: A Possible Echo." *PQ* 29 (1950): 367–74. Greville is second only to Sidney among the English authors mentioned by Bruno. The chorus tertius of *Mustapha* has echoes of the *Spaccio della bestia trionfante* and other passages in Greville reflect his close reading of Bruno.

Ure, Peter. "Fulke Greville's Dramatic Characters." *RES* 1 (1950): 308–23. "The emphasis on the correlation between outward weakness and crime and their origin within the creature is the essential psychological principle upon which Greville's *personae* are constructed." He is "pre-eminently the dramatist of the inward man."

———. "A Note on 'Opinion' in Daniel, Greville, and Chapman." *MLR* 46 (1951): 331–38. For Greville, "to trust to outward opinion was to forsake the task of creating an inward discipline of virtue."

Jacquot, Jean. "Religion et raison d'état dans l'oeuvre de Fulke Greville." *EA* 5 (1952): 211–22. The focus is on the plays, especially on the religious attitudes they reflect. Greville believes in predestination; he is also a very enigmatic author. "Il y a en lui une voix qué murmure contre la dureté de la loi du Ciel; une autre lui dit que peut-être après tout Lucrèce a raison."

MacLean, Hugh N. "Fulke Greville: Kingship and Sovereignty." *HLQ* 16 (1953): 237–71. Greville "specifically rejects both aristocratic and democratic forms of government." He accepts some and rejects other ideas associated with divine right, but he has a consistent passion for order and always maintains that "a benevolent central power is highly preferable to even a semi-democratic regime."

Wilkes, G. A. "The Sources of Fulke Greville's *Mustapha*." *N&Q* 5 (1958): 329–30. A pamphlet source is included in vol. 2 of Painter's *Palace of Pleasure* (1575); Greville need not have depended on the later edition and the play may be significantly earlier than the accepted date of 1603 or 1604.

———. "The Sequence of the Writings of Fulke Greville, Lord Brooke." *SP* 56 (1959): 489–503. A closely argued chronology for the full canon is presented.

Oras, Ants. "Fulke Greville's *Mustapha* and Robert Wilmot's *Tancred and Gismund*." *N&Q* 7 (1960): 24-25. Act V, scene ii, of *Mustapha* borrows from and improves on *Tancred*.

Morris, Ivor. "The Tragic Vision of Fulke Greville." *ShS* 14 (1961): 66-75. Greville's sense of tragedy, which is defined, may offer insights into Shakespearean tragedy.

Bullough, Geoffrey. "Sénèque, Greville et le jeune Shakespeare." In *Les tragedies de Sénèque et la théâtre de la renaissance,* ed. Jean Jacquot and Marcel Oddon (1964), pp. 189-201. Greville's and Shakespeare's use of a common source are compared.

LaGuardia, Eric. "Figural Imitation in English Renaissance Poetry." In *Actes du IV congrès de l'association internationale de littèrature comparée,* ed. François Jost, 2 vols. (1966), vol. 2, pp. 844-54. Examples from Greville, including his plays, figure in a discussion of the roles of the ideal and mundane worlds in Renaissance mimetic poetry.

Muir, Kenneth. *Introduction to Elizabethan Literature.* 1967. *Alaham* and *Mustapha* are "abortive as dramas" but "contain some of Greville's finest poetry."

Gunn, Thom, ed. *Selected Poems of Fulke Greville.* 1968. There is a brief general introduction; choruses from the plays are included.

Farmer, Norman, Jr. "Fulke Greville and Sir John Coke: An Exchange of Letters on a History Lecture and Certain Latin Verses on Sir Philip Sidney." *HLQ* 33 (1970): 217-36. Greville's letters to Coke and a draft of a Coke reply provide several biographical details and insight into Greville's theories about history.

Kelliher, W. Hilton. "The Warwick Manuscripts of Fulke Greville." *British Museum Quarterly* 34 (1970): 107-21. The largest extant authorized manuscript text for an Elizabethan author is described and analyzed.

Rebholz, Ronald A. *The Life of Fulke Greville, First Lord Brooke.* 1971. The extensive biographical material is comprehensively presented with a consistent critical interpretation of the canon. Most significant earlier scholarship and criticism is incorporated here.

Rees, Joan. *Fulke Greville, Lord Brooke, 1554-1628: A Critical Biography.* 1971. A selective rather than a comprehensive approach is used. The plays are discussed in a full chapter which considers the possibility of revisions. "*Mustapha* illustrates the dangers of government by a tyrant, *Alaham* the perils of a state ruled over by a weak king."

Bennett, Paula. "Recent Studies in Greville." *English Literary Renaissance* 2 (1972): 376-82. Scholarship on Greville, including material on the nondramatic works, published between 1945 and 1971 is surveyed; the format is based on that used for major dramatists in this series.

Levy, F. J. "Fulke Greville: The Courtier as Philosophic Poet." *MLQ* 33 (1972): 433-48. Although Greville was not always as moral as he pretends (he was an accessory to Suffolk's peculation of royal funds), the plays reflect his dissatisfaction with the immorality of James's court.

Waller, G. F. "Fulke Greville's Struggle with Calvinism." *Studia Neophilologica* 44 (1972): 295-314. "Greville's God has the power of the earthly tyrants in his dramas, plus—a feature denied to earthly monarchs—an incomprehensible impregnability." Greville's domination by a tyrannical God "results in his vision being capable of neither glory nor tragedy."

Rees, Joan, ed. *Selected Writings of Fulke Greville.* 1973. Selections from *Alaham* and the full text of *Mustapha* are included.

GERVASE MARKHAM

Silbermann, Abraham Moritz. *Untersuchungen über die Quellen des Dramas "The True Tragedy of Herod and Antipater with the Death of Faire Mariam," by Gervase Markham and William Sampson (1622).* N. d. [1927?]. Parallels to other Jacobean plays are noted. The main source is probably not Josephus but Peter Morwyng's *History of the Jewes Commune Weale* (1558).

Valency, Maurice. *The Tragedies of Herod and Miriamne.* 1940. Forty dramatizations, written from the Renaissance to the present, are studied comparatively.

Mullett, Charles F. "Gervase Markham: Scientific Amateur." *Isis* 35 (1944): 106-18. Markham's scientific and literary accomplishments are surveyed.

Thayer, C. G. "Ben Jonson, Markham, and Shakespeare." *N&Q* 1 (1954): 469-70. Jonson closely follows a passage in Markham's *Cavelarice* for the description of Win-the-Fight Littlewit, *Bartholemew Fair,* IV.v.21-27.

Gittings, Robert. *Shakespeare's Rival: A Study in Three Parts.* 1960. Evidence, chiefly allusions, is offered to establish Markham as the rival poet of Shakespeare's sonnets.

Muir, Kenneth. "Some Words in *Devoreux*." *N&Q* 9 (1962): 207. The poem may provide the key to identifying Markham as the rival poet in Shakespeare's sonnets.

Poynter, F. N. L. *A Bibliography of Gervase Markham, 1568?–1637.* 1962. The introduction gives a careful reappraisal of Markham's life and works. Detailed information, including locations, is provided about the early editions.

————. "Gervase Markham." *E&S* 15 (1962): 27-39. Markham does not deserve his reputation as a hack; his works show real talent and his contribution to popular education was significant.

Scragg, Leah. "Shakespearian Influence in *Herod and Antipater*." *N&Q* 15 (1968): 258-62. Antipater, a bastard in the play, is legitimate in the sources; "the characterization of Antipater, certain elements of the plot, and a number of verbal echoes suggest that the play is particularly indebted to the sub-plot of *King Lear* and that the characterization of Antipater is based upon that of Edmund."

JOHN MASON

Wadsworth, Frank W. "The Relationship of *Lust's Dominion* and John Mason's *The Turke*." *ELH* 20 (1953): 194-99. "Similarities in the conception and handling of character, situation, and plot devices which go far beyond the obvious resemblances arising from two tragedies' being part of a contemporary 'villain play' tradition" suggest that Mason used the earlier tragedy as a model.

ALEXANDER MONTGOMERY

See the discussion of Philotus *in the Anonymous Plays section of this volume.*

Mill, A. J., ed. *Philotus.* In *Miscellany Volume,* Scottish Text Society, 3d ser., vol. 4 (1933), pp. 83-158. Neither contemporary historical nor internal literary evidence provides clues for authorship. Robert Semple's claim is dismissed. The editor discusses the relationship of the play to its source, *Riche His Farewell,* and their relationship to a common source, *Gli Ingannati,* without reaching a conclusion. The edition is a reprint of the 1603 quarto; it includes variants from the 1612 edition and a glossary.

Dilworth, Mark. "New Light on Alexander Montgomerie." *Bibliotheck* 4 (1965): 230-35. Previously unknown information about the life and death of Montgomery after he was outlawed in 1597 is revealed in commemorative Latin funeral poems by a Scots monk, Thomas Duff.

Shire, Helena M. "Alexander Montgomerie, 'The Oppositione of the Court to Conscience': 'Court and Conscience wallis not weill.'" *Studies in Scottish Literature* 3 (1966): 144-50. Shire gives a close prose translation of Thomas Duff's Latin funeral poems for Montgomery.

Jack, Ronald D. S. "Montgomerie and the Pirates." *Studies in Scottish Literature* 5 (1967): 133-36. Two entries from *The Calendar of State Papers (Foreign)* provide biographical details for 1586-90, a hazy period for previous biographers. Montgomery was caught at sea by the English in 1586, suspected of piracy and Catholic sympathies, and possibly imprisoned.

McDiarmid, M. P. "*Philotus:* A Play of the Scottish Renaissance." *Forum for Modern Language Studies* 3 (1967): 223-35. The source is "Of Phylotus and Emilia," the eighth tale in Barnaby Rich's *Rich His Farewell to Military Profession.* Montgomery has an "indisputable claim" to authorship "by the tests of a common spirit, style, language, and phrasing." Robert Semple's style, in the Lindseian school, "forbids any notion" of his authorship. Previous arguments for the date of the play are considered and rejected; the evidence points to 1583-86. Montgomery's career also accords with this dating.

Shire, Helena Mennie. *Song, Dance, and Poetry of the Court of Scotland under King James VI.* 1969. Contains a twenty-page survey of Montgomery's life.

WILLIAM PERCY

Dodds, Madeleine Hope. "William Percy and Charles Fitzjeffrey." *N&Q* 160 (1931): 420-22. The date of the action of the main plot, Percy's friendship with Fitzjeffrey, and other details support a date for a first version of *The Cuckqueans and Cuckolds Errants* "soon after 1590." The play parodies Senecan drama. [The *Annals* assigns a date of 1601.]

―――. "William Percy and James I." *N&Q* 161 (1931): 13-14. Allusions in *The Fairy Pastoral* (which has "no redeeming features whatsoever") make it "fairly certain" that the play was written for and probably performed during James's visit with the Duke of Northumberland in 1603.

―――. "William Percy's *Aphrodysial.*" *N&Q* 161 (1931): 236-40, 257-61. Percy wrote the play for the christening of a nephew in 1602. He "revised this and all his other plays [for] performance by the Children of Paul's." Evidence for alteration is found in the stage directions, which are reprinted in full. Four plot details are imitated from *The Merry Wives of Windsor.*

―――. "*A Dreame of a Drye Yeare.*" *JEGP* 32 (1933): 172-95. Locates three manuscript volumes of Percy's plays, describes their contents, summarizes the plot of *A Dreame,* and cites academic influences and contemporary allusions. Details about the Near East in the play are compared to those in contemporary and modern accounts. William Basse's *Urania,* a long narrative poem (1603-12), is indebted to the play, which is dated 1601. [The *Annals* cites this play by the title *Arabia Sitiens, or a Dream of a Dry Year.*]

Hillebrand, Harold N. "William Percy: An Elizabethan Amateur." *HLQ* 1 (1938): 391-416. A full biography and a description of the manuscripts at the Huntington Library and Alnwick Castle precede a survey of criticism of the plays. The plays, written for adult actors, were performed for a private audience. The dates of the plays in the manuscripts are correct. A summary of *A Country Tragedy* and *Necromantes* concludes the article.

Dodds, Madeleine Hope. "*A Forrest Tragaedye in Vacunium.*" *MLR* 40 (1945): 246-58. The play reveals Italian influence in the Chorus. Percy uses Boccaccio, an Italian tragedy, and *Gismond of Salerne* as sources for the main plot, and contemporary French politics for the subplot. The play has value as social history, since it reflects the "manners, the interests, and the gossip of the period 1601-3." [The *Annals* cites this play by the title *A Country Tragedy in Vacunium.*]

Hughes, Leo, and Arthur H. Scouten. "Some Theatrical Adaptations of a Picaresque Tale." *Studies in English* (Univ. of Texas) 25 (1945-46): 98-114. Percy's manuscript play *Cuckqueans and Cuckolds Errants* appears to be the "first attempt to make dramatic use of a story which was to persist in the theater for two centuries and more." Subsequent uses of the story by Marston and other dramatists of the seventeenth and eighteenth centuries are discussed.

Race, Sydney. "John Payne Collier." *N&Q* 195 (1950): 21. The late date of authorial transcription and other details arouse suspicion that the Alnwick manuscripts containing the plays are not genuine.

Wright, Herbert G. *Boccaccio in England from Chaucer to Tennyson.* 1957. The sources for the opening and the main plot of *A Forest Tragedy in Vacunium* are Boccaccio's *Il Sacrificio* and the *Decameron.* [The *Annals* cites *A Forest Tragedy* by the title *A Country Tragedy in Vacunium.*]

Greenfield, Thelma N. *The Induction in Elizabethan Drama.* 1969. Descriptions of stage decor, properties, and costumes in the Huntington Library manuscript of *A Country Tragedy in Vacunium* illuminate Percy's use of "several types of induction materials to symbolize and to explain his play and finally to defend it."

JOHN SANSBURYE

Harbage, Alfred. "The Authorship of *The Christmas Prince.*" *MLN* 50 (1935): 501-5. *Periander,* included in a manuscript called *The Christmas Prince,* could be by Sansburye; the play imitates *Lear* at points.

EDWARD SHARPHAM

Nicoll, Allardyce, ed. *Cupid's Whirligig.* 1926. The copy text is the 1607 quarto; variants from the 1611, 1616, and 1630 quartos are listed.

The criticism in the introduction is sharply qualified. *Whirligig* is "a coarse play, coarse in theme, coarse in character-delineation, and coarse in texture."

Leech, Clifford. "The Plays of Edward Sharpham: Alterations Accomplished and Projected." *RES* 11 (1935): 69–74. Sharpham made extensive revisions in both the plays firmly ascribed to him. The revisions are sloppy but they show Sharpham working to meet the demands of the stage.

ROBERT TAILOR

Albright, Evelyn May. "A Stage Cartoon of the Mayor of London in 1613." *The Manly Anniversary Studies in Language and Literature* (1923), pp. 113-26. *The Hog Hath Lost His Pearl* (1614) satirizes the greed of the Lord Mayor of London, Sir John Swinnerton, and secondarily burlesques recent plays (in allusions, ludicrous mingling of two lines of action, and the "farcically overdone romanticism of the minor plot"), especially Dekker's *If It Be Not Good, the Devil Is in It.* Swinnerton connived to acquire the grant of patents on wines—the "pearl" alluded to in the title.

McKenzie, D. F., ed. *The Hogge Hath Lost His Pearl.* 1972, for 1967. The introduction to this Malone Society edition describes the 1614 quarto and its printing history, reprints Sir Henry Wotton's letter about the furor caused by the first production, and explains the reasons for the furor—satire on the Lord Mayor, Sir John Swinnerton.

THOMAS TOMKIS

Tilley, Morris P. "The Comedy *Lingua* and the *Fairie Queene.*" *MLN* 42 (1927): 150-57. The *Fairie Queene* is "the immediate source" of the play's main action and most of its allegory.

———. "The Comedy *Lingua* and Du Bartas's *La Sepmaine.*" *MLN* 42 (1927): 293-99. Tomkis borrows heavily from Du Bartas.

———. "The Comedy *Lingua* and Sir John Davies's *Nosce Teipsum.*" *MLN* 44 (1929): 36-39. Borrowings from Davies's poem appear only in the fourth act of the play.

Dick, Hugh G. "Presentation Copy of Tomkis's *Albumanzar*." *N&Q* 178 (1940): 10. Furnivall notes having seen an inscribed copy of one of the two 1615 editions; its location is now uncertain.

————. "The Lover in a Cask: A Tale of a Tub." *Italica* 18 (1941): 12-13. Giambattista della Porta's *Lo astrologo* has an altered version of a tale from the *Decameron;* Tomkis further alters the story in *Albumanzar.*

————, ed. *Albumanzar: A Comedy [1615]*. 1944. The introduction includes an account of Tomkis's life, a stage history, and a critical assessment.

Mander, Gerald P. "Thomas Tomkis." *TLS,* 31 March 1945, p. 151. Dick's edition of *Albumanzar* provides an occasion for a review of the known facts about Tomkis and speculation about his career after he left London and the theaters.

Turner, Robert K., Jr. "Standing Type in Tomkis's *Albumanzar.*" *Library* 13 (1958): 175-85. The first quarto is analyzed in detail; the second quarto of 1615 may have used some standing type from the first.

Sale, Arthur, ed. *The Alchemist,* by Ben Jonson. 1969. Act II, scene iii, and Act III, scene ii of *Albumanzar* are printed in an appendix for comparative purposes.

Hale, David G. "*Coriolanus:* The Death of a Political Metaphor." *SQ* 22 (1971): 197-202. *Lingua* uses a traditional analogy as "a consistent frame for the action, but without making the analogy itself the object of laughter." In contrast, "*Coriolanus* clearly shows the failure of the metaphor of the body politic."

LIST OF CONTRIBUTORS

CHARLES R. FORKER is Professor of English at Indiana University.

WILLIAM L. GODSHALK is Professor of English at the University of Cincinnati. He would like to thank his students Catherine Hall, Dinesh-kumar Hassan, Jeanne Leiman, and Stephen Wellmeier for their help in compiling and checking.

ANNE LANCASHIRE is Professor of English at University College, University of Toronto.

JILL LEVENSON is Associate Professor of English at the University of Toronto.

TERENCE P. LOGAN is Associate Professor of English at the University of New Hampshire.

CECIL M. MCCULLEY is Professor of English at the College of William and Mary.

DENZELL S. SMITH is Professor of English at Idaho State University.

INDEX
PERSONS

343

INDEX
PLAYS

Alphabetization and modernized spelling follow the "Index of English Plays" in Alfred Harbage, Annals of English Drama, 975-1700 (*1940; rev. S. Schoenbaum, 1964*). *Unusually long titles have been abbreviated.*